The Ellington Century

David Schiff

UNIVERSITY OF CALIFORNIA PRESS
Berkeley · Los Angeles · London

Passages from the Duke Ellington poem discussed in
chapter 6 courtesy of the Estate of Mercer K. Ellington
and its executor, Paul M. Ellington.

University of California Press, one of the most distinguished university presses in the United States, enriches
lives around the world by advancing scholarship in the
humanities, social sciences, and natural sciences. Its activities are supported by the UC Press Foundation and by
philanthropic contributions from individuals and institutions. For more information, visit www.ucpress.edu.

University of California Press
Berkeley and Los Angeles, California

University of California Press, Ltd.
London, England

Library of Congress Cataloging-in-Publication Data

Schiff, David.
    The Ellington century / David Schiff.
        p.   cm.
    Includes bibliographical references and index.
    ISBN 978-0-520-24587-7 (cloth : alk. paper)
    1. Jazz—History and criticism.   2. Jazz—Analysis,
appreciation.   3. Ellington, Duke, 1899–1974—
Criticism and interpretation.   4. Music—20th century—
History and criticism.   I. Title.
    ML3506.S287   2012
    780.9'04—dc23   2011034123

Manufactured in the United States of America

20   19   18   17   16   15   14   13   12
10   9   8   7   6   5   4   3   2   1

In keeping with a commitment to support environmen-
tally responsible and sustainable printing practices,
UC Press has printed this book on Rolland Enviro100,
a 100 percent postconsumer fiber paper that is FSC
certified, deinked, processed chlorine-free, and manufactured with renewable biogas energy. It is acid-free
and EcoLogo certified.

To Judy

Contents

Preface

As a composer I spend the better part of my life happily adrift with only the haziest idea of what I'm doing. Composing veers from the directionless to the inevitable (calm sea to prosperous voyage) so suddenly that both phases seem beyond my control. Writing *about* music, for me, is most enjoyable when it feels similarly unwilled and when, like Columbus, I end up in a different place from the one I thought I was trying to reach. For better or worse, that is what happened many times in the course of writing this book.

The initial impulse for *The Ellington Century* sprang from my love for Duke Ellington's music (a devotion that began in high school when, browsing through the record store bins between Miles Davis and Maynard Ferguson, I came upon the LPs *At His Very Best* and *Daybreak Express* and which later was magnified by the pioneering research of Gunther Schuller and Mark Tucker) and my consequent dissatisfaction with most histories of twentieth-century music. Ellington's name rarely appeared in these accounts, and when it did he figured as an anomaly, a composer in a genre defined by improvisation, a "serious" popular musician who, unlike George Gershwin, never crossed over to the forms of the concert hall or opera house, a successful song writer who worked far from the commercial machinery of Tin Pan Alley and who never composed a hit Broadway musical. Music history conceived as separate stories about classical music, musical theater, and popular song placed Ellington's music on the periphery, somehow extraneous despite its undeniable appeal. With every rehearing, though, I came to feel that this music belonged at the center of a cross-categorical story that had yet to be written.

The distance that my own view of things had drifted from mainstream opinion became clear when, on the eve of the millennium, the *New York Times* asked me to write a retrospective article on the passing century. I opened my article by asserting that Ravel, Bartók, and Ellington were universally acknowledged as the three greatest composers of the century. Apparently finding my claim perversely idiosyncratic, an editor at the *Times* advised me to drop that opening and recenter the piece on Stravinsky and Schoenberg or Webern and Cage. I realize now that my initial lead, consigned until now to the *Times'* trash basket, was both provocative and overoptimistic (and idiosyncratic, though hardly perverse), but making a short list of "greats" taught me a lot about my own sensibility. Today the Ravel/Bartók/Ellington trinity stands even higher in my critical estimation, but I realize that I came to value Ravel and Bartók by first absorbing Debussy and Stravinsky; I listened to their music, particularly *La Mer* and *Agon,* so much in my early years that now I simply take their influence for granted. (Just so you know how strange I was: in high school I used to walk around singing the twelve-tone "Surge, aquilo" aria from Stravinsky's *Canticum Sacrum,* and I would play through whole acts from *Pelléas* in my head from memory. No wonder I wasn't popular.) A decade of round-the-clock Mahler a little later on left a similar indelible mark, as did an intense Zappa phase (which, regrettably, never surfaces in this book). Before I began to listen to Ellington, I had steeped myself in the three M's: Mingus, Monk, and Miles; I was fortunate to hear all three perform live many times, and I think I've gone through seven copies—LPs, tapes, and CDs—of *Kind of Blue.* All these musicians shaped my musical proclivities before the age of twenty. Over the years my taste in music has expanded widely and unpredictably, though I still have plenty of blind spots, as my students will be happy to tell you.

The first sketch for this book attempted a revisionist history of a short "Ellington century" from 1899 to 1974, but I soon realized that I was not a historian either by training or by temperament; the book would be a composer's view, not a historian's (though, reader be warned, my previous life as a student of English literature has also left its mark). I also consciously decided not to build the project on a foundation of gripes. I wanted to talk about the music I liked, not quibble with

Adorno or Boulez. The music I liked included works from genres that are usually treated separately, and unequally. I hoped to punch some holes in the walls between them, but I gradually came to appreciate the full force of Ellington's dictum: "It's all music." The old categories of high and low, elite and vernacular, even of European and American and black and white, misrepresented a shared worldwide project: imagining and creating music that illuminated the unprecedented conditions of modern life.

One day, after I had mapped out a chronological outline of the century with some flashy chapter headings, an alternative approach suddenly came to mind and defined the task at hand. Instead of doing battle with history I would write a nonhistory. Instead of organizing the book chronologically I would talk about music in terms of color, rhythm, melody, and harmony. Instead of trying to cover all the important music of the century in textbook fashion, I would just talk about particular works that illuminated these facets of musical expression, to which I later added three areas of musical representation: love, history, and God. For each of these areas I found it easy to identify music by Ellington that exemplified expressive and technical pursuits shared with many other composers. An Ellington century then took shape (relatively) effortlessly.

That was where I started; where did I end up? Nothing in my prospectus implied a method, much less the kind of theoretical apparatus that scholars are expected to announce in advance these days. I knew what I wanted to do, but I had no idea how I would achieve my goal—and that's where writing this book became like composing. I allowed myself to be disorderly and intuitive, as if I were improvising on the keyboard or singing in the shower. I read all sorts of books and articles, stories and poems, some of them very far afield from my intended topics. And I *listened:* all the time, and all over the musical map. The more intently I listened, the more time I spent alone with the music, the happier I became. At some point I realized that my own pleasure would give the book its method. I listened and I wrote and then I listened some more. Instead of writing history I composed a disorderly and highly personal bundle of love letters to my favorite works of music—sprinkled with occasional lovers' quarrels.

Throughout all my labors on this book, the vast legacy of the Ellington Orchestra sustained and animated my efforts. In the past, when I have finished writing an article or teaching a class about a composer, I have sometimes felt the need for a change of scenery and have given the music a short (or occasionally even permanent) vacation, but, despite all the time I have put into researching and writing this book, I can't imagine a day in my life without the joyous revelations of the Ellington (and Co.) playlist.

Acknowledgments

Writing this book has increased my appreciation of a vast number of wise and supportive colleagues, friends, and institutions. My first thanks go to Reed College for awarding me an essential yearlong sabbatical leave, and also for encouraging my work and stimulating my mind for over thirty years. My Reed colleagues Virginia Hancock (proofreader par excellence), Mark Burford, Jacqueline Dirks, Roger Porter, and Pancho Savery offered helpful advice and, even better, asked me hard questions. Jim Holmes and Erin Conor in the Reed Library helped me track down material and document it.

My second institutional thanks goes to the wonderful staff at the Archive Center of the Smithsonian Museum of American History, always knowledgeable and generous in sharing their treasures. Particular thanks go to Reuben Jackson, who told me that I handled original documents like a musician; I think it was intended as a compliment.

I have been very fortunate to be able to discuss the book with a group of eminent and erudite musicians, including Marty Ehrlich, Anthony Coleman, David Taylor, Larry Karush, David Berger, John Schott, Peter Kogan, Ellen Taaffe Zwilich, and Hollis Taylor. I have also benefited greatly from suggestions made by scholars such as Carol Oja, Anne Shreffler, Judith Tick, Geoffrey Block, John Howland, Benjamin Piekut, Anna Celenza, and John Wriggle. And I was guided and aided immeasurably by Mary Francis, Suzanne Knott, Sharron Wood, and Eric Schmidt at the University of California Press.

This book also depends upon a much wider group of teachers, friends, and family who inspired and shaped my musical calling. Some of them have been dead for a long time, but I feel their influence every day: Ralph Friedman, my first maestro at Roosevelt Elementary School; Cantor Lawrence Avery, my sweet-singing gateway to Jewish music; my piano teachers Kenneth Wentworth, James Wimer (my own private Boulanger), Helen Kasin, Harry Coleman, and William Daghlian; Maestro Dr. Richard Karp, the first conductor to acknowledge that I was a composer; friends and teachers at Columbia University, including N.J. Garrett, Jack Beeson, Nicholas England, Alfred Ladzekpo, and Richard Goodman; Irwin Stahl (my own private Schoenberg); friends and teachers at Cambridge University, including Roger Smalley, Tim Souster, Penny Souster, Hugh Macdonald, Peter Britton, Simon Emmerson, and John Street; my teachers at the Manhattan School of Music, Ludmila Ulehla, John Corigliano, and Ursula Mamlok; my composition teacher at Juilliard, Elliott Carter; and my main maestros, James DePreist, Amy Kaiser, Kenneth Kiesler, George Manahan, David Zinman, and Gerard Schwarz.

Finally, this book would not have been possible without the love, encouragement, and especially the patience of my family. My parents, Jack and Lillian Schiff, did not live to see it appear but steered me in the right direction. My children, Daniel and Jamie, struggled valiantly to make me appear cooler than I am. And, above all, my wife Judy gave me the life support that has allowed me to realize so many of my dreams.

PART ONE

Overture: *Such Sweet Thunder*

I went to college on the G.I. Bill to study composition, and
we studied every composer and every system of arranging
and writing—Berlioz, Strauss, Schoenberg, and so forth. I was
then to learn that there was this link between Schoenberg and
Ellington. They'd lived apart, never been associated with each
other, were practically ignorant of each other's works, yet
there was an absolute parallel.

—Mercer Ellington

The century of aeroplanes has a right to a music of its own.

—Claude Debussy

Let's begin medias res fashion, midway through that up-in-the-air century, on April 28, 1957, a day before Duke Ellington's fifty-eighth birthday, when *Such Sweet Thunder* premiered at New York's Town Hall.

With its brash, brassy, backbeat-driven opening, "Such Sweet Thunder," the title track of the twelve-movement suite by Duke Ellington
and Billy Strayhorn, drops us off at the vibrant center of twentieth-
century music, the intersection of high art and popular entertainment:
African, American, and European traditions, improvised performance,
and rigorous composition. A "Shakespeherean" blues, with echoes
of the "Habanera" from Bizet's *Carmen* and Fats Domino's 1956 recording of "Blueberry Hill," it draws on jazz, rock, and Latin rhythms
all the while retelling the story of Othello, the Moor of Venice, and
Desdemona, the original satin doll, and, as Ellington always told the

audience, all the fun they must have had. Just over three minutes long, "Such Sweet Thunder" amplifies the text and subtexts of Shakespeare's most intimate tragedy and also mirrors its own historical moment, the untranquilized '50s already squirming from the hormones of pubescent boomers and the as-yet-unenforced consequences of *Brown v. Board of Education*. High time for Othello to tell the story his way.

Like most of Ellington's music, "Such Sweet Thunder" is compact: six blues choruses (each twelve bars long) in G (flickering between major and minor) at a moderate tempo with a four-bar transition (composed by Billy Strayhorn) inserted to create a more fearful asymmetry (or, in live performances, a louder outro). The music, commanding your attention from its first notes, is taut, concise, compressed, logical. At every point you hear two or more different ideas juxtaposed (form) or superimposed (counterpoint). Each chorus builds on an element from the previous one, moving the plot forward with dramatic inevitability. It's a well-wrought urn—with an attitude.

On the third or fourth hearing, as the terse deployment of musical symbols becomes clear, you may begin to discern bits of the story. Like the play, the music contrasts exteriors and interiors, public piazzas and private boudoirs, power and vulnerability. It hides its most intimate utterance, the shadowy, erotic fifth chorus, beneath a mask of deceptive bravado. In the first chorus the Moor's reputation precedes his entrance, as often happens with tragic heroes; the swaggering brass snarls, "Don't mess with this Moor!" With his blaring entrance in the second chorus Othello, like Ellington at the Cotton Club, flaunts his primitive, jungle nature ("Rude am I in my speech") both to intimidate his white patrons and to satisfy their prejudices. (Desdemona's father, you'll recall, says that "against all rules of nature" she fell "in love with what she fear'd to look on.") The groove may sound primitive, but the reversed habanera rhythm (long short/short long) suggests a self-conscious irony. The sax section discords of the third chorus, reminiscent of the fierce harmonies of Ellington's 1940 masterpiece "Ko-Ko," show that the idea of the "primitive" is in the mind of the beholder; to borrow Alfred Appel Jr.'s useful phrase, that's "jazz modernism." And then, in the fourth chorus, the "jungle" speaks, but gently. Ray Nance's assuredly nonchalant trumpet solo, the one slot in the design left open for improvisation, must be one of Othello's wondrous tales:

> Of the Cannibals, that each other eat;
> The Anthropophagi, and men whose heads
> Do grow beneath their shoulders.

That's quite a prelude to a kiss, yet it is still an audience-conscious public performance, an erotic shtick. Then Strayhorn's well-coiled rude interlude suddenly explodes; could it be a display of Desdemona's "downright violence and scorn of fortune"? So much for blushing white femininity; it takes two to habanera. In the fifth chorus swagger gives way to shadowy *tendresse*. When the reprised second chorus returns the action to the harsh light of the public sphere, we may visualize the two levels of the music, the hootch in the treble and cootch in the bass, as our two leading characters, both of them free of the categories that would define them. At least for a while. (For much, much more on *Such Sweet Thunder*, see chapter 5.)

And so, in 1957, the year of Little Rock, and Governor Faubus, and high-finned, Dagmar-bumpered V-8s, Edward K. Ellington and William Strayhorn launched their Shakespeare suite, originally intended for the Shakespeare Festival in Stratford, Ontario, with a blazing and sensual blues/fanfare, a celebratory tone parallel to the ultimate deed of integration that Jim Crow, still well entrenched south of the Canadian border, was designed to prevent, intimidate, and punish with horrific violence.

The political daring and musical synthesis of *Such Sweet Thunder* were not isolated phenomena. In the post-McCarthy years both jazz and the Bard blossomed in the hothouse setting of summer festivals. The late Renaissance provided an elegant cover for timely political provocation. Joseph Papp first brought free Shakespeare to Central Park in the summer of '57. Five months after the New York premiere of *Such Sweet Thunder*, the musical *West Side Story* opened on Broadway. Two months after that, *Agon*, with music by Stravinsky and choreography by Balanchine, premiered at the City Center (twelve blocks north of Town Hall). Like the Ellington/Strayhorn suite, *West Side Story* retold a Shakespearean story of ill-fated interethnic love with intercultural music that drew on jazz and Latin rhythms. *Agon*, like *Such Sweet Thunder* a suite of twelve short movements, featured at its core an erotic pas de deux danced by the white Diana Adams and the black Arthur Mitchell. Stravinsky based the music on French court dances from the sixteenth and seventeenth centuries found in De Lauze's *Apologie de la danse*— dances that would not be out of place in a production of *Othello* or *Romeo and Juliet*.

Risky cultural criticism required teamwork. *Such Sweet Thunder*, *West Side Story*, and *Agon* were collaborative creations: Leonard Bernstein, Jerome Robbins, Stephen Sondheim, Arthur Laurents, and Harold Prince (along with orchestrators Sid Ramin and Irwin Kostal) resituated *Romeo and Juliet. Agon,* written at the suggestion of Lincoln Kirstein, was Stravinsky's first twelve-tone ballet score and a posthumous collaboration. Stravinsky had attended a performance of Schoenberg's Serenade op. 24 conducted by his assistant, Robert Craft, on April 14, 1952. The coda of the *Agon* "Pas de deux," a duet for mandolin and harp, is a deep bow to the Serenade's nervously twanging mandolin and guitar. The "Pas de deux" crossed previously sacrosanct musical boundaries, juxtaposing a quotation from Webern's Variations for Orchestra, op. 30 with a recollection of the "Sacrificial Dance" from the *Rite of Spring.* Stravinsky was breaching the stylistic wall that had separated the music of Paris and Vienna throughout the previous half century. But much of *Agon* also suggests that Stravinsky was listening to recent jazz: the middle section of the Bransle Double evokes the cool West Coast style of the time. (In his next work, *Threni,* Stravinsky would co-opt Shorty Rogers's trademark flügelhorn.) Balanchine's choreography embodied the musical mélange as visual jazz. The critic Edwin Denby wrote that one of the male dancers displayed the timing of a "New York Latin in a leather jacket."[1]

At the same historical moment, a jazz suite, a Broadway show, and a classical ballet took on the hot-button issue of racial integration through similar strategies of stylistic synthesis and juxtaposition and transhistorical, cross-cultural conversation. These works also challenged the era's official culture of sexual repression, although the musical's gay subtext ("Somewhere") remained unnoticed for years, at least outside of Christopher Street and West Hollywood. Billy Strayhorn's "Up and Down and Up and Down (I Will Lead Them Up and Down)," the most original movement in *Such Sweet Thunder,* also dealt covertly with sexual difference; we can hear it as a self-portrait, Strayhorn as Puck, to set beside Ellington's self-depiction as Othello in the opening track. Boy love drives the plot of *A Midsummer Night's Dream:*

> The king doth keep his revels here to-night:
> Take heed the queen come not within his sight;
> For Oberon is passing fell and wrath,
> Because that she as her attendant hath
> A lovely boy, stolen from an Indian king;
> She never had so sweet a changeling;
> And jealous Oberon would have the child
> Knight of his train, to trace the forests wild.

Strayhorn's self-portrait as the impish fairy Puck suavely symbolized multiple aspects of his life. He was openly gay, and at the same time he was often an invisible instigator of musical spells; he usually remained in New York while the band toured, phoning in musical fixes as needed. A classically trained musical wunderkind, sixteen years younger than Ellington, Strayhorn could compose songs that sounded completely Ellingtonian (like "Day Dream") or create music whose advanced harmonies and structure were uniquely his own. "Up and Down" is a virtuosic display of nearly atonal contrapuntal juggling pairs of players impersonating the disoriented lovers of Shakespeare's dream.

Strayhorn's special relationship with the band may have given him a certain Puck-like objectivity. When, at the end of "Up and Down," Strayhorn asks Clark Terry to intone Puck's line "Lord, what fools these mortals be," these mortals might be heterosexuals or fellow homosexuals or fellow musicians. Strayhorn's sexual theme was both literarily astute and politically daring. We may recall how scandalous it seemed back in the '50s for Robert Lowell to devote a stanza of his 1956 confessional poem "Skunk Hour" to a "fairy decorator" who is considering marriage, the "cure" for inversion prescribed by the conformist psychotherapy of the era. Years before Stonewall the integration of straight and gay sensibilities, so hard for America even to contemplate at the time, was an essential part of the Ellington Orchestra's musical language.

Integration: I begin this book with *Such Sweet Thunder* because it represents a shared cultural space either ignored or dismissed by purists of all stripes. Purism, sorting alleged sheep from imaginary goats, can seduce with an appearance of rigor, but it can also mask snobbery or even racism. Historians on both the jazz and the classical sides who divide twentieth-century music before, say, 1970 into "separate but equal" musical territories perpetuate, consciously or not, hackneyed musical judgments that are racial stereotypes. These prejudices include the supposed opposition of commercial popularity and artistic integrity, difficulty and accessibility, intellectual control and spontaneity. Forty years after Ellington was denied a Pulitzer Prize, music journalists still keep alive this form of segregation by covering either classical music or jazz; classical critics cross this line only when a jazz figure seems to be doing something that can be described in classical terms, or, more recently, to profess their admiration for the artier rock bands. The picture of an unbridgeable high/low, art/entertainment, or black/white divide persists—this despite ample evidence to the contrary. At its premiere, for instance, *Such Sweet Thunder* shared the program with Kurt Weill's Violin Concerto, played by Anahid Ajemian, conducted by Dmitri Mitropoulos.

An alternative view of twentieth-century music can emerge once we think of musicians not as warring clans or isolated monads but as collaborators in the shared cultural project foreseen by Debussy, the invention of a music that reflected the new technical and social realities of the time. This project consumed the talents of composers and performers, urban tunesmiths and lone outcasts, popular entertainers and obscure eccentrics, reactionaries and conservatives, progressives and radicals, critics and listeners. What we term "modern" or "modernistic" music was an evolving series of hypotheses, experiments, and reevaluations. Irving Berlin's "Putting on the Ritz" is as much of a rhythmic experiment as the "Monoritmica" from Berg's *Lulu* or Dizzy Gillespie's "Things to Come." If we measure the success of experiments in terms of their broad impact, the collected solos of Louis Armstrong become the mother lode of the century's rhythmic research. And, although some musicians worked only in a particular milieu, many others crossed stylistic and social lines all the time. From James Reese Europe to Wynton Marsalis, jazz musicians have challenged the idea that their music is inherently "low," and the list of classical composers who appropriated ideas from jazz would include just about every major European and American figure. James P. Johnson, master of the stride piano and composer of the Charleston, also wrote two piano concertos, a symphony, and two operas. George Gershwin asked Alban Berg to autograph his copy of the *Lyric Suite*. Schoenberg praised Gershwin's music and imitated its sound in his Theme and Variations for band. Charlie Parker quoted *Le sacre du printemps* whenever he spotted Stravinsky in the audience. Leonard Bernstein jammed (once) with Miles Davis. Frank Zappa worshipped the music of Edgard Varèse; Vladimir Horowitz admired and envied Art Tatum's technical prowess. Stravinsky lifted a few bars from "Goosey Gander" when he wrote his *Ebony Concerto* for Woody Herman, and, according to Mercer Ellington, was a regular visitor to the Cotton Club. And Ellington shared the stage with Mitropoulos—who knew?

No single oeuvre spans the full cross-categorical range of mid–twentieth-century music better than the vast repertory of the Duke Ellington Orchestra, most of it composed by Ellington and Strayhorn. This rich body of music, written over nearly fifty years, includes enduring songs, instrumental "tone parallels," jazz concertos, extended suites, ballet music, film music, and sacred music. Just consider this alphabetical list, far from complete, of Ellingtonian classics:

Across the Track Blues

All Too Soon

Anatomy of a Murder

Are You Sticking?

Awful Sad

Battle of Swing

Birmingham Breakdown

Black and Tan Fantasy

Black Beauty

Black, Brown and Beige

Blood Count

Blue Cellophane

Blue Light

Blue Serge

The Blues I Love to Sing

The Blues with a Feeling

Bojangles

Boy Meets Horn

Braggin' in Brass

C Jam Blues

Chelsea Bridge

Clarinet Lament

Clothed Woman

Concerto for Cootie

Controversial Suite

Cotton Tail

Creole Love Call

Creole Rhapsody

Day Dream

Daybreak Express

Deep South Suite

Delta Serenade

Diminuendo in Blue and Crescendo in Blue

Dusk

East St. Louis Toodle-Oo

Echoes of Harlem

Echoes of the Jungle

Far East Suite

Giddybug Gallop

Harlem Airshaft

Hot and Bothered

Immigration Blues

In a Mellotone

In a Sentimental Mood

It Don't Mean a Thing (If It Ain't Got That Swing)

It's Glory

Jack the Bear

Jubilee Stomp

Jump for Joy

Ko-Ko

Liberian Suite

Lotus Blossom

Main Stem

Merry Go Round

Misty Morning

The Mooche

Mood Indigo

Moon Mist

The Mystery Song

New Orleans Suite

Night Creature

The Nutcracker Suite

Old Man Blues

On a Turquoise Cloud

Perfume Suite

A Portrait of Bert Williams

Prelude to a Kiss

Queen's Suite

Rain Check

Reminiscing in Tempo

Ring Dem Bells

The River

Rockin' in Rhythm

Rocky Mountain Blues

Rude Interlude

Satin Doll

Saturday Night Function

Second Sacred Concert

Sepia Panorama

Showboat Shuffle

Sloppy Joe

Solitude

Sophisticated Lady

Such Sweet Thunder

Suite Thursday

Symphony in Black

Take the A Train

Tattooed Bride

Tiger Rag (arr.)

A Tone Parallel to Harlem

U.M.M.G

Warm Valley

Washington Wabble

Someday scholars will refer to these works by the equivalent of Köchel numbers. They bring together the popular and the serious, improvisation and composition, African rhythms and European harmonies in ways that, I would propose, can shed some unexpected light on the more category-bound, or similarly unbounded, music around them from Berg to Zappa. In the chapters that follow a single Ellingtonian work will lead into a broader exploration of different technical aspects of music, color, rhythm, melody, and harmony, and different realms, both profane and sacred, of musical representation.

SEGUE: THE MUSIC OF SOUND

The "century of aeroplanes" is a catchy rubric, but what would its music sound like? For some composers the answer was literal: it would sound like an airplane, as in George Antheil's *Ballet mécanique,* whose orchestra featured a giant propeller. But the airplane could also be a metaphor—for speed, freedom, anxiety, change. It suggested new harmonies, colors, rhythms. The airplane soared across boundaries and Maginot lines, connected once-distant places and cultures in a matter of hours.

For other composers the new music would sound like sound itself, freed from its traditional burden of connotations and associations. The third of Schoenberg's Five Pieces for Orchestra, op. 16, originally titled "Farben" (Colors) and later retitled "Summer Morning by a Lake," may be the earliest "sound" piece. It seems, at first hearing, to lack melody, rhythm, and harmony so that all that remains is tone color. If we ignore Schoenberg's later palliative attempt to associate the color with a time and place, we can enjoy a kind of categorical (and Cagean) vertigo as we ask ourselves how this "color" is any more musical than the random sounds in the room. Later examples of "sound" music, whether by Webern or Varèse or Xenakis, similarly push us against the imagined boundary between musical and nonmusical sounds, which calls into question the legitimacy of the border line. What forces determine the kinds of sound that will be admitted to the realm of music? What sounds and voices does the boundary line wall out?

The third movement, Andante, of Ruth Crawford's String Quartet (1931) shows how the disorienting power of sound can allow a new, previously suppressed voice to emerge. Crawford highlighted the special character of this movement by surrounding it with contrapuntal movements made up of splattered, splintered, or polarized elements. In the Andante this broken discourse yields to a "complex veil of sound."[2] For most of the movement the four instruments knit a tight harmonic fabric based on half steps that slowly ascend in pitch. The individual swelling dynamics imbue this harmonic idea with a sense of breath and pulse, as if the sound itself were a living organism, a breathing body. As the four instruments blend in what Crawford termed a "heterophony of dynamics"[3] they also articulate a melodic line that passes from one instrument to another, creating one voice out of many. The sound not only breathes, it sings. As Judith Tick explains, this effect was so novel that Crawford felt compelled to revise the score repeatedly; seven years after she started she inserted a three-bar episode in which the four instrumental lines suddenly come unglued and then just as suddenly fuse on two shrieking tone clusters. Is this the sound of tragic struggle or the birth pangs of a voice from within the female body?

If the airplane defied gravity and redefined space, the new sound technologies— recording, radio, and sound-on-film—allowed music to defy and redefine time. It is only possible to contemplate *Such Sweet Thunder* fifty years after its creation because it was recorded; from the earliest days of his band Ellington understood the importance of broadcasting his music and of putting music on disc with the highest possible illusion of fidelity. Edison's 1877 invention (first used for music right around the beginning of the twentieth century) changed music economically and conceptually, far more so than "mechanical reproduction" impacted the visual arts. Unlike the unique visual artwork, with its defining "aura," a work of music exists *only* as a reproduction; every performance is a reenactment of an idea. Ever since the invention of the reed flute and lyre in antiquity, musical machines—instruments—have reproduced the sound of the voice, or the sound of each other. Even as the development of a symphonic culture in the nineteenth century conferred an "aura" on a small group of works performed in concert halls and opera houses, these works were being re-created on the parlor piano, by amateur string quartets, by a band in the park, or by the organ grinder in the street. Listeners accepted recordings as *music* (not as some defective facsimile) almost from the beginning. Tone tests sponsored by the Edison Company between 1915 and 1926 challenged listeners to distinguish live and recorded sounds and proved, as Emily Thompson claims, that "the act of listening to reproduction was implicitly accepted as culturally equivalent to the act of listening to live performers."[4] A recording of an opera aria (Caruso was the biggest star of early recordings) conveyed that aria far more convincingly and conveniently than most amateur performances could. With the arrival of cheap record players during the First World War and radio broadcasts of music in the 1920s, almost anyone could reproduce a musical work at home.

The first recordings, however primitive, were the first electronic music. The new sound technologies translated all music, regardless of origin, into electric impulses and then back to sound emanating from some kind of loudspeaker. Increasingly, the manipulation of sound, previously attainable only through intermediary performers or instruments, came to be seen as the essence of music. It makes sense, then, to begin our journey across the categorical boundaries of twentieth-century music with a discussion of timbre, the color of sound, and its connotations, the sounds of color.

CHAPTER I

"Blue Light": Color

Ellington plays the piano but his real instrument is his band.
Each member of his band is to him a distinctive tone color
and set of emotions which he mixes with others equally
distinctive to produce a third thing which I like to call the
Ellington Effect.

—Billy Strayhorn

In modern orchestration clarity and definition of sonorous
image are usually the goal. There exists, however, another
kind of orchestral magic dependent on a certain ambiguity
of effect. Not to be able to identify immediately how
a particular color combination is arrived at adds to its
attractiveness. I live to be intrigued by unusual sounds that
force me to exclaim: Now I wonder how the composer does
that?

—Aaron Copland

Stan Kenton can stand in front of a thousand fiddles and
a thousand brass and make a dramatic gesture and every
studio arranger can nod his head and say, "O yes, that's done
like this." But Duke merely lifts a finger, three horns make a
sound, and I don't know what it is.

—André Previn

One thing that I learned from Ellington is that you can
make the group you play with sing if you realize each of the
instruments has a distinctive personality; and you can bring
out the singing aspect of that personality if you use the right
timbre for the instruments.

—Cecil Taylor

Now if it is possible to create patterns out of tone colors that are differentiated according to pitch, patterns we call melodies.. . . . then it must also be possible to create such progressions out of the tone colors of the other dimension, out of that which we call simply "tone color."
—Arnold Schoenberg

Hear with your eyes and see with your ears.
—Charlie Parker

Duke Ellington, born on April 29, 1899, could easily have become a painter rather than a musician. Though he began piano studies, with Marietta Clinkscales, when he was seven, he later recalled that "all through grade school, I had a genuine interest in drawing and painting, and I realized I had a sort of talent for them."[1] In 1963 he even helped paint the sets for *My People,* a multimedia theater piece marking the centenary of the Emancipation Proclamation. Ellington called many of his compositions "tone parallels" or "portraits"; his music linked sounds and images. Coloristic titles located the music on a chromatic spectrum: azure, magenta, turquoise, indigo, black, sepia, beige, and tan. Ellington's palette of many colors *signified:* blue of whatever shade referred to the musical form, expressive vocabulary, and social function of the blues; the gradations leading from tan to black announced the central subject of his creative work, the history, experience, and culture of African Americans. Just consider this panchromatic catalogue of Ellington titles:

Azure	*Black, Brown and Beige*	Blue Cellophane
Beige		Blue Goose
Black	Black Butterfly	Blue Harlem
Black and Tan Fantasy	Blue Belles of Harlem	Blue Light
		Blue Pepper
Black Beauty	Blue Bubbles	Blue Ramble

Blue Serge

Blutopia

Brown

Brown Betty

Brown Skin Gal

Café au lait

Creamy Brown

Crescendo in Blue

Diminuendo in Blue

Ebony Rhapsody

The Gold Broom and the Green Apple

Golden Cress

Golden Feather

Lady in Blue

Lady of the Lavender Mist

Magenta Haze

Midnight Indigo

Mood Indigo

Moon Mist

Multicolored Blue

On a Turquoise Cloud

Purple Gazelle

Sepia Panorama

Transblucency

Ultra-violet

Violet Blue

Ellington's gift for translating visual colors into tone colors set his music apart early on. By the time the Duke Ellington and his Kentucky Club Orchestra recorded "East St. Louis Toodle-Oo" on November 29, 1926, the better-known bands of Paul Whiteman and Fletcher Henderson had already configured the standard sound of large ensemble jazz. In 1925 the Whiteman band had twenty-six players: six violins, two violas, two cellos (including the young William Schuman), string bass, three trumpets, three trombones, tuba, four saxes, banjo, guitar, drums and piano[2]—no wonder they called this style of jazz "symphonic." For its highly influential 1926 recording of "The Stampede" the Henderson band had eleven players: one trumpet, two cornets, one trombone, tuba, three saxes (all doubling clarinet), banjo, drums, and piano. Despite the difference in size, both Whiteman and Henderson configured their bands in instrumental choirs (reeds, brass, and, for Whiteman, strings), a method codified as early as 1924 in Arthur Lange's *Arranging for the Modern Dance Orchestra*. Classical composers had similarly deployed the orchestra in terms of instrumental choirs, winds, brass, and strings, the better to synchronize articulations and intonation. Hybrid sonorities, mixing instrumental families, can sound muddy if they are not well rehearsed. Or they can sound magical.

Although Ellington's early "orchestra" was smaller than Henderson's by just one trumpet, this slight difference meant that the Ellington band really had only one full section, the reeds. Instead of playing choir against choir and hot soloists against sidemen, Ellington treated every member of the band as a soloist and blended the sounds of different instruments and players.

The contrast of Bubber Miley's muted, growling trumpet and the smoldering accompaniment in the baritone sax and tuba, blue against black, "East St. Louis Toodle-Oo" put Ellington's distinctive approach to timbre on the map. By the time of its third recording, on December 19, 1927, the interplay of Miley, Harry Carney (baritone sax), Joe Nanton (muted trombone), and Rudy Jackson (growling low clarinet) formed a terse study in shades of brown that matched Miley's visual parallel for the piece: "This is an old man, tired from working in the field since sunup, coming up the road in the sunset on his way home to dinner. He's tired but strong, and humming in time with his broken gait."[3] Fine-tuning the color balance as the piece evolved, Ellington abridged the statements of a contrasting theme (reminiscent of A. J. Piron's song "I Wish I Could Shimmy Like My Sister Kate") in this third recorded version. Foreshortened and refocused, the conventional "sweet" coloring now set the gritty darkness of the rest of the composition in starker relief. Ellington was composing in colors—like Matisse.

Though he may have used the band as his palette, timbre for Ellington was neither abstract nor dehumanizing. Colors were also human voices. Ellington hired players with idiosyncratic and instantly recognizable playing styles, and composed parts for specific players rather than instruments. The musicians of the band formed a spectrum of strongly characterized timbre styles: Miley's aggressively rough sound contrasted with Arthur Whetsol's almost humming introversion; the liquid croon of Johnny Hodges's alto played against the rude honk of Harry Carney's baritone. Within a few years the trombone section of Nanton, Lawrence Brown, and Juan Tizol produced three completely different timbres: raspy, smooth, Latin.

Early on Ellington saw that the new mechanisms for amplification and recording could enhance coloristic explorations. Long before the advent of recording "production," let alone of electronic music, Ellington revealed his genius for technologically enabled sound synthesis in "Mood Indigo," first recorded on October 17, 1930, but written especially for the "microphonic transmission" of a radio broadcast.[4] In a radio interview in 1962 Ellington recalled the radical role played by the microphone as a lucky accident: "When we made 'Black and Tan Fantasy' . . . [we used] the plunger mute in the trumpet and in the trombone in that duet and always got a 'mike' sound. . . . They hadn't conquered this yet, and they messed up a lot of masters because every time they'd get the mike they'd throw it out." For the recording session of "Mood Indigo" in 1930 "the aim was to employ these instruments in such a way, at such a distance, that the mike tone would set itself in definite pitch—so that it wouldn't spoil the recording. Lucky again, it happened."[5]

To signify the deepest "blue" in "Mood Indigo" Ellington scored the opening melody in a choralelike texture for three players: Whetsol (trumpet), Barney Bigard (clarinet) and Nanton (muted trombone). He painted his mood with the three instrumental colors found in New Orleans jazz but arranged them counterintuitively with the trumpet on top, the trombone a third below it, in its highest register, and the clarinet an octave and a fourth lower than the trombone, an acoustic gap labeled an "error" in the conservatories that Ellington, fortunately, never attended.[6] The apparently upside-down scoring demonstrates Ellington's astute command of the acoustical properties of each instrument and of the individual styles of each performer, the haunting, hollow quality Bigard brought to the clarinet's low register, Whetsol's plaintive lyricism, Nanton's insidiously sliding speechlike inflections. It shows his prophetic instinct for technology as well: together the three sounds blend into a whisper that would be undetectable without amplification. No wonder that Billy Strayhorn dubbed such timbral magic "the Ellington effect."

"BLUE LIGHT"

A slow, intimate blues recorded in 1938, "Blue Light" demonstrates how Ellington used tone color to shape mood and form. From its first meditative, bell-like chords on the piano, it suggests the indigo atmosphere of the last set in some nearly deserted nightclub; just one couple remains on the dance floor, perhaps with nowhere else to go, clinging to each other in the blue-tinted, smoke-filled air. "Blue Light" is that rare kind of music that evokes a specific time of day, temperature, and atmospheric condition. "The most neglected and least known of Ellington's masterpieces,"[7] "Blue Light" was recorded twice on December 22, 1938, by an eight-man subgroup of the Ellington Orchestra: Bigard, clarinet; Carney, clarinet (?); Wallace Jones, trumpet (?); Brown, trombone; Fred Guy, guitar; Billy Taylor, bass; Sonny Greer, drums; and Ellington, piano.[8] Here's an outline of the form:

Intro: Piano solo four bars.

Chorus 1: twelve-bar blues. Clarinet solo with piano fills.

Chorus 2: twelve-bar blues. Trio for muted trumpet, muted trombone, and clarinet with piano fills.

Chorus 3: twelve-bar blues. Trombone solo with reed accompaniment. (Trombone melody composed by Lawrence Brown.)

Chorus 4: Piano solo.

Borrowing Schoenberg's term, we might term "Blue Light" a *klang-farbenmelodie* blues, a formal expansion of the color synthesis of "Mood Indigo." Each chorus presents a different kind of blue: the smoky middle range of Bigard's clarinet, the "indigo" scoring of the trio, the vibrato-rich warmth of Brown's trombone (set in relief by a low reed trio in the background), and Ellington's restrained pianism (with a brief homage, to my ear, to Earl Hines). Each timbre evokes a different aspect of the blues. Ellington's brief intro sounds urbane and modernistic; his first chord replicates exactly (if not intentionally) the opening harmony of Berg's Piano Sonata op. 1. Bigard's solo, by contrast, is roots music, straight out of New Orleans and Sidney Bechet. The trio, more muted and rhythmically steady, choralelike, than in "Mood Indigo," also has the ghostly gaslight sonority Ellington had used in his "Mystery Song" in 1931. Brown's solo, by contrast, feels fully embodied, like a warm embrace. In 1933 Spike Hughes had complained that Brown's sophisticated sound was out of place in "Duke's essentially direct and simple music,"[9] thereby underestimating both musicians, but Brown's lyricism here illustrates how Ellington could paint a jazz panorama (from Bechet to Tommy Dorsey) even within such a small framework. Ellington's closing solo chorus begins with the dissonant major-minor chord he habitually used to signify "the blues," momentarily muses on a fragment from Earl Hines's solo in "West End Blues," then turns out the lights.

"BLUE LIGHT" AS BLUES

A meticulously balanced tone-color composition, "Blue Light" is also a blues, although not in a way that devotees of, say, B. B. King might recognize. The term "blues" itself appears in bewilderingly various ways; it is used narrowly, to denote a chord progression, or grandly, as in Albert Murray's *Stomping the Blues,* to characterize an entire culture. Historically, the blues emerged after the Civil War from the sorrow songs of the antebellum period.[10] As much a poetic as a musical genre, it has its own verse form, syntax, vocabulary, imagery, and subject matter:

When a woman gets the blues she hangs her head and cries,
When a woman gets the blues she hangs her head and cries,
But when a man gets the blues, he grabs a train and flies.[11]

We can parse this blues stanza as follows:

Form: a thought stated, repeated, completed (surprisingly)

Syntax: lines broken midway by a caesura, and at the end by a comma; these breaks usually filled with a guitar response

Imagery: Love, tears, the railway

Subject: Suffering and escape from suffering

Most recorded blues consist of five or six stanzas that tell a story, though usually more as a sequence of images rather than a linear narrative. Jazz musicians refer to these stanza structures as choruses.

Often blind or lame, and so excluded from manual labor, early blues performers, or "blues men," sang to their own guitar accompaniment. At once outsiders and shamanic representatives of the community, they sang about themselves, and about everyone. Within African American culture the blues formed part of a larger musical landscape that included work songs, religious songs, and ragtime. These genres denoted class and region, the sacred and profane. Until around 1900 the blues was heard only in the Deep South, and in Mississippi and Louisiana in particular. Growing up in Washington, D.C., Ellington did not hear the blues until he encountered Sidney Bechet: "I shall never forget the first time I heard him play, at the Howard Theatre in Washington around 1921. I had never heard anything like it. It was a completely new sound."[12]

Some jazz musicians, like Louis Armstrong and Lester Young, were born into the blues environment, while others, like Ellington and Coleman Hawkins, had to acquire the idiom consciously. The ease with which blues traveled and the very possibility that musicians from widely different backgrounds could master it suggests that blues was just part of a more widespread African American musical inheritance, and also that it was a transportable, itinerant music built for travel, whether on a train, or through the media of radio and recording. It was a kind of music that was everywhere, if you knew where to listen. As Ellington wrote, "I went on studying, of course, but I could also hear people whistling, and I got all the Negro music that way. You can't learn that in any school."[13]

The blues, stylized verse in song, is both a poetic idiom and a distinctive musical sound. Blues singing, as ethnomusicologist Jeff Todd Titon observed, employed a particular kind of vocal production: "The tone quality of early downhome blues singing largely resulted from the way the singer enunciated his words. Singing with an open throat, he relaxed his lips and mouth and kept his tongue loose, low, and toward the back of his mouth. This position favored certain kinds of vowels and consonants and made it somewhat difficult to produce others."[14] Titon noted that blues singers employ nasal, rasping sounds not used in their ordinary speaking voices, effects that can be traced to the "heterogeneous sound ideal" or "timbral mosaic" of African music.[15] In the blues, speech and song mix; in instrumental blues, the instrument always has a vocal quality: "the nasal, foggy, hoarse texture that delivered the elisions, hums, growls, blue notes and falsetto, and the percussive oral effects of their ancestors."[16] In his classic study *Stomping the Blues* Albert Murray uses the terms *blues* and *jazz* interchangeably, but the blues encompasses many musical idioms beyond the usual boundaries of jazz. Buddy Bolden, often cited as the musician who brought the streams of ragtime and blues together, as well as the secular and the sacred, and the spoken and sung elements in African American music, played "with a moan in his cornet that went all through you, just like you were in church or something . . . made a spiritual feeling go through you. He had a cup, a special cup, that made that cornet moan like a Baptist preacher."[17] Bolden's playing also took its timbre from the streets, from the sounds of itinerant ragmen playing long tin horns, party instruments that produced blues sounds later imitated on the trumpet.[18] The translation of blues from voice to instrument therefore was not an artistic elevation of a folk form into an art genre, but rather a complex process of interweaving many oral and aural traditions to pass on a body of experience and wisdom—folk songs without words.

Within the realm of jazz the blues retains its poetic and timbral character, but it also serves as the basis of instrumental improvisation. When jazz musicians play the blues, they conceptualize the form in terms of a twelve-bar phrase structure, or "chorus," divided into three four-bar phrases, following the stanza form. They create melodic lines using the pitches of a "blues scale," which is usually understood to include major and minor versions of the third, seventh, and sometimes fifth degrees of the scale, and they follow a standard harmonic pattern, such as (one chord per measure):

I–IV7–I–I7
IV–iv–I–VI
ii–V–I–I

Because all blues restate the same harmonic and poetic patterns over and over again, they are all genetically related, though perhaps at different removes. These degrees of separation might be termed stylizations; we might, accordingly, listen to "Blue Light" the way we hear Chopin's mazurkas. But that would extract them from the intertextual continuum of their own culture, in which, as we have seen, different genres mingled easily. To see how "Blue Light" dialogues with other kinds of blues we can listen to it alongside a vocal blues recorded by Jimmy Rushing and Count Basie, and an instrumental blues by Sidney Bechet.

Though Ellington's band never included a real blues singer like Basie's Jimmy Rushing (as we will see, Ellington often preferred more classical-sounding singers), it is still instructive to compare "Blue Light" to "Blues in the Dark," an equally atmospheric number recorded by the Count Basie Orchestra with Rushing in January 1938. Around that time, the influential jazz critic and promoter John Hammond championed Basie's blues-based jazz against what he perceived as Ellington's betrayal of the idiom: Ellington, Hammond wrote in 1943, "has introduced complex harmonies solely for effect and has experimented with material farther and farther away from dance music."[19] Ellington and Basie knew better, and these two examples of the blues reveal similar elements. The similarities, though, are surprising. Rushing's "hot" voice sounds like Brown's "sweet" trombone: they both seem to rise out of the soil like a mighty oak. By contrast, Bigard's clarinet and Buck Clayton's muted trumpet dart and spin like a pair of dragonflies. The lyrics Rushing sings might provide a subtext for "Blue Light":

> Kind treatment make me love you, be mean and you'll drive me away.
> Kind treatment make me love you, be mean and you'll drive me away.
> You gonna long for me baby, one of these long rainy days.
>
> Did you ever dream lucky baby, and wake up cold in hand?
> Did you ever dream lucky baby, and wake up cold in hand?
> You didn't have a dollar, somebody had your woman.

Basie frames three choruses of blues in E♭ (two for Rushing, one for Basie) with a c minor blues in growling "jungle" style recalling Ellington's "Black and Tan Fantasy." The two pieces and the two titled bandleaders seem to be conversing; listening to them side by side reveals that the blues is a form of dialogue both internally and intertextually. Basie's southwestern country style and Ellington's urbane Harlem idiom are dialects of the same language.

We can also hear "Blue Light" as a conversation with Sidney Bechet; Ellington called Bechet the "epitome of jazz,"[20] and both Barney Bigard and Johnny Hodges were Bechet disciples. Bechet's "Blue Horizon," which received canonic status on the Smithsonian Collection of Classic Jazz, perfectly illustrates the central role that tone color plays in shaping blues as dialogue, even within an instrumental solo. Bechet recorded "Blue Horizon" in December 1944 with a quintet of distinguished New Orleans musicians: Wilbur de Paris, trumpet; Vic Dickenson, trombone; Manzie Johnson, drums; Pops Foster, bass; and Art Hodes, piano. Although his preferred instrument was the soprano sax, Bechet played clarinet here, or perhaps it would be more accurate to say he constructed an entire piece out of the particular timbral qualities of the clarinet, much as Stravinsky had done in 1920 in his *Three Pieces for Solo Clarinet,* written either after hearing Bechet play (possible but not certain) or after reading his friend Ernest Ansermet's ecstatic praise of Bechet as "the first of his race to have composed perfectly formed blues."[21] In constructing "Blue Horizon," a six-chorus blues in E♭, which uses only the pitches of an E♭ blues scale (E♭ major plus a lowered third, G♭, and a lowered seventh, D♭), Bechet contrasted the three distinct registers of the clarinet. He spread an extended melodic line over a range of three octaves (from the E♭ below middle C to the E♭ two octaves and a third above middle C). The low (called "chalumeau"), middle, and upper (clarion) ranges of the clarinet sound almost like different instruments. Bechet placed each chorus within one or two of these ranges:

Chorus 1: chalumeau

Chorus 2: middle register

Chorus 3 chalumeau

Chorus 4: middle and chalumeau in call-and-response

Chorus 5: middle

Chorus 6: clarion

In each chorus Bechet returned to the low chalumeau register for the third phrase, which serves as a refrain, unifying the piece but also bringing it back home to the timbre that is closest to speech. We might say that "Blue Horizon" is a *klangfarbenmelodie* for a single instrument, but its timbres differ from the classical clarinet sound, and that difference points to the particular way tone color functions in the blues. Bechet's clarinet does not sound like anyone else's. In the blues idiom the individual player's sound is far more important than an idealized notion of how an instrument should sound. Bechet's sound has a distinctive wide vibrato, but that is just one of its special sonorities. Bechet's lower register for instance, does not have the hollow, disembodied quality produced by classical clarinetists; it is a full, fat sound, almost like a trombone. Similarly the middle range is sweet, not pallid; the clarion register is trumpetlike, not shrill. Bechet also colored his sound with three ornaments, a slow downward slide, a more than usually pronounced vibrato, and a "blues" inflection, a flattening and bending of pitch that he reserves for the pitch G♭. Each of these ornaments points to what we might term a "blues sound ideal" of varying the color within a note rather than sustaining a single timbre all the way through. In the blues the timbre changes as much within one note as from one note to the next; every tone sounds unpredictably alive.

Both polyvocal and polytimbral, Bechet's clarinet portrays a community of voices speaking and singing that are linked by a refrain that pulls their differences back to a common source. In "Blue Light" Ellington's piano plays a very similar function, responding, completing, and summarizing the other instruments. Both pieces seem formally self-contained yet open-ended. Blues stanzas roll on in an endless narrative; individual blues performances or compositions take up a story that has already begun and then pass it along to the next speaker.

THEME AND VARIATIONS: A BLUES GALLERY

Ellington reworked "Blue Light" over a decade, creating a variegated gallery of related nocturnes: "Subtle Lament," "Dusk," "Transblucency," and "On a Turquoise Cloud." Like Monet's series of haystack paintings, these works bathe identical subjects in changing light; heard back-to-back they might be termed "blues-as-process." They demonstrate how small changes in instrumental combinations or in their ordering can transform musical signification. They also reveal the range of Ellington's creative process, from informal on-the-spot improvisation to contrapuntal construction. Rex Stewart wrote that Ellington might arrive at a recording session, listen to a run-through, and then call for changes, "perhaps starting with bar sixteen, playing eight bars, then back to letter C, and when we got to letter E he'd call a halt. Then he'd sit at the piano and play something, have a consultation with Tom Whaley [the band's copyist], and some new music would be scored on the spot."[22] Ellington's sketches, preserved at the Smithsonian, show that the music was usually written out in detail before such impromptu reshuffling.

"Subtle Lament," a moderate blues in G recorded on March 20, 1939, and again in the fall of 1940,[23] sounds at first like an informal rearrangement of "Blue Light" with the "Mood Indigo" chorus placed right after a new piano and bass intro and rescored for four reed instruments.[24] Following is a call-and-response chorus for piano (using material similar to the intro to "Blue Light") and trombone trio, a solo chorus for Rex Stewart (cornet using half-valve muting) over a low reed background in place of Lawrence Brown's chorus but without his melody, a chorus for trombone trio, a chorus by Barney Bigard with brass and reed accompaniment, and a four-bar restatement of the "Mood Indigo" section as outro. Moving the furniture around, however, Ellington altered the structure and timbre. The "Mood Indigo" chorale now became the binding element. It appears three times: at the beginning and end, but also as a background to the Stewart and Bigard solos. As it increases in thematic importance, however, the chorale also sheds its mysterious coloration; it is now played within a single instrumental choir, not as a hybrid color. Ellington compensated for this loss by introducing a new timbral contrast of low trombone trio against the high reeds. The three trombones become the mysterious element through the blend of their sounds (Brown, Nanton, and Tizol had sharply contrasting styles of playing) and also through their unexpected Debussyan harmonies.

Heard as a nocturne, "Subtle Lament" seems to depict midnight rather than the 3 A.M. of "Blue Light." On May 28, 1940, moving the clock and the quality of light back by several hours, Ellington recorded "Dusk," a considerable reworking of the elements in those two predecessors and of their template, "Mood Indigo." Like "Mood Indigo," "Dusk" is in B♭ and has a sixteen-bar AABA phrase structure that nevertheless sounds like a twelve-bar blues. It begins with a piano and bass intro very similar to "Subtle Lament." The first chorus is a chromatic melody scored in the "Mood Indigo" voicing, with muted trumpet and muted trombone in thirds, with a clarinet an octave and a half below, and, like "Indigo," with a ripe late romantic altered dominant ninth as its second chord. As in "Subtle Lament," Rex Stewart has a solo chorus, and in the third chorus the low trombone trio counters the high reed choir, but here the reeds sound like a tree full of birds chirping at sunset. The timbral heart of "Dusk," the last phrase of the third chorus, however, is new and also carefully composed for the entire band.[25] Here Ellington blended five reeds and six muted brass in darkly dissonant harmonies that nevertheless produce a luminous tone color. This example of the "Ellington effect" has inspired superlatives ever since it appeared: "I know of no other work for jazz orchestra that conveys such an impression of tranquility on the verge of tears."[26]

Ellington, however, had even more changes to ring on his nocturnal theme in general, and on "Blue Light" in particular. On January 4, 1946, he premiered "Transblucency" (a.k.a. "Transbluency," a.k.a. "A Blue Fog That You Can Almost See Through") at Carnegie Hall. Essentially, "Transblucency" is an overt variant of "Blue Light," significantly transposed upward from G to Bb. Here, though, nonchalant improvisation evolved into a classical-sounding, contrapuntally strict composition. Ellington signaled the classical turn by rescoring the "Mood Indigo" trio, replacing the trumpet with a wordless soprano (Kay Davis).[27] Davis's vocal purity would suit Rachmaninoff's famous "Vocalise." The second chorus brings back Lawrence Brown's tune, even creamier and croonier than it was in "Blue Light" thanks to the upward transposition. Here, though, Ellington gives Brown's melody a Bach-like treatment.[28] It serves as the cantus firmus for two choruses, the first a duet for soprano and clarinet (Jimmy Hamilton, whose classical tone blends perfectly with Davis's voice), the soprano intoning the cantus, the clarinet playing a new counterpoint; and the second with the cantus in the low reeds and brass with the soprano singing a new counterpoint. Sketches preserved in the Ellington Archive show how carefully Ellington planned the contrapuntal devices. Ellington's slightly frantic piano intro and outro have an impromptu air that contrasts tellingly with the work's contrapuntal and coloristic logic.

"On a Turquoise Cloud," premiered at Carnegie Hall on December 27, 1947, might be termed an encore for "Transblucency." It uses all the same elements (adding the color of the bass clarinet), but now they are employed in a delightfully informal fashion, transposed down to a mellow Db, yet built on a new color, the floating timbre of Kay Davis's high Abs (and singular high Bb). No longer a blues, somewhere between a pop tune and an opera aria, it is a siren song. The only further steps Ellington would make in this direction move upward to celestial realms: Mahalia Jackson's wordless humming after "The Twenty-Third Psalm" and Alice Babs's coloratura in "Heaven."

"KO-KO": THE COLOR BLACK

Shades of blue make up one half of Ellington's color spectrum; variants of black, from café au lait to ebony, form their complement. The breathy but warm sound of the New Orleans clarinet, with Bechet as the foundation amplified by Bigard and Hodges, signified blue. The dark growl of Miley's trumpet, Nanton's trombone, and Carney's baritone sax, all derived from the sound of Joe Oliver's cornet, connoted black. Ellington uses both blue and black timbres in music that belongs, in form and gesture, to the genre of the blues, though often the black pieces state the blues harmonic progression in the minor mode. Ellington's *noir* style (branded—some say by George Gershwin—as "Jungle Music" at the Cotton Club) portrayed characters who are more African than American, representing the resilience and strength that existed before slavery and that survived beyond it. The black-to-tan spectrum also represented two momentous events in the African American experience, the traumatic Middle Passage from Africa to America and the Great Migration from the rural South to the urban North. Ellington sounded this theme in the 1920s with "East St. Louis Toodle-Oo" and "Black and Tan Fantasy," in the '30s with "The Saddest Tale," "Echoes of Harlem" and "Menilek," and in the '50s with "Such Sweet Thunder." Throughout his career he referred to an operatic presentation of the theme, called *Boola,* "which tells the story of the Negro in America."[29] In 1941 Ellington told Almena Davis, an interviewer for a black newspaper, the California *Eagle,* that he had "practically finished a full-length opera based on the history of the American Negro, and is readying a synopsis of it to submit to a prospective producer."[30] The opera never appeared, but, according to Barry Ulanov, Ellington drew two of his most important works of the 1940s, "Ko-Ko" and *Black, Brown and Beige,* from the operatic sketches.[31] Both works reflect Ellington's political engagement, which reached a peak of militancy in the early 1940s, when the United States entered a war against racism without addressing racism on the home front. Because of its scale and ambition, *Black, Brown and Beige* will receive its own chapter, but here "Ko-Ko" can exemplify the color black, with all its resonances, very well on its own.

Ellington recorded "Ko-Ko" for the first time on March 6, 1940, at the first Victor recording session of what has come to be known as the Blanton-Webster Band because of the revivifying arrivals of Jimmy Blanton on bass and Ben Webster on tenor sax. The session also produced "Jack the Bear" and "Morning Glory."[32]

In form, "Ko-Ko" is eight blues choruses in e♭ minor (the blackest possible key, at the furthest remove from the white harmony of C major) preceded by an eight-bar intro. Each chorus is in call-and-response format:

Intro. Baritone sax (Carney) answered by trombones (eight bars)

1. Bass trombone (Tizol) answered by saxes

2. Saxes answered by plunger-muted trombone (Nanton) assisted by muted brass

3. Same as 2 but with higher-pitched trombone responses

4. Saxes answered by muted brass and piano

5. Trumpets answered by saxes and trombones

6. Brass answered by solo bass

7. Shout chorus; brass (and clarinet) answered by saxes

8. Eight bars same as chorus 1; four-bar coda

Almost every chorus begins with the Beethovenian rhythmic figure:

♪ ♪ ♪ ♩[33]

This motive is pounded out first on the tom-toms, then intoned by the baritone sax; in the first chorus it becomes a four-note melodic figure in the valve trombone. It provides the rhythm for the saxophone, trumpet, and trombone calls in choruses three through six. Thematic urgency mirrors the massive, dense coloration of the score. Except for the piano, the only solo voices heard are dark and deep: tom-tom, baritone sax, bass trombone, muted trombone, string bass. Higher-pitched colors appear as doubled melodies or as chords that become increasingly dissonant sounding as the piece progresses, reaching a peak with the first chord of the shout chorus, an E♭ minor eleventh chord made up of all the black notes on the piano. Even at the beginning, though, the parallel triads in the trombones have a modernistic sting, an aspect of the piece pushed further in the jabbing chords and wailing whole-tone scales of the piano.

While "Blue Light" emphasized the contrasting timbres of individual players, "Ko-Ko" draws its color from massed instrumental groupings. It treats saxes, trumpets, and trombones as if each section were a single voice and gradually fuses these three elements together in the sixth chorus with three increasingly dissonant fanfarelike chords. In the technical terms of the European tradition, Ellington scored "Ko-Ko" in a *tutti* style, exploiting the massed timbral possibilities of the entire ensemble. This approach to the orchestra, like the rhythmic motto, reminds the listener of the heroic side of Beethoven, the Third, Fifth, Seventh, and Ninth symphonies. To continue the Beethoven analogy, we might say that the sound of "Ko-Ko" is a Promethean theft, a defiant transfer of the image of heroism from white to black. Ellington composed "Ko-Ko" in 1939. Its heroic coloring anticipates some of the most important classical works of the war years that made similarly symbolic use of Beethoven's rhythms, in particular Schoenberg's *Ode to Napoleon* (1942) and Stravinsky's Symphony in Three Movements (1945). Precociously postcolonial with a vengeance, "Ko-Ko" reclaimed and rewrote the primitivism of early modern classical music and the tom-tom-grooved "jungle" numbers that white audiences demanded from black entertainers, using the most esteemed devices of European art music as emblems of African American integrity, pride, and power.[34]

Ellington composed music with color in order to write a "colored" music; throughout his career he defined his artistic project as giving musical expression to the experience of African Americans. Although much of his music evolved in the dubious "plantation" atmosphere of the segregated Cotton Club, Ellington's painterly titles were not floor show gimmicks; they directed listeners to the music's timbral essence. He told one interviewer that his orchestra played "unadulterated American Negro music," not jazz or swing. Ellington was acutely conscious of art's responsibility to represent experience and of the inability of European forms of music and media to represent the particular experiences of his life. The forms of his music and the sounds of his orchestra presented an alternative system of representation based in sound, form, and social function on the blues. Altering a musical culture at a most basic level meant rewiring the way music was perceived and processed: Ellington's music asks us to see with our ears and hear with our eyes. This disruption of the habitual sensory pathways makes Ellington a "nationalist" in the way Bartók or Falla were, but it also makes him a quintessential modernist like Debussy and Schoenberg, who similarly sought to transform the experience of music by fusing sound and sight.

SEGUE: AFTERNOON OF THE XYLOPHONE

A few notes of music, a tapping, a faint
hum: you girls, so warm and so silent,

dance the taste of the fruit you have known!
Dance the orange.
—Rainer Maria Rilke

A noir, E blanc, I rouge, U vert, O bleu: voyelles. . . .
—Rimbaud, "Voyelles"

These days every shoemaker's apprentice can orchestrate to
perfection.
—Mahler to Alma on Puccini's *Tosca*

Firstly, hanging from the ceiling, were Smyrna carpets with complex
patterns picked out on a red background. Then on all four sides were
door-curtains from Kerman and Syria, striped with green, yellow and
vermilion. Coarser door-curtains from Kiarbekir, rough to the touch
like a shepherd's cloak; and still more carpets which could be used
as hangings, long carpets from Isphahan, Tehran, and Kermanshah,
the wider carpets of Shumaka or Madras, strange flowerings of
peonies and palms where the imagination was let loose in the garden
of dreams. On the floor, which was strewn with thick fleeces, there
were more carpets: in the center, an Agra, an astonishing piece with
a wide, soft, blue border against a white background, on which
were exquisitely imagined patterns in a blueish violet. After that,
wonders were displayed on all sides. . . . Here were Turkey, Arabia,
Persia and India: palaces had been emptied, mosques and bazaars
ransacked. . . . Visions of the East hovered beneath the extravagance
of this savage art amid the strong scent that this ancient wool had
kept from lands of sun and vermin.
—Zola, *Au bonheurs des dames*

Between 1905 and 1910 the spectrum of European music shifted
from somber Victorian mauve to riotous fauve. The mournful hues of
Brahms and Bruckner gave way to the extravagant glitter of Ravel's
Shéhérazade, Strauss's *Salome,* Puccini's *Madama Butterfly,* Debussy's
Ibéria, Mahler's *Das Lied von der Erde,* Stravinsky's *Firebird.* Shim-
mering orchestral effects, erotic subject matter, and exotic geographic
settings mirrored looming issues of the fin de siècle: imperialism, ori-
entalism, Decadence, Symbolism, the occult, the primitive, and what
Elaine Showalter termed "sexual anarchy." More than a matter of
"sound for sound's sake," the heightened intensity of timbre presaged
changes in the way music represented ideas and feelings, changes, as
well, in its social function.

These riotous new timbres heralded the musical onset of modernism (a.k.a. Symbolism or Decadence in fin de siècle parlance). Unlike
romantic music, Symbolist music did not conjure up easily identifiable
emotions. Instead it was evocative, evasive, even deliberately obscure.
Treating human nature as an unfamiliar terrain, it placed the human

subject (you and me) within a complex web of sensory associations. The self became an Other.

By mimicking, however superficially, non-European musical styles (Chinese, Japanese, or Balinese), composers undermined the assumption that the ideas and emotions represented in European music were universal categories. European music, like Zola's department store, had already begun to trade in exotic colors (think of *Aida* and *Carmen*) without the composers realizing how such appropriation might transform the appropriators. The xylophone, a rogue instrument with Asian/African origins, can help track the fin de siècle shift of timbre and its unforeseen consequences. Long before its first clattering appearance in European concert music, in Saint-Saëns's *Danse macabre* of 1874, the xylophone assumed the role of a menacing outsider. Originating in Southeast Asia and developed in Africa, it reached Europe in the fifteenth century: "The earliest pictorial evidence of the xylophone is found in a woodcut from the collection *Totentanz* [*Dance of death*, 1511] by Holbein the Younger, depicting Death carrying the instrument hanging from a shoulder strap."[35] An alien, skeletal instrument played by itinerant musicians, the xylophone signified otherness; in the 1890s its dry, cackling tone propelled a broomstick-borne witch in *Hansel and Gretel* and gave a tinselly glitter to the countercultural street life of Montmartre in *La Bohème*.

Placed within the plush romantic orchestra, the alien xylophone sounded unvocal and immiscible. Its diabolical death rattle mocked the sound ideal of European music, the expressive voice. It did not breathe or vibrate, it just clonked. In the first decade of the twentieth century the xylophone became an emblem of the new as well as the Other. Its sound evoked states of being that were alternative geographically, racially, or psychologically. In Strauss's *Salome* it paced the frantic belly-shaking coda of the Dance of the Seven Veils; in Debussy's *Ibéria*, it initiated the sultry habanera of *"les parfums de la nuit"*; in *Gigues* it punctured the sound of a whining carousel like a throbbing migraine; and in *Jeux* it mocked middle-class morals with a shockingly modern *romance à trois*. It etched its alien imprint on Mahler's Symphony no. 6 (*danses macabres* and hard-driven death marches), Ravel's *Mother Goose Suite* (evoking the Balinese gamelan) and *Daphnis et Chloé* (satyrs), Schoenberg's Five Pieces for Orchestra, op. 16 (sinister premonitions), Berg's Altenberg Lieder, op. 4 (snow and, later, unmeasurable pain), and Stravinsky's *Firebird* (the infernal Kastchei) and *Petrouchka* (the fatal interracial fight between Petrouchka and the Moor).

In all these works the xylophone's harsh matter-of-factness eroded the aesthetic foundation of European music, which could be summed up in the word *expression*. Music was supposed to be a simple voice-like communication, speech turned into song. Heeding Wordsworth's notion that a poet was a "man speaking to men," nineteenth-century listeners imagined a symphony or concerto as a gendered lyrical utterance, a man *singing* to men. Composers emphasized instruments most reminiscent of the human (particularly the male) voice, including cello, horn, and clarinet, to make the entire orchestra sound like a magnified lyric baritone. Audience members felt that the music spoke to them directly in terms they immediately grasped, a condition I'll call "intersubjectivity." Assuming that the emotions expressed in the music, from the *pathétique* to the *eroica*, were universals, theorists and acousticians claimed that the devices for representing these emotions were not the conventions of a particular idiom or culture but sprang from the facts of physics and biology—an idea that remains surprisingly alive today.

The xylophone's antivoice drove the center of musical aesthetics away from human expression and toward tone color, whose relation to human consciousness was more mysterious than the familiar signals of feelings. Bypassing the ideal of expression, Debussy defined music as "colors and rhythmicized time."[36] Schoenberg's "Farben" (Colors), the third of his Five Pieces for Orchestra, elevated tone color above melody, harmony, or rhythm. In his *Harmonielehre* of 1911 he predicted that the music of the future would make melodies not out of pitches but of colors: *klangfarbenmelodie*. A quarter of a century later, Ravel's *Bolero*, an epic *klangfarbenmelodie*, confirmed the triumph of timbre over expression—and quickly achieved worldwide popularity.

The development of recording further aided and abetted the new primacy of sound. *Bolero*, popular as it was in the concert hall, came into its own with the advent of hi-fi stereophonic recording technology. Although the pursuit of high fidelity seemed like a technological development, recording changed all aspects of musical culture. By allowing any kind of music to be played at home, it undermined the brick-and-mortar hierarchy that placed the highest forms of musical art in concert halls and opera houses, the lowest in bars and brothels. Recorded music, reproduced without recourse to notation, erased the distinction between calculated composition and spontaneous improvisation. Its technology also determined musical form; Ellington built his "three-minute masterpieces" to fill one side of a 78 rpm, just as Stravinsky composed the movements (one to a side) of his Serenade in A.[37] Soon enough, the evolving capacities for sound storage and organization fed back on acoustical sound itself, so that live performances increasingly aspired to the sound and ambience of recordings. The art of orchestration now collaborated with the artistry of the recording engineer; classical and popular musicians alike would need to master both roles.

KIND OF WHITE: PIERROT LUNAIRE

Like Duke Ellington, Arnold Schoenberg was, at times, a painter as well as a composer. However, while Ellington's music merged aural and visual sensations effortlessly, in Schoenberg's music they collided explosively. The resulting music and paintings retain their power to disturb. Critics have treated them either as artistic breakthroughs toward a new representational system, or as medical data, the diaries of a mad musician, but choosing either one of these escape routes trivializes the music. Schoenberg's short-lived exaltation of musical color over melody and harmony, like Ellington's lifelong pursuit of the blues, sprang from a fundamental dissatisfaction with the framework of reality as it had come to be understood in European culture.

In 1905 Arnold Schoenberg struck up a fatal friendship with the painter Richard Gerstl at a Mahler concert in Vienna. Discussions with Gerstl soon led Schoenberg to try painting himself. In 1907 Gerstl moved in with Schoenberg's family and then ran off with Schoenberg's wife, Mathilde, mother of his two children and sister of his friend and teacher Alexander von Zemlinsky. When Mathilde returned to her husband, Gerstl committed suicide, on November 5, 1908. Even before Gerstl's death, Schoenberg's music was moving toward the "emancipation of the dissonance" that had been forecast, though not yet attained, in the final movement of his Second String Quartet (which he dedicated to Mathilde after the affair had ended). At the premiere, a month after the suicide, hostile members of the audience made catcalls and whistled into their house keys in protest, even though the quartet cadenced conventionally enough in F♯ major.

In the face of such vehement resistance to his music Schoenberg suddenly considered pursuing a career as a painter—a delusion perhaps born from a kind of Stockholm syndrome after the Gerstl affair. At the same time though he pushed the "emancipation of the dissonance" further in a series of increasingly radical compositions: Three Pieces for Piano, op. 11, *The Book of the Hanging Gardens,* op. 15 (song cycle), Five Pieces for Orchestra, op. 16 (the first piece entitled "Premonitions," the third, "Colors"), and the monodrama *Erwartung,* op. 17, all composed in 1908 and 1909.[38]

After this creative explosion Schoenberg entered a dry spell. His sense of isolation had deepened with Mahler's departure from Vienna in 1907 and his death in 1911. He feared that even his staunchest supporters, his two students, Berg and Webern, were becoming rivals more than disciples. Ever resourceful, Schoenberg took advantage of his composer's block by completing his *Harmonielehre* (Theory of Harmony), mainly traditional save for speculative talk about constructing chords in fourths rather than thirds (which Schoenberg had already demonstrated in his *Kammersinfonie,* op. 9) and constructing melodies from tone colors rather than pitches, or *klangfarbenmelodie.* Schoenberg's compositional floodgates would reopen only after another momentous encounter with a painter, Wassily Kandinsky.

Kandinsky and other artists associated with the journal *The Blue Rider* attended an all-Schoenberg concert in Munich on January 2, 1911. Kandinsky commemorated the concert in his painting "Impression III (concert)," which evolved from a realistic doodle to an abstraction in which, as Fred Wassermann writes, "the piano has become a dominant mass of black (bisected by a white band), smashing up against and vibrating with the overwhelming intensity of the yellow that envelops most of the painting."[39] The concert included the recent Second Quartet, op. 10 and Three Piano Pieces, op. 11. On January 18, Kandinsky wrote Schoenberg, whom he had never met, a letter with a portfolio of his works, proclaiming that "what we are striving for and our whole manner of thought and feeling have so much in common that I feel completely justified in expressing my empathy.[40] Schoenberg responded on January 24 as if he had been thrown a lifeline:

> I am sure that our work has much in common—and indeed in the most important respects: In what you call the unlogical and I call the "elimination of the conscious will in art." I also agree with what you write about the constructive element. Every formal procedure which aspires to traditional effects is not completely free from conscious motivation. But art belongs to the *unconscious!* One must express *oneself!* Express oneself *directly!* Not one's taste, or one's upbringing, or one's intelligence, knowledge or skill. Not all these *acquired* characteristics, but that which is *inborn, instinctive.*[41]

Schoenberg and Kandinsky met in person in September 1911. Kandinsky had been planning to publish "an almanac that would present a synthesis of the arts by mixing the radical new work of an international group of modern artists and musicians with folk art, Asian art and 'primitive' art."[42] Schoenberg contributed the essay "The Relationship to the Text" and the score of *Herzgewächse,* a setting of a symbolist poem by Maeterlinck for high soprano, celesta, harmonium, and harp for the publication. Four of his paintings appeared at the first Blue Rider exhibition in December 1911.

Herzgewächse, with its otherworldly, séance-style sonority and super-high F on the word *mystisches* was the first indication of Kandinsky's influence on Schoenberg. The composer had come to this new artistic alliance already steeped in the Viennese expressionism of Klimt and Kokoschka, and he was devoted to the notions of the instinctual basis of life found in the writings of Strindberg and especially Otto Weininger, the suicidal author of *Sex and Character,* to whose memory Schoenberg had originally dedicated his *Harmonielehre.*

As Carl Schorske chronicled, the fin de siècle Viennese vanguard saw their society as fundamentally deceptive. But what was the truth behind the false appearances? Schoenberg may have found an answer in Kandinsky's *Concerning the Spiritual in Art.* The painter presented the composer with an inscribed copy of his book on December 9, 1911. Just before publication he had added these words: "Schoenberg's music leads us into a new realm, where musical experiences are no longer acoustic, but purely spiritual. Here begins the 'music of the future."[43] A trained musician, Kandinsky also praised the compositions of Debussy and Scriabin.

Kandinsky's speculative theoretical writings could not be more different from Schoenberg's textbooklike *Harmonielehre.* In "The Relation to the Text," however, Schoenberg not only extolled *Concerning the Spiritual in Art* as a book he had read "with great joy," but he developed Kandinsky's distinction between appearances and reality: "The outward correspondence between music and text, as exhibited in declamation, tempo and dynamics, has but little to do with the inner correspondence, and belongs to the same stage of primitive nature as the copying of a model."[44] Kandinsky's book presented three arguments. First he called for an art that would rise above "materialism," with its concern only for appearances and "shapeless emotions such as fear, joy, grief, etc." The new art would express "lofty emotions beyond the reach of words" in pursuit of "the internal truth which only art can divine, which only art can express by those means of expression which are hers alone."[45] Next he described a "spiritual revolution" using the figure of a triangle moving onward and upward. At the center of this argument he cited Madame Blavatsky and the Theosophical Society, a movement that approached "the problem of the spirit by way of the *inner* knowledge."[46] Finally, Kandinsky discussed at length "the psychological working of color" as a way toward a fusion of the arts involving musical movement, pictorial movement, and physical movement. (Not surprisingly, Kandinsky's search for a *Gesamtkunstwerk* sprang from his experience of Wagner's *Lohengrin*.)[47] Although, unlike Scriabin, he did not actually experience synesthesia, Kandinsky catalogued the effects of colors in terms of musical sounds:

> A light blue is like a flute, a darker blue a cello; a still darker a thunderous double bass and the darkest blue of all—an organ.
> . . . absolute green is represented by the placid, middle notes of the violin.
> White . . . has this harmony of silence, which works upon us negatively, like many pauses in music that break temporarily the melody.
> In music black is represented by one of those profound and final pauses. . . . The silence of black is the silence of death.
> Light warm red . . . is a sound of trumpets, strong, harsh, and ringing.
> Violet is . . . an English horn, or the deep notes of wood instruments (e.g. the bassoon).[48]

The purely spiritual was no vague region; psychic explorers from Swedenborg to Blavatsky had mapped it out in terms of numbers and colors.[49] The Theosophical Society attached particular importance to the numbers three and seven; the society defined its mission in terms of three large aims and pictured the universe as seven bodies of spirit/matter.

During his brief but intense friendship with Kandinsky (which terminated with the outbreak of the First World War), Schoenberg applied occult ideas of the spirit to two major works, one, *Die glückliche Hand* (The Lucky Hand), a one-act opera already in progress, the other, *Pierrot Lunaire*, an unforeseen opportunity. *Die glückliche Hand* was begun in 1910 as a pairing to *Erwartung*, a contrast of masculine genius to feminine instinct straight out of Weininger. At curtain rise, the protagonist, simply called "Der Mann," lies facedown: "On his back crouches a cat-like, fantastic animal (hyena with enormous, bat-like wings) that seems to have sunk its teeth into his neck." Following the example of Kandinsky's opera *Der gelbe Klang*, written in 1909 with music by Thomas von Hartmann (a Russian composer who later became a follower of Gurdieff) and published in *The Blue Rider* in 1912, Schoenberg represented the creative work of Der Mann through a "color crescendo": "It begins with dull red light (from above) that turns to brown and then a dirty green. Next it changes to a dark blue-gray, followed by violet. This grows, in turn, into an intensely dark red which becomes ever brighter and more glaring until, after reaching a blood-red, it is mixed more and more with orange and then bright yellow; finally a glaring yellow light alone remains and inundates the second grotto from all sides."[50]

In January 1912 Albertine Zehme, a onetime Wagnerian soprano who had become a *diseuse,* asked Schoenberg to write music to accompany her recitation of poems from *Pierrot Lunaire,* a collection of fifty poems by the Belgian Parnassian Albert Giraud in the German translation of Otto Erich Hartleben. Zehme promised twenty to thirty performances and Schoenberg at first viewed the commission mainly as a business opportunity, but he soon found himself engaged in his most original composition to date.

Usually discussed in term of its *sprechstimme* performance style midway between speech and song, its contrapuntal structures (including passacaglia and fugue), and its brilliant instrumental writing, *Pierrot* owes much of its sound and structure to Kandinsky. Schoenberg constructed it systematically from colors and numbers, the "inner values" behind external appearance, as Kandinsky had written in his introduction to *Der gelbe Klang:* "The means belonging to the different arts are externally quite different. Sound, color, words! . . . In the last essentials, these means are wholly alike: the final goal extinguishes the external dissimilarities and reveals the inner identity."[51]

On *Sesame Street* they might say that *Pierrot Lunaire* is brought to you by the (Blavatskian) numbers three and seven and the colors white, black, and red. Schoenberg, who chose and arranged the text from Giraud's volume, subtitled the cycle "Three Times Seven Poems"; there are three parts, with seven poems in each. It opens with a seven-note motive, a rhythmic idea that returns in various guises throughout, most dramatically at the close of "Die Kreuzen" (The Crosses), which ends part II.

There are four explicit "color" movements: "4. Eine blasse Wäscherin" (white), "8. Nacht" (black), "11. Rote Messe" (red), and "18. Der Mondfleck" (white again). The movements share numerology as well. Number 4 begins with seven three-note chords, scored for flute, clarinet, and violin. Number 8 is a passacaglia built on a repeated three-note theme. In number 11 each line of the poem has seven syllables. To evoke the colors, Schoenberg mixed instrumental timbres just as Ellington would do in "Mood Indigo," but with his own tricks. He revoiced the trio of instruments in number 4 from chord to chord, so, for instance, in the first chord the clarinet plays the top note, the flute the bottom, and the violin the middle, while in the next chord the flute is on top, clarinet is on the bottom, and in the next, violin is on top, and so on. In the score he asked that the three instruments "play at completely equal volume and without expression" to produce a composite, disembodied sonority, a "white" sound.

In "Nacht" Schoenberg combined the sounds of the bass clarinet, cello, and the piano in its low register to represent "giant black moth wings killing off the sun's radiance" as night descends. The middle section of this movement, as vapors begin to rise, counterpoints flutter-tongued clarinet, the cello playing tremolos on the bridge, more squeaks than pitches, and staccato notes on the piano, a swirl of shadows. For "Rote Messe" Schoenberg contrasted high squeaks (piccolo and the upper register of the piano) and low mutters (bass clarinet, viola, and cello), a comic effect, almost like cartoon music, to paint a gruesome scene: Pierrot reveals the dripping red Host to the congregation by dipping his fingers in his heart's blood.

"Rote Messe," like much of *Pierrot Lunaire,* feels at once lurid and funny, qualities not much evident in Schoenberg's earlier work. By employing Kandinsky's mystical symbolism in place of the attempts at direct expression found in *Erwartung,* Schoenberg took his music to new and unexpected (and not particularly Kandinskian) places: objectivity and satire, with expression itself, the coin of the realm of romantic music, exposed (as it is in Kafka's "Hunger Artist") as an addictive codependency between the artist (up on the cross) and the audience who get their kicks watching the bloody spectacle, then crawl back to their humdrum everyday lives.

To replace the *weltschmerz* that died on the cross at the end of part II, Schoenberg ratcheted up the colors and the comedy in part III. Here Pierrot returns to the daylight world (lit by a green sun) in a kind of sadomasochistic vaudeville. In number 18, "Der Mondspeck," the color white, earlier a benign image of the imagination, returns as a symptom of obsessive compulsion as Pierrot vainly attempts to remove a speck of moonlight from the back of his coat. The instruments parody his pointless attempts to wipe the speck (genius? guilt? both?) away, "*Wischt und wischt,*" with a five-part double fugue scored mostly in the upper register; its twin subjects might be called Itchy and Scratchy. The song reduces the esoteric "devices" of fugal writing, imitation, stretto, canon, augmentation, retrograde, to so many nervous tics, deconstructing pedantry with pedantry. What remains, though, dazzles. All the counterpoint just turns into brilliant glitter, white like a diamond.

There is no indication that Kandinsky ever heard *Pierrot Lunaire*. In a letter to Kandinsky on August 19, 1912, Schoenberg referred to *Pierrot* semi-apologetically as "perhaps no heartfelt necessity as regards its theme, its content [Giraud's *Pierrot Lunaire*], but certainly as regards its form" and mentions his next project based on Balzac's Swedenborgian novel *Seraphita*. That project resulted in two works that mark the terminus of Schoenberg's colorized spiritualism. First came the orchestral song "Seraphita," op. 22, no. 1, to a poem of Ernest Dowson, scored for an unusual ensemble of voice, twenty-four violins, twelve cellos, nine basses, six clarinets, one trumpet, three trombones, tuba, timpani, cymbals, xylophone (of course), and tam-tam. Whether its precise instrumental proportions reflect acoustical concerns or numerological symbolism, the song has a unique otherworldly but sensuous timbre.

Schoenberg spent most of the war years working on a huge oratorio, *Die Jakobsleiter*, that might have fulfilled Kandinsky's prophecy of a higher art form. Like the contemporary visionary compositions, Scriabin's *Mysterium* and Ives's *Universe Symphony*, both intended for performances on mountaintops, Schoenberg's oratorio seems planned from the outset as a spiritual exercise whose dimensions would preclude actual performance. In the course of work on the oratorio, however, Schoenberg began to conceive a different way of relating the surface of music to an inner structure, the twelve-tone system, which would make its official debut in the unspiritual setting of a waltz, the last of Schoenberg's Five Pieces for Piano, op. 23, written in 1921.

INTERMEZZO: A PALER SHADE OF WHITE

The occult spiritualism of Schoenberg and Kandinsky (and early Stravinsky) ended, musically, with the arrival of jazz, first heard in France as played by James Reese Europe's 369th Infantry Hellfighters Band. Within a few years most European composers abandoned expressionism for jazz-tinged "objective" styles such as neoclassicism or Neue Sachlichkeit.[52] Although at first perceived as just another exotic fad, jazz confronted European music with a pertinent, persuasive rendering of contemporary experience that proved to be surprisingly tenacious and, at first, seductive. Euro-jazz by Milhaud, Ravel, Hindemith, Krenek, and Weill dominated the new music scene of the 1920s.

The eruption of jazz in European music incited a series of backlashes, both musical and political. Tone color and skin color remained linked, as evidenced by the discourse surrounding the 1928 Stravinsky/ Balanchine ballet *Apollon musagète,* conceived as an apotheosis of whiteness. Balanchine's choreography followed Stravinsky's description of his score as a *"ballet blanc,"*[53] that is, with dancers in tutus. In his *Autobiography* Stravinsky wrote that he had "pictured it to myself as danced in short white ballet skirts in a severely conventionalized theatrical landscape devoid of all fantastic embellishment."[54] The music, which evinced its whiteness by using only strings, began with the tonal emblem of whiteness, a simple cadence in C major. The timbre and tonality bore a heavy ethical message, which Stravinsky made explicit in his *Poetics of Music,* delivered at Harvard in 1939 (just as Ellington was composing "Ko-Ko"): "My freedom will be so much the greater and more meaningful the more narrowly I limit my field of action and the more I surround myself with obstacles. Whatever diminished constraint diminished strength. The more constraints one imposes, the more one frees one's self of the chains that shackle the spirit."[55] The music and choreography for *Apollon musagète* (a.k.a. *Apollo*) have become classics of high modernism, but it is edifying to view them as a statement of European essentialism (not without protofascist overtones). But don't take my word for it:

> *George Balanchine:* I myself think of Apollo as white music, in places as white-on-white. . . . For me the whiteness is something positive (it has in itself an essence) and at the same time abstract.[56]

> *Lincoln Kirstein:* In its grave sequence Balanchine carved four cameos in three dimensions: Calliope portrayed the metric and caesura of spoken verse; Polyhymnia described mimicry and spectacular gesture; Terpsichore, the activity, declaration, and inversion of academic dancing itself. These are all subservient to Apollo, animator and driver; they are his handmaidens, creatures, harem and household.
>
> With Lifar, Balanchine had been given a boy who might conceivably become a young man. In America, with Lew Christenson (who danced the role in New York in 1937), he found a young man who could be credited as a potential divinity. Praxitelean head and body, imperceptibly musculated but firmly and largely proportioned, blond hair and bland air recalled Greek marbles and a calm inhabitant of Nicolas Poussin's pastorals.[57]

Boris de Schloezer: "Whatever may have been the circumstances which led to the birth of *Apollo*, the work reveals to us its author's secret, his thirst for renunciation, his need for purity and serenity."[58]

It's not easy being white.

SOUNDS AND PERFUMES: SYMBOLISM IN WHITE AND BLACK

Kandinsky's theories about the relation of music, color, and words were a belated summation of the larger artistic movement, Symbolism, whose aesthetic ideology shaped the modernist literature of Charles Baudelaire, Paul Verlaine, Arthur Rimbaud, Stéphane Mallarmé, Paul Valéry, Stefan George, Georg Trakl, Rainer Maria Rilke, Aleksandr Blok, Andrei Belyi, William Butler Yeats, T. S. Eliot, James Joyce, Ezra Pound, and Wallace Stevens, among many others.[59] Symbolist literature aspired to the condition of music. It often cloaked this goal, however, in a mask of obscurantism. In the compositions of Debussy and Ellington Symbolist aesthetic ideas became far more accessible to everyday life. Arcane modernism became "jazz modernism."

Debussy's music is key to understanding the newly exalted role played by tone color as a means of representation. In his oeuvre Debussy gave musical form to the complex interplay of sensual perception and imaginary evocation that Baudelaire termed "correspondences":

> La Nature est un temple où de vivants piliers
> Laissen parfois sortir de confuses paroles;
> L'homme y passe à travers des forêts de symboles
> Qui l'observent avec des regards familiers.

> Nature is a temple of living pillars
> where often words emerge, confused and dim;
> and man goes through this forest, with familiar
> eyes of symbols always watching him.[60]

In this forest of symbols the human subject does not control meaning rationally but perceives it through sensory association as an endless chain of metaphors.

Debussy imbibed this Symbolist creed, further elaborated in Verlaine's "Art poétique," Rimbaud's "Voyelles," and J.K. Huysmans's novel *A Rebours,* and in the preface to Oscar Wilde's *Picture of Dorian Gray,* at the famous "Tuesdays" at Mallarmé's apartment and, on

Fridays at the Chat Noir.[61] In the 1880s Debussy set poems by Mallarmé, Verlaine, and Baudelaire, developing a richly allusive idiom of musical symbolism. Sounds became symbols.

In his songs Debussy often employed a symbolic sonority in the accompaniment to "read" the text. In "En Sourdine," the first song in the Verlaine cycle *Fêtes galantes,* composed in 1891, a leitmotif beginning with three repeated notes sounds throughout the first section; it disappears and then returns at the end where the singer names its symbolic role: "Voix de notre désespoir,/Le rossignol chantera" (Voice of our despair,/the nightingale shall sing). In retrospect, we realize that the motive represents the nightingale's call, but as a symbol of despair, not a scenic effect. The repeated note itself is a double metaphor: the piano sounds like a flute that sounds like a nightingale. But the song has grander, even more esoteric echoes. The voice of despair springs from a forbidden love; the poem depicts Verlaine and Rimbaud hiding amorously in the bushes. The poem, mirroring a mirror, also replicates in a very condensed form the entire second act of *Tristan,* the lovers' tryst, in which Brangäne, the voice of despair, warns of the inevitable intrusion of the real world. The nightingale's motive frames the central intimacy just as Brangäne's admonitions form a kind of protective wall around the great love duet. In case we might miss this tone parallel, Debussy launched the song with the famous "Tristan chord," the exact pitches heard at the opening of Wagner's opera but transposed an octave higher, one sound symbol evoking another.

Debussy tried his hand at writing Symbolist poetry, or rather prose, in his *Proses lyriques,* published in 1895. Here he pushed the piano-as–orchestra to an extreme, so that the second song, "De grève . . ." (Of the Shore . . .), forecasts the sound of *La Mer* composed a decade later. In terms of sound-as-symbol, however, the most interesting song is the last, "De soir . . ." (Of the Evening . . .). We might retitle it "Sunday in Paris with Claude," for, like Seurat's contemporary "Sunday Afternoon on the Island of La Grande Jatte," it is a painting of "modern life"—the earliest piece of music depicting the hustling "leisure" of the weekend city, including an excursion by train to the suburbs.[62]

In "De soir . . ." the piano sounds less like an orchestral reduction than an imaginary superorchestra. The contrapuntal *moto perpetuo* accompaniment rolls out a ceaseless stream of sound evocations all drawn from a short motive. As the motive evolves, its visual correlatives change as well. At first it evokes a clamor of church bells. Then, augmented in a dotted rhythm, it suggests the rattling bounce of a suburban train. As the train is "devoured" by a tunnel a new contrapuntal texture appears, waves of sixteenth notes in the right hand against a grandly rising and falling arch in the left, all played on the black keys of the piano. Though the black keys may indicate the darkness of the tunnel, they also produce a pentatonic scale. The scale and rhythmic counterpoint sound like gamelan music. The significance of this occidental/oriental double image becomes clear when Debussy inverts the counterpoint, lifting the slow arch motive to the upper register of the piano as the words speak of "Dimanche, dans le bleu de mes rêves" (Sunday in the blue of my dreams), as if the day trip to the outskirts of Paris were just a poor substitute for more exotic travel. (Des Esseintes, the hero of *A Rebours,* preferred imaginary travel to the real thing.) As evening settles on the city the arch motive turns back into bell sounds, no longer clangorous but distant, nostalgic, slowly fading as the speaker falls asleep.

The Symbolist songs prepared Debussy for the full expression of textless musical symbolism in the *Prélude à l'après-midi d'un faune,* an orchestral work inspired by Mallarmé's poem. The *Prélude* is not a tone poem but what Ellington would term a "tone parallel." Debussy explained to a critic that the music was "perhaps the dream left over at the bottom of the faun's flute."[63] Debussy reduced Mallarmé's almost inscrutable text to its essential sonoric value, an unaccompanied C♯ on the flute in its breathy, slightly muted middle register, a pitch "naturally out of tune on French flutes of the period."[64] The unaccompanied flute solo that begins the *Prélude* is not a diegetic sound within the action (real or dreamed) of the poem but a floating sound symbol poised to take on any of the poem's inflections. Placing the sound of the flute first before addressing, however indirectly, the action of the poem, Debussy was implementing Verlaine's instruction: "De la musique avant toute chose" (Music first!).

Debussy's most sophisticated works of timbral symbolism, though, are not his songs or orchestral pieces but his piano compositions, especially Book I of the *Préludes,* a set of twelve "tone parallels" published in 1910. Debussy here applied the techniques of musical Symbolism to the central idea of Impressionist painting, the fleeting character of sensory experience. As in Turner and Monet, wind and water present images of constant change, but Debussy chose subjects that also placed those elements in relation to other works of art. Each prelude poses the question of how art can resist and embrace temporality. To indicate the thematic interplay of the enduring and the perishable Debussy framed the first book of *Préludes* with two dances, one from ancient Greece, preserved on a frieze in the Louvre, the other from contemporary America, a ragtime Debussy had heard performed by street musicians (probably in blackface) while on vacation in England.

Debussy's piano never sounds simply like a piano but creates sonic metaphors. Lockspeiser describes Debussy's approach to the piano as illusionistic: "To both Marguerite Long and Louise Liebich [Debussy] insisted that the piano was to sound as if it were 'an instrument without hammers' and he wanted the fingers on the keyboard to appear to 'penetrate into the notes.' The illusion was to be complete. Nothing was to be allowed to destroy the impression that the mechanical piano, a mere 'box of hammers and strings' was not a piano."[65] Illusionism is not the same as illustration; it would be a mistake to hear these pieces as musical depictions. The sound images evoked in the *Préludes* are themselves symbols; the music is part of the symbolic forest in which humankind wanders, a forest Debussy had evoked at the very opening of his opera *Pelléas et Mélisande*.

Debussy signaled the complex symbolism of these relatively simple pieces by the placing and selection of titles. Titles appear in parentheses at the end of each prelude rather than at the top of the first page, as if they were just tentative, transient associations. Seven of the titles link the music to artworks, making the preludes reflections of reflections. "Danseuses de Delphes" refers to a Greek caryatid in the Louvre, "a support column sculpted in the form of a female figure."[66] "Voiles" may refer either to the dancer Loïe Fuller or to sailboats, depending on the gender assigned to the title word. "Le vent dans la plaine" begins a line of a poem by Favart that serves as an epigram for Paul Verlaine's "C'est l'extase langoureuse," which Debussy had set to music in his *Ariettes oubliées*. "Les sons et les parfums tournent dans l'air du soir" is a line from Baudelaire's "Harmonie du soir," which Debussy had set to music in 1885. "La fille aux cheveux de lin" takes its title from a poem by Leconte de Lisle, itself based on a poem by Robert Burns. "La Cathédrale engloutie" refers to a Breton myth that formed the basis of the opera *Le Roi d'Ys* by Edouard Lalo. Shakespeare's *A Midsummer Night's Dream*, as illustrated by Arthur Rackham, is the source of "La Danse de Puck." Of the remaining five, three, "Les collines d'Anacapri," "La Sérénade interrompue," and "Minstrels," are portraits of popular music (Italian, Spanish, and American, respectively). Scholars have yet to nail down specific references for the remaining two preludes, the violent "Ce qu'a vu le vent d'ouest" and the desolate "Des pas sur la neige,"[67] whose title could have sprung from any number of

Impressionist snow scenes, a favorite genre of Monet and Sisley in particular (see, for example, Sisley's "Snow at Louveciennes" at the Musée d'Orsay).[68]

The titular interpretations listed above are found in most program notes; these also usually divide the preludes between those based on artworks and those based on nature without seeing that the two groups are connected metaphorically to the central theme of temporality, which received its most monumental treatment in "La Cathédrale engloutie," a fresco of stone, seawater, and metallic bells. Debussy placed its *Parsifal*-paced unfolding between two more fleeting visions that could be termed salon music à la Grieg (a composer whom Debussy pretended to dislike): the interrupted serenade and Puck's dance. Just as each prelude associates sound with sight, each also evokes the sense of touch. Each title suggests a different physical material: stone, feathers, water, snow, flaxen hair, wind gusts, fairy cobwebs, guitar strings, drum skins, the scents of plants or perfume; each material suggests a different physical connection between pianist and keyboard.

To see how Debussy used tone color symbolically, let's examine "Danseuses de Delphes" and "Des pas sur la neige" in more detail. The title "Danseuses de Delphes" presents a conundrum similar to that of Keats's "Ode on a Grecian Urn" in its suggestion of life suspended in fired clay:

> O Attic shape! fair attitude! with breed
> Of marble men and maidens overwrought,
> With forest branches and the trodden weed;
> Thou, silent form! dost tease us out of thought
> As doth eternity: Cold Pastoral!

Debussy similarly represented a dance set in stone. The score tells the performer that the music should be *"doux et soutenu,"* at once sweet and sustained, no easy task, but the words encapsulate the almost impossible simultaneous evocation of grace and gravitas. The melody, an ascending legato line, hides between a bass figure in octaves and a rising chorale of three-note chords. The two framing figures are counterintuitively both slurred and marked staccato. The counterpoint demands a scrupulously controlled touch from the pianist, who must balance the three voices and also bring out the melody, all within a soft dynamic—as if the keyboard were made of modeling clay just beginning to set. Further expanding the varieties of touch, Debussy contrasts the airy heaviness of the opening texture with a cadential phrase to be played even more quietly, like a distant harp or lyre—perhaps this is the music that the dancers themselves are hearing. In the next phrase Debussy repeats what we have just heard but stretches out each figure across the keyboard, as if he were reorchestrating. The accompaniment suddenly suggests the sound of finger cymbals or crotales, which Debussy had also used as a classical Greek color in "Afternoon of a Faun." Debussy gradually animates his three lines into a complex hand-over-hand choreography at bars 15 to 17, where the interplay of elements is finally, though briefly, heard at a *forte* dynamic. After this climax recedes the last three bars reiterate a single harmony in three contrasting colors: a seven-note statement of a B♭ major triad is sounded once *forte*, then repeated *pianissimo*, then underscored with a single B♭ at the very bottom of the keyboard, which must be released while the pedal sustains the upper chords—a *klangfarbenmelodie* that is also a melody of touch.

Debussy gave touch an even more complex symbolic treatment in "Des pas sur la neige." The piece is built on an evolving ostinato, a short motive with a curiously nervous rhythm on which the composer placed a heavy synesthetic burden: "Ce rythme doit avoir la valeur sonore d'un fond de paysage triste et glacé" (this rhythm should have the tonal color of the depths of a bleak, frozen landscape). The motive sounds twice in each bar, the second statement one note higher in the scale, forming a rising four-note idea that recalls a similarly freighted motive in Wagner. Both the ostinato and the plaintive melody that rises above it sound like they are trying to restate the opening of the Prelude to the third act of *Tristan,* and indeed Debussy's prelude retraces the steps of Wagner's phrase by phrase. Debussy indicates the complexity of the allusion by mirroring Wagner's consoling second theme, a downward chromatic drift, with a diatonic theme in G♭ major that is not only as distant from the d minor tonic as possible but is also played mainly on the black keys, above the symbolic snow line.[69]

The submerged intertextual links, though, reinforce the central theme of the *Préludes.* Replacing romantic heat and humidity with a brittle chill, Debussy recast Wagner's heaving emotion-laden notes as black markings on a white page, evanescent as footprints in the snow. Once we hear the snowy landscape as a metaphor for the piano keyboard itself, the prelude becomes a commentary on the relation of piano and orchestra. The piano, essentially a percussion instrument, cannot simulate the swelling string crescendo (with all violins on the open G string) that begins Wagner's prelude. By comparison with that warm sound, the piano is a treacherous icy timbral landscape; the pianist's touch, skating on thin ice, must assert illusion over physics. Yet, as Lockspeiser points out, the piano's physical limitation relative to the orchestra is also a strength: "It was sometimes to be an instrument that drew music from the circumambient air, or that could project patterns made up of myriads of little sounds. It was never admitted to be an instrument inferior, in the range of shadings of its dynamics, to wind or string instruments. Its defects were its virtues."[70] Transforming Wagner's warm sounds to an icy *"valeur sonore"* no orchestra could produce, the piano asserts its symbolic superiority.

Debussy's musical symbolism rests on two strategies that suggest parallels with Ellington. The first is intertextuality, usually between the music and some other artwork. The second is the sound metaphor, the evocation of one timbre through another. Debussy's symbolic techniques inform the musical languages of such later and different works as Stravinsky's Sererade in A, Bartok's *Out of Doors,* Messiaen's *Vingt Regards,* or any of the preludes in Shostakovich's op. 87. But, even though the Cotton Club may have existed in a different universe from Mallarmé's exclusive symbolist gatherings, Debussy's aesthetic ideas perhaps found their richest application in the music of the Ellington Orchestra. From his earliest compositions to his last recordings, the blues provided Ellington with an intertextual discourse; his band was the source of sound symbols. Let's see if we can come up with a list of Ellington "preludes." If we exclude the genres of songs, concertos, and extended compositions (and give Strayhorn and Tizol their own lists), and limit ourselves to pieces with a distinctive timbre, we might easily arrive at two volumes of twenty-four preludes, a Bachian "48" to set beside Debussy's three dozen:

1. Black and Tan Fantasy
2. Black Beauty
3. Immigration Blues
4. East St. Louis Toodle-Oo
5. The Mooche
6. Creole Love Call
7. Awful Sad
8. Jubilee Stomp
9. The Mystery Song
10. Echoes of the Jungle
11. Mood Indigo
12. Old Man Blues
13. Eerie Moan
14. In a Sentimental Mood
15. Delta Serenade
16. Daybreak Express
17. Menilek
18. Blue Light

19. Subtle Lament
20. Jack the Bear
21. Ko-Ko
22. Across the Track Blues
23. Harlem Airshaft
24. Bojangles
25. A Portrait of Bert Williams
26. Sepia Panorama
27. Dusk
28. Warm Valley
29. Blue Serge (Mercer Ellington)
30. Clothed Woman
31. Moon Mist (Mercer Ellington)
32. Dancers in Love
33. Happy-Go-Lucky Local
34. Transblucency
35. On a Turquoise Cloud
36. Such Sweet Thunder
37. Madness in Great Ones
38. Where's the Music
39. Single Petal of a Rose
40. Zweet Zurzday
41. Afro Bossa
42. Bonga
43. La Plus Belle Africaine
44. Depk
45. Amad
46. The Sleeping Lady and the Giant Who Watches over Her
47. Portrait of Wellman Braud
48. Second Line

While we're at it, here are a dozen Strayhorn preludes:

1. Chelsea Bridge
2. Take the "A" Train
3. Balcony Serenade
4. Johnny Come Lately
5. Hear Say
6. Star-Crossed Lovers
7. Bluebird of Delhi
8. Agra
9. Isfahan
10. Lotus Blossom
11. Blood Count
12. U.M.M.G.

OUTRO: SOUNDS RECAPTURED

The "Ellington effect" is a particular instance of a much wider twentieth-century soundscape, a constructed environment of sound that always has both physical and semiotic dimensions. As Emily Thompson points out, the idea of acoustical engineering itself arose in response to the idea of "noise pollution." Noise was a ubiquitous by-product of ever-encroaching industrialism, but it also symbolized "the many perils of the modern American city, including overcrowded tenements, epidemic disease, and industrial pollution."[71] Similarly, a "good" acoustic environment was not a simple question of physics and reverberation time but a matter of taste, and therefore a matter of class and race as well. The acoustics of Symphony Hall in Boston, for instance, were designed for an orchestra manager, Henry Higginson, who preferred "older music" to "very noisy music" (in other words, Beethoven over Strauss), part of a broader notion of the solemn, serious qualities—ethical qualities—that Higginson and others of his time associated with good music. Concertgoing, according to Theodore Thomas, was "an elevating mental recreation which is not an amusement."[72] Good acoustics could symbolize an entire value system.

Just a few years after the opening of Symphony Hall in 1900 its carefully controlled environment would be an anachronism. The argument about good and bad music and good and bad sound quality shifted from the concert hall to the living room and later to the kitchen, the den, and, most worryingly, the automobile. And to the movie theater as well. For most of the people most of the time, musical sound in the twentieth century meant recorded and/or broadcast sound, the revolutionary consequence of Edison's 1877 invention (and Marconi's 1895 discovery), when, as Ira Gershwin would put it, "they all laughed"— but not for long.

The surprisingly rapid acceptance of recorded music as the equivalent of live performance may appear less surprising when we realize that, at least in middle-class households, the piano already played the same cultural role in the nineteenth century that the phonograph would play in the twentieth. Through transcriptions and reductions, the piano, like the phonograph, brought into the home the orchestra and the opera house, as well as genres such as ragtime, which otherwise might only be encountered in questionable surroundings. Prefiguring the direction that recording would follow, the piano evolved in order to translate instrumental sounds with the ever-greater illusion of fidelity. Piano builders, composers, and performers took an interest in the "production" of piano sound, not just its renderings of pitches and rhythms but also its atmospherics. Debussy's use of the piano to suggest distant sounds, cultures, and sensations makes him a precursor for recording engineers. Recording allowed the esoteric researches of symbolism to shape the sound of everyday life, including the "sound" of music.

While the sound of recorded jazz reflected changes in technology as well as ongoing trade-offs between sound, convenience, and price, it was also a subliminal, symbolic "correspondence" to the way people conceptualized jazz. When Ellington's music was associated with inaccessible and exotic venues like the Cotton Club, recordings were made in a "you are there" mode (often with Irving Mills simulating the role of emcee). When jazz listeners sought to capture the nonrepeatable essence of jazz, improvisation, they would tolerate bad microphone placement and erratic balances as long as the results sounded "live." For listeners, like John Hammond, predisposed to view jazz as a kind of folk music, a rough acoustic was a badge of honor. And when jazz became a classical music, the recording ambience had to suggest the calm, well-balanced resonance of the concert hall.

There are Ellington recordings to match all of these approaches; the Blanton-Webster recordings made for Victor in 1940 and 1941 and the live recording made at the Crystal Ballroom in Fargo, North Dakota, on November 7, 1940, demonstrate how contrasting styles of recording can cast completely different lights on the same repertory and players. Dick Burris and Jack Towers made the Fargo recordings on a portable disk-cutting recorder. The sound is distant, balances are erratic, and some recordings break off in the middle of a performance. It says volumes about the notion of jazz "authenticity" that many listeners accept the judgment of Alexander Coleman, cited in the Book-of-the-Month Club rerelease, that this "recording is the jazz equivalent of the Holy Grail." For its admirers, the Fargo set represents the way the Ellington band "really" sounded, in the moment. By contrast, not only is the sound of the Victor recordings (made in Chicago, Hollywood, and New York) clearer and more evenly balanced, but the performances are more classical as well, that is, slower, even though they were mainly single takes. For a different kind of listener, these studio recordings of the Blanton/Webster band are the firmest evidence of the "masterpiece" status of most of the pieces (interestingly, the same listeners rarely give the vocals the same respect as the instrumental pieces).

We can hear a similar divide in recording styles in canonic albums made in 1959 by two of Ellington's most important successors: Charles Mingus's *Blues and Roots,* produced by Nesuhi Ertegun for Atlantic, and the Miles Davis/Gil Evans *Sketches of Spain,* produced for Columbia by Teo Macero and Irving Townsend. It's not an accident that Atlantic is best known for their recordings of Ray Charles and Aretha Franklin, while Columbia was associated with the sounds of the Philadelphia Orchestra and the New York Philharmonic. The ambience (or lack of it) of the Mingus recording screams authenticity. You feel like you are in the front row at the Five Spot. There seems to be no reverb, no room sound, no microphones, nothing between you and the music. The sound perfectly suits the gospel style of the music; it tells us that we are in a jazz church, as far from the commercial realm of Mammon as it is possible to be.

Sketches of Spain is renowned for its first track, Evans's sixteen-minute reworking of the slow movement of Rodrigo's *Concierto de Aranjuez,* originally for guitar and orchestra, as a concerto for trumpet and a twenty-six-player jazz orchestra (including flutes, oboe, and harp). The arrangement united Davis, Evans, and Rodrigo and invited Debussy, Ravel, Falla, and Juan Tizol to the party, and Nelson Riddle and Henry Mancini as well. Given the crossover nature of the music, the sound ambience here aptly bespeaks hybridity. From the first sounds of a distant harp and castanets, the music seems to float in a highly engineered imaginary space at once resonant and intimate, where instrumental sounds drift in and out, in sharp or soft focus. The sound suits the mood of romantic exoticism, but, even more, it supports Davis's vocal approach to the music, "the jazzman as confessional poet," as Gary Giddins put it.[73] As soon as jazz singing embraced the microphone, the recording of jazz required some attention to the balance of amplified and unamplified elements, the synthetic intimacy of the voice and the acoustic space of the instruments. Nelson Riddle turned this problem into an art form in the albums he made with Frank Sinatra in the mid-1950s, *In the Wee Small Hours* and *Only the Lonely.* Evans's three concerto albums for Davis, *Miles Ahead, Porgy and Bess,* and *Sketches of Spain,* can be heard as a fusion of Ellington/Strayhorn tone parallel and concerto genres and Riddle's way of wrapping the voice in instrumental opulence.

Blues and Roots and *Sketches of Spain* present contrasting pictures of jazz as a music of roots and a music of branches. Mingus's music here explores the black side of the Ellington spectrum, while Davis and Evans pursue the blue side beyond "Transblucency." Though Ellington rarely engaged in the kind of evolved production heard on *Sketches of Spain,* even in albums marketed as "hi-fi," his innovative approach to timbre as sound and symbol could inspire musicians working in styles that might seem distant from jazz. We might even detect the influence in the music of Brian Wilson. Rock historians usually place the highly composed ambient sound of "Good Vibrations" within the framework of Phil Spector's "wall of sound" first heard in the 1963 recording of "Be My Baby" by The Ronettes, and the Beatles' recording of "Strawberry Fields." Spector created an "overall sound tapestry" by "combining layers of electronically processed sound—miked, amplified, recorded, filtered, compressed, synthesized, and so on."[74] In "Strawberry Fields," the producer George Martin mixed a simple guitar/bass/drums accompaniment with music for trumpets and cellos "and the strange sucking timbres produced by recording various percussion instruments with the tape reversed."[75] For the album *Pet Sounds* and the single "Good Vibrations," Wilson similarly created a background track of staccato chords using recorded sounds of organ, harpsichord, piano, sleigh bells, and pizzicato strings[76] and the electronic sound of the theremin. If we compare the sound of "Good Vibrations" with classic earlier Beach Boys recordings like "Little Deuce Coupe," the difference reproduces (by other technical means) the contrasting modes of "authenticity" and "hybridity" we heard in the Mingus and Davis/Evans albums, similarly recasting Wilson from "real" beach boy to surreal rock poet. "Good Vibrations" might just be Californian for *klangfarbenmelodie*.

CHAPTER 2

"Cotton Tail": Rhythm

The presence of rhythm and lack of symmetry are
paradoxical, but there they are. Both are present to a
marked degree. There is always rhythm, but it is the rhythm
of segments. Each unit has a rhythm of its own, but when
the whole is assembled it is lacking in symmetry. But easily
workable to a Negro who is accustomed to the break in
going from one part to another, so that he adjusts himself
to the new tempo.

—Zora Neale Hurston

The incantation must be so percussion oriented that it
disposes the listeners to bump and bounce, to slow grind
and steady shuffle, to grind, hop, jump, kick, rock, roll,
shout, stomp and otherwise wing the blues away.

—Albert Murray

What good is melody?

—Irving Mills, lyrics to "Don't Mean a Thing
(If It Ain't Got That Swing)"—also attributed to Bubber Miley

In the early years of the twentieth century the tempo of life sped up
sharply, as if someone had suddenly stepped on a global gas pedal.
Urban life seemed faster, noisier, less predictable. The hopped-up pace
felt exhilarating and dizzying: "Everything around man jumps, dances,
gallops in a movement out of phase with his own."[1] Even before the
century turned its musical soundtrack crackled with a new rhythm.

Scott Joplin's "Maple Leaf Rag," published in 1899, the year of Duke Ellington's birth, quickly became a worldwide sensation. Ragtime was not just another form of exoticism in an era that cultivated the exotic; Europeans (wowed by the performances of the touring Sousa band) and Americans alike embraced ragtime as the emblem of their accelerating everyday lives: "We make love to ragtime and we die to it."[2] Like the first Wright Brothers' plane, however, ragtime was just the lift-off phase of ever-faster existence; in a few decades people would move at the speed of sound and communicate at the speed of light. And they would dance: every increment of speed set bodies in new kinds of motion, from rag to rap. The eighteenth century danced the minuet, the nineteenth waltzed, but in the twentieth each decade branded itself with a dance rhythm: the one-step, the fox-trot, the Charleston, the Lindy, the mambo, the twist, disco, salsa—all of them African American in origin.

Between the two world wars jazz musicians imbued the new dance rhythms with an equally new quality called swing. Where ragtime had mirrored the nervous jolts and jostle of the city streets, swing, disseminated at lightning speed through radio, celebrated the freedoms that accelerated motion brought to daily life, freedoms made visible in the sleekly urbane dancing of Fred Astaire and Ginger Rogers and the gravity-defying acrobatics of the Nicholas Brothers. Today the term *swing* sounds geriatric (swing dance classes for senior citizens); we have to remind ourselves that swing was as radical a concept for music as relativity was for physics.

Swing remains oddly ineffable. Even in the twenty-first century it still eludes the grasp of most classically trained musicians. And of the dictionary as well. Even a well-honed definition seems to beg a few questions: "A sensation of pull and momentum found in jazz. It appears to result partly from the push and pull between layers of syncopated rhythms and the constant underlying beat."[3] More than the sum of technical devices (such as syncopation and "swung" eighths), more than a particular stylistic phase of jazz, swing, ultimately, is an *ethical* ideal, a temporal image of liberation, or, as Albert Murray says, "purification and celebration/affirmation."[4]

Swing first appeared as an extraordinary quality of solo playing, heard mainly in short "breaks." Instrumentalists, arrangers, and composers quickly learned ways to insinuate swing into performances by big bands as well as soloists. A handful of much-anthologized moments usually serves to chart its development: Jelly Roll Morton's swung performance of "Maple Leaf Rag," Louis Armstrong's 1924 solos (in "Go

'Long Mule" or "Copenhagen") in the relatively unswinging Fletcher Henderson band, the 1932 recording of "Moten Swing," in which every member of the Bennie Moten Orchestra captures the quality.

While in the view of many jazz historians, the Ellington band, for all its formal and expressive distinction, was rarely in the forefront of rhythmic propulsion, jazz critics single out "Cotton Tail" as an acme of swing, a groundbreaking rhythmic achievement that "changed the face of jazz."[5] In "Cotton Tail" rhythm plays a formal role comparable to its function in Beethoven's symphonies.

"COTTON TAIL"

Did you ever hear that story about that rabbit in the briar patch?
And they caught him and some shit what he was doing wrong. They
said, "We'll fix you—we're going to throw you in the briar patch."
And the rabbit, "Oh, mister, please, please, don't throw me in
there." Yes! They threw him in there and he said, "You can all kiss
my ass. That's where I wanted to be all the time!" Then he cut out,
ya know. Well, that's the way it is.

—Louis Armstrong

The Ellington Orchestra first recorded "Cotton Tail" in Hollywood on May 4, 1940. The recording features the tenor saxophonist Ben Webster, who had joined the band just five months earlier. Webster's unusually spacious two-chorus solo started out as an improvisation but became a fixed feature; in Ellington's music improvisation was often the road to composition. The solo became Webster's signature tune, but it would remain largely intact in later performances of "Cotton Tail," when Paul Gonsalves occupied the solo tenor chair.[6]

Throughout his career Duke Ellington worked synergistically with the members of his band. The taut structural logic of "Cotton Tail" is characteristically Ellingtonian, clearly related, as we shall see, to older Ellington charts based on "Tiger Rag," but its effortless drive (and many of its notes) depend on two musicians who had recently joined the band: Webster and bassist Jimmy Blanton. Some listeners might also detect the influence of composer/arranger/pianist Billy Strayhorn (who joined the band a year earlier and was already Ellington's alter ego) in the fierce dissonances of some of the brass chords.

Webster had worked with Ellington occasionally in 1935 and '36 (he can be heard on recordings of "Truckin'" and "In a Jam"), but until his arrival in January 1940 the band had never had a regular tenor soloist to fill the gap between Johnny Hodges on alto and Harry Carney on baritone. Now there were five reed players: Barney Bigard played clarinet and, when needed, second, nonsoloing tenor, and Otto Hardwick was a nonsoloing alto. Since the Ellington book was conceived for a four-man reed section, Webster at first had to create his own parts; it would have made sense, therefore, for him to compose (or propose) an entire chorus in which the five saxophones would play an improvisatory-sounding group solo, at once harmony and melody.[7] The reed section solo device descends from the clarinet trios in Don Redman's arrangements for Fletcher Henderson in the 1920s such as "The Stampede" of 1926 (and on Ellington's "The Mooche" of 1930) and in many Benny Carter charts in the 1930s (Webster had played with Carter).[8]

"Cotton Tail" exists both as a thirty-two-bar head to be followed by improvised choruses and as a six-chorus composition in which the head serves as a frame. You can find the head in most fake books, though often in the key of A♭ rather than the B♭ heard on Ellington's recordings.[9] "Cotton Tail" as a composition, not just the head, consists of six choruses of "rhythm changes" in B♭, a format that many bands of the time could have filled out without a written arrangement (as a head arrangement). However spontaneous it may sound it is not a head arrangement but a tightly compressed composition in which every note counts. Its phrase structure and scoring develop a dialogue of reeds and brass toward an escalating rhythmic and dynamic tension that reaches a high point in the "tutti" shout of the final chorus.

In jazz parlance "rhythm changes" denotes a thirty-two-bar harmonic pattern derived from Gershwin's "I Got Rhythm." Throughout the 1930s jazz players appropriated the harmonic patterns of popular songs, transforming them into variants of the blues (the Moten band turned "Sweet Sue, That's You" into "Toby," and the Lunceford Band transformed Gershwin's early tune "Do It Again" into "Swinging Uptown"). Ethel Merman put "I Got Rhythm" on the map in the 1930 Gershwin musical *Girl Crazy;* within a few years rhythm changes were second only to the twelve-bar blues pattern as the basis of jazz improvisation. Five years before "Cotton Tail" Ben Webster had recorded a very swinging rhythm changes chart, "Hotter than 'ell," by Horace Henderson with the Fletcher Henderson Orchestra. Virtually contemporary with "Cotton Tail" are such famous rhythm changes charts as the Basie band's "Lester Leaps In" and "Lunceford Special." Pieces based on rhythm changes are, like the blues, a series of isomorphic stanzas, but where a blues stanza (or chorus) contains three four-bar lines, AAB, a "rhythm" stanza has four eight-bar lines: AABA. (The template of rhythm changes does not use the final extended "Who could ask for anything more?" phrase of the Gershwin song.) In a blues the B serves to complete the thought:

> I've got the choo-choo blues, had 'em all night and day.
> I've got the choo-choo blues, had 'em all night and day.
> 'Cause the Panama Limited carried my man away.[10]

In rhythm changes the B,

> Old man trouble,
> I don't mind him.
> You won't find him
> Round my door

also called the "bridge" or "release," sets up melodic contrast and harmonic tension resolved by the final A.

A masterwork of compression, "Cotton Tail" consists of twenty-four (6 × 4) phrases, only three of which state the "head." No two phrases are exactly the same. Following is a phrase-by-phrase outline. The personnel for the May 1940 recording were:

Reeds: Otto Hardwick and Johnny Hodges, alto sax; Barney Bigard, tenor sax and clarinet; Ben Webster, tenor sax; Harry Carney, baritone sax

Brass: Cootie Williams, Wallace Jones, Rex Stewart, trumpets; Joe Nanton, Lawrence Brown, Juan Tizol, trombones

Rhythm: Duke Ellington, piano; Fred Guy, guitar; Jimmy Blanton, bass; Sonny Greer, drums

Chorus I: "Head" AA'BX

A: "Head" played in unison by one alto sax, baritone sax, plunger-muted trumpet (Williams), and trombone (Nanton)

A': "Head" with brass chords added

B: Reversed call-and-response between the five-sax choir and Williams's growled trumpet solo

X: A four-bar contrapuntal riff for reeds and brass taking the place of the expected eight-bar A

Chorus II: "Webster solo part I" AA'BA"

A: Webster and the rhythm section

A': Webster continues

B: Reverse call-and–response between clarinet + brass and Webster

A″: Webster continues solo, two bars of emphatic brass punctuation at the énd

Chorus III: "Webster solo part II" XA′BA″

X: Webster and rhythm section. Eight bars outside the harmonic progression, using instead a single diminished seventh chord

A′: Webster continues

B: Webster continues; six-note brass chords played on downbeats of every other bar

A″: Webster continues

Chorus IV: "Brass" AA′BX

A: A riff-style chordal melody for the brass section

A′: Brass continues

B: Baritone sax solo

X: Piano solo

Chorus V: "Sax section" AA′BA″

A: Harmonized melody played by five saxes

A′: Sax section continues

B: Sax section continues; melody here seems to allude to the Gershwin tune

A″: Sax section continues

Chorus VI: "Shout" AA′BA

A: Call-and-response between brass and sax choirs

A′: Call-and-response extended (brass repeats, saxes vary)

B: Climactic phrase with reeds and brass together

A: Head

In the outline above, the letters attached to phrases refer to harmonic structure, not melody. Note that Ellington's head does not return after each bridge but only at the end of the entire piece. Melodic development takes the place of repetition, just as it does in Beethoven or Brahms. Or the blues.

At once circular (reiterating its phrase structure in the manner of the blues) and linear, "Cotton Tail" builds phrase by phrase, chorus by chorus, to the climactic "tutti" proclamation of VI B. Its form is subtly, systematically asymmetrical: the six choruses are grouped 1 + 2 + 3 (an expanding Fibonacci series that would have pleased Bartók). Three structural anomalies (X) elide the six choruses into a seamless, seismic whole. The last phrase of chorus one, four bars shorter than the expected eight, serves as a jump cut to Webster's entrance. The cropped phrasing tilts the entire structure; everything thereafter seems to arrive ahead of schedule.

Harmonically static, Webster's first solo phrase in chorus two seems to extend the previous stanza as well as beginning a new one. Its structural ambiguity turns Webster's double chorus solo into an asymmetrically subdivided single phrase, 40 + 24 (AABAXABA). The last phrase of chorus four similarly jettisons rhythm changes in favor of a blues oscillation on the piano that sets up the supersax supermelody of chorus five. Although Ellington's static, out-of-time solo comes two thirds of the way through the piece, it feels like its center, the eye of the storm. Form is also a manifestation of rhythm; these strategic formal asymmetries are slo-mo versions of faster off-kilter patterns.

Listening to "Cotton Tail" we can detect five different kinds of rhythm:

1. Pulse rhythm: bass, drums, piano
2. Melodic rhythm: beginning with the head
3. Soloistic (supermelodic) rhythm: first heard in Cootie Williams's plunger solo I B
4. Riff or shout rhythm: first heard emerging in the trombones in I A and A'
5. Harmonic rhythm: the regularly paced temporal exposition of rhythm changes

Each of these rhythms has its own physiognomy, speed, and ancestry. The steady stream of harmonic rhythm, the chord change that happens every two beats like clockwork, is European in origin. The unpredictably exploding shout rhythm, derived from the "ring shout," has African roots. The steady pulse (234 beats per minute) heard nonstop in the bass and drums relates to two continents, the walking bass of European baroque basso continuo and the "metronome sense" of African drummers. Theorists of rhythm in both European and African music tell us that rhythm is layered, simultaneously horizontal and vertical. The rhythmic engine driving "Cotton Tail" onward and ever upward counterpoints rhythms and cultures.

Tracking each rhythmic strand in isolation through the piece shows that each one tells its own story.

Pulse Rhythm

Bass (Jimmy Blanton) and drums (Sonny Greer), both improvising, lay down a carpet of steady beats, four to a bar. Unlike the walking bass lines in baroque music (the Prelude in B Minor from *The Well-Tempered Clavier,* Book I, for instance), the inflection of the four beats changes often and unpredictably in both instruments; it's a springy carpet. Between one extreme of four evenly accented beats and the other of two heavy backbeats (one *and* two *and*), Greer also punches the fourth beat at times and ushers in the last phrase of chorus two with a four-note break that says "I Got Rhythm." Similarly, Blanton varies the inflection by playing either two pairs of notes or four different notes in each bar. The double articulation of pulse by pitched and unpitched instruments, as rhythm and melody, makes the drums speak, the capability for which they were banned during the time of slavery.

Melodic Rhythm

From its first note the head melody bounces off the pulse far more often than it coincides with it; it falls on the downbeat in only three of its eight bars, all even-numbered, structurally weak. This pattern subtly alludes to the melody of "I Got Rhythm," which similarly avoids the downbeats of strong bars and stresses them in the weak ones. Where the Gershwin song states the same rhythmic pattern three times, normalizing its African cross-rhythms and ending with the reassuring squareness of "Who could ask for anything more?" "Cotton Tail" slyly moves the "anything more" to its fourth bar and then skitters to its close with four over-the-bar-line syncopations.

The head is what musicologists term a "contrafact"—a new melody constructed on an older harmonic progression. The term emits an unfortunate odor of fraudulence that hides the sophisticated musical and cultural transactions at play. As a form of blues, jazz always sets new melodies atop a preexisting harmonic pattern. Contrafacts apply this strategy to popular tunes, but a distinction may be drawn between a contrafact that is a new popular tune, such as "Meet the Flintstones," and jazz heads like "Moten Swing" (based on "You, You're Driving Me Crazy") or Thelonious Monk's "In Walked Bud" (based on "Blue Skies") or "Lester Leaps In," Parker's "Anthropology" and "Moose the Mooche," Sonny Rollins's "Oleo," Monk's "Rhythm-a-ning," and "Cotton Tail"—all based on "I Got Rhythm." These heads do not replace one pop tune with another. Instead, they erect a jazz melody on the ruins, so to speak, of a pop tune, a more complicated and devious kind of melody in conspicuously contentious relation to its pop prototype. This kind of jazz melody reappropriates musical elements back from popular song, exposing a history that the song had relegated to amnesia. Which is the real contrafact?

The bounding melodic pattern of the head, repeatedly sidestepping the downbeat, is an eight-bar rhythmic palimpsest, a jazz rhythm built on a pop rhythm (I-got-rhy-thm) derived from a ragtime hook (Hold-that-ti-ger) that conjures up West African origins. You can hear Ellington as musical archaeologist at the opening of the "String Session" version of "Cotton Tail"; by emphasizing the oddly placed repetitions of the opening pitch within the melody, he makes it sound like an Afro-Cuban clave or West African handbell. One step higher in the scale than it should be and famously hopping off the downbeat, that first melody note sounds a radically African accent against the American pop tune scaffolding adumbrated by the bass in the absence of chords. That accent erupts more emphatically in the fifth bar when a flatted fifth, ricocheting off the beat, defines the melodic curve.

Supermelody

Jazz melody bounces off the beat; soloistic supermelody freewheels on the offbeats. Webster's two-chorus solo exemplifies supermelody here, darting and hovering beyond the already loosened rhythms of the head. Ellington frames Webster's improvised supermelodies with composed ones: Cootie Williams's plunger solo in I B,[11] Harry Carney's solo in IV B, and then two "supersax" choruses that in effect turn the entire sax section into a single instrument.

Shout

Shout rhythm appears in bursting two- or three-note riffs throughout the piece, gradually emerging from a subservient supporting role (trombones, sneaking in at the end of I A and building in the follow-ing phrase) to lead the call-and-response (in I B, II B, and III B) to the epiphanic glory in VI B. In chorus four the trumpet section, taking up an idea they first announced in I X, builds a riff melody that climaxes in a shower of two-note shouts. Unlike the other rhythmic styles, shout rhythm is always played by instrumental choirs—as a community.

Swing arises—somehow—from the interaction between these differ-ent rhythmic elements. One way to get at how this works is by listen-ing closely to each rhythmic strand, starting with the way Sonny Greer shapes the rhythm by "feathering" the bass drum and playing accents on the drum rim. Students learning to play jazz spend a lot of time going to school with recordings like this one, transcribing and playing solos. But we can also think of swing less as a technical phenomenon than as a cultural, or cross-cultural, one. Swing is as much a matter of cultural perception as of instrumental physics. Let's look at the sources of that perception.

CONTINUO VERSUS CLAVE

The rhythmic language of "Cotton Tail" fuses European and African elements for which I'll use the shorthand terms *continuo* and *clave*. "Continuo" denotes the rhythm of harmonic change. In its harmonic function the rhythm section of a jazz band (guitar, piano, bass, drums) resembles the continuo section of European baroque music (keyboard and bass). As Ned Sublette argues, the appearance of the continuo in European music after 1600 coincided with the popularity of dances like the sarabande and chaconne, which had traveled (with the slave trade) from Africa to the Caribbean and then to Spain.[12] Europeans reinforced the African rhythms with repeated patterns of harmonic motion (basso ostinato, or ground bass) articulated by the bass and keyboard. In ba-roque music and later European styles the slow and predictable mo-tion of harmonic progressions served as the foundation for more rapid and varied melodic motion; in Bach's Goldberg Variations, a *summa* of ground bass composition, a thirty-two-bar harmonic progression underlies thirty-one pieces that are otherwise completely different in melodic rhythm, tempo, and meter. The rhythm of harmonic change—continuo—shapes twentieth-century American popular songs, and the jazz compositions and improvisations based on them.

West African–derived elements in the rhythmic language of "Cot-ton Tail" appear in the offbeat rhythms of melody, supermelody, and shout. Though they may appear complicated, unpredictable, and asymmetric in transcription, these rhythms don't *sound* irregular or disruptive, qualities associated with syncopation in European music (think of those roof-rattling offbeat chords in the first movement of the *Eroica*). Essential rather than secondary, expected rather than exceptional, these asymmetries derive from patterns played by the metal handbell in West African music and the wooden *clave* in Cuban music. West African music is organized around a repeated figure played on a high-pitched metal handbell (*gankogui* in Ewe); in Caribbean music like the Cuban *son* the wooden clave sticks take over this function, while in the United States, where dancing and drumming by slaves was largely banned, hand clapping preserved the African rhythms in patterns such as the familiar "Bo Diddley" rhythm of rock music. For convenience I'll term all the different forms of this rhythm "clave."

Unlike the beat patterns of European music, clave beats have different lengths. Also unlike European rhythms, which are predominantly based on units of two or four beats, clave patterns are usually in three, five, or seven beats; these asymmetric figures are always felt or played contrapuntally against regular duple foot or drum patterns. Five familiar clave patterns are:

3 + 3 + 2 ♩. ♩. ♩ called *tresillo* in Cuban music

2 + 1 + 2 + 1 + 2 ♩ ♪ ♩ ♪ ♩ called *cinquillo* in Cuban music

3 + 3 + 2 + (2) + 2 + 2 + (2) ♩. ♩. ♩ ♩ ♩ Bo Diddley or *son* rhythm

3 + 3 + 2 + (2) + 3 + 3 ♩. ♩. ♩ ♩. ♩. bossa nova

2 + 2 + 1 + 2 + 2 + 2 + 1 ♩ ♩ ♪ ♩ ♩ ♩ ♪ West African pattern also heard in salsa

All these patterns add up to either eight, twelve, or sixteen eighth notes, which usually equals either two or four steps.[13]

When studying West African music the first thing you learn is the handbell pattern; you then learn, very slowly, how to coordinate that pattern with different figures played on each drum or rattle and also with song and dance. Most of the drums, each of which plays its own rhythmic pattern, are pitched and are played in such a way that their rhythmic patterns also form pitch melodies. The master drummer, overseeing the entire ensemble, indicates changes in sections of a dance and also (uniquely) plays a variety of figures. As you progress, you may come to realize that the terms most often used to describe the rhythms—syncopation, cross-rhythm, and polyrhythm—are misleading.[14] There are indeed many different rhythmic figures performed simultaneously, but they are precisely linked components of an overall rhythmic pattern. Or an overall *melodic* pattern, but therein lies a tale. Allow me to share an experiential anecdote of the moment when I got (African) rhythm.

Back in the disco decade, when I was a graduate student at Columbia, I played Ewe music (from southeastern Ghana) for a few years under the guidance of master drummer Alfred Ladzekpo and Professor Nicholas England. We began our study with some simple children's songs, first learning to clap the handbell pattern. Over a period of months I learned to play (in rising order of difficulty) *axatse* (rattle), *kagan* (highest-pitched drum), and *kidi* (medium-pitched drum). The drums were more difficult because, in addition to pounding out a rhythm, I had to manipulate the pitch by using one stick to change the tension of the drumhead. Meanwhile, I would listen carefully for the *gankogui* pattern, which I thought of as corresponding to a European $\frac{12}{8}$ measure; indeed, it is often transcribed that way, misleadingly, because Ewe musicians do not learn their music from notation. To detect the pattern I tried to hear a downbeat; if I could find "one," then everything else would fall into place, just as it did when I played tuba in my high school marching band. I should have realized that I was in trouble when my perception of $\frac{12}{8}$, a four-beat pattern, would suddenly shift into $\frac{3}{2}$, the same number of eighth-note beats divided into three slower half-note beats.

One evening, when I had already advanced to playing the *kidi*, the "one" disappeared right in the middle of a song—or, rather, I sensed with gut-wrenching horror that it had never been there in the first place. There was no regular harmonic rhythm to simplify the welter of drumbeats that surrounded me. I could no longer feel the handbell rhythm, either in $\frac{12}{8}$ or $\frac{3}{2}$. I had no idea where to play my pattern. For a very long couple of minutes I was, like Alice tumbling down the rabbit hole, in rhythmic freefall.[15]

Immediately hearing that I was in trouble (and that I was screwing up the performance), Alfred came over and began to beat my correct drum figure on my shoulders. Suddenly the overall pattern was again clear. Later, disabused of any notion that I had a natural affinity for Ewe music, I asked him how he heard the connection between the different rhythms without a sense of "one." His answer took me by surprise: "I hear it all as a single melody." While I was perceiving discrete patterns (cross-rhythms, polyrhythms) and keeping separate track of rhythm and pitch, he was hearing the whole cloth: not incidentally, the Ewe people are equally famed for their music and their textiles. The ethnomusicologist John Miller Chernoff terms this "single melody" a "cross-rhythmic fabric";[16] in this music the drums, rattle, hands, feet, and voices are threads woven together—and so are rhythm and pitch, pitch and speech: the carefully tuned pitches of the drums link the music to the Ewe language, which is tonal.[17] Each separate element interweaves with the uneven, asymmetric, odd-numbered beats of the handbell by filling in spaces between beats. This interlocking of multiple patterns gives the music its particular dynamic drive, as Chernoff says, and also serves its communal function. There are no listeners here; anyone who is clapping or stepping (correctly) becomes part of the musical tapestry.

The many rhythmic idioms of African diasporic music (including Caribbean and North and South American styles) all negotiated different balances between their European and West African inheritances. In the United States, where dancing and drumming by slaves were banned, the clave pattern wore a variety of disguises; it became a rhythmic trickster. In ragtime, for instance, clave hides out in the right hand, which sounds West African, while the left hand usually marches along European-style. Yet while African American musicians found ever-new ways to keep the African element alive in their music, the impact of European harmony was not simply repressive. The complex patterns of West African rhythm had been kept in place by a hierarchic order; the role of master drummer was passed on from generation to generation within particular families, and only the master drummer could improvise. Regularly repeated slow patterns of harmonic rhythm simplified the complex West African rhythmic tapestry and so in a way democratized them, allowing for more widespread improvisation and innovation. At the same time, though, the Africanization of European-based popular tunes in jazz composition and improvisation endowed them with a quality of communal celebration; jazz performance reenacted the moment of liberation, the passage from bondage to freedom. Swing, as Albert Murray reminds us, celebrates and affirms that moment. If you doubt his words just listen, to start, to "Daybreak Express."

DIGGING FOR SWING

Classically trained musicians are taught to hear the historical foundations of their repertory; they learn the importance of hearing the Bach and Beethoven in Brahms, the Brahms in Schoenberg. A similar consciousness can illuminate African American music as well. For a historical perspective on the inner workings of "Cotton Tail," let's move from a kind of phenomenology to an informal kind of "primary source" history, pursuing two hints in the music: the legacy of the ring shout and the hidden presence of "Tiger Rag." We'll proceed archaeologically in roughly reverse chronology, from "Tiger Rag," to "Carolina Shout," to the shout "Run Old Jeremiah"—there's a lot to dig.

"Tiger Rag"

I-got-rhy-thm; hold-that-ti-ger: "Tiger Rag" is where the Gershwins got rhythm—or at least *that* rhythm. The origins, authorship, and even the identity of "Tiger Rag" are a little shady. At his 1938 Library of Congress sessions Jelly Roll Morton demonstrated how he had created it from "an old quadrille" consisting of an introduction, a waltz, a "mazooka," and "a two-four time," and he also took credit for the title. Black and white bands in New Orleans played "Tiger Rag" under various names, but it first reached a wide public with the 1918 recording by the Original Dixieland Jazz Band (ODJB), whose leader, Nick LaRocca, copyrighted it. The sheet music bears only a vague relation to what the ODJB recorded, let alone what later performers considered "Tiger Rag."[18] For one thing, it lacks the "Hold-that-ti-ger" hook. But their recording, a much more impressive performance than the primitive "Livery Stable Blues" that launched them (and jazz) to international fame the previous year, imprinted that hook, with its memorable downward trombone slide, on jazz history. In August 1922, the Friars Society Orchestra, soon to be renamed the New Orleans Rhythm Kings, recorded their version of "Tiger Rag," reducing the opening three strains to a mere introduction, playing the Tiger hook almost exactly as ODJB had, but then adding two hot choruses based on the hook, one for clarinetist Leon Roppolo ("considered the best white clarinetist in New Orleans"),[19] the second a New Orleans–style free-for-all. "Tiger Rag" now consisted of some kind of vamp to set up multiple repetitions of the thirty-two-bar "trio"—the tail had become the body.[20] The length of the "trio," moreover, made it a perfect platform for extended solos. By December 1927 "Tiger Rag," now a mere platform and renamed "Hotter than That," supported one of the most astonishing series of solos in jazz to that time: Louis Armstrong both playing and scat singing with Johnny Dodds on clarinet, Lonnie Johnson on guitar, and Kid Ory on trombone.[21] While Dodds and Ory worked within a rhythmic frame-work clearly related to ragtime, Armstrong and Johnson, improvising simultaneously in $\frac{3}{4}$ and $\frac{4}{4}$ (as Schuller describes it), pushed beyond the furthest frontiers of swing.

Improbably, given his non–New Orleans origins, "Tiger Rag" served as a pillar of Ellington's repertory through the late 1930s. Ellington first used "Tiger Rag" in 1928 as a harmonic framework in "Hot and Both-ered," which was praised by R. D. Darrell for its "fury and intensity"[22] (it was paired with "The Mooche" on Okeh 8623).[23] The English critic Constant Lambert famously lauded "Hot and Bothered" and its com-poser in more cultivated terms: "I know of nothing in Ravel so dexter-ous in treatment as the varied solos in the middle of the ebullient 'Hot and Bothered' and nothing in Stravinsky more dynamic than the final section."[24] A "cultivated" observation, but not off the mark; the solos by Hodges, Whetsol, Miley, and Baby Cox (the latter two in a dueling duet), Bigard, Lonnie Johnson (guitar), and Hodges, again, are richly in-ventive, and the closing shout chorus has a cumulative rhythmic punch comparable to the ending of Stravinsky's *Pulcinella*.[25] Lambert does not seem to have realized, though, that the solo sections were improvised (as is apparent by a comparison with the 1930 recording released on Vel-vetone with new solos by Hodges, Nanton, and, in particular, Freddy Jenkins). The harmonic changes of the final strain of "Tiger Rag" were as much a proving ground for supermelodic improvising in the 1920s as "How High the Moon" would become in the 1940s.

Before looking at Ellington's series of "Tiger Rag" pieces, however, let's pause, listen, and pay homage to the ne plus ultra of "Tiger Rag" interpreters: Art Tatum. Tatum recorded his definitive version of the piece in March 1933, eight months before Ellington recorded "Day-break Express," which it seems to foretell. He begins with an ultra-modernistic slow prelude and then demonstrates the extreme virtuosic possibilities of every piano style of the era. Tatum, to the displeasure of some critics,[26] continued to play something very close to this version for the rest of his career, but what they seem to take for mere showing off is one of the greatest piano compositions of the century, an astonishing assertion of hope at the very depths of the Great Depression.

Like Tatum, Ellington appreciated from early on that "Tiger Rag" was built for strutting your stuff or, as he put it in 1938, "Braggin' in Brass." In some ways Ellington's four variations on the theme form a continuous piece spread out over a decade:

"Hot and Bothered," October 2, 1928

"Tiger Rag," January 8, 1929

"Daybreak Express," December 4, 1933

"Braggin' in Brass," March 3, 1938

These "Tiger Rag" variants, all of them concert numbers designed for listening rather than dancing, reveal how Ellington expanded the solo swing of Armstrong into a composed ensemble rhythmic style. "Hot and Bothered," as we saw before, frames a series of solos with a composed intro and final shout. On the 1930 recording of "Hot and Bothered" trumpeter Freddy Jenkins played a dazzlingly complicated figure that was either written out or was part of a well-established solo: in either case, Ellington would seize on it eight years later.

Ellington recorded "Tiger Rag," under its own title, as his first extended work, filling two sides of a 78-rpm disc. Although this is mostly a series of solos ("a staggering array of non-gimmicky, highly individual solos"),[27] there are two composed ensemble choruses, the first for the saxes and the second, at the beginning of side two, for the trumpets, which take direct aim at Gershwin's *Rhapsody in Blue;* the gesture announces a compositional cutting contest that Ellington would pursue the following year in his *Creole Rhapsody.* Both of the ensemble sections are in the "supersax" texture of a melody played in chords, and both make a section sound like a single improvising player. The closing shout chorus begins as a call-and-response but snowballs as saxes and trumpets bring back ideas from their ensemble phrases.

In "Braggin' in Brass," perhaps written in response to Benny Goodman's popular 1936 recording of "Bugle Call Rag," Ellington elevated the supersax idea to even more virtuosic heights by rearranging Jenkins's "Hot and Bothered" solo for three perfectly synchronized trumpets; he kicked up this effect with what Schuller terms a "hocket-style" passage for the three trombones. In medieval music a hocket (the word means "hiccup") was a melody whose notes were split into staccato shards between singers; here, the trombones sound more like three tuned drums in rapid-fire alternation. Both of these stunts blur the line between improvisation and composition. Ellington could play his orchestra with the same rhythmic abandon that Tatum brought to the piano because he was writing for players who could swing both on their own and together.

In the early 1930s sleek, superfast "killer dillers" like "Casa Loma Stomp" and "Chinatown" (Henderson), "White Heat" (Lunceford), and "Toby" (Moten) were all the rage; in retrospect, the genre was a bridge between hot jazz and swing. Ellington's response, "Daybreak Express," turned "Tiger Rag" into a killer-diller tone poem, a shout exalted to a freedom ride. An ensemble piece from beginning to end, "Daybreak Express" has a more complicated structure than its "Tiger Rag"–based predecessors: the opening section, with its famous accelerating pulse in the brass, is conspicuously modernistic, with parallel harmonies over a bass ostinato and a real train whistle (perhaps mimicking the taxi horns in *An American in Paris*); its chugging mechanism heats up with the entry of a 3 + 3 + 2 clave figure in the brass. A blues-inflected call from Nanton (sounding like the train's porter) serves as a link to three "Tiger Rag" choruses, the first for saxes in A♭, the others in D♭. This modulation opens up the tonal expanse of the piece, heightening the evocation of a transformative journey.

The sax chorus (part of which is transcribed in Gunther Schuller's *The Swing Era,* p. 63) is an intensified version of its counterpart in "Tiger Rag," part I, with a repeated $\frac{3}{2}$ cross-rhythm (a nine-note clave):

♪ ♪ ♪ ♩ ♪ ♪ ♪ ♪ 𝄾

that recalls the repeated $\frac{3}{4}$ figure (against a $\frac{2}{2}$ meter)

♩ ♩

in Armstrong's scat chorus in "Hotter Than That."

The last two choruses are call-and-response shouts: the first, led by Cootie Williams's repeated high B♭s (the added sixth of the harmony), proclaims the "Hold-that-ti-ger" motive jubilantly, like a battle anthem; the second phrase reverses the call-and-response with the saxes wailing on a minor third, suggestive of a church spiritual. The symbolic train simultaneously carries the music to the edge of the promised land and back home. Then someone slams on the brakes and Freddy Jenkins issues a sigh on his half-valved trumpet; freedom remains a "dream deferred."

By the late 1930s "Tiger Rag," along with just about any other rag, felt retro; its harmonies were old hat even when the sheet music appeared in 1917. It had also become wildly popular, in recordings by Benny Goodman, Bob Crosby, and Glenn Miller, as a frantic jitterbug novelty with conspicuous allusions to the ODJB recording that recalled its "Dixieland" origins at a time when the revival of the older New Orleans style under the "Dixieland" rubric was just taking off. The ODJB echoes surrounded the piece with a suspect, magnolia-scented nostalgia for the Old South, which Ellington would later demolish in his *Deep South Suite*. It was time to retire "Tiger Rag." Ellington had already embarked on a rivalry with Gershwin, so why not up the stakes by transferring the cultural resonances of "Tiger Rag" to a new foundation, Gershwin's signature tune, which had "Tiger Rag" in its musical DNA? Hold-that-ti-ger; I-got-rhy-thm. "Cotton Tail" leapt out of their dry bones.

"Carolina Shout"

"Carolina Shout," arguably the most influential American piano composition of the twentieth century, showed the way to a musical future while at the same time capturing a fast-receding past. Ellington learned to play James P. Johnson's composition from the piano roll in 1920 and performed it for the composer, already the reigning monarch of Harlem stride piano, the following year.[28] According to its composer, "Carolina Shout" re-created a lost world:

> My mother was from Virginia and somewhere in her blood was an instinct for doing country and set dances—what were called "read [or 'reel'] shoutings." My "Carolina Shout" and Carolina Balmoral are real southern set or square dances.[29]

> These Charleston people and the other Southerners had just come to New York. They were country people and they felt homesick. When they got tired of two-steps and schottisches (which they danced with a lot of spieling), they'd yell: "Let's go back home!" . . . "Let's do a set!" . . . or, "Now, put us in the alley!"[30]

Johnson evoked the old dances, "the squares and jubas danced to mouth harps, bones, Jew's harps, and other makeshift musical instruments of the core culture."[31]

Yet in reviving the past, Johnson was also creating a new music. I'm tempted to retype that as NEW MUSIC because the seminal rhythmic innovation "Carolina Shout" made it an American counterpart to Stravinsky's *Danse sacrale* (which twitches, reels, jerks, and stumbles but never swings). Just as every young classical composer in Europe circa 1920 felt obliged to come to terms with *Le sacre,* every aspiring jazz pianist in New York had to master Johnson's "test piece." "Carolina Shout" set the bar for Johnson's successors in stride piano royalty, Waller and Tatum, and it was also foundational for Ellington and Basie both as pianists and arrangers.

"Carolina Shout" exists in variant forms on piano rolls, recordings made from 1921 to 1944, and printed scores, but the similarities between the sources outweigh their differences. It consists of five sixteen-bar "strains" ABCDED (the same formal plan found in Sousa's "Liberty Bell," a.k.a. the Monty Python theme) framed by an intro and a stunningly "modernistic" outro that suddenly reminds us that the music heard up to that point has been evoking an earlier era. Any of the strains might be repeated with varied ornamentation; on the 1921 recording James P. Johnson takes A and C twice; the wonderful Fats Waller recordings similarly move a lot of the furniture around without wrecking the room. Perhaps because of all the variorums most of the written analyses seem inaccurate: most hear four strains (the usual Joplin form) rather than five and detect one shout chorus, C, where I hear two, C and E, with E (the trio section of the second half of the piece) the climactic phrase. This second shout, with a strong family resemblance to the famous final phrase of Morton's "King Porter Stomp," also recalls the ecstatic wail heard in the later parts of "Run Old Jeremiah" (see below).

As composer and performer Johnson cultivated a broad stylistic range that extended from contemporary Broadway songs like Gershwin's "Liza" and Cole Porter's "What Is This Thing Called Love?" back through W. C. Handy and Scott Joplin and their predecessors (as in "The Dream," a New Orleans Spanish-tinged piece said to date from 1890), to the much older spiritual themes that occur in his extended 1927 composition *Yamekraw*. His performances of older pieces help set his own innovations in perspective. "Carolina Shout" is not just faster than, say, "Maple Leaf Rag," but it is also far more virtuosic (its performance restricted to a stride elite), aggressive and self-consciously modernistic. Its formal design dramatizes a changing balance of power between continuo and clave patterns. The striding left hand starts off from a comfortably bouncing "one-and-two-and" oompah then shifts to a less symmetrical but still decorous 3 + 3 + 2. The diatonic Bach-like harmonies similarly convey a sense of a nostalgically idealized past. When the first shout (C) arrives, the rhythm tilts decisively in the clave direction with both hands playing off the beat in interlocked "syncopated" figures. By the second part of the piece (DED), asymmetry becomes the norm as the right hand smashes a dissonant cluster between the already irregular left-hand beat. The climactic E phrase transfers this smash to the left hand, where it sounds like a whole trombone section. And in the coda modernist ninth-chord harmonies announce the final triumph of clave rhythm, which finally takes its Afro-Caribbean form of 3 + 3 + 2 at twice the speed heard in the A section of the left hand.

We can think of "Carolina Shout" as the link between the ring shout and the shout chorus, which would become a convention of big band compositions in the 1930s. You can hear this device develop in the evolving rearrangements of "King Porter Stomp" as recorded by the Fletcher Henderson Orchestra between 1928 and 1933.[32] Henderson turned Morton's stomp into a call-and-response shout between brass and reed choirs; Gunther Schuller claimed that this "would become the single most influential ensemble idea in the entire Swing Era."[33] By the early '30s this idea took off, especially in the super–high tempo "killer dillers," where, however, the device of the shout chorus often lost contact with its older religious origins, and also its connections to the multiple-strain form of ragtime. The more modern-sounding numbers were modeled not on old quadrilles but on hit tunes: "Toby" is built on "Sweet Sue Just You" (by Will Harris and Victor Young), and the even more advanced "Moten Swing" covers (barely) "You, You're Driving Me Crazy" (Walter Donaldson), both popularized by Bing Crosby, while Henderson's enormously influential "Wrappin' It Up" follows the ABAC design of many Broadway songs. These appropriations of the "sweet" repertory kept the shout alive. The pop-oriented format, with the "bridge" kicking up the harmonic tension, heightened its celebratory power.

"Run Old Jeremiah"

"Carolina Shout" linked jazz to its roots in an earlier African American music and its African antecedents: before there was swing, before there was jazz or even ragtime, there was the shout, or ring shout, first described in 1799 by a traveler to New Orleans who saw "vast number of slaves . . . dancing in large rings."[34] Joseph F. Watson, in his book *Methodist Error* in 1819, reported that following a camp meeting Negroes would accompany their singing with audible footsteps and thigh slaps.[35] Another observer (Robert Todd) reported "great billows of sound from the tornado of praise" and "leaping, shuffling and dancing, after the order of David before the ark when his wife thought he was crazy," an image recaptured in Ellington's *Second Sacred Concert*. An account from 1867 notes the practice of dancing in a circle: "Old and young, men and women . . . all stand up in the middle of the floor, and when the 'sperchil' [spiritual] is struck up, begin first walking and by-and-by shuffling round, one after the other, in a ring."[36] Only in Place Congo in New Orleans did observers note the presence of drums, which were banned elsewhere.

There is scant recorded evidence of the ring shout, but two ear-opening examples are easy to find on the web: "Knee Bone," sung by Joe Armstrong and group, and, with a couple of caveats,[37] "Run Old Jeremiah," recorded in Jennings, Louisiana, by John and Alan Lomax in 1934 and conveniently accessible on the web.[38]

Both of these recordings demonstrate the call-and-response format central to African American music, and they both have complexly woven rhythmic fabrics. On "Knee Bone" you hear two clapped rhythms: a *tresillo* clave pattern plus a steady backbeat that combine to form the rhythmic figure heard at the opening of Charles Mingus's epic and Ellingtonian composition *Black Saint and the Sinner Lady*. "Run Old Jeremiah" begins with the instruction "You got to run," then later jumps on a train:

One mornin'
Before the evening
Sun was goin' down (× 3)
Behind them western hills. (× 3)
Old number 12
Comin' down the track. (× 3)
See that black smoke.
See that old engineer.
See that engineer. (× 2)
Tol' that old fireman
Ring his ol' bell
With his hand.
Rung his engine bell. (× 2)

The lyrics and the rising rhythmic excitement anticipate Ellington's "Daybreak Express." Both celebrate the escape from bondage.[39]

If we hear these recordings only as documents of primitive styles from which jazz evolved, we forget that many jazz musicians considered the shouts of their ancestors as a sacred repertory whose memory they attempted to evoke and honor in their own compositions and performances. Dancing in a ring was, as Samuel Floyd writes, "a symbol of community, solidarity, affirmation and catharsis."[40] The quality that would be called swing was a lifeline to the past for people repeatedly robbed of their ancestry by the mechanisms of slavery and racism. Shout also linked jazz and religion, as Willie "The Lion" Smith explained, "Shouts are stride piano—when James P. and Fats and I would get a romp-down shout going, that was playing rocky, just like the Baptist people sing. You don't just play a chord to that—you got to move it and the piano-players do the same thing in the churches, and there's ragtime in the preaching. Want to see a ring shout? Go out to the Convent Avenue Baptist Church any Sunday."[41]

POST-DIG

We have dug down from "Cotton Tail" to "Run Old Jeremiah." Now we can come up for air and give "Cotton Tail" another hearing. The rhythmic language of "Cotton Tail," call it swing, exists:

- "in the moment," the product of minutely coordinated muscular action by fifteen performing musicians.
- as a structure, imagined and implemented by composer(s).
- as a strategy of cultural negotiation and as a reanimator of historical memory.

All that in three minutes! This may seem like a heavy burden to place on a "foxtrot" (as the original record label identified it), but any work of music that commands relistening multitasks in analogous ways. The historical echoes of shout in jazz are as powerful as the reverberations of plainchant in the canon of European art music from Léonin to Messiaen. Rhythm is at once an occurrence in time, a representation of temporal experience, and an agent of historical retrospection and revaluation. As listeners we hear rhythm more acutely, and as performers we articulate rhythm more evocatively, when we consider its full representational scope.

CUBIST RHYTHM

Jazz is a different fraternity altogether, a wholly different kind of music making. It has nothing to do with composed music and when it seeks to be influenced by contemporary music it isn't jazz and it isn't good. . . . The point of interest is instrumental virtuosity, instrumental personality, not melody, not harmony and certainly

not rhythm. Rhythm doesn't exist really because no rhythmic
proportion or relaxation exists. Instead of rhythm there is "beat."
The players beat all the time merely to keep up and know which
side of the beat they are on.

—Igor Stravinsky

Stravinsky did evince preoccupation with jazz music. He talked
about it. He wrote a series of compositions with titles referring
to "ragtime," but no evidence of the preoccupation appears in
the actual music, honestly examined, honestly listened to. That
preoccupation was purely verbal.

—Gene Krupa

A jazz influence, in blanket terms can be found throughout
my music.

—Igor Stravinsky

Certainly, it is not impossible to see immediately the kinship between
Slav and African, and how one must inevitably pass to the other;
and how the utmost end of one development is not unsympathetic
to the other.

—George Antheil

Stravinsky used to come by and sit and listen to the band from
time to time in the Cotton Club days. They got to know each other
pretty well.

—Mercer Ellington

Classical composers at the turn of the twentieth century cohabited the
newly sped-up world, and their music, too, began to mirror modern
urban life. The jittery traffic jam scherzos in Schoenberg's Chamber
Symphony (1906) and Second Quartet (1907) and Ives's *Central Park
in the Dark* (1906) are perhaps the first examples of the new city music;
even at this early date, Ives employed ragtime as an emblem of modernity. Although books about twentieth-century music often bemoan the
moribund state of rhythm at the end of the nineteenth century, European
concert music was technically well equipped to represent the quickened
pulse of modernity. Any score by Mahler, Strauss, or Debussy reveals
rhythmic idioms rich in subtlety and nuance; many otherwise progressive composers of the twentieth century felt little need to go beyond the
sophisticated rhythmic practices of these masters, which included polyrhythms, changing meters, irregular phrase lengths, and a performance
style in which tempo and pulse were in a continuous, expressive state of
flux. All of these subtleties of composition (which Schoenberg summed
up in the phrase "musical prose") and performance, moreover, were
easily represented by musical notation.

Classical composers had the technical resources for rhythmic innovation; the challenge, for some, was to find a fresh new groove. Mahler and Strauss, for all their innovative energy, were still writing either waltzes or marches. As they had done in pursuit of new tone colors, composers looked to the edges of Europe for untapped raw material, to Spain, to Eastern Europe, and beyond them to Africa and the Far East. Many soon realized, however, that a new rhythm had already arrived—from America. Well before the 1913 premiere of *Le sacre du printemps,* Europeans were dancing the habanera, the tango, and the cakewalk. When Erik Satie needed to represent the most advanced sound of his time for *Parade,* the Satie/Cocteau/Picasso/Massine avant-garde sensation of 1917, he simply pasted in a bit of Irving Berlin's "That Mysterious Rag."

While Satie appropriated African American rhythms, other composers, most notably Stravinsky, stylized them into what I'll call cubist rhythms. Much as cubist painters analyzed objects in terms of a few basic geometric shapes (cubes, spheres, cylinders, cones), Stravinsky, as cubist composer, constructed rhythms on the basis of twos and threes, relative durational or accentual values heard either horizontally, with changing meters, or vertically, as in the two-against-three cross-rhythm called hemiola; his *Symphonies of Wind Instruments,* composed in 1920, exploits these rhythmic proportions throughout. Just as cubist art quickly evolved from the emulation of Iberian and African "folk" sculpture to become a system for representing contemporary spatial discontinuity, cubist rhythm, though launched in *Le sacre* as an atavistic evocation of an imaginary Slavic past, seemed to capture the newly altered temporality of modern life. In music as in painting, the trinkets of imperialism morphed into emblems of European progress. European and European-American rhythmic innovations counted as "rhythmic research," to use Virgil Thomson's phrase, while African American rhythms were figured as products of instinct. Even the jazz-loving, jazz-influenced Stravinsky would succumb to this unconscious mind/body racism when claiming that jazz lacked "rhythmic proportion or relaxation." Through most of the century the imitators took credit for the original.

The cubist two-and-three rhythms heard in the music of Stravinsky, Bartók, and Copland strongly resembled the clave patterns of African and Afro-Cuban music, and the "Spanish-tinged" 3 + 3 + 2 of Jelly Roll Morton's music. The "modernism" of African American rhythm had surfaced as a trope in European music as early as Debussy's "Golliwog," which used "Under the Bamboo Tree," written in 1902 by the African

American composer Bob Cole, to mock the outdated romanticism of *Tristan*. The radicalizing potentials of African American music became even more apparent as soon as the music called jazz arrived in Europe in 1918 with James Reese Europe's Hellfighters Band and Will Marion Cook's Southern Syncopated Orchestra. Within a few years European modernists were traveling to Harlem to hear the real thing (their accounts often sound like Conradian voyages up the Congo) and composing foxtrots and shimmies fitted out with devices like polytonality and metric changes that conspicuously transformed the "real thing" into European art. Rather than go to school with jazz musicians, classical composers reduced the new idiom to a few devices that signaled modernity. Stravinsky's *Piano Rag Music* of 1920 is a Chaplinesque picture of modern times, mechanized, disjointed, oppressive, far from the jaunty celebratory spirit of James P. Johnson's 1915 "Carolina Shout."

Adding insult to appropriation, some modernists used cubist ideas to explain jazz to the classical audience. In an essay that appeared in *Modern Music* in 1927, Aaron Copland claimed that the eight eighth-note pattern, 1–2–3 : 1–2–3 : 1–2 was "the molecule of jazz." "The peculiar excitement they produce by clashing two definitely and regularly marked rhythms is unprecedented in occidental music. Its polyrhythm is the real contribution to jazz."[42] Though Copland's description (which he repeated with few changes throughout his life) fit the conspicuous syncopations of songs like "Fascinating Rhythm" and "Puttin' on the Ritz" or of Zez Confrey's novelty piano compositions like "Stumbling" much better than most of what we now call the jazz of the period, it shows how modernist composers conceptualized jazz rhythms reductively in order to appropriate them for their own purposes.

We might term many of the rhythmic innovations of modernist concert music "jazz by other means," (or "Euro-jazz") though I'll call them cubist rhythms instead. Was this kind of rhythm as inimical to jazz as both Stravinsky and Gene Krupa, from opposite sides of the lines, would have us believe? There's no doubt that European composers were thinking about jazz and, perhaps, listening to it, though few followed the developments of jazz closely enough to distinguish its most important figures; discussions of jazz by Stravinsky and Copland never mention Louis Armstrong. Measured by the number of composers who suddenly added a saxophone to their orchestras (including Berg, Schoenberg, and Webern), the generic impact of jazz on European concert music and, of course, American as well was huge, but also, by the same measurement, short-lived. Modernist composers, moreover, were ambivalent about jazz. For some it was an alien style that could only be assimilated in unmediated fashion through collage, as Satie did in *Parade,* or Ives did in *Central Park in the Dark* with its quotations from "Hello My Baby!" (a hit tune from 1899 by Joseph Howard and Ida Emerson); or it could serve as a convenient vehicle for anarchic "wrong-note" irony, as in the piano ragtimes of Ives, Stravinsky, and Hindemith, instances of rag rage that treat the new idiom with a violent, distorting irreverence. (By comparison, Stravinsky handled Pergolesi's music with kid gloves.) But while the outer trappings of jazz-age jazz soon faded, jazzlike rhythmic devices remained an essential part of the modernist idiom, even when they appeared in music labeled Bulgarian (Bartók's Fifth Quartet) or Mexican (Copland's *El Salón México*) or classically Greek (Stravinsky's *Apollo, Orpheus,* and *Agon.*)[43]

Before we examine some examples of cubist rhythm by Bartók and Stravinsky, we need a sidebar to deal with the issue—the red herring, actually—of notation. In jazz circles discussion about rhythm usually focuses on "feel," the subtleties of performance; when modernist composers talk about rhythm they usually have a mental picture of some page from the score of *Le sacre* in which the meter changes every bar, even though some of the most rhythmically sophisticated movements in the modernist canon, the first movement of Bartók's Fourth Quartet (1928), the first movement of Webern's Symphony (1930), the first movement of Schoenberg's Fourth Quartet (1937), and the first movement of Stravinsky's Symphony in C (1939), are written in $\frac{4}{4}$ throughout. (Bartók sketched first in changing meters, then renotated in $\frac{4}{4}$.) Two rhythmically vibrant parts of *Le sacre,* the "Augurs of Spring" and "Dancing Out of the Earth," are similarly devoid of meter changes.

The opposition of feel and notation, however, replays the racist stereotypes of instinct versus culture. The rhythms of jazz and modernist music share more common ground than either Stravinsky or Krupa suspected. To locate that common ground let's look at two canonized and high-spirited modernist concert works both written around the swing era, neither explicitly related to jazz: Bartók's Fifth String Quartet (1934) and Stravinsky's Concerto in E♭, "Dumbarton Oaks" (1938)—with an inevitable detour through *Le sacre.*

BARTÓK: STRING QUARTET NO. 5

The rhythms of Bartók and Stravinsky often approximate the woven, multilayered texture of jazz, but from Eastern European vantage points.

Their music, like Ellington's, illustrates the way rhythm functions as both sound and symbol. According to the dates in the score, Bartók composed his great String Quartet No. 5 in a month (August 6 to September 6, 1934), and few works of twentieth-century concert music can match its feeling of rhythmic spontaneity. And yet it applies the principles of rhythmic cubism (threes and twos combined horizontally and vertically) with a systematic logic. The thematic material of the first movement contrasts groupings of three and two and of five (3 + 2) and often builds up a rhythmic counterpoint either by superimposing two or three rhythmic patterns or through strettos, overlapping passages of imitation. Played idiomatically (as in the recordings by the Vegh Quartet), the ingeniously constructed music nevertheless has the improvisatory lilt of folk music.

Bartók, of course, knew a thing or two about folk music; he dedicated years of his life to recording, transcribing, and analyzing music from Hungary, the Balkans, Turkey, and North Africa. His studies of folk music, and of natural phenomena as well, were not simply empirical. Many Bartók scholars find that he conceived his music in terms of a vast dialectical project symbolized by the numbers two and three. The goals of the project have been stated most broadly by Leon Botstein: "Bartók uniquely managed to reconcile the claims of formal musical aesthetics and the ideology of progressive musical modernism with the cultural politics of identity and subjective particularity;"[44]—well, perhaps not so uniquely, since, if we include jazz within the realm of "progressive musical modernism," the description fits Ellington as well.

Bartók's music set out to synthesize Beethoven's dynamic classicism and Debussy's static impressionism, Schoenbergian chromaticism and the modal diatonicism of Hungarian folk melodies, culture (with a capital "C") and nature (with a capital "N"), and, reducing this project to its rhythmic essentials, *two* and *three*. Not since medieval music, when triple rhythms *(tempus perfectum)* signified the divine and duple rhythms *(tempus imperfectum)* the human, have the smallest building blocks of rhythm carried such philosophical weight.[45]

Bartók worked out the symbolic dialogue of twos and threes in many ways. It first appears as a large-scale structural symbolism, I think, in the Second Quartet, a three-movement work. The calmly meditative first movement begins in $\frac{9}{8}$ time (3 × 3); the despairing third movement is in $\frac{4}{4}$ (2 × 2). Between them, a scherzo inspired by the music Bartók heard in Biskra, Algeria, at times savage, at times grotesque, begins in two, but in its compressed recapitulation its themes are refashioned in a whirling triple meter. In the Fourth Quartet Bartók used a five-movement arch structure, with the first and fifth movements in duple meters ($\frac{4}{4}$ and $\frac{2}{4}$), the second and fourth in triple meters ($\frac{6}{8}$ and $\frac{3}{4}$); the central movement, in the Bartókian genre of "night music," sounds almost a-metric, outside of time.

In the Fifth Quartet Bartók pursued metric symbolism even further. Again there are five movements, but the corresponding outer movements are in contrasting meters, the first mainly in $\frac{12}{8}$, the fifth in $\frac{2}{4}$. The second and fourth movements can be heard as a theme in $\frac{4}{4}$ and a variation in $\frac{3}{4}$. At the center is a scherzo marked "Alla bulgarese," and it, too, is in an arch form, with the outer section in bars of nine eighth notes divided as 4 + 2 + 3, while the central section, the very heart of the entire quartet, is in $\frac{10}{8}$ divided as 3 + 2 + 2 + 3. To make things even more systematic, Bartók associates his duple rhythms with the interval of the fourth, his triplet rhythms with thirds; the nine-beat scherzo is a cascade of thirds.

Bartók became fascinated with Bulgarian rhythms in the 1930s; he may have felt that they were evidence, in nature, of the larger symbolic order. These dance rhythms are based on "slow" and "quick" beats, beats of different lengths. Although ethnomusicologists disagree about the relation of the beat lengths, especially when at rapid tempos, Bartók heard the beat patterns in terms of a 3:2 ratio, represented by fast beats of quarter notes (two eighths) and slower beats of dotted quarters (three eighths). Bartók pursued possible combinations of beats in a variety of compositions. Two studies in Bulgarian rhythm appear in the fourth volume of *Mikrokosmos,* and the sixth volume concludes with Six Dances in Bulgarian Rhythm. They present rhythms of 3 + 2, 2 + 2 + 3, 4 + 2 + 3, 2 + 3, 3 + 2 + 3, 2 + 2 + 2 + 3, and our old friend 3 + 3 + 2. Similar rhythms also appear in *Music for Strings, Percussion and Celesta* (fourth movement 3 + 3 + 2), the Sonata for Two Pianos and Percussion (first movement 3 + 2 + 2 + 2), *Contrasts* (third movement 3 + 2 + 3 + 2 + 3), and the Concerto for Orchestra (fourth movement 2 + 2 + 2 + 3).

Apart from their possible symbolic function and evident musical charm, these Bulgarian rhythms have a few notable properties. First, in Bartók's usage they are real meters, regularly occurring accentual patterns articulated through harmonic change, not the variably accented figures found elsewhere in Bartók's music (such as the "Syncopation" study no. 133 in *Mikrokosmos,* volume 5) or in Copland or Stravinsky. Unlike clave-based music, where hand and feet have different, complementary rhythms, in Bulgarian music they coincide. A Cuban *son* pattern puts three unequal beats of the clave against two equal foot beats. In Bulgarian rhythm the 3 + 3 + 2 pattern is heard as three steps; in "I Got Rhythm" it has two (or four).

Although Bartók was one of the few European composers to appear untouched by jazz in the 1920s, he nevertheless realized that Bulgarian meters bore an uncanny relation to jazz, and he took advantage of the connection in 1938 when he composed *Contrasts* for Joseph Szigeti and Benny Goodman. The King of Swing was also a serious classical clarinetist; his jazz style, moreover had Eastern European klezmer overtones (most obviously in Ziggy Elman's "And the Angels Sing" based on the klezmer tune "Der Shtiler Bulgar"). Goodman comfortably crossed over to Bartók's world; a year later Bartók moved into Goodman's territory with the fourth and sixth of the Bulgarian dances, both written, as Bartók himself pointed out, in the blues-inflected style of Gershwin. The Hungarian composer must have known *Rhapsody in Blue* and the *Preludes,* which are full of 3 + 3 + 2 patterns.[46]

Jazz fans know Bulgarian rhythms through Dave Brubeck's "Take Five" (written by Paul Desmond), "Unsquare Dance," and particularly "Blue Rondo à la Turk," with a theme written as three bars of 2 + 2 + 2 + 3 plus one in 3 + 3 + 3. Though some jazz critics viewed Brubeck's hugely popular experiments as heavy-handed gimmicks,[47] they could more sympathetically be heard (as many of Bartók's works can be heard) as anticipations of world music parallel to the global outreach of Ellington's *Far East Suite.*

Many jazz players (and rock musicians as well) have continued Brubeck's experiments (and "Take Five" became a jazz standard), but these rhythms can become ponderous, especially when players slam the downbeats. Bartók's treatment of the rhythms in his "Alla bulgarese" shows more finesse, and perhaps more of a jazz feel. He begins his melody off the beat and phrases it in call-and-response two-bar units. Instead of repeating the opening phrase Bartók turns the rhythmic shape around by making the "call" in the cello sound like an upbeat to the "response" in the violin and viola. In the recapitulation Bartók intensifies the rhythmic development, stretching and contracting the phrases over the bar lines and creating new cross-rhythmic counterpoints. From a classical point of view we might say that Bartók is developing his rhythms very much in the way Beethoven would; from a jazz point of view we might say that he is pushing them in the direction of supermelodic liberation, with a shoutlike ecstasy in the final crescendo (bar 74), followed by an ending as quietly concise as the last phrase of "Cotton Tail."

STRAVINSKY: CONCERTO IN E♭, "DUMBARTON OAKS"

In the concert and ballet worlds Stravinsky's name is synonymous with rhythm; not surprisingly, he borrowed from jazz, as he admitted, throughout his life. Jazz musicians, especially in the bebop period, liked to show their respect to the Russian master by inserting a phrase of *Petrouchka* or *Le sacre* into a solo, especially when their composer was present. The young Billy Strayhorn introduced *Le sacre* (along with *La Mer* and *Alborada del gracioso*) to Lena Horne; it was difficult, but she liked it "when I'm a little juiced."[48] As the "separate but equal" remark at the top of the section shows, Stravinsky didn't exactly return the compliment, at least not when sober. Or when composing: *Ebony Concerto,* written for Woody Herman and full of details lovingly lifted from some of the Herd's greatest hits, remains the highest, hippest compliment that classical musical modernism paid to the jazz world.

Stravinsky's waspish statement about jazz from the first *Conversation* book uses the dismissive tone he often employed to deal with serious rivals, but his distinction between "rhythm" and "beat" sheds light on his idiosyncratic methods for creating cubist rhythms. Where Bartók often worked from music he heard in the field, Stravinsky always worked from written sources, whether they were transcriptions of folk music or scores by other composers, from Gesualdo to Webern. Where the Hungarian composer thought of basic rhythmic shapes almost like atoms, as part of the essential material of music, Stravinsky conceived musical ideas, or *"matières sonores,"* as static but malleable objects, to be twisted, extended, chopped; rhythm was not inherent in those materials but was a way of shaping them. To compose he would find a sound, a chord, an instrumental effect, or an entire existing piece of music, then animate it with a varied collection of techniques that I'll call Igor's tool kit.

For Stravinsky, the temporal was also spatial. Composition was a matter of shuffling, repositioning, cutting, pasting, juxtaposing and superimposing—disruptive processes that, nevertheless, like the magician's spell in *Petrouchka,* endowed static material with dynamic life; often at the end of the piece Stravinsky (again as magician) would restore them to their pretemporal condition.

Many of Stravinsky's rhythmic techniques had their roots in earlier Russian music. Unusual and changing meters, protocubist rhythms, were common in the music of the Russian nationalist school. Richard Taruskin shows how Glinka, in *Ruslan and Lyudmila*, set pentasyllabic folk poetry "isochronously" in a quintuple meter.[49] Rimsky-Korsakov, Stravinsky's teacher, similarly wrote the final chorus of his opera *Snegurochka* in $\frac{11}{4}$. The "scientific" anthology of Russian folk songs by Istomin and Lyapunov transcribed folk melodies with constantly changing meters, a way of hearing already transfigured into art music in the Promenade sections of Mussorgsky's *Pictures at an Exhibition*.

We can designate the inherited technique of irregular meter as "rhythmic tool number one" and note its handiwork throughout *Le sacre*, most obviously at the opening of "Spring Rounds," in which a simple melody unfolds in groupings of $\frac{5}{4}$, $\frac{7}{4}$, and $\frac{6}{4}$, quite similar in effect to a Mussorgsky Promenade. This technique of rhythmic variation applies to melody; according to Taruskin, it springs from prosody, and we might compare it to vers libre, the poetic technique that uses a different meter in every line. But melody usually needs an accompaniment; Stravinsky used two additional rhythmic tools for this purpose.[50] In the main part of the "Spring Rounds" a syncopated figure in the bass interlocks with the melodic phrases and expands or contracts along with them: rhythmic tool number two. This technique of synchronized irregularity also served Stravinsky's purpose in the far more irregular "Naming and Honoring of the Chosen One" and the "Sacrificial Dance," in which the melody bounces off changing accents in the bass.

Stravinsky had a far more devious rhythmic tool (number three) in his kit. Under the *irregular* metric groups of the melody ($\frac{4}{4}$, $\frac{2}{4}$, $\frac{4}{4}$, $\frac{3}{4}$, $\frac{4}{4}$, $\frac{5}{4}$, $\frac{3}{4}$, $\frac{3}{4}$) in the "Mystic Circle of the Young Girls," he placed a *regular* pattern of four eighth notes that goes out of phase with the melody midway through. The clash between a regular ostinato and a changing accentual pattern occurs throughout Stravinsky's oeuvre, from the "Royal March" in *Histoire* to the "Bransle Gay" in *Agon*. Stravinsky often chose to notate this type-three rhythmic counterpoint in a way that emphasized the irregular element rather than the steady one. This notation calls attention to the distinct characters of the two rhythmic elements but makes it harder to see how they synchronize. We might say that it makes the "beat" secondary to the "rhythm."

Superimposed rhythmic patterns, some more regular than others, produce some of the most exciting moments in *Le sacre;* I'm thinking in particular of the phrases after rehearsal number 28 in "Les augures printaniers," in which two ostinatos, one of four eighth notes, the other of six, appear under two melodies, a fast one in the high winds, a slower one in the trumpets, whose phrase lengths vary in the Mussorgskian way; and the even more complicated layering at rehearsal number 67, "Procession of the Oldest and Wisest One," particularly at 70, when the guiro enters in a 4:3 ratio with the bass—but since when was the guiro a Russian instrument? Or—to ask a bigger question—what connects these polyrhythmic textures to the idioms of any of Stravinsky's putative nationalist predecessors? They sound more like West African music, or perhaps like a mating of Russian melody and West African drumming, than a little reminiscent of jazz: Irving Berlin and George Gershwin also had Russian origins, after all.

The most rhythmically charged sections of *Le sacre,* the "Dancing Out of the Earth," which ends part 1, "The Naming and Honoring of the Chosen One," which begins the *Totentanz* of part 2, and the final "Sacrificial Dance" display intriguingly West African rhythmic patterns and textures. "Dancing Out of the Earth" piles up rhythmic element in eighth notes, triplets, and then sixteenths, with each rhythmic strand assigned its own harmonic identity: whole tone, quartal, and octatonic. On top of this volcanic rumble Stravinsky sounds a rhythmic figure derived from the infamously off-accented "Sacre chords" from the "Augurs of Spring" in part 1:

I can think of no precedent for this kind of rhythm in Russian or European music, but it strongly resembles the West African Husago dance transcribed by A. M. Jones.[51] African sculpture was the rage among Parisian cubist painters at the time; African music was imported as well.

The off-kilter shuffled meters of "Naming and Honoring" and "Sacrificial Dance" relate to African music in a different way—through Spain and the New World. In both sections I hear the strong influence harmonically and rhythmically of Ravel's *Alborada del gracioso* (that favorite, you'll recall, of Billy Strayhorn and Lena Horne) in particular the asymmetric $\frac{6}{8}$ rhythm (2 + 2 + 2 + 3) heard at measure 31 and after: this figure forecasts the terrified leaps and falls of Stravinsky's victim. The "Sacrificial Dance" turns the rhythmic tension several notches tighter toward vertigo. Stravinsky said that he heard this rhythm before he figured out how to notate it and he revised the notation later in his life, as did conductors like Koussevitzky and Bernstein. The spasmodic notation masks the regular and (dare I say it) ragtime element lurking in the dance. As Pieter van den Toorn noted, the main rhythmic figure, represented in a phrase unit of $\frac{2}{16}, \frac{3}{16}, \frac{3}{16}, \frac{2}{8}$, adds up to twelve sixteenths, also known as $\frac{3}{4}$:

If you heard them against a regular quarter pulse (and snapped your fingers on the eighths) you would feel a rhythm with a family resemblance to, say, Joplin's familiar "Entertainer":

In distancing himself from jazz, Stravinsky may have been protesting too much. Ragtime arrived in Paris a decade before Stravinsky; he did not have to wait until 1918 to compose a piece with that title, but he did have to find himself removed, as he was by a war and a revolution, from Russia and its traditions. Stravinsky throughout his life was a compositional magpie seizing on whatever musical objects he "loved." From *Histoire du soldat* onward, jazz was part of his *matières sonores;* he would even give the sound of Shorty Rogers's flügelhorn a prominent role in the austere, sacred, and serial setting of *Threni*.

Richard Taruskin quashed the idea that Stravinsky was influenced by jazz with the perceptive statement, "What makes Stravinsky's rhythm fascinating and delightful . . . is its metrical ambiguity—that is, the doubts the composer continually and deliberately sows . . . precisely about what jazz takes for granted."[52] Let's test Taruskin's statement by looking at a bit of prime swing-era Stravinsky, the Concerto in E♭, "Dumbarton Oaks," composed in 1938.

The concerto is syncretistic in style and rhythmic devices. The first movement pits Bach against ragtime (in the violins at rehearsal number 2). The second movement replaces the back-to-baroque style with a teasing little tune from Verdi's *Falstaff* and a Rossinian flute solo. The third movement begins like a brisk march, slows down for some "Arabian" music à la Tchaikovsky, and ends like a speeding locomotive. Its opening displays the rhythmic ambiguity Taruskin describes—but more so. There are three simultaneous rhythmic patterns: a six-note theme in the horn, played twice with slightly different rhythmic values; a pulse rhythm ostinato in the bass in groups of three or four quarter notes; and an unheard conducted rhythm of changing meters that coincides with neither of the heard patterns, but which places the two statements of the melody in contrasting relations to the bar lines (an example of *augenmusik*). The first note of the tune begins on the second beat of a $\frac{2}{4}$ bar as an upbeat but returns as the downbeat of a $\frac{3}{4}$. If we don't watch the score or the conductor it will sound the other way around because we would assume (listening to the bass) that the first note was the downbeat of a $\frac{2}{2}$ bar, but because the theme is eleven beats long, the second statement would sound off the beat. While this diabolically manufactured rhythmic shift would not happen in jazz, its layered structure (tune, pulse, and feel) is a cognate of jazz. The asymmetry of the phrase, one half coinciding with the strong beat, the other bouncing off it, could be thought of as an extended hemiola ($\frac{3}{4}$ against $\frac{6}{8}$), similar to the 5 + 7 division of the West African handbell pattern.

Stravinsky asserted himself as time shaper by cropping the lengths of phrases in either odd or even numbers of beats, the odd beats serving as syncopating irritants and the even patterns as a resolution, though this resolution may be more apparent to the ear than the eye. At the end of the movement Stravinsky built his little tune almost to an anthem, superimposing it on a chugging *moto perpetuo* figure of four eighth notes in the strings. In the final phrase, a repeated unit forty-six beats long, Stravinsky superimposed three rhythmic ideas: in the winds, the upper strings, and the lower strings, in changing meters that correspond mainly to accents in the wind melody. If instead of following the bar lines you let the steady four eighth-note figure in the violins organize the rhythm (say, by tapping your foot on the first note and snapping a finger on the third), you will notice that the music suddenly takes wing, its irregular chop turned into an infectious bounce. Once you hear the music this way, you will also discover that Stravinsky's notation of the last five notes (ta-ta-ta-ta-TA) misrepresents the joyful groove so apparent to the fingers and toes but hidden from the eye. Keep on snapping and the last five notes become ta-ta-TA-ta-ta, with the last note no longer a plodding downbeat but a ricocheting bounce.

European music, torn loose from its older harmonic moorings, needed to acquire something of the rhythmic backbone of jazz; African American music, evolving from an array of regional folk styles toward a sophisticated form of artistic expression, at times looked to European modernism for inspiration. The cultural exchange is best understood as a trade between equals, not between sophisticates and primitives. We might say that the achievements of European musical modernism challenged jazz musicians in general, and Duke Ellington in particular, to take the modernity of their own music more seriously, to plumb its expressive and representational resources more fully as a cultural and political instrument. Yet, given the many ways in which European music and jazz interacted, any notion of European precedence seems questionable, and even an appearance of influence may be deceptive or at least redundant. Ellington's 1937 "Diminuendo in Blue" and "Crescendo in Blue" sport half-classical titles that accurately mirror their structural designs and that ask us to listen to them formalistically as "modern music"; at the same time these paired pieces exemplify both the blues and swing.[53] These paired works, testing the boundaries, are classics of both jazz and modern music. As is "Cotton Tail."

OUTRO: EXPERIMENTAL RHYTHM

The large literature on American experimental music usually credits rhythmic progress to the vanguard (white) composers whom Virgil Thomson called the "rhythmic research fellows":[54] Henry Cowell, Edgard Varèse, and, by extension, John Cage, Lou Harrison, and Conlon Nancarrow. This alliance, formed in the 1920s, called themselves "ultra-modernists." Thomson, with slightly more accuracy than he brought to the phenomenon of swing, characterized them by their "arithmetical structures, which are about the only structures available to non-tonal music."[55] Henry Cowell, without reference to any existing style of music, proposed rhythms derived from the fractional structure ($\frac{1}{2}$, $\frac{1}{3}$, $\frac{1}{4}$, $\frac{1}{5}$, etc.) of the overtone series in his *New Musical Resources,* published in 1930 as an ultra-modernist bible.[56]

One of the finest applications of Cowell's rhythmic ideas appeared in the last movement of Ruth Crawford Seeger's 1931 String Quartet, whose structure is a rhythmic numbers game. The first violin plays one note, the remaining trio plays twenty notes, then the first violin plays two notes, the trio, nineteen, and so on, and then they reverse course.[57] We might call it a rhythmic diminuendo and crescendo, but the formalistic exercise also sounds like a wicked mad-scientist parody of obsessive compulsion—an experiment that worked.

Beyond the "ultras" Cowell's ear-stretching rhythmic proposals had little influence until the 1940s when composers in Europe and America began to reconsider their rhythmic practice especially under the influence of serialism. Emerging composers like Boulez were dismayed by the apparent discrepancy between Schoenberg's radical method of organizing pitches and his traditional-sounding rhythmic idiom. Applying simple durational algorithms to a pitch series, Messiaen and Boulez "serialized rhythm" in "Modes de valeurs et d'intensité" and *Structures I,* respectively; Milton Babbitt made a similar move in his *Composition for Four Instruments.* For about twenty years Cowell-like "arithmetic structures," often devoid of any feeling of pulse or meter, dominated advanced concert music.

After 1950 John Cage went even further, replacing any traditional notion of rhythm with determinedly "meaningless" clock time, mere temporal data. Cage's antipsychological strategies showed a futuristic understanding of the new recording and broadcasting technologies that were transforming the way music was produced and perceived. In works, like Cage's *Williams Mix,* of *musique concrète,* composed through tape manipulation, rhythm was a function of tape length and playback speed: "The score resembles a dressmaker's pattern, from which the tapes were cut to size and shape."[58]

Throughout his career, though, Cage either ignored jazz or described it as a naïve folk style.[59] Equating the experimental with the conceptual, Cage denied jazz, however free, any conceptual content or experimental capacity; not surprisingly, when the free jazz of Sun Ra, Ornette Coleman, Eric Dolphy, Don Cherry, Cecil Taylor, and John Coltrane first appeared, some critics assumed, as they had with Ellington's jazz innovations, that it was trying to catch up with the advances of classical modernism, especially with Cage. A typical bracketing of Cage and Coleman appears in Frank Tirro's *Jazz: A History.* Tirro juxtaposes Cage ("I try to arrange my composing means so that I won't have any knowledge of what might happen. . . . My purpose is to eliminate purpose") with Coleman ("I don't tell the members of my group what to do. I want them to play what they hear in the piece for themselves. I let everyone express himself just as he wants to. The musicians have complete freedom, and so, of course, our final results depend entirely on the musicianship, emotional make-up, and taste of the individual member").[60] If Coleman was reacting to Cage, he was reacting selectively. Musicianship, emotional makeup, and taste, all forms of purpose, were three factors that Cage systematically excluded from his music.

Despite Cage's virtual silence on the subject of jazz, however, the rhythmic research of Charlie Parker, Dizzy Gillespie, Max Roach, Art Blakey, Thelonious Monk, and Bud Powell also reverberated with advanced styles in painting, poetry, and even concert music. Painters like Jackson Pollock played bebop recordings in their studios; poets like

Frank O'Hara emulated its spontaneous-sounding phrase shapes; and composers as different as Leonard Bernstein, Elliott Carter, and Stefan Wolpe emulated its high-voltage rhythmic energy.

We might designate all jazz, from Buddy Bolden onward, as rhythmic research, but what were the particular rhythmic innovations of bebop and post-bebop styles? Many of the musicians shared a desire to break the ties with American popular song. Though the two genres were intimately entwined from the time of Louis Armstrong's 1929 rendition of "I Can't Give You Anything But Love" to his chart-topping recording of "Hello Dolly" in 1964, by the late 1940s the marriage was already on the rocks.

Bebop musicians often transformed Broadway material radically, as Charlie Parker did with "Embraceable You," Miles Davis did with "Surrey with the Fringe on Top," and Coltrane did, on an epic scale, with "My Favorite Things." By calling attention to the gap between Broadway and Birdland renditions of the same tunes, jazz musicians declared an ironic musical independence. Less ironically, they also developed an alternative jazz songbook to replace the Broadway-born standards, a strategy of Ellington's career from the beginning. Instead of playing Gershwin or Rodgers tunes they performed a copious new jazz songbook composed by Tadd Dameron, Thelonious Monk, Errol Garner, John Lewis, Charles Mingus, Miles Davis, or Sonny Rollins. Or they abandoned the thirty-two-bar structure of the pop tune altogether, along with the harmonic role of the rhythm section. The 1959 Ornette Coleman quartet (Coleman on white plastic alto sax, Don Cherry on pocket trumpet, Charlie Haden on bass, and Billy Higgins on drums) was eccentric in a lot of ways, but especially in the absence of a harmony instrument, piano or guitar. The loosened-up texture of their music, though, had precedents in the opening bars of the Parker/Gillespie "Ko-Ko," and, as we have already heard, in the first phrase of "Cotton Tail."

Moving away from the pop tune, jazz musicians reconnected with other genres of African American music, like the gospel music heard in many compositions of Charles Mingus or the funk rhythms in Miles Davis's *On the Corner*. They put their music to school with other traditions of improvisation: Indian music (John Coltrane and Alice Coltrane) or African music (Randy Weston and, in his extended composition for jazz orchestra and Ghanaian musicians, *Congo Square*, Wynton Marsalis). Or they just went "out."

Jazz historians trace the birth of the "out" to the atonal sections of Ellington's "Clothed Woman" of 1947, but the impulse was also present around the same time in the music of Lennie Tristano and the futuristic pieces, like "City of Glass," that Robert Graettinger wrote for Stan Kenton and which Ellington parodied wickedly in his *Controversial Suite* of 1951, which also took a parting shot at the "Dixieland" revivalists.[61] Ornette Coleman's 1959 performances at the Five Spot turned these marginal efforts into a new movement that came to be called, after Coleman's 1960 album, free jazz.[62]

Eric Dolphy's *Out to Lunch*, recorded in 1964, is an early but classic example of the idiom. Its personnel are: Eric Dolphy, bass clarinet, flute, and alto sax; Freddie Hubbard, trumpet; Bobby Hutcherson, vibraphone; Richard Davis, bass; and Tony Williams, drums. (Astonishingly, Williams was just eighteen years old when the recording was made.) Of all the free jazz musicians, Dolphy had the strongest connections with advanced classical composition. He performed Varèse's flute solo *Density 21.5,* and he dedicated the third work on this album to Severino Gazzelloni, the Italian avant-garde flautist. Though all five tracks of *Out to Lunch* repay close study, let's look at the opening number, "Hat and Beard," an homage (or "tone parallel") to Thelonious Monk.

"Hat and Beard" is a study in odd-numbered asymmetry. It is in five sections and begins with a nine-beat, nine-pitch ostinato divided into 5 + 4 (C–B♭–A♭–G♭–F; E–B–G–D♭). The two melodic units imply the oscillating harmonies of Monk's theme song "Epistrophy." The opening section states the ostinato in various transformations twenty-two times, lasting about ninety seconds. The closing section also restates the ostinato but reverses the order of variants from the opening and compresses them to sixty seconds (a Bartókian structure and, roughly speaking, proportional relationship). The rhythm of the ostinato is square but goofy, like Monk's "Misterioso."

The three central sections are solos for Dolphy (bass clarinet), Hubbard, and Hutcherson, with Davis and Williams maintaining the 5 + 4 beat pattern throughout, aided by Hutcherson, when he's not soloing. What might have been a rhythmic straitjacket in lesser hands becomes a marvel of unpredictable cross-accentuation, especially in the "knots and gnarls" of Williams' ceaselessly creative drumming.[63] The rhythm section plays "supermelodically" without losing the pulse. Dolphy's solo, a darting series of swirls, wails, and shrieks, defies any simple relation to the pulse; though many of its sounds come from the repertory of "extended technique" cultivated by European avant-garde wind players like Gazzelloni and Heinz Holliger, every sound Dolphy makes stems from the blues. Hubbard develops Dolphy's fragments into longer, sustained lyrical lines that sound in turn like bebop and Arabian music. Hutcherson begins his section sparely, delineating the scalar structures of the ostinato. Instead of building on this, Hutcherson forgoes a star turn and instead weaves a trio with the bass and drums, quietly evoking bells and birdcalls—a little "night music."

There is not a single moment in "Hat and Beard" where the rhythmic patterns suggest the expected patterns of bebop, let alone swing. Yet it swings. The rhythmic layering and the vocabulary of rhythmic gestures in play all stem from the jazz tradition, and the exquisite timing and phrasing of the five performers sum up generations of rhythmic experiment by musicians predating even Bechet and Armstrong. The loss of pop tune harmonic progressions seems no loss at all; on the contrary, they feel like an unnecessary encumbrance, mere scaffolding. The rhythmic and harmonic implications of the ostinato theme seem more rigorous and apt in their demands on the players. There's life after rhythm changes.

"Out" in "Hat and Beard" is a happy, utopian state. It does not take the listener outside of time, nor, despite the album title, is it in any way crazy. But it does lead us "out" of constraining categories like classical, jazz, and even avant-garde (and it reminds us that all of those categories are constraining). As Ellington put it, the art is not in the categories, but "in the cooking."[64]

CHAPTER 3

"Prelude to a Kiss": Melody

In the advanced industrial countries pop music is defined
by standardization; its prototype is the song hit. A popular
American textbook on writing and selling such hits
confessed that with disarming missionary zeal some thirty
years ago. The main difference between a pop song and a
serious or—in the beautifully paradoxical language of that
manual—"standard" song is said to be that pop melodies
and lyrics must stick to an unmercifully rigid pattern while
the composer of serious songs is permitted free, autonomous
creation. The textbook writers do not hesitate to call popular
music "custom-built," a predicate usually reserved for
automobiles.

—T. W. Adorno

Play a simple melody.

—Irving Berlin

INTRO: THE MELODY BIZ

Melody was a touchy subject for the grandees of modern music. In his
1939 Norton Lectures Stravinsky conceded, grandly, that the public
was right about melody and he was wrong: "I am beginning to think,
in full agreement with the general public, that melody must keep its
place at the summit of the hierarchy of elements that make up music."[1]
Once he had bowed to the wisdom of his Harvard audience, however,
Stravinsky sternly corrected it: "but that is no reason to be beclouded
by melody to the point of losing balance and of forgetting that the art of

music speaks to us in many voices at once. Let me once again call your attention to Beethoven, whose greatness derives from a stubborn battle with rebellious melody."

Schoenberg similarly presented himself as a misunderstood melodist: "It is perhaps necessary to show also some melodies of my later period, especially of the composition with twelve tones, which has earned me the title of constructionist, engineer, mathematician, etc., meaning that these compositions are produced exclusively by the brain without the slightest participation of the heart."[2] Attempting to appear warm and fuzzy, Schoenberg cited as a melodic illustration of "heart" a twelve-tone theme from his Third String Quartet that most listeners would file under "brain." The rhythm of this theme (from the opening of the Intermezzo movement) has a certain Viennese lilt, but its pitches have all the charm of an atonal ear-training exercise.

Melody, a fighting word, can set the cultured elite against the general public, the brain against the heart, the human against the unhumanly mechanical. In wrestling with the subject, Stravinsky, Schoenberg, and Adorno, each in his own way, tried to put out a persistent antimodern brush fire. For their opponents the absence of melody, more than any other factor, explained the ever-widening distance between modern music and the concert audience. The decline and fall of melody epitomized the "agony of modern music," to quote the title of Henry Pleasants's 1955 antimodern, projazz polemic.

But what made melody such a hot potato? My trusty 1969 *Harvard Dictionary of Music* locates the tensions within the term itself. Its definition begins with bland objectivity: "In the broadest sense, a succession of musical tones, as opposed to harmony, i.e., musical tones sounded simultaneously." Down a few paragraphs, though, we find a surprisingly reception-oriented definition: "Melody is the only element in common to music of all times and all peoples, and . . . the cornerstone and touchstone of artistic quality." As a yardstick of quality, not simply an acoustical fact, melody empowers the listener. No wonder the term pushed composers' buttons! If melodic quality is measured by royalties, only a bare handful of classical melodies written since, say, 1920 have come anywhere near the earning power of popular songs. Perhaps the modernists should have just admitted flat out that they were handing melody over to Tin Pan Alley while they pursued loftier goals.

Tin Pan Alley was the name Monroe Rosenfield gave to a block on West 28th Street where M. Witmark, publisher of the 1891 hit "The Picture That's Turned to the Wall," had its headquarters.[3] Tin Pan Alley devoted itself exclusively to publishing and promoting popular songs. Its business took off rapidly through ties to emerging media: cheap sheet music, cabarets, variety shows, vaudeville, and the player piano.

Unlike most modernists, Tin Pan Alley understood the commercial value of its product and the makeup of its market. Adorno did not need to invent the idea that there was a mechanical formula for song production; the industry issued its own recipes for success. Charles K. Harris, both composer and publisher of the 1892 hit "After the Ball," advised composers to "take note of public demand" and "avoid slang and vulgarisms" as well as "many-syllabled words." He summed up his whole aesthetic creed in one sentence: "Simplicity in melody is one of the great secrets of success."[4]

At the outset, Tin Pan Alley's idea of simplicity caused its composers to turn out products that seemed merely crude, with simple hymnbook harmonies and cloying lyrics. Comparing these songs with the European art music of the time, Charles Hamm relates the rise of Tin Pan Alley in the 1890s to a wider split in musical culture: "The first Tin Pan Alley composers were contemporaries of Claude Debussy, Richard Strauss, Gustav Mahler, and Arnold Schoenberg; there was almost no common ground now between popular and classical music, no possibility that a piece of contemporary art music could be fashioned into a popular song."[5]

We could replay this "melody gap" throughout the twentieth century: the 1950s, for instance, were the decade of both Boulez and Buddy Holly. But a contrast of the crude if catchy "After the Ball" and the utterly refined *Das Lied von der Erde* omits important parts of the story. By the late 1890s Tin Pan Alley was also selling cakewalks and ragtimes, many by African American composers, often under the racist rubric of "coonsongs." However offensively packaged, ragtime enlivened the marketing mix of sentimental ballads and Bowery waltzes with raffish, rhythmic songs like Ben Harney's "You've Been a Good Old Wagon But You Done Broke Down" (1895) and Joseph Howard's "Hello! Ma Baby" (1899). As Hamm points out, the melodic market also had room for the operatic sounds of Reginald De Koven, Victor Herbert, and Ethelbert Nevin, whose songs spoke a language not all that distant from Strauss or Mahler.

At the beginning of the twentieth century popular music was a mélange of cakewalks, sentimental ballads, novelty tunes, Gilbert and Sullivan, and Viennese operettas, and the broad eclecticism of popular music has continued ever since. The Alley's megamart approach also embraced contemporary classical works. Debussy's "Rêverie" became "My Reverie"; Rachmaninoff's Second Piano Concerto was reborn as "Full Moon and Empty Arms"; Puccini's *Tosca* provided melodic inspiration for "Avalon" (1920, credited to Al Jolson) and "Smile" (1936, by Charlie Chaplin); and Stan Kenton lifted his theme song, "Artistry in Rhythm," right out of Ravel. By 1914 popular tunesmiths like Irving Berlin and Jerome Kern were writing songs that were not one-season ephemera. For some early critics of popular culture, like Gilbert Seldes in *The Seven Lively Arts* (1924), "Alexander's Ragtime Band" and "They Didn't Believe Me" marked the arrival of a new art form. For much of the classical world, however, they were just more "Moon/June" rubbish.

With the appearance of Ella Fitzgerald's "song book" albums in the late 1950s and the publication of Alec Wilder's *American Popular Song* in 1972, the much-maligned output of Tin Pan Alley became the much-acclaimed Great American Songbook. Wilder's book, written by a practitioner, demonstrated on every page that the creators of popular song were craftsmen, not hacks. They pursued aesthetic ideals, not just monetary gain. Today opera stars like Renée Fleming and Jessye Norman perform these songs as certified classics, but the rise of the Great American Songbook from the flotsam of Tin Pan Alley owed much to interpretations by jazz singers and instrumentalists. Louis Armstrong initiated this cross-genre, cross-race collaboration in his 1933 recording of "I Got a Right to Sing the Blues," by Harold Arlen and Ted Koehler. The African American Armstrong strutted his right to sing a popular song by two Jewish Americans who proclaimed their right to compose in an African American genre.

The collusion of jazz and popular song produced new ways of composing melodies, new ways of performing them, and a new form of melodic elaboration, beyond embellishment, which I call "supermelody." The Ellington repertory richly illustrates the full range of these melodic innovations. Songs from "Solitude" to "Satin Doll," and soloists as gifted as Johnny Hodges, Cootie Williams, and Lawrence Brown, exalted melody far beyond the habitual dualisms of high and low or brain and heart.[6]

THE DUKE ELLINGTON (& CO.) SONGBOOK

Although the *Duke Ellington Songbook* came third in Ella Fitzgerald's recordings (after Cole Porter and Rodgers and Hart, but before Irving Berlin, the Gershwins, Harold Arlen, Jerome Kern, and Johnny

Mercer), his place of honor in the Great American Songbook was far from obvious at the time. Alec Wilder devoted just a few pages to Ellington toward the back of his book; he prefaced his praises (for the music) by claiming that "the only problem with discussing his songs is that very few of them are essentially songs, nor were they meant to be."[7] The statement is both true and false. As a band leader and an African American, Ellington lived a very different life from the rest of the song-writing fraternity. Unlike the Mighty Six, he did regularly write songs for Broadway shows and Hollywood movies. Many of his songs, like "Mood Indigo," first became popular as instrumental compositions. Once they were launched, Irving Mills or a staff lyricist, like Mitchell Parish at Mills Music, would add lyrics.

On Broadway most lyricists and composers worked closely together, usually writing the music first and words second. As Philip Furia points out, this method allowed the lyrics to bounce off the syncopated rhythms and echo the "ragged" quality of contemporary American speech. Even after he broke with Mills, however, Ellington never sustained a hand-and-glove collaboration with a lyricist, although in 1939 he hired Billy Strayhorn for that purpose. Ellington soon discovered that writing great lyrics, like those Strayhorn had already penned for his song "Lush Life," was just one of Strayhorn's many talents.[8]

Although Wilder assumed that all of Ellington's songs were by-products of his band's instrumental repertory, the young, unknown Ellington had worked as a songwriter when he first came to New York.[9] In 1925, a year before the recording of "East St. Louis Toodle-Oo" put his band on the map, he composed three songs for the all-black review *Chocolate Kiddies*. African American songwriters, following in the foot-steps of Shelton Brooks ("Some of These Days" and "The Darktown Strutters' Ball") and Chris Smith ("Ballin' the Jack") scored notable successes in the early 1920s. Eubie Blake and Noble Sissle wrote "I'm Just Wild about Harry" for their popular review *Shuffle Along*. Turner Layton Jr. and Henry Creamer wrote "Way Down Yonder in New Orleans," and James P. Johnson and Cecil Mack launched the most important dance craze of the decade with "Charleston" from the 1923 show *Runnin' Wild*. Ellington's song "Jig Walk" quoted "Charleston" explicitly (as did Gershwin's Piano Concerto in F, written in the same year), but it already revealed a personal voice hinting at the "jungle" style that would soon appear.[10]

Ellington, however, pursued a different path from other black song-writers. Although all-black reviews, beginning with Sissle and Blake's

Shuffle Along, were popular and influential, they were marginalized. The music industry was segregated, either as a matter of law, or marketing strategy, or custom. Broadway happily assimilated the musical advances of the all-black reviews (Gershwin, for instance, turned the catchy rhythm of "I'm Just Wild about Harry" into "Love Is Sweeping the Country"), but African American musicians like W. C. Handy, Eubie Blake, Will Vodery, and William Grant Still were kept at a remove from the commercial machinery that turned Broadway melodies into money-making hits. Even at the Cotton Club, where performers were black but the audience was white, except for a few seats in the back reserved for black celebrities, white composers and lyricists like Jimmy McHugh, Harold Arlen, and Dorothy Fields wrote "black" songs. As the film *Black and Tan Fantasy* shows, the Ellington Orchestra provided music for dance numbers, but not songs.

Ellington and Mills sized up this situation early and gave popular song a specific economic function in relation to a broader marketing strategy designed to set Ellington apart from the competition and to appeal to white listeners as well as black. In his 1933 advertising manual[11] Mills instructed his agents not to "treat Duke Ellington as just another jazz bandleader. . . . Ellington's genius as a composer, arranger and musician has won him the respect and admiration of such authorities as Percy Grainger . . . Leopold Stokowski . . . Paul Whiteman . . . and many others." As a "great artist" and "musical genius" Ellington recorded for the prestigious mass-market Victor label, not for labels aimed only at the "race" market. The songs, published as sheet music, aimed for the wide—that is, white—audience. The lyrics of "Sophisticated Lady," "Solitude," and "In a Sentimental Mood" were dreamy, romantic, and racially nonspecific. The sophisticated lady portrayed on the cover of the original sheet music could be white. Ellington and Mills tailored the songs for general use. Their unmarked racial character allowed them to cross over to romantically erotic territory not usually open to black male vocalists until the arrival of Billy Eckstine and Nat "King" Cole. Not surprisingly, "Solitude" became a big national hit for Benny Goodman, not Ellington. American dance halls, like its churches, would remain segregated either by law or custom for most of Ellington's life.

As a reproof to Wilder's dismissive assessment of Ellington's songwriting, Gary Giddins pointed out that though Ellington only composed one-twelfth the number of songs written by Jerome Kern, they produced an equal number of "standards." Here is his list of Ellington "standards":[12]

All Too Soon

Azure

Caravan (by Juan Tizol)

Come Sunday

Do Nothing Till You Hear from Me

Don't Get around Much Anymore

I Didn't Know About You

I Got It Bad and That Ain't Good

I Let a Song Go Out of My Heart

I'm Beginning to See the Light

I'm Just a Lucky So-and-so

In a Mellotone

In a Sentimental Mood

Jump for Joy

Lost in Meditation

Prelude to a Kiss

Rocks in My Bed

Satin Doll

Solitude

Sophisticated Lady

But wait, there are more (if we add some Strayhorn and Tizol tunes). Here are additional songs on Ella's recording:

Bli-Blip

Chelsea Bridge (Strayhorn)

Day Dream (Strayhorn)

Drop Me Off in Harlem

Everything But You

I Ain't Got Nothin' But the Blues

I Didn't Know About You

It Don't Mean a Thing (If It Ain't Got That Swing)

Just A-Sittin' and A-Rockin' (Lee Gaines, Strayhorn)

Just Squeeze Me (But Please Don't Tease Me)

Love You Madly

Lush Life (Strayhorn)

Mood Indigo

Perdido (Tizol)

Rocks in My Bed

Squatty Roo (Hodges)

Take the "A" Train (Strayhorn)

This list still does not include "Black Butterfly" or "It Shouldn't Happen to a Dream" or such later standards as "Heaven," nor does it list many great instrumental melodies, such as "Black Beauty" and "Warm Valley," which were never given lyrics. By any measure Ellington (& Co.) was a prodigious melodist.

Because many of his early works either quoted existing melodies ("Black and Tan Fantasy," "Creole Love Call") or shared credits with Bubber Miley, it is hard to pinpoint the first Ellingtonian melody. "The

Mooche," recorded in October 1928 and for many years the band's theme song, presented Ellington's trademark combination of jungle beat and chromaticism. In the spring of 1928, Ellington recorded, as a piano solo, an equally individual yet completely different melody, "Black Beauty." Although the authorship is also shared with Miley, its style is more in the character of other lyrical pieces written for, with, or by Ellington's "sweet" trumpeter Arthur Whetsol such as "Awful Sad," "Take it Easy," "Zonky Blues," and "Misty Mornin'." All these melodies build a plaintive mood on gliding chromatic harmonies.

With its first melodic interval, a downward leap of a minor seventh, "Black Beauty" announced Ellington's uninhibited approach to melody. The tune unfolds without repetition, leaping back up a major ninth to end its first phrase. Its melodic notes enrich the harmony and insinuate the blues. Although the main phrase of melody doesn't seem to allude to the blues, its two accidentals, the flatted third and flatted seventh, come from the blues scale. Ellington, though, avoided the stereotypical blues markers that Gershwin depended on; the blues feeling saturates "Black Beauty" without calling attention to itself.[13]

Ellington must have been particularly proud of "Black Beauty." It is featured in the central art deco dance sequence in the short film "Black and Tan," and it remained in the band's book for years. "Awful Sad" (also from 1928), by contrast, is a nearly forgotten gem. Its even more modernistic harmonies have led some critics to suspect the influence of Bix Beiderbecke's impressionistic "In a Mist,"[14] but as the title of James P. Johnson's tune "You've Got to Be Modernistic" implies, modernistic chords were very much à la mode. What was not in the air, at least not for another forty years, is the melodic line that, in its easy grace, sounds more like Brian Wilson's "God Only Knows" than like anything from the 1920s.

"PRELUDE TO A KISS"

With two of his earliest hit songs, "Mood Indigo" (1931, coauthored with Barney Bigard) and "Sophisticated Lady" (1933), Ellington already demonstrated a style of melodic writing that set his songs apart from those of contemporaries, even those as adventurous as Gershwin and Arlen. "Mood Indigo" begins with a typical device of indicating a "blue note" by wavering between the major and minor third of the key (A♭ in the sheet music version). In the second phrase, though, to the words

You ain't been blue,
Till you've had that mood indigo

the tune seems to fly off the tonal rails as the harmony shifts to E major. This harmonic move is not as weird as it first looks, but its sinuous chromaticism sounds more like Bartók than Chopin.

True to its title, "Sophisticated Lady" is even more up-to-date. The sheet music version, also in A♭, begins with an altered F♭ dominant seventh chord with the fifth lowered so that all the notes are part of a whole-tone scale. The ultrasophisticated chord is an emblematic modernistic touch, the first of more to come. The tune begins by climbing up in thirds, F–A♭–C–E♭–G♭, to outline the dissonant interval of a minor ninth, from F to G♭; it then proceeds chromatically downward, with the harmony moving in parallel with the melody, in nonfunctional dominant seventh chords. Like the whole-tone scale, this device is conspicuously Debussyan. Ellington sustains the harmonic tension in the "bridge" of the song, later given the words

Smoking, drinking,
Never thinking
Of tomorrow, nonchalant.

The harmonic progression (I–vi–ii–V) is an Alley cliché and might sound harmonically uninteresting if Ellington had not placed it in the key of G major, far distant in tonal terms from the A♭ tonality of the other phrases. Even though the Broadway tunesmiths prided themselves on the harmonic deviousness of the "bridge" (Rodgers's "Have You Met Miss Jones?" is the classic example), few can match Ellington's nonchalant chromatic elegance here.

Alec Wilder termed "Prelude to a Kiss" (1938) "another chromatic idea supported by very gratifying, satisfying harmony" and granted that "except for a totally instrumental release, it comes close to being a song. Even the lyrics by Irving Gordon (in lock step with Irving Mills) have a few moments, though the image of a 'flower crying for the dew' somehow fails."[15] The tune appeared almost simultaneously as both an instrumental and a vocal recording (August 8, 1938, for the instrumental, August 24 for the vocal by Mary McHugh, accompanied by Johnny Hodges and His Orchestra).[16]

"Prelude to a Kiss" is a thirty-two-bar AABA song. Although this format is typical, by Alley standards the melody of "Prelude to a Kiss" is indecently chromatic. Its sensuous chromatic descent recalls erotic arias like the "Habanera" from *Carmen* or *"Mon Coeur s'ouvre à ta voix"* from *Samson et Dalila*. While the two French examples begin on the tonic and outline the tonic triad clearly, Ellington's melody starts on the dissonant seventh degree of the tonic C major scale and does not settle down tonally for eight bars, where it comes to rest not on the tonic C but on an A, the "added six" floating above the dominant. Ellington goes even further at the bridge, belying the lyrics ("Though it's just a simple melody") with a jump into a distant key (E major) and approaching every note in that key with a half-step chromatic "neighbor tone." The interval of the half step, the building block of the chromatic scale, becomes a subliminal melodic motive, or what Schoenberg might term a *Grundgestalt,* a basic shape. The downward curve of D♯–C♯–B–A–C♮ (which then resolves up to C♯) is so devious that even Ella Fitzgerald (or whoever copied the music for her) felt the need to "correct" it, making that low C♮ a C♯. Ellington here turned the pitch C, which should be the most consonant note, into the strongest dissonance, a diminished ninth that resolves upward to a slightly milder dissonance (major ninth) rather than downward to an octave.

Harmonies heat up the melody's seductive moves. Ellington set the initial pitch, B, atop a D dominant-ninth chord to form the interval of a thirteenth above the bass, the highest possible upper addition to a triad. The thirteenth is a double dissonance, one seventh (upward from C to B) stacked on another (from D to C). Music theory terms these combinations of tones dissonances, but they sound sensuous, not harsh. Every note of this melody is either a dissonance, or part of a dissonant chord. In the seven notes of the opening phrase the dissonances are as follows:

B over a D ninth: a thirteenth

B♭: a passing tone forming a diminished thirteenth

A over a G ninth (with a raised fifth): a ninth

A♭: a passing tone forming a diminished ninth

G: a fifth over a C dominant ninth

A: an "escape tone" forming a thirteenth

E: the major seventh of an F major seventh chord

For the next phrase Ellington transposed the notes and chords just heard down a minor third, seemingly even further from any vestige of C major, but landing on a d minor triad, the first three-note harmony of the song, which, as any jazz pianist can tell you, will easily lead to

C major through the progression ii–V–I. Ellington, however, stretched that familiar move out with an upward melodic leap of a ninth on "se-re-*na-ding* you."

All these dissonances may look like early Schoenberg, but they sound more like those of Schoenberg's tennis partner, George Gershwin, just as the lyrics tell us. (Gershwin died in July 1937; perhaps this song was Ellington's musical eulogy.) Indeed the rich chord progression resembles that of "Nice Work If You Can Get It," written a year earlier for Fred Astaire in *A Damsel in Distress*. Ellington's melody is more deviously sensual than Gershwin's bromidic glide.

The eccentricities of "Prelude to a Kiss"—its chromaticism, high dissonance level, and systematic exploitation of the interval of a half step as a thematic idea— mask what we might term its skeletal structure. These good bones become visible once we pare the song down to its two outer lines and remove the many pitches outside the C major scale. Such a reduction reveals how the melody and the bass move steadily (yet evasively) toward the tonic. The melody descends sequentially: B–A–G–E; G–F–E–D. Ellington delays the arrival of the tonic note C so that the melody had to keep moving. When the melody finally completes the move downward to C, it leaps up a ninth so that the descent has to begin all over again. The bass line likewise moves in the time-honored pattern of the circle of fifths, but where another composer might have traced that circle from C to C, Ellington began the circle on D, one note above the tonic (D–G–C–F–B–E–A–D), keeping the harmony in suspense.

Though Ellington's style was distinctive, his songs employed the same idiom as that used by his Broadway-based colleagues, not a distant jazz world dialect. To better discern the similarities and differences, let's compare "Prelude to a Kiss" to a song that would seem to be its opposite, "My Romance," by Richard Rodgers and Lorenz Hart. It appeared in their 1935 show *Jumbo* and was revived as a jazz standard by Bill Evans. "My Romance" appears as plain as "Prelude to a Kiss" seems extravagantly fancy, but perhaps the differences are just skin-deep.

Celebrating a lack of ornament ("My romance doesn't have to have a moon in the sky"), Rodgers's tune is conspicuously "white." The entire melody for the chorus uses only the notes of the C major scale. As in "Prelude to a Kiss," the "chorus" of "My Romance" is thirty-two bars long, but in a different configuration, ABAC, more typical of theater-based songs. ABAC songs save their biggest punch for the ending rather than the bridge. They present two similar statements with different endings, the first tentative, the second assured. Where the overall arc of Ellington's tune moves downward to resolution on the low C, Rodgers's tune is a series of upward scales that reach a climax in the final phrase when the opening three notes, the hook that states the title, blaze forth, transposed up a sixth to state and reiterate the melody's highest note.

Beneath their surfaces, though, "My Romance" and "Prelude to a Kiss" are nearly identical. Both melodies state an idea then restate it a third lower. Both melodies create tension by moves from the tonic, C, to the submediant, E. Ignoring for a moment the differences between their AABA and ABAC designs, we might even say that Rodgers's diatonic chords and melody represent the harmonic analysis of Ellington's tune. It would be hard to reduce the tune or chords of "My Romance" the way we did for "Prelude to a Kiss"; like a shellfish, its skeleton is on the surface.

If we flip that observation around we can see why the tunes encourage different jazz treatment. To a jazz player, "My Romance" is a blank slate, just waiting for its harmonies to be enriched, its rhythms enlivened. As printed there is not a single jazz rhythm in the entire song apart from its fox-trot feeling, and yet if a player just moves the notes forward half a beat, as Bill Evans does, it becomes effortless jazz. "Prelude to a Kiss," by contrast, doesn't have to be turned into jazz. Its melody comes already richly ornamented. Its rhythms subtly alternate bars of fox-trot and bars of Charleston so that it swings even played as written. Johnny Hodges doesn't turn it into jazz; he just turns it into Hodges.

UNDRESSED MELODIES: SEX AND RACE

The pop tune flourished within a particular time frame, let's say 1911–70, in a particular place, melting pot, mongrel Manhattan, and it served particular social functions, including the definition of national and generational identities. Eighty-five percent of the time (according to Furia) its overt subject, though, was romance ("I love you in thirty-two bars"): not medieval romance, but the American kind where boy meets girl and, if things work out, they check into a small hotel, but, as "There's a Small Hotel" says, only in the "bridal suite." Romance included sex, love, and marriage; the friction and frustration generated by these categories kept the subject and the songs interesting.

Popular songs represented romance with four scales: major, minor, blues, and chromatic. The major scale conveyed an ideal of untroubled, "normal" innocence: "Do-re-mi." Like Mozart, Schubert, and Brahms, however, the tunesmiths knew how to give a song a bittersweet quality by making the major scale sound minor. Here are four mixed-mode examples (of many, many others) you can play through in your head: "My Heart Stood Still" (Rodgers and Hart), "Embraceable You" (the Gershwins), "What'll I Do?" (Berlin), and "Yesterday" (Lennon and McCartney). The first two songs emphasize minor-sounding segments of the major scale. "What'll I Do?" draws its poignancy from just one pitch borrowed from the minor mode, the flat sixth. "Yesterday" hovers between major and relative minor. None of these songs uses blues devices, but the minor mode makes them sound blue. Love, after all, isn't easy, but at least in pop tunes the minor usually gives way to the major.

Until rhythm and blues crossed over to become rock and roll, the blues scale functioned as a racial marker in pop tunes. The blues scale indicated that a song, like "Stormy Weather," was intended for black performers because it portrayed emotions that "they" had but "we" could not express, or it portrayed a "mongrel" condition, like that portrayed by mixed-race Julie in *Show Boat* when she sings "Can't Help Lovin' That Man of Mine." The blues scale in particular became a fixture of torch songs, from "The Man I Love" to "The Man That Got Away," sung by women who had "gone south" and paid the price. The presence of the blues, even in just a passing chord, as in "Somebody Loves Me," denotes an unsettling, subversive feeling summed up in the phrase "low down." Although Harold Arlen specialized in songs with a blues tinge, there's not a trace of the blues in his most "American" score, for *The Wizard of Oz*. In the Emerald City, Dorothy may not be in Kansas anymore, but she is also far from the un-American terrain of Harlem.

In classical music and popular music alike the chromatic scale often denotes sexuality. Tin Pan Alley's chromatic inhibition therefore may have been more than a question of singability. In a marketplace where songs appeared in the censored media of the movies and radio, full frontal sexuality was both unsingable and unspeakable. Without sex, though, love songs become, in the words of Dorothy Fields, "as cold as yesterday's mashed potatoes." The solution appeared in songs like "How Long Has This Been Going On," which floated a diatonic melody atop a chromatic accompaniment, an upstairs/downstairs scalar divide. This device appears in "The Girl Friend" (Rodgers and Hart, 1926), a paean of "terrible honesty": "Homely wrecks appeal/When their checks appeal,/But she has sex appeal." The girlfriend in question is both good and bad: "She's knockout, she's regal,/her beauty's illegal." Rodgers divides her licit and illicit aspects between the melody and the bass, keeping the erotic element subconsciously below the waist.

Gershwin pushed the diatonic/chromatic split even farther in "Liza" (1929) and "Boy What Love Has Done to Me" (1930). The title of the second song speaks for itself, but "Liza" is a more complex cocktail. It appeared in "Show Girl," a short-lived "Dixieland" extravaganza dreamed up by Flo Ziegfeld that featured both the Ellington Orchestra (playing its own music) and a ballet based on Gershwin's *An American in Paris*.[17] "Liza" was Gershwin's response to Ziegfeld's request for a "minstrel number in the second act with one hundred beautiful girls seated on steps that cover the entire stage."[18] The gimmick was that just as Ruby Keller was about to begin the song, Al Jolson, her new husband, would leap out of the audience to serenade her and sing the song himself.[19] The song had to be black, white, and blackface all at the same time. To code this racial mélange, Gershwin used three scales. The first phrase ("Liza, Liza, skies are gray") pits a minstrel-style pentatonic melody against a rising chromatic bass line. Both lines turn diatonic in the second half of the phrase ("But if you'll smile on me/All the clouds'll roll away"). The white-note music mirrors the Kernesque sweetness alluded to in the lyrics; it also allows Keeler and Jolson to sing in their own white voices.

Once we see how the harmonic language of the Great American Songbook encoded race and sex, we can hear the chromaticism of Ellington's melodies as more than a stylistic refinement. Brandishing its chromaticism rather than hiding it in the bass line, the melody of "Prelude to a Kiss" exposed the code and spoke the unspeakable. The melody made the erotic audible. Consciousness of the codes also shed light on the subversive strategy behind Ellington's own mythology, such as the story of composing "In a Sentimental Mood": "That was written very spontaneously. One playing—zhwoop!—just like that. The occasion was in Durham, North Carolina. . . . It was a rather gay party with the exception of two girls and one fellow. . . . So I had two chicks, one on each side of me, and I said 'Just listen to this. You girls are too good friends to let anything like this come between you,' And this is what I played for them. I played it and I remembered it, and then I put it down."[20] It's a lovely story, but a cunning one as well. "In a Sentimental Mood" is one of the most sophisticated songs Ellington wrote, even more than "Prelude to a Kiss." It also takes direct aim at Gershwin, lifting its first seven notes from "Someone to Watch Over Me," then exposing the squareness of Gershwin's song through a masterful deployment of two Gershwin devices, the chromatic bass and the passing allusion to the blues, a single A♭ that tints the entire melody. Where Gershwin had built his melody by repeating the same rhythm in a descending melodic sequence (longing to see/I know that he/'s waiting for me), Ellington's tune curls unpredictably, arpeggiating up a ninth when you least expect it. Compared to the Gershwin, it sounds improvised whether or not it actually was. (The performance to hear is by John Coltrane.) Dave Brubeck's nearly as spontaneous-sounding homage, "The Duke," begins with the melodic inversion of "In a Sentimental Mood," a technique usually associated with serialism rather than jazz.

The great popular tunes, particularly the ballads, conveyed the contradictory tenets of urban life: sexual liberation versus "family values," freedom versus anomie, enlightened sophistication versus abiding prejudice. The closer we look at the songs, the more their craft appears as ways of registering social friction through musical and verbal frissons, dissonances, and uncertainties that, while rarely rising to political protest, absolve them from the Adornian charge of mindless escapism. Their full complexity, though, demanded new styles of performance that would replace literal reproduction with looser reinterpretation. They needed, as we will see, to be sung with a blues voice, as blues.

"DAY DREAM": SINGING THE BLUES, BLUEING THE SONG

Musically, not legally, who owns a melody? If you listen to three tenors—yes, *those* three tenors—sing, say, "Nessun dorma," each version will contain the same pitches and pretty much the same rhythms. Even the sounds of their voices will differ only enough so that an experienced opera lover could tell them apart. Puccini still calls almost all the shots. By contrast, when you hear Bessie Smith and Billie Holiday sing the "St. Louis Blues," their pitches, rhythms, and even some of the words differ sharply from the printed sheet music. W. C. Handy may have received royalties, but both singers felt free to remake his song in their own images. And if you listen to Sarah Vaughan stretch the last phrase of "My Funny Valentine" into infinity, there will be no question of who owns *that* melody. Unlike concert audiences, listeners to jazz and popular music expect performers to style a song distinctively. Historically, though, the contrast of composers' and performers' prerogatives has not always been so clear-cut. On recordings of Broadway musicals from the 1920s, singers like Gertrude Lawrence perform great Gershwin tunes with (to our ears) a genteel literalism; much of the music termed "jazz" in the 1920s was played as written from mass-produced stock arrangements.[21] Opera singers in the baroque and bel canto eras added ornaments and embellishments to arias; concerto soloists were similarly expected to improvise cadenzas.

The conformity of classical music stems from the power of the printed score as a legal restraint and an aesthetic one, a power asserted by music publishers in the nineteenth century, put into copyright law early in the twentieth, and turned into an aesthetic cause by performers and scholars. Even before Toscanini proclaimed that his performances were *come scritto*, classical music was getting hooked on literalism. The score was the music. In the face of such textual power the performer's room for interpretation has grown ever narrower.

Popular singing, by contrast, gradually became ever freer in execution. Exactly how this happened is a complicated story involving many different styles of vocal performance and changing technology,[22] but it certainly had a lot to do with the two great waves of blues popularity, first as sheet music in 1914 and then as recordings in 1920. Today we take the link between blues and popular music for granted, but they would have seemed inimical a century ago, and not just racially. Popular songs were designed for mechanical reproduction as sheet music or piano rolls, and they were carefully branded with hooks or novelty subject matter to differentiate themselves from competing projects. Developed in an oral culture, the blues, by contrast, put a premium on the individual singer's bardlike ability to embellish within a common musical and poetic vocabulary. The essence of blues was elaborated repetition, both within a blues stanza where a single line would be sung twice with different inflections, and between songs that shared structure and subject matter. Publication placed the blues at a crossroads. Would the blues now be performed as written, like most popular songs? Actually, there were fairly literal blues performances, at least to judge by Eva Taylor's recording of Joe Oliver's "West End Blues," which sounds demurely text-bound compared to the famous recording by Louis Armstrong.[23]

The blues began to transform the performance style of popular music through recordings by less restrained "blueswomen," including Ma Rainey and Bessie Smith. Mamie Smith (one of many unrelated blues-singing Smiths) launched the craze with her intensely wailed rendition of Perry Bradford's "Crazy Blues," which sold seventy-five thousand copies within four weeks of its release in October 1920.[24] Anyone who owned a copy of the sheet music would have seen at once that Bradford's song was not being sung *come scritto.* The blueswomen certainly employed forms of embellishment and ornamentation not found in popular song performance of the time judging by the few recordings we have of musicals in the 1920s, not on Broadway, where operetta-style singing mingled with cabaret-style *Sprechstimme* and the minstrel show "mammyisms" of Al Jolson. For conservative listeners, even in the realm of popular music the sounds of blues vocalism were repellant. When Louis Armstrong appeared in London in 1932, *Melody Maker* dismissed his singing of popular tunes like "Them There Eyes" or "When You're Smiling" as "savage growling."[25] Today these performances sound like classics of coloratura, the fine art of melodic elaboration.

We can hear contrasting versions of blues coloratura in three wonderful performances of "St. Louis Blues," the famous January 14, 1925, Bessie Smith recording with Louis Armstrong on cornet and Fred Longshaw on reed organ; Billie Holiday's recording from October 15, 1940, with the Benny Carter Orchestra; and a lesser-known recording from February 9, 1932, by Bing Crosby with the Ellington Orchestra. It's not surprising that Bessie Smith's recording, with its harmonium accompaniment, slow tempo, and trumpet obbligato has become a sacred text in jazz history; it has the weight of a Bach aria. In her first phrase ("I hate to see that evening sun go down"), Smith called attention to the way she sings each note by compressing the notes of the melody, following its four-note motto, within the range of a minor third, between the tonic E♭ and G♭. We might categorize her embellishments as introductory, a slide to the main pitch; concluding, a fall from the main pitch; or internal, a wavering of the pitch within the note, particularly noticeable on the many G♭s, especially on the word "sun." There are also notes that are sung almost *parlando,* and others that are sung straight and trumpetlike, matching Armstrong's tone. In the second phrase ("Feelin' tomorrow like I feel today"), she used the two syllables of "mor-row," which take the place in the melody of the one syllable "see," to color the pitch F instead of G♭. In relation to her singing, the term "blue note" has to be applied to a whole family of ornaments that she applied to different steps of the scale, not just the third.

Smith produced a different timbre for each of the song's three strains. By compressing the melody in the first part she saved the B♭ for the opening of the second, tango-rhythm part, and to further dramatize that entrance she delayed it, singing "St. Louis Woman" right on the beat rather than as three upbeats. And then in the third section she makes her voice smile just by adding a touch of a growl. Armstrong responds to this phrase ("Got the St. Louis Blues jes blue as I can be") with a melody so ripe for the plucking that Ellington stole it for the opening of his "Clarinet Lament."

Billie Holiday recorded "St. Louis Blues" at an easy bounce tempo and sang it in C. Although this is lower than Smith's recording, it sounds higher because Holiday's style is microphone-based. She sings the notes in this relatively low register as if she were speaking them, without using the chest voice needed in acoustic singing. Her style sounds so relaxed that you don't notice that she has extended the range of the melody to a major ninth, from G to A. The faster tempo allows Holiday to sing two stanzas of the last section, first using a compressed melody similar to Bessie Smith's and then, following Benny Carter's clarinet solo, a more extroverted version as befits the unexpectedly hip lyrics ("I love that man like a school boy loves his pie, like a Kentucky colonel loves his mint and rye"). Holiday brings several new elements of ornamentation into play. In her singing, as in that of opera singers of the past, vibrato is an ornament with many different shapes (steady, increasing, decreasing, or added suddenly). It allows her to apply a wide spectrum of vocal colors, from the spoken to the instrumental, to just a few pitches. Another ornament is a muted sound caused by darkening the vowel, which makes the note less forward sounding, almost as if it were hummed. And finally there is rubato, a rhythmic ornament. In European music rubato, in which the tempo seems to slow down and speed up almost from note to note, is associated with performances of romantic piano music (Chopin) or opera. In a Puccini aria, for instance, the singer will often give every beat a different value, and the conductor has to be careful to line up the orchestral accompaniment with the unsteady pulse. In Holiday's performance the tempo stays constant but her melody lags behind much of the time, a more complicated, contrapuntal situation. Putting melody and harmony out of phase, this type of rubato is both a rhythmic and harmonic embellishment.

Historians of popular song credit the blend of blues and pop singing into a new style to Louis Armstrong and Bing Crosby, who recorded similar repertory in similar styles around 1930, thereby proving that the new style was not tied to race, region, or repertory. Crosby's singular recording with Ellington, an extended four-and-a-half-minute arrangement of "St. Louis Blues," celebrates that synthesis. Crosby's performance combines aspects of the Bessie Smith recording with Louis

Armstrong's uptempo rendition, recorded in 1929, but it also sounds recognizably like Crosby.

Ellington placed Crosby's vocal in dialogue with hot solos by Cootie Williams, Joe Nanton, and Johnny Hodges. The arrangement is in three parts, a slow section in B♭ with Williams playing the first strain of Handy's song and Nanton growling; the second, tango, strain, a central section in F ushered in by modulating arpeggios from Ellington, where Crosby sings all three strains; and a fast concluding section back in B♭ launched by Hodges with Crosby scat singing along. Ellington and Crosby turned Handy's tune into a stylistic panorama, a symphonic showcase for Crosby's three singing styles. Crosby moves easily between a fairly literal performance of the melody to much freer singing that is similar to the way Armstrong sang Hoagy Carmichael's "Rockin' Chair," which he first recorded with the composer in 1930. Crosby leaps over into what was once jazz territory when he starts to scat. Armstrong had put scat singing on the map with his 1926 recording of "Heebie Jeebies" and expanded its expressive range in "Hotter Than That" and "West End Blues." The technique made the voice an instrument, freeing it from the words to pursue instrumental-style melodic improvisation, a step beyond melodic embellishment. (Ellington first used the device as a compositional color for Adelaide Hall in "Creole Love Call" and "The Blues I Love to Sing" in 1927.)

Gary Giddins and Will Friedwald have claimed that Crosby and Armstrong were learning from each other. Crosby, who had sung with Paul Whiteman since 1926, assimilated Armstrong's rhythmic freedom and blues ornamentation so that he could improvise like a jazz instrumentalist. Armstrong entered the field of popular song with his 1928 recording of Fats Waller's "Ain't Misbehavin'." In the early 1930s he covered most of the songs made popular by Guy Lombardo. These recordings demolished the line between sweet and hot styles. In "I'm Confessin' That I Love You" (1930) Armstrong begins with a laid-back Crosby-like vocal laced with a Hawaiian guitar accompaniment but then issues a shot across the bow with one of his hottest and highest trumpet solos to date. Through emulation and competition Armstrong and Crosby helped define a new fusion of pop material and jazz performance, which Will Friedwald nicely dubs the "jazz ballad."[26] In his arrangement of "St Louis Blues" Ellington just put the icing on the cake.

Ellington's resident master of the jazz ballad was not a singer but a saxophone player, Johnny Hodges. (To my taste, Ivie Anderson was more compelling on rhythm songs like "Don't Mean a Thing" and

"Killin' Myself" than on ballads.) Although Hodges had a wide stylistic range, including rough-and-tumble numbers like "Jeeps Blues" and "The Gal from Joe's," he inspired Ellington and Strayhorn to compose a series of slow ballads that range in expression from the erotic ("Warm Valley") to the tragic ("Blood Count"). Strayhorn's "Day Dream" was Hodges's signature tune, and there are four outstanding recordings:

1. With his own orchestra (actually an octet of Williams, Brown, Hodges, Carney, Ellington, Blanton, and Greer), on November 2, 1940

2. A live performance with the Ellington Orchestra at Carnegie Hall on January 3, 1943

3. With Ella Fitzgerald and the Ellington Orchestra on June 24, 1957 (recorded for the *Songbook* album)[27]

4. With the Ellington Orchestra on November 15 or 16, 1967, issued on *And His Mother Called Him Bill;* most of the other tracks were recorded in August 1967 after Strayhorn's death

In ballads Hodges assumed the role of a jazz diva; Charlie Parker dubbed him "Johnny Lily Pons Hodges."[28] Playing without any sign of emotion on his face, he would scour out every drop of feeling in a tune. Listeners who assume that jazz is about getting as far as possible from the original melody may be surprised by Hodges's respect for the composed line. A comparison of the 1940 and 1967 versions of "Day Dream" shows how decades of experience with the tune allowed him to play it even straighter.

I hear three components of Hodges's ballad style. First is his shaping of the phrases of the melody; second is the selective application of ornaments, which often became fixed additions to the tune; and third is the elaboration of connecting phrases, usually fast, fluttering, and spontaneous sounding. The ornaments Hodges added to a tune were fixed but never inert. He would often bend the second note of "Day Dream," turning an octave into a blue note, but he would never do it the same way twice. Most of his ballad recordings are in the format AABABA, with the second half of the tune returning in a highly ornamented variation. Usually Hodges would save his "connecting" phrases for this section so that the listener could hear them retrospectively as a counterpoint to the original. Hodges uses vibrato and rubato in very similar ways. They seem ever-present in his playing but they actually come and go with unexpected results. On the 1967 recording, for instance, he makes the opening two notes of the song sound more soulful by play-ing them *straighter* than the sheet music. Just imagine what "Lily Pons Hodges" could have done with "Nessun dorma"—even though Puc-cini's melody sounds a tad cheesy next to Strayhorn's.

"U.M.M.G.": THE ART OF THE JAZZ HEAD

If you drop by your local jazz club or tune into your local jazz station, if you're lucky enough to have one, the music you hear will most likely be improvised on the basis of the blues or some popular tune or on a distinctive subgenre of melody I'll call a jazz head. Where pop tunes were designed for the marketplace, jazz heads are esoteric. They have titles but not hooks or lyrics, unless someone adds them later. For the uninitiated the titles can seem as arcane as those for abstract paintings such as De Kooning's "Ruth's Zowie." In form they may follow the blues format, or one of the pop outlines, or the composer's whim. Their raison d'être is provocation, laying down a challenge. They may just set a rhythmic impetus in motion, or plot out a harmonic conundrum. The rest is up to the performers. You hear the head once or twice and then it disappears into the whirl of improvised solos, only to return twenty minutes later to put the cat back in the bag.

Ellington's "C Jam Blues" is the platonic model of the jazz head, as minimal as a composition can be. First recorded as "C Blues" by Barney Bigard and His Orchestra (with Strayhorn at the piano) in September 1941, and soon rearranged as a three-minute big band composition by Strayhorn, recorded by the Ellington Orchestra as "C Jam Blues" in January 1942, it morphed into a vocal called "Duke's Place" in 1958 and has lived a successful triple life (as head, arrangement, and song) ever since as one of the most played tunes in the jazz repertory.[29] It uses just two pitches, G and C, and a single simple riff played identi-cally three times, marking the three phrases of the blues. The jazz reper-tory is full of riff tunes, like "Stompin' at the Savoy," "Jumpin' at the Woodside," "In a Mellotone," and "So What," but "C Jam Blues" is so stripped down that it's a wonder it ever got copyright protection. More than a riff, though, it is an elegantly mathematical demonstration of the blues essence:

Rhythm: One bar to establish the breath, one bar to establish the beat, one bar to announce African origins with a Charleston rhythm, and one bar of silence, to leave room for a response.

Pitch: Two pitches define the tonality. Each of three statements colors the pitches with a different harmony. The G appears first as the fifth of the tonic triad, then more dissonantly as the ninth of the subdominant, then even more dissonantly as the eleventh of the supertonic.

Form: One phrase three times tells a story. That's the blues boiled down to a Zen koan.

In blues heads like "Misterioso," "Blue Monk," and "Straight, No Chaser," Thelonious Monk, Zen master of the jazz head, pushed the conceptual provocations of "C Jam Blues" even farther. The last of these could be the jazz version of Ives's *Unanswered Question*, though its first five notes seem to quote *Till Eulenspiegel*, also an apt comparison. It states this riff motive eleven times over twelve bars. The motive expands to ten notes or contracts to four, sprouting up in weedlike defiance of the bar lines, the chord changes, and even the tripartite phrase structure of the blues. As the riff bounces and bumps against the fixed matrix of the blues its pitches and rhythms are constantly reinflected, consonant here, dissonant there, on the beat or off the beat. It's a head that messes with your head.

"C Jam Blues" reduces the melodic content to a single interval, the perfect fourth. In "Misterioso" Monk similarly wrote a blues exclusively in sixths that amble up and down in nonstop, nonswinging even eighth notes. The sixths also outline a four-note rising-falling melodic motive (D–E♭–F–F♭) that appears in subtle variations. These mutant restatements gain in intensity in the last four bars until the pattern finally breaks with five ascending notes in a row ending on the flat seven. The final sixth, C and A♭ over a B♭ bass, is the only syncopation (and only enriched harmony) in a piece whose mystery resides in the way it implies a jazz feel with rhythms and a groove that should produce only a geometric squareness. In twelve bars Monk lays out a conceptual parable about the most basic aspects of the blues.

If Monk ran with Ellington's minimalist side, Billy Strayhorn took his complexities up a notch or ten. As early as "Day Dream," written in 1939 while he was living in Ellington's apartment and studying his scores,[30] Strayhorn expanded the chromatic boundaries of the newly minted "Prelude to a Kiss" with an opening phrase that outlined an augmented octave and ended with an augmented triad and a bridge that used eleven of the twelve tones. The weird intervals nevertheless sound effortlessly romantic.

Listeners to NPR know the first eight notes of Strayhorn's "Rain Check" from the "All Things Considered" theme; they are also buried inside The Beatles' "I Will." It's not easy to write a tune that sounds like common property. What you can't hear in these near quotations is the way Strayhorn planted the seeds for the whole melody with a two-chord introductory fanfare. Where Ellington composed through montagelike contrast, Strayhorn constructed pieces through similarity, generating new-sounding episodes from unexpected aspects of an opening premise. In form the melody of "Rain Check" is not the expected AABA, with its sharp contrast of two ideas, but instead ABAC, the theatrical form rarely used in jazz heads, a double statement with different outcomes. The B phrase begins as if it were just repeating the opening (making us expect an AABA), then modulates surprisingly up a major third from F to A. The structure seems at once comfortably familiar and intriguingly eccentric; it forms a harmonic loop that a soloist will want to traverse over and over.

When I hear "U.M.M.G." (1954) I get the impression that Strayhorn had been listening to Cole Porter's "All of You" (which had just debuted in *Silk Stockings*) and Brahms's Second Piano Concerto (specifically the consoling cello solo that opens the slow movement) and decided he could improve on both. The title refers to the Upper Manhattan Medical Group (run by Strayhorn's friend and Ellington's personal physician, Dr. Arthur Logan), but unlike Strayhorn's terminal medical ballad "Blood Count" (1967)—which, as Walter van de Leur writes, "conjures the devastating consequences of Strayhorn's progressing cancer"—"U.M.M.G." is an uptempo celebration of life.[31] Like "All of You," "U.M.M.G." hovers between major and minor, but at a riskier tonal altitude. Every stressed note in the melody sits "high in the chord," to use the language of bebop. The very first note, B♭, is an eleventh over an already dissonant F half-diminished seventh chord (a.k.a. the *Tristan* chord). The B♭ resolves briefly then bounces up to a C♭, heard as the minor ninth over a B♭ seventh chord. The first half of the opening phrase moves in small intervals like the Brahms theme, but its second half rockets upward in thirds from a low A♮ to a high E♭. When the phrase repeats (the song is an AABA) it shoots even higher to a G♭, so that the melody spans almost two octaves. While the bridge seems to relax the tension with a surprising move to F major in its first four bars, it ratchets up the tension with a sequence that transposes the pitches up a half step to a piercing climax on a D♭ perched dissonantly atop an E♭♭.

This melodic high-wire act seems to rely on the safety net of a pre-dictable tonal progression until we notice that the opening phrase never settles on a tonic chord. Here Strayhorn employed a Brahmsian tech-nique that Schoenberg dubbed *"schwebende Tonalität,"* or "suspended harmony." The tonal balance wavers between D♭ major and G♭ major without settling on either one until the end, when it just melts into D♭. If you played the melody slowly and began with a consonant G♭ major triad instead of that provocative *Tristan* chord, the tune would sound dolefully Brahmsian. Counterintuitively, though, Strayhorn propelled this weighty harmonic material with a suave, nonchalant Porteresque bounce. Such nonchalance is no easier to achieve on Sugar Hill than at the Waldorf.

THE ART OF·THE SUPERTUNE: IMPROVISED MELODIES

For many listeners the ne plus ultra of jazz is not Ellington's "Ko-Ko," as *ultra* as that work may be, but the unrelated Charlie Parker composi-tion "Koko," which is erected on the chord changes of "Cherokee" (a sturdy pop tune by the non-Cherokee English band leader Ray Noble.) Parker's "Koko" can serve us here as an exemplary "supermelody," a neologism I define in three ways. First a supermelody is composed on top of a preexisting melody. Second, it sounds not like a substitute melody but like melody raised to a higher power. Third, like Superman, a supermelody flies. It may be preplanned, and its components may be a set of preexisting melodic figures and phrases, but the actual assemblage happens as it is performed.

The Smithsonian Collection of Classic Jazz and most overviews of jazz history map the subject as a mountain range of daunting, dizzying peaks, the great improvised solos from Bechet to Rollins and from Arm-strong to Marsalis, with either Parker or Coltrane as Mount Everest. You can find answers to the question of how jazz performers impro-vise in many how-to textbooks and in Paul Berliner's monumental and revelatory *Thinking in Jazz*. One recurring theme in all these studies is the mixture of preparation and spontaneity. To a greater or lesser extent, jazz improvisers are not just doing what comes naturally. Most jazz players live up to the old title "professor" that once designated the resident pianist at a bordello. They know more about music theory than anyone else in the business, and they practice as systematically as the most competitive concert violinists. The cult of technique goes back to the earliest days of cutting contests between the great Harlem pianists. John Coltrane owned a copy of Nicolas Slonimsky's *Thesaurus of Scales and Melodic Patterns*,[32] and it remains a jazz bible to this day, even though it was not intended for this purpose but as an aide for avant-garde atonalists.[33] But at a certain point all that erudition and woodshedding has to be put aside.

A different way of looking at the experiential dualism of improvising would be to see it as a mixture of two cultural forms. Jazz improvisers are simultaneously playing the blues, even when the chord changes are by Richard Rodgers, and employing a technique that Renaissance and baroque musicians termed "divisions," using shorter, faster subdivisions of the beat and thereby doubling, tripling, or quadrupling the speed of the original melody. They are, as the saying goes, telling a story (that's the blues side), and at the same time they have to play the right notes. Blues playing, stemming from the call-and-response of the bluesman and his guitar, is itself dualistic; improvising, according to Lonnie Hillyer, "is really like a guy having a conversation with himself."[34] The dialogue can appear in phrasing, in contrasts in register that simulate polyphony within a single line, and also through intertextual quotations.

At the same time, though, most jazz performers conceptualize a piece in terms of its harmonic progression, the essential framework for improvisation. In the blues, and in most popular tunes, the harmony changes once or twice per bar. In many places in "Koko," Parker plays eighth notes against a single harmony from "Cherokee." This kind of melodic line resembles the nonstop arabesque of the D major prelude from Book I of Bach's *Well-Tempered Clavier,* where the right hand plays sixteenth notes and the harmony changes every two beats. Organists of Bach's time, and even today, were taught to improvise pieces like this following the principles of Renaissance polyphony (called either sixteenth-century or species counterpoint today) and the baroque basso continuo. The first approach, which emphasizes stepwise motion, might be termed horizontal, the second, which emphasizes clear definition of the harmony, is more vertical. Both concepts taught musicians how to combine consonant and dissonant notes, notes that were part of the harmony and certain notes that were not, into a fluent melodic line.[35]

In the opening bars of Parker's solo the continuous eighth notes outline a melodic curve down an octave from B♭ and then jump back up. Parker placed a dissonance on the downbeat of each bar, and in the first two bars he resolved the dissonance on the third beat, connecting dissonance and resolution by playing a "double neighbor" figure, playing the notes just above and below the resolution. Bach more likely would have put the consonances on the strongest beat, but the pattern of tension and release is the same. In the third bar, though, Parker *begins* on a dissonant note, the same B♭ now sounded against an f minor harmony, and then jumps up an octave and then ascends to an even more dissonant note, G♭. Bach might not have approved at first, but Parker was using a sanctioned technique, anticipating the next harmony, B♭7, in which the pitch B♭ is perfectly consonant by Bach standards and the G♭ sounds like an augmented fifth, legitimate by bop standards.

I'm pointing out the theoretical basis of jazz improvisation because it offers a way of analyzing not just the notes of a solo but its style and strategies, and also to demystify the lines between jazz and classical musicians. Jazz theory differs from classical theory in vocabulary but not in grammar. Classically trained musicians, especially keyboard players, can learn all they need to know about choosing notes for an improvisation from the repertory they play (from Bach and Chopin in particular) as well as from theory courses. If they can't jam it's not a problem of theory illiteracy or not being able to make music in the moment. It's a question, rather, of cultural illiteracy; they just need to spend some serious time, as jazz players do, with the blues. They need to study Sonny Rollins as closely as they study Mozart.

When classical players ask me where to begin, though, I usually suggest *Kind of Blue*. With more than five million copies sold, *Kind of Blue* is probably in your collection, and there is a published transcription of the entire album.[36] I have been listening to it (on at least seven different well-worn copies) with undiminished pleasure for fifty years. Let's concentrate on the second track, "Freddie Freeloader."

Bill Evans (the pianist on all the tracks aside from "Freddie") compared the premise of the album to "a Japanese visual art in which the artist is forced to be spontaneous."[37] Davis and Evans seem to have shaped the "Japanese" sensibility of the album together in advance and without much warning to the others. Conditions, therefore, mixed the familiar and the unexpected. None of the solos paraphrases a familiar melody. They are all supermelodies.

A twelve-bar blues in B♭, "Freddie" was the first track to be recorded for the album and also its most conventional tune, yet it provoked five extraordinary solos by (in order) Wynton Kelly, piano; Miles Davis, trumpet; John Coltrane, tenor saxophone; Cannonball Adderley, alto saxophone; and Paul Chambers, bass. (Drummer Jimmy Cobb did not solo.) The head is a call-and-response blues, a kind of updated

"Stompin' at the Savoy," with trumpet and saxes playing a simple two-note motive, a descending whole step, and the piano responding more casually. The chord changes are simple, avoiding boppish interpolations of enriched harmonies. The only surprise comes in the last two bars, where an A♭7 takes the place of the expected B♭ or turnaround harmonies. The progression is:

B♭7 (four bars);

E♭7 (two bars), B♭7 (two bars);

F7 (one bar), E♭7 (one bar); A♭7 (two bars).

The head divides these twelve bars into two unequal sections. In the first eight bars the melodic instruments play the two-note theme in parallel first inversion triads, G minor and F minor over the B♭7 harmony; C minor and B♭ minor over the E♭7 harmony. In the last four bars the melody moves in half steps rather than whole steps, and instead of playing mellow triads the trio plays the bare, acidic harmony of a tritone. The head thus divides asymmetrically between passivity and agitation. Despite its laid-back quality, the opening two-note—or, really, two-chord—theme puts the modal side of *Kind of Blue* right on the table by interpreting a B♭7 harmony as a six-note scale: F–G–A♭–B♭–C–D (F Dorian without the seventh). Moreover, the two triads of the theme are deceptively consonant sounding. Heard in terms of the B♭7 harmony, each triad contains a dissonant note: the G of the first chord is the thirteenth; the C of the second is the ninth. Each soloist responds to the theme with a precise consideration of its special qualities yet in a distinctive voice:

Wynton Kelly (four choruses). Kelly's solo emphasizes the blues roots of the head. Its opening bars announce the gospel-tinged style of "hard bop funky regression"; it could be played on a Hammond B3, and, gospel-style, it builds to a climactic shout chorus that emphasizes the defining notes of the blues scale, flat third, flat fifth, and flat seventh. Kelly, however, constantly keeps the melodic identity of the head in the foreground even as he leads it into his own stylistic territory. He ornaments the two-note G-F motive with neighbor tones and passing tones and dramatizes the half-step motive of the closing four bars through rhythmic displacement. Kelly also subtly honors the modal concept of the piece. When he first comes to the A♭7 chord he plays a B♭ arpeggio over it, turning the tonic triad into a Lydian mode upper extension. In his second chorus he uses a similar Lydian harmony over the E♭7 chord and follows up this modernistic touch with an aptly Parkeresque flourish. Kelly's trump card, however, is what classical musicians call a "rocket" figure, a rising arpeggio, first heard here as an upbeat to the last phrase of the first chorus. It recurs in varied form four times more, pushing the spirit of the solo ever higher toward its climactic shout.

Miles Davis (six choruses). With Davis's entrance the style suddenly swerves from Ray Charles to Erik Satie. He plays short *Gymnopédie*-esque phrases, moving in small intervals that are punctuated with spacious rests. This would simply sound tentative if the pitches were not so carefully chosen to invoke the head. Davis emphasizes the two dissonant pitches of the opening chordal motive, G and C, stretching out the melodic resolution of the G to F over eight bars. Where Kelly brought out the chromatic tension of the last four bars, Davis seems at first to bury it in a chantlike oscillation that ends in a bop-harmony rocket, the first sign of tension beneath the calm surface. Gradually Davis turns Kelly's strategy inside out so that by his last chorus, with its apogee on a high D♭, he is just as down home as his pianist.

John Coltrane (six choruses). Shifting the emotional balance from passive to active, Coltrane launches his solo with three upward flourishes, each time cresting on the high C, the dissonant element in the second chord of the head motive. This gesture announces a tone of ecstatic celebration magnified through all six choruses. The majority of Coltrane's phrases are two-bar arabesques describing a convex melodic curve or its concave inversion. These long phrases are the temporal equivalent of Coltrane's huge sound; both make his solo the center of gravity of the whole track. Coltrane sets off most of his melodic flights with a rest, springing off the downbeat as if it were a diving board. This mannerism serves to shape the whole solo when its final chorus begins assertively right on the beat. His repeated high B♭s here resolve the high Cs that opened the solo.

Julian "Cannonball" Adderley (five choruses). Where Coltrane's solo was monumental, Adderley's is sly and sinuous. Unpredictable in the length and character of his phrases, Adderley pulls the music back toward classic free-associational bebop with fluent Parker licks and intertextual stylistic allusions.[38] Adderley underscores the sense of unrestricted freedom by eliding most of his phrases over the bar lines, anticipating chord changes or building a melodic curve around them rather than rebounding off a new harmony. He saves his most virtuosic passagework for the furious close, which nevertheless highlights the pitches E♭, D♭, and D, which imparted a tritonic sting to the cadence of the head.

Paul Chambers (two choruses). Less a solo than a necessary transition back to the mood of the head after such a far-flung journey, Chambers's two choruses reinstate two structural pillars, the simple blues progression and the call-and-response phrase format, through a simple dialogue of walking bass quarter notes and ornamental guitarlike triplet eighths.

Each of these supermelodies shapes thematic, stylistic, expressive, tonal, and rhythmic ideas. Why not just call them melodies? I think they are best thought of as melodies raised to a higher power. They all refer in some way to the original head, so that they are reflective rather than merely assertive, lunar rather than solar. Because they build on an existing structure, though, they are also much less repetitive; the head established its identity by stating the two-note motive five times; none of the solos repeats a single phrase.

Borrowing the terminology of Roland Barthes, we might say that a tune is "readerly" while a supermelody is "writerly." A tune presents a powerfully compelling statement, while a supermelody mirrors our own strategies for grasping and interpreting that statement. Supermelodies enact listening as spontaneous composition; ruminating in ever-widening circles, they are interpretations caught in the act of becoming texts.

OUTRO: A FEW SIMPLE SONGS

We might divide successful twentieth-century classical melodies between simple songs (like "a Simple Song" from Leonard Bernstein's *Mass*) and cosmic melodies, not excluding the possibility that the simple can also be cosmic and vice versa. (Ellington proves both points with his simple song "Come Sunday" and his cosmic melody "Heaven.") The simplifying side of twentieth-century classical music fell into obscurity in the midcentury narrative of ever-increasing complexity. In the past twenty years, though, performers and scholars have shown more respect for the melodic gifts of composers like Prokofiev and Barber and have also paid more attention to the ideology-based simplifications of Hanns Eisler and his American disciples Aaron Copland and Mark Blitzstein, but there is still a tendency to frame any melodic simplicity as retrogressive or commercial. Two of the most powerful musical responses to the Second

World War demonstrate the expressive power of a good, simple tune: Kurt Weill's "Und was bekam des Soldaten Weib?" (words by Brecht) and Francis Poulenc's "C" (words by Louis Aragon). The songs are in the cabaret styles, of, respectively, pre-Hitler Berlin and wartime Paris. The Weill song harkens back to "Surabaya Johnny" and even further back to Schumann's "Die beiden Grenadiere," while stylistically Poulenc's is just a few steps away from "Autumn Leaves" (or "Les feuilles mortes," music by Joseph Kosma, words by Jacques Prévert, first recorded in 1945).

The Brecht/Weill song, a catalogue of the booty a German soldier has sent his wife from the plundered capitals of Prague, Oslo, Amsterdam, Brussels, Paris, and Bucharest, is strophic, with a repeated three-phrase AAB section in b minor followed by a concluding restatement of A in the major that reports her final gift, a widow's veil sent from the Russian front. The tune follows the Tin Pan Alley principles of melodic writing in terms of range, repetition, and catchiness, but its phrases extend beyond the expected eight bars to a discomfortingly odd eleven, with a subtle alienation effect. The A phrases contain a rising question phrase, harmonized with just two chords, b minor and a bluesy G7, followed by a falling answer where the accented notes of the melody form clichéd appoggiatura dissonances against sentimental secondary dominant harmonies the soldier's wife might have heard on the radio. The final stanza forecasts a Russian victory (the song was probably written in 1943) and celebrates the soldier's death with an ironic turn to major. The grimly reassuring harmony suggests that the widow arrived at the soldier's funeral decked out in all her ill-gotten gifts.

"C" describes the flight of Frenchmen southward, out of the path of Nazi occupation, through a series of images of an imagined past (the castle of a mad duke) and the newsreel present (overturned cars and defused weapons), held together by the French sound "C" *(say)*. Like the Weill, it exploits a contrast between minor and major and the power of a refrain. The most memorably café-style phrase, drifting from D♭ major to C♭ major, appears twice, first with the idealized imagery of an eternal fiancée dancing in a meadow, and then with a picture of impotent weaponry and tears that cannot be rubbed away. Poulenc sets the eight-syllable lines with great finesse so that the final syllables, all of them pronounced "C," toll like bells heard in the distance.

Both the Weill and Poulenc songs subtly camouflage their artistry and their seriousness. They could easily be programmed along with other hits of the war years such as Frank Loesser's "Spring Will Be a

Little Late This Year" or Ellington's "I'm Beginning to See the Light."
Or they could share the stage with heavier music of the time, like the
"Lamentation" from Bernstein's *Jeremiah Symphony* or Britten's settings of the Holy Sonnets by John Donne. If you played Poulenc's song
very, very slowly it would begin to sound like a contemporaneous simple melody that responded to the same events in a less vernacular manner, the final movement from Olivier Messiaen's *Quartet for the End of
Time*, "Louange à l'Immortalité de Jésus." Both composers employed
a chordal vocabulary not far from what you can find in Ellington or
Cole Porter. But the tempo makes all the difference. In performance
Messiaen's thirty-three four-beat bars last just over seven minutes. At
that pace (each beat lasting five seconds), the conventional sequential
and symmetrical structure of the melody melts into the sublime and
an added E major sixth chord, usually associated with elevator music,
sounds like the voice of God.

CHAPTER 4

"Satin Doll": Harmony

I had a kind of harmony inside me, which is part of my race, but I needed harmony that has no race at all but is universal.
—Duke Ellington

The kaleidoscope blending and interchanging of twelve semitones within the three-mirror tube of Taste, Emotion and Intention—the essential feature of the harmony of to-day.

The harmony of to-day, and not for long, for all signs presage a revolution, and a next step toward that "eternal harmony." Let us again call to mind, that in this latter the gradation of the octave is infinite, and let us strive to draw nearer to infinitude.

—Ferruccio Busoni

We thus no longer find ourselves in the framework of classic tonality in the scholastic sense of the word. It is not we who have created this state of affairs, and it is not our fault if we find ourselves confronted with a new logic of music that would have appeared unthinkable to the masters of the past. And this new logic has opened our eyes to riches whose existence we never suspected.

—Igor Stravinsky

INTRO: HOW JAZZ TAUGHT ME HARMONY (AND EVEN MADE ME LOVE IT): A SHORT CONFESSIONAL

Harmony is the most academically discussed and least generally understood element in twentieth-century music and, so far, twenty-first-century music as well. Despite the persistent myth of harmonic progress, the infinite expansion of harmonic resources forecast by Busoni and others somewhere along the line turned into a contracting black hole. Today most composers, from neotonalists to microtonalists, work in the harmonic dark, and music theorists, still hooked on Brahms, offer little in the way of ideas to elucidate most of the music from Debussy to Radiohead. The dark, I have found, is sometimes the best place to be, but I only began to see the light through a belated discovery of jazz harmony.

In 1965 the Pulitzer Prize board, headed by the president of Columbia University, overturned the recommendation of the music jury and refused to honor Ellington with the prize. In 1967, however, Columbia honored me with a Kellett Fellowship for two years of study at Cambridge, and in 1973 Columbia belatedly granted Ellington an honorary doctorate. At Clare College, as at Columbia, I studied English literature while surrounding myself with musically stimulating friends, in particular the composers Roger Smalley and Tim Souster, who introduced me to the music of Messiaen and Stockhausen. England had suddenly become the hot spot of new music; Boulez was conducting the BBC Symphony Orchestra and the Beatles even put Stockhausen's face on the cover of *Sgt. Pepper*. In London I heard Boulez conduct *Pelléas* and *Wozzeck* and Stockhausen's *Gruppen* and also attended the London premiere of Elliott Carter's Piano Concerto. I spent any spare money on buying contemporary scores, which were much cheaper in England than back home. Though I didn't pay much attention to the rising star on the British rock scene, Jimi Hendrix, I did go to see Cecil Taylor play a kind of jazz that emptied the hall in about ten minutes. I loved that power to offend; I was in my hard-core avant-garde phase. In the spring of 1970 Tim, Roger, Peter Britton, and I even gave the Cambridge premiere of Terry Riley's *Keyboard Studies*.

Halfway through my first year I decided to switch to the study of music, even though the department was far more traditional than the one at Columbia. The Cambridge music curriculum was amorphous by American standards. There were no required courses or activities, no classes in musicianship or solfège. You were expected to spend the year preparing, with the help of a faculty supervisor, for six three-hour exams, called the Tripos. In music these exams consisted entirely of a single kind of exercise. They gave you the beginnings of pieces ranging from the fourteenth century (Machaut) to the twentieth (Poulenc), and you were asked to complete them—at your examination desk. (The composer Nicolas Flagello later told me that when students at the more humane setting of Rome's Accademia Nazionale di Santa Cecilia took a similar examination they would be locked in a studio with a piano and provided with as much spaghetti as needed to get through.) Previous exams were made available so I knew what to expect, but no one could explain how I might prepare myself for this daunting task. As good English empiricists the music dons at Cambridge viewed music theory as a suspiciously Germanic form of speculation. They seemed to believe that you could pass the exam on the basis of listening and intuition alone.

Before I could get too panicky, though, fate intervened in the form of the Vietnam War. In the spring of 1968 the draft laws changed; graduate study no longer deferred me from service. I soon learned, though, that New York City was setting up a crash program to train teachers, who were still qualified for deferral. I sailed home to learn, in eight weeks, how to teach at a junior high school.

My year at J.H.S. 118 in the south Bronx, which was also the year of a protracted New York teachers' strike, Woodstock, and the moon landing, was, needless to say, interesting, but once I drew a high number in the draft lottery my thoughts anxiously returned to the Tripos. My brother Andy recommended that I call his jazz piano teacher, Irwin Stahl, for advice. I brought Irwin a copy of an old exam. He asked if anyone at Cambridge had taught a way of analyzing the music in order to complete the incipits —but, of course, they had not. In that case Irwin suggested that I study harmony and counterpoint with him. In just a few months he taught me everything I have ever needed to know about both subjects. His understanding of harmony was stunningly lucid. "There are just three chords," he told me. "Everything else is a just a substitution." Irwin, who wrote the liner notes for the great *Art Tatum Solo Masterpieces* collection, showed me how to think about harmony from a jazz perspective, even though we were not studying jazz.

I later learned that his approach to harmony was nearly identical to that of Schoenberg's textbooks. Irwin had me compose progressions, not pastiche imitations of Bach chorales or Mozart minuets, just different combinations of those three chords: the subdominant, the dominant, and the tonic, or, in jazz terms, ii, V, and I. Once I understood the relationship between these chords I could expand their potential. Changing the note in the bass by "inverting" a chord allowed the music to flow more smoothly. Replacing a chord with its relative minor or major made the harmony sound richer. Preceding any chord with its dominant increased the sense of urgency. Adding a fourth pitch to triads, making them into seventh chords, turned a Bach-like progression into jazz. Preceding the dominant with the subdominant (ii) made any chord progression sound like bebop. Using only four-pitch chords that did not contain the fifth turned cocktail piano into Bill Evans. The only problem with harmony, I discovered, was the way it was usually taught. But what could I do with this knowledge other than hope that it would get me through the Tripos? Though I never pictured myself as a real jazz pianist I got a fake book. I learned to play "Satin Doll" in different jazz styles, at different tempos, and with different voicings. Schoenberg once said that there was still a lot of music to be written in C major. I used to think that was a joke but now I took it as prophecy.

"SATIN DOLL" OR JAZZ PIANO 101

[Parental warning: from here on things get a little technical.]

Jazz harmony is largely the domain of pianists, and its concepts today still derive from the 1930s keyboard styles of Teddy Wilson and Art Tatum. Viewed broadly, it differs from classical tonality only in requiring that all chords contain at least four different pitches. In other words, it is based on seventh chords rather than triads. Like classical harmony, jazz harmony recognizes three different chord functions: tonic, dominant, and subdominant. In classical theory these would all be the major triads (in a major key) I, V, and IV, or, in the key of C, C major, G major, and F major. The dominant creates harmonic tension that needs to be resolved by the tonic. It is therefore usually played as a four-pitch dominant seventh chord, or V7. By contrast the subdominant sounds more relaxed than the tonic, and it also has a certain antique and sacred quality associated with what musicians call a "plagal cadence," usually heard in church when the congregation sings "Amen."

In jazz harmony the three functions appear as three different kinds of seventh chords, a major seventh for the tonic, a dominant seventh for the dominant, and a minor seventh for the subdominant. The subdominant function in jazz is heard with the chord on the second degree of the scale, ii7, rather than the closely related IV in classical practice. Jazz pianists, however, rarely use these chords in their simple forms. They usually add the sixth and ninth to the tonic chord, the eleventh to the subdominant, and a variety of altered tones—flat ninths, augmented ninths, sharp elevenths, and thirteenths—to the dominant. You never hear a plain vanilla V7 chord in jazz (though it sounds fine in boogie-woogie or rock).

"Satin Doll," Ellington's closing theme song from its appearance in 1953, can serve as a jazz harmony paradigm; in its deceptive simplicity,

"Satin Doll" is, as the saying goes, as good as good bread. If you look at a lead sheet for "Satin Doll" (credited to Ellington and Strayhorn, with lyrics added later by Johnny Mercer), you will see that every chord name written above the melody except one has a "7" attached to it. The exception is the tonic chord C, but no jazz pianist would play this as a simple triad. The chords alternate between minor seventh chords and dominant sevenths, a series of ii–V progressions. (To evoke the sound of a ii–V progression just hum the opening bars of "Tea for Two.") The harmonies begin close to the tonic key with d minor 7 and G7, which would usually resolve on C. The tune postpones that resolution with a series of moves that seem to take the harmony increasingly far from the tonic home base. Before resolving, the harmony moves to three dominant chords that don't occur within the seven pitches of the C major scale, A7, D7, and D♭7, each preceded by a subdominant. To a classical theorist several things might look odd. Most of the dominant sevenths don't resolve to a tonic, and the final cadence reaches C major by way of a D♭7 rather than the expected G7.

Jazz theory unlocks the mystery of this progression through the concept of substitution. The paired ii–V chords are taking the place of their implied resolution, so that we might say that the d minor 7 to G7 progression is filling in for the tonic C major chord. Likewise, e minor 7–A7 implies the subdominant (d minor 7), and a minor 7–D7 implies the dominant G7. In the fifth bar of the tune there is a subtle substitute for the a minor 7, a "borrowed" chord (either c minor 7 or a half-diminished 7) from the g minor scale, a device for harmonic darkening common in Brahms. The last two chords, the exotic-sounding A♭ minor 7 and D♭7, are what jazz theory terms "tritone substitutes," taking the place of chords an augmented fourth away, d minor 7 and G7. The idea of the tritone substitution comes from a common jazz practice of flatting the fifth in a dominant seventh chord, for instance, playing G, B, D♭, and F as a G7. These four pitches, however, are the very same ones you would play for a D♭7 chord with a flat fifth: D♭, F, G, and B. Two chords that seem far apart turn out to be interchangeable. Once we understand how chords substitute for others we can see that the harmonic outline of "Satin Doll" is really a Bach-like I–ii–V–I.

You wouldn't need to know any of this if jazz performance were simply a question of playing the sheet music as written. Jazz theory books label playing the tune in a way that even resembles the sheet music as "cocktail piano," a tentative first step toward actual jazz performance. The way a jazz pianist interprets the song, however, depends on whether it is a solo performance or, as is more usual, the pianist is accompanied by bass and drums. In either case the pianist is expected to recast the music while preserving its basic structure, introducing further substitutions and different arrangements of the notes in the chord, or what jazz musicians refer to as "voicing." Chord voicings receive considerable attention in jazz piano textbooks because they will give an interpretation a personal sound, and also because of the relation of the piano to the bass. In order to keep out of the bassist's way, the pianist's left hand usually stays around middle C and avoids playing the root note of the harmony. When a jazz chart asks for a G7 chord the pianist's left hand therefore may play the pitches F, A, B, and E, but not the G. This takes both physical and mental practice.

"GOODBYE PORK PIE HAT": HARMONY IN BLUE

While jazz musicians absorbed the "universal" harmony of European tonality they also inflected and enriched that idiom by applying it to the blues. Based on scales and tunings not found in European music, the blues, sung with guitar accompaniment in its rural folk style, presented a particular challenge for the pianist who could not bend pitches, an essential aspect of blues performance. Pianists had to find ways to square the blues style with the well-tempered tuning of the piano and also with the habitual harmonic patterns and voice leading of classical keyboard harmony. The blue note, especially the blue third, was part of a tonal idiom that the piano could not reproduce but could only simulate by using harmonies from the major or minor modes.

The clash of blues melody and piano harmony proved to be highly productive. Boogie-woogie piano styles emulated the blues guitar by using chords that were as much rhythm as harmony. This direction led to rhythm and blues and rock. The jazz piano tradition that came out of ragtime, Jelly Roll Morton and the Harlem stride pianists, James P. Johnson, Willy "The Lion" Smith, and Luckey Roberts was more engaged with what were known as "modernistic harmonies": ninth chords, parallel motion, chromaticism. Stride piano, the stylistic foundation for both Ellington and Basie, reached its most sophisticated form in the virtuosic extravaganzas of Art Tatum. In the late 1920s Earl Hines perfected an alternative, more melodic approach, often called a trumpet style, to jazz piano playing; in the 1930s Teddy Wilson extended Hines's style. Billy Strayhorn synthesized his distinctive harmonic style from Tatum and Wilson. Since the 1940s jazz piano has developed dialectically between styles that extended harmonic modernism (Lennie Tristano, John Lewis, Bill Evans) and those that pulled back to the blues (Horace Silver, Wynton Kelly); both tendencies, however, are usually present in jazz harmony.

The persistent interplay between modernism and blues suggests that they were perhaps more related than opposed. There is much evidence to suggest that certain practices of European modern harmony, including added notes, polymodality, and polytonality, began as responses to jazz (or its predecessor, ragtime) rather than the other way around. This may be less a question of precedence than of parallel development. Like Bartók and Stravinsky, rag and jazz pianists were inventing an urbane harmonic style out of pretonal rural melodic material. The relation of rural and urban styles in both jazz and classical music is less a matter of replication than representation. Works like Stravinsky's *Pribaoutki* (1918) and Bartók's *Improvisations on Hungarian Peasant Songs* (1920) translated the nonclassical aspects of peasant music into jarring dissonances: double-inflection chords combining major and minor thirds, bitonality, and tone clusters. All these devices appeared as well when Stravinsky first imitated jazz in his *Ragtime* (1918) and *Piano Rag* (1919), harmonically gritty scores miles away from Joplin. Dissonance served as an emblem of the "primitive"; discords ironically represented the triads and seventh chords of Stravinsky's models. Jazz composers, by contrast, represented urban experience, the new African American milieu created by the Great Migration out of the South, with sophisticated-sounding harmonies that signaled modernity. Ellington built early works like "Black and Tan Fantasy," "East St. Louis Toodle-Oo" and "The Mooche" out of this contrast. In both European music and jazz the modern appeared as an atavism of the primitive. "The Mooche" was simultaneously modernistic music and jungle music. The European modernists were trying to bypass bourgeois values. Ellington was subverting the South.

The harmonic changes of the blues served to indicate its AAB poetic phrase structure by marking the caesura within a line and the end of a line:

I hate to see   de evening sun go down

Harmonic change also aided rereading of the first line when it was repeated:

Hate to see   de evening sun go down

and the completion of the thought:

Cause my baby   he done lef dis town.

In the 1914 sheet music W.C. Handy harmonized this phrase (in G major) using only chords built on I, IV, and V:

G7 C7 G7 /
C6 C7 G /
D7 / G /

This harmonization simulated the blues third in several different ways. Handy used a grace note A♯ to color the B♮ in the G major or seventh chords. The blue third appears as a B♭ in the C7 chord, but also in the D7 chord where it sounds like an augmented fifth. If you listen to Bessie Smith you will hear that she also treated the added A in the C6 chord as a blue note. In a sense the pitches that Handy notated as B, A♯, and B♭ were stand-ins for a blue third that the piano cannot play. The frequent harmonic reinterpretation of those pitches gave them something of a blue quality.

Ellington employed an even simpler harmony in the opening of "Black and Tan Fantasy" (credited to Ellington and Bubber Miley). The first strain of the piece is a minor blues, and until its third four-bar phrase it only uses triadic harmony (in B♭ minor): b♭ minor (i) and e♭ minor (iv). A seventh chord only appears with the V7, which is decorated with the one moment of fancy harmony, a G♭7 neighbor chord. The sparseness of the harmony reflects the melody, which is not a blues and does not contain blue notes but is a church hymn, "The Holy City."[1] The piece combines two "down-home" sounds by superimposing a sacred melody on a secular phrase pattern. In the next phrase, however, it jumps to a different world, entering B♭ major by way of a G♭ ninth chord. The richer harmony hinted at in passing now blossoms. This contrasting phrase presents a series of modernistic markers: a minor seventh chord, a dominant seventh with augmented fifth, a cross rhythm of $\frac{3}{8}$ against the $\frac{4}{4}$, and an eight-chord circle of fifths progression packed into two bars with the right hand moving in parallel tritones. The piece reconfigures its stylistic opposition in its two most famous phrases: Bubber Miley's plunger-muted blues chorus, primitivism made modern through interjections of augmented-fifth seventh chords, and the closing quotation of Chopin's Funeral March. The music juggles "dicty" and down-home, North and South.

A challenge for many jazz musicians in the 1920s was to reinterpret the blues through modernism rather than in opposition to it. A strikingly modernized blues appears in "Sloppy Joe," a rarely discussed but fascinating Ellington work from 1929 (co-credited to Barney Bigard). This piece sounds like a response (either as homage or parody) to the famous recording of "West End Blues" with Louis Armstrong and Earl Hines that had appeared the year before. It follows a similar format of solos, including a chorus of scat singing by Sonny Greer. But the highlight is Ellington's piano solo; it illustrates what Hines had to teach him. Ellington alternated bars in stride piano style with modernistic measures using five-note harmonies in parallel motion with the right hand voiced in fourths. These modern-sounding chords slide into the blues harmony from a third above or below. In the second phrase, Ellington used the logic of the harmonic sequence to repeat a bar on the expected IV chord down a step to a ninth chord on the flat third, outside the key but bluer than blue. In two final Hines-isms he implied a double-time feel for a trumpet-style piano arabesque and, for his final cadence, jumped (rather than slid) between two modern-voiced chords with the right hand stacking fourths and the left hand in an open seventh. Ellington could have played this solo twenty years later without it sounding in any way dated.

The blues progression found in "The St. Louis Blues" has survived for almost a century. It could be elaborated with ever more complicated chords, as in Art Tatum's versions of "Aunt Hagar's Blues";[2] or it could be fitted out with many substitute chords, as in Charlie Parker's "Blues for Alice," where the harmony changes twice per bar; or it could be further simplified, as in Miles Davis's "All Blues." As an example of a later blues, at once rooted in tradition and exploratory, let's examine "Goodbye Pork Pie Hat," Charles Mingus's elegy for Lester Young first recorded in 1959.

When you first look at the lead sheet, the chord structure looks bewildering.[3] Traveling far from the three-chord blues, Mingus used nine different chords. The names of the chords and the notation of the melody also seem bizarre. The first chord is an E♭7 with an augmented ninth, the second a B dominant thirteenth, which would not appear to be in the key of E♭. Actually, though, it is a chord also heard in "Black and Tan Fantasy," the lowered VI chord, borrowed from E♭ minor, but when "Goodbye" continues with chords of E and A we start to run out of enharmonic fixes, and we have to begin invoking the idea of the tritone substitution. Mingus further confused things through the phrase structure, which sounds like 4 + 3 + 5 rather than the expected three phrases of four bars. All this fancy harmony, though, served a purpose very similar to the harmonic changes in "St. Louis Blues." They constantly reinflect the blue third, the pitch G♭, which appears in every bar. I'll tabulate the ways the pitch appears in each chord:

E♭7	augmented ninth
B9	fifth
E major 9	third
D♭9 sus	fourth (sus)
A♭ minor 7	seventh
F minor 7 flat 5	minor ninth
B♭7 sharp 5	sharp fifth
C13	sharp eleventh
A7	thirteenth

If you sing the pitch G♭ against each of the chords you will naturally find yourself adjusting the intonation in response to the varying degrees of tension between the root of the chord and the position of the G♭, and you will hear how Mingus's melody is a sustained keening wail on E♭ and G♭.

HOMMAGE À RAVEL

Play "Satin Doll" as a slow waltz and it will suddenly sound like a *valse sentimentale* of Ravel. Though his name rarely appears in jazz theory books, you can hear the influence of Ravel clearly in the music of Billy Strayhorn ("Chelsea Bridge") and Bill Evans ("Waltz for Debby"). Ravel prophetically employed a jazzlike harmony based on seventh chords in some of his earliest works, like the song "Sainte" and the "Pavane pour une infante défunte." By 1903, with the orchestral song cycle *Shéhérezade,* Ravel had mapped out all the harmonies that Burt Bacharach and Stephen Sondheim would use seventy years later; Sondheim's 1986 musical *Into the Woods* sounds Ravelian from beginning to end. I even hear Ravel (via Miles Davis and Gil Evans) in Steve Reich's *Music for 18 Musicians.* You would have to go back to Corelli to find a harmonic style with a comparable impact.

Ravel reached his full harmonic maturity in *Valses nobles et sentimentales,* published in 1911. A century after that scandal these eight waltzes remain a living thesaurus of harmonic devices that stay just within the boundaries of functional harmony and yet employ a wide variety of dissonances. You can hear Ravel's relevance for jazz most clearly in the fifth waltz of the set, written in an exquisitely spiced E major. The eight-bar phrase beginning at measure 17 sounds like the bridge of a popular song, and with good reason. The harmonic progression is a ii–V–I in F♯ major that is then repeated, transposed up a step, in A♭. This is exactly the same progression found in the bridge of "Satin Doll" and many other jazz standards.

Ravel's way of creating dissonances appears in a nutshell in bars 17 and 18. The music is written in a three-voice texture. If you just play the outer voices you'll see that they are not particularly dissonant in relation to each other. In the first bar only two of the six melody notes are dissonant, and both fall on unaccented parts of the beat. In bar 18 Ravel repeats the melody exactly but changes the bass to imply a harmony a perfect fifth lower. This device (often used by Debussy as well) turns consonant notes into dissonances, placing the dissonances on accented beats. Adding the inner voice you will see that it creates dissonances at nearly every point where the upper voice was consonant. This means that there is some kind of dissonance present on eleven out of the twelve eighth notes of these two bars. Yet the only egregiously illegitimate-sounding dissonance in both bars falls on the last eighth note where the right hand has a C♯♯ and E♯ against a D♯ in bar 17 and a C♯ in 18. In general Ravel is as scrupulous in resolving dissonances as were Bach and Chopin, though at times he was far more devious than his predecessors.

A different technique equally pertinent to jazz appears in the first eight bars. The melody decorates the pitch G♯ while the bass moves downward. The G♯ sounds dissonant against the A in the bass, more dissonant when the bass move down to F♯, and more dissonant still when the bass moves down to a D♮. The bass seems to outline a D major triad that fits with the C and D in the inner voices but clashes with the G♯ and E♯ in the melody. At the end of the third bar, though, everything changes. The C and D slide up a half step, the bass moves down to B, and the harmony suddenly comes into focus as the dominant of E major. The deceptively dissonant G♯ turns out to have been the consonant element in a series of what theorists term appoggiatura harmonies, illusional chords created out of nonharmonic tones, dissonances substituting for consonances. In the next four bars the melody repeats but the harmony changes, again in a jazzlike way. For the second bar, which could have been harmonized with the dominant B7, Ravel used instead an altered E♯ dominant chord, in other words, the tritone substitute. No wonder jazz pianists pay attention.

Ravel's music converses with jazz because he thought like a jazz musician, from the bass up. We know this from the evidence of his sketches and also a few short examples of self-analysis.[4] Though his harmonies shocked his contemporaries, Ravel arrived at them through a method he had learned at the conservatory. He habitually used the baroque shorthand of the figured bass, sketching the structural outer lines before adding inner voices. In other words, he started with a lead sheet. His music nevertheless sounds unbaroque because he often used types of parallel motion banned in older harmony but common in Debussy's music and because he did not always resolve a dissonance in an obvious way if he felt that it already implied its resolution. A dissonance could, in effect, substitute for a consonance.

Here are some highlights of harmonic devices in the waltzes:

I (G major). The opening measure flings harmonic provocations at the audience: a chord of six pitches (all the white keys except E) followed by an even more dissonant chord of five pitches, the apparently nonsensical piling of a d♯ minor 7 over a D♮. The next bar resolves these chords slightly with a consonant five-tone chord, which is followed, however, by the sharpest sound yet, an apparently unidentifiable combination of the pitches A♯, C♯, D♯, and E. When you live with the progression for a little while, however, its shock value recedes to reveal a linear logic. The dissonant notes of each chord, once you figure out which they are, resolve by step, just as they would in Bach harmony, but the steps have been displaced up an octave so that, for instance, the C♮, which seems out of place in the first chord, moves up a half step plus an octave to C♯ in the second chord and then comes to rest on D, back down a major seventh, at the beginning of bar 2. The opening phrase reaches its peak in three statements of a modern dominant, a stack of thirds from the root to the thirteenth, omitting only the third of the chord; jazz musician call this a "sus" chord. The harmony for the rest of this waltz mixes these newly spiced consonances with even more challenging combinations of notes that at first sound discordant. The most notorious progression occurs in the eight-bar passage leading back to the recapitulation. Here the bass line goes clear around the circle of fifths (and through all twelve tones of the chromatic scale). The bass powers high-voltage chords of clashing major and minor thirds, or major and minor sevenths. You can find just about every chord needed for jazz piano in this one phrase.

II (G minor). This slow waltz begins with a forecast of Billy Strayhorn's "Chelsea Bridge" and then goes into a *gymnopédie*-style homage to Erik Satie by using the Dorian mode instead of the usual minor. Although the main phrase sounds consonant compared to the din of the first waltz, it too predicts jazz practice by using a g minor 7 as the tonic and a d minor 11 as a combined tonic/subdominant. A closing phrase seems to wrap the Satie tribute in a warm embrace and pulls the waltz into the major mode. After a brief midsection (all the waltzes are in ternary ABA form), Ravel recasts the *gymnopédie* by immobilizing the bass line and compressing the major third (C–E) of the second harmony so that it sounds like a major second (C♯–E♭). With this whole-tone harmony Debussy joins the party.

III (e minor–G major). The sound of the major second, introduced in the last third of the previous waltz, now defines the sonority of a whole movement. In his *Jazz Harmony at the Piano*, John Mehegan refers to Ravel-inspired voicings based on seconds rather than sevenths, and this waltz is one possible source. Its piquant quality is further enhanced by the use of Aeolian mode or natural minor, which gives a slightly bitonal feeling to the opening sixteen bars; the right hand sounds like it is in G major, but the left hand sits on the pitch E.

IV (A♭, vaguely). This waltz teeters on the edge of atonality by contrasting nonfunctional harmonic progression based on thirds with more traditional moves based on fifths. Its cadences in A♭, C, and E feel like arbitrary resting points, each one a plausible tonic. It begins with what a jazz pianist might term a dominant thirteen with both a flat and augmented ninth, in other words, a blues dominant with both major and minor thirds.

V (E major). Already discussed, but note how Ravel here picks up the sliding triads from the closing phrase of Waltz II. These neighbor progressions set up a network of thematic connections but also anticipate the polytonality of Waltz VII.

VI (C major). We might call this "kitten on the keys," if that title were not already in use. The wrong-note half-step melodic figure, played by the thumb, sounds accidental until we realize that it develops the sliding triad theme of the previous waltz. Again we hear second harmonies, but here Ravel develops a contrast of melodic minor seconds and harmonic major seconds into a blur that disguises a simple V–I progression in C major.

VII (A major). This is the most elaborate of the waltzes and the one that Ravel cited as most characteristic; he later incorporated parts of it into *La Valse,* the waltz to end all waltzes. The main tune appears as a thickened melody of three-note chords that eventually swells to become a melody of seventh chords. The ultimate harmonic shock comes in the middle section, which seems to superimpose a melody in E major on a bass in F. Ravel analyzed this passage as an example of "unresolved appoggiaturas," which he illustrated, tellingly, using a figured bass and compared to the opening chord in Beethoven's Piano Sonata op. 31, no. 3.[5] He may have been joking. Because the melody in the right hand sounds tonally close to the A major of the outer section, it feels consonant while the bass seems "wrong," a half step too high. Not surprisingly, the surreal, dreamlike effect of this superimposition proved useful in Hollywood, but it also appears in several Richard Rodgers standards such as "Spring Is Here" and "The Sound of Music."

VIII "Épilogue" (G major). A new melody, voiced in parallel triads, drifts slowly over a nearly static bass line that, halfway through, comes to rest on a low G. Between reorchestrated and reharmonized recurrences of the melody, reminiscences of all the waltzes flash by against a tolling B. The music comes to rest with the return of the mysterious passage from the end of Waltz II, cadencing, just as it would in jazz, not on a tonic chord but on a dominant ninth.

Ravel's harmonic discoveries did not end with *Valses nobles et sentimentales*. In later works he absorbed influences from Stravinsky, Schoenberg, Bartók, and Gershwin; but this was a kind of payback since he had already influenced all of those composers except for Schoenberg. Ravel's oeuvre provides models for harmonic idioms by composers from Bartók and Berg to Mingus and Monk that retain a functional bass line and a sense of progression while pushing the envelope of dissonance. I hear a particular connection between Ravel's sensibility and Billy Strayhorn's (though Strayhorn's distinctive harmonic style also resembles Alban Berg's at times). Strayhorn began "Lush Life," composed in 1933 when he was eighteen, with an unusual harmonic progression, a major seventh on the tonic moving, out of the key, to a major seventh on the flat seventh degree, straight out of Ravel's *Sonatine.* "Chelsea Bridge," with its parallel augmented eleventh chords, is perhaps the most obvious homage, but I also hear a tribute to Ravel in Strayhorn's own *valse sentimentale*, "Lotus Blossom," Ellington's favorite composition by his alter ego.

GOING MODAL: DEBUSSY AND SHOSTAKOVICH

In 1959 Miles Davis's Mixolydian "All Blues" launched modal jazz, and just a few years later the Beatles gave popular music a modal makeover in "Eleanor Rigby" and "Norwegian Wood." When music theorists speak about modes, they mean scale patterns that differ from the usual major and minor, although technically speaking those are modes also. The scale from D to D on the white keys of the piano is called Dorian; E to E, Phrygian; F to F, Lydian; G to G, Mixolydian; A to A, Aeolian. (The names of the modes derive from a misreading of Greek music theory, not from actual ancient Greek music.) If you build triads on the notes of each mode you will see that compared to the major scale they do not have major triads on the fourth and fifth scale degrees. They do not produce the usual IV–V–I progression needed to define the key. Harmonies based on modal scales either have a looser sense of harmonic progression or find different ways of producing tonal function. In "Lush Life" and in many Beatles songs the major triad a step below the tonic (the flat seven from the Mixolydian mode) substitutes for the usual dominant. In jazz the use of modal scales emerged from the rich harmonies of bebop, in which chords often contained five or six pitches. Thinking modally, jazz players treated the subdominant not as a ii7 chord, which, by adding thirds, might contain (in C major) the pitches D, F, A, C, E, G, and B, but as the Dorian mode, which contains these same pitches. Modal harmony helped jazz musicians conceive their music more linearly, less chordally. Just as they had done in Impressionist music, the modes cleared the air.

In French music modal harmony came back to life with the three *Gymnopédies* of Erik Satie, composed in 1888. The first twenty bars of the first *Gymnopédie* employ only the pitches of the D major scale, but they don't sound like D major. The harmony rocks between two major seventh chords built on G and D; since there are no dominant-sounding chords we could be in either D major or G Lydian. Satie avoided major triads that would strengthen a sense of key; for a final cadence on D he used a minor chord as the dominant rather than the usual major triad or dominant seventh chord. In the third *Gymnopédie* the melodic line stays on the white keys throughout and the harmony falls on the white keys except for a few B♭s, which support a general strategy of avoiding major triads. Even though the piece sounds harmonically simple, it uses only one major triad, an inverted one at that, and only one dominant chord, a dominant ninth on G, which does not resolve in tonal fashion to C. Dominant progressions made music march; Satie's harmonies allowed music to float. You could draw up a long list of his imitators, beginning with Debussy, who orchestrated the *Gymnopédies,* and Ravel, who imitated them in his *Mother Goose* as well as in the *Valses nobles.*

Debussy's most rigorously modal composition is the first movement, "Pour invoquer Pan, dieu du vent d'été," of his *Six épigraphes antiques.* The music appeared as a piano duet in 1914, but it had been composed in 1900, at the height of Debussy's association with Satie, as (unpublished) background music for recitations of the faux Greek *Chansons de Bilitis* by Debussy's friend Pierre Louÿs. (Satie had established a precedent for using the "Greek" modes to illustrate Greek subjects in the *Gymnopédies* and *Gnossiennes.*) The movement uses only the notes of the G Dorian scale; its opening melody, presented unharmonized, is pentatonic, omitting the E and B♭ of the mode. These excluded notes form the interval of the tritone, which would tend to focus the harmony on the tonality of F. The pentatonic subset of G Dorian, lacking that dissonant interval, is tonally ambiguous. It could be harmonized in C major, or F major, or any of the modes derived from those keys. Debussy, however, further limited the harmonic possibilities by allowing no chromatic alteration of the pitches of G Dorian. He nevertheless shifted the tonal center of gravity from one phrase to the next, so that at first we hear the piece in C Mixolydian, then B♭ Lydian, then D Aeolian. Only at the end is there a cadence on G, and it is set up with a progression of major triads on B♭ and C (III and IV) playing the roles of subdominant and dominant, respectively. Throughout the movement Debussy breaks rules of academic tonality just as he had begun to do back in his conservatory days, with parallel fifths and unresolved ninths, but the overall effect is of a rediscovered consonance, music minus anxiety.

There are many later examples of "white key" music in the twentieth century. Prokofiev in particular liked to give diatonic melodies his own personal stamp. In the first piece, a slow waltz, of his *Visions fugitives,* op. 22, written between 1915 and 1917, the melody sits entirely on the white keys except for a single D♭ six bars before the end that is marked *misterioso.* Prokofiev harmonized the melody with a counterpoint of seventh chords that move in parallel but don't resolve or define a key. When the phrase repeats a new chromatic inner voice adds a little spice but no tonal direction. This time the phrase drifts downward to a b♭ minor triad, which turns (by way of the logic of tritone substitution) into a kind of dominant. It allows the music to close on e minor, where, it turns out, it actually began.

The name of Keith Jarrett became associated with modal jazz in the 1970s especially thanks to the recording of his solo concert in Cologne. Not incidentally, Jarrett later recorded the complete Preludes and Fugues, op. 87 of Shostakovich, composed in 1950–51. It took the insights and devotion of a great jazz musician to unlock a work that was still a buried treasure for most classical pianists. This massive cycle is a summation of Shostakovich's musical universe and also a commentary, at times satiric, on many aspects of twentieth-century music, including Stravinsky's neoclassicism (Fugue no. 2 in A minor) and twelve-tone composition (Fugue no. 15 in D♭).

Jarrett's critics sometimes accused him of, in effect, rolling an orange on the white keys. The first fugue of the Shostakovich cycle can serve as a response to their accusations. It is a model of absolute white-key composition that shows how much musical coherence can be found in just seven pitches. Within that limitation Shostakovich followed Bach's practice closely. The fugue is in four voices. The subject is eight bars long and uses just six of the available seven pitches, so that it retains its exact intervals when transposed up a fifth to become the answer. The answer imitates the subject at the fifth, and there are two countersubjects (counterpoints to the subject or answers that return rigorously). As in many Bach fugues there are also a couple of canons and pedal points, all part of the usual fugal machinery. Bach, however, would have constructed the harmonies of the fugue through a tour of related keys, going, say, from C major to G major, to a minor, to F major, and then back to C. In each of these harmonic regions he would use pitches from the chromatic scale not present in the C major scale. Shostakovich also visits different regions, but because he does not use any accidentals, they appear as modes. We hear statements of the subject in E Phrygian, B Locrian, A Aeolian, and D Dorian before we get back to C major, but Shostakovich saved the F Lydian for the end, where it seems to challenge the tonic key; the final cadence feels more suspended than resolved. Each of the fugue's modal regions has its own harmonic weight and flavor, so that the self-imposed harmonic constraints of the fugue feel like an expansion of resources. Only in the Lydian section, however, does Shostakovich allow modal logic, and the contrapuntal logic of a canon, to produce dissonant-sounding tritone clashes that threaten, in passing, the mood of calm objectivity.

"THE CLOTHED WOMAN," OR WHAT IS THIS THING CALLED ATONALITY?

After the Second World War the history of European art music in the twentieth century was rewritten, first in Paris, then at Princeton, as an inevitable evolution from tonality to "free" atonality to serialism. Somewhere along the line this tale of harmonic progress became interwoven with T. W. Adorno's jeremiads against popular music and jazz, which branded these genres as infantile empty-calorie musical junk food manufactured by the culture industry. These views began to change (at least outside France) as early as the 1960s, when rock music seemed at least as interesting, both musically and politically, as much of the new art music. With the rise of the civil rights movement, the '60s were also a fertile and contentious period for African American music in a wide range of styles, from the gospel-inspired soul music of Aretha Franklin to the free jazz of John Coltrane. Ellington's *Far East Suite* and Sacred Concerts were very much part of that politically charged panorama.

Free jazz, often played without reference to harmonic progressions, provoked a new debate about atonality. When the style first appeared, with Ornette Coleman Quartet's gig at the Five Spot in late 1959, some critics heard the new jazz as a belated response to the European avant-garde, while others emphasized its political radicalism. Some heard it as a response to Stockhausen, others as a resurgence of primitive blues untainted by popular music. LeRoi Jones summed up the debate in *Blues People*: "[Cecil] Taylor and [Ornette] Coleman know the music of Anton Webern and are responsible to it intellectually, as they would be to any stimulating art form. But they are not responsible to it emotionally, as an extramusical catalytic form. The emotional significance of most Negro music has been its separation from the emotional and philosophical attitudes of classical music." Jones advised that avant-garde techniques "be *used* not canonized" by African American musicians.[6]

Ellington anticipated this controversy by more than a decade. At his December 27, 1947, Carnegie Hall concert he announced, without much ado, that he would now play "The Clothed Woman," sat down at the keyboard, and let loose the most outside piano solo he or anyone else had imagined up to that time. Actually only the opening and ending sections of the piece are so far out, and Ellington never revealed if their eccentric sounds were meant to describe a woman getting clothed or unclothed. Ellington recorded the piece twice in 1947, and the music was later published. The sheet music rather oddly claims to be Marian McPartland's arrangement of the piece, yet "like the Ellington original involves little improvisation." Perhaps the sheet music is an arrangement in that it transforms the original, which was scored for piano and band, into a piano solo. The printed music, lacking indications of tempo and dynamics, is useful only if you listen first to the Ellington recordings. Its outer sections look like a random collage of arpeggios, blues riffs, and dense polychords sprinkled with seemingly incongruous F major triads. You wonder if Ellington had composed it Cage-style by consulting the *I Ching*. When you listen to Ellington's performance, however, these fragmented, discordant gestures reveal themselves as a slow and slinky blues in F, the apt prelude and postlude to the central stomp in B♭, as harmonically mainstream as the framing episodes are not. Ellington's musical cocktail complicates any sense of distinction we might have between atonal and tonal, European and African American, out and in, extraordinary and everyday, pop and art. In its suave subversion of "category" it leapfrogs over the historical determinism of the decades that followed its premiere to a later eclecticism that didn't take shape as an artistic movement until after Ellington's death. But even though postmodernists treat atonality as an option rather than an imperative, it remains ill defined technically and culturally, and it is still very much tied to the works and ideas of Arnold Schoenberg, even though there is a lot of atonal music, by Scriabin, Debussy, Ives, or Ellington, that has little to do with Viennese expressionism and its aftermath. A century after its first appearances atonality still sounds out—and that remains its attraction.

Critics and theorists have applied the slippery term *atonality* to music ranging from the late works of Liszt to art rock, from music that departs ever so slightly from nineteenth-century textbook rules to music that doesn't even employ pitches. For the general public it denotes music that is both nasty sounding and deliberately obscure, the product of some diabolical system. To be sure, many twentieth-century composers from Scriabin on propounded harmonic systems or generated speculative compositional procedures. Evaluating the results of systems as different as those of Hindemith and Cage is complicated by the fact that ideas can sometimes be fascinating in their own right.

Some of the most admired music of the later twentieth century, like the works of Lutosławski and Steve Reich, sprang from the ideas of John Cage rather than the sound of his music. I have always found the music of Xenakis compelling at the gut level, though I don't understand the mathematics behind it at all.

Perhaps we can grasp atonality better if we go through the back door and briefly reexamine tonality. Theorists usually apply the term *tonal harmony* to European music written between, say, 1675 and 1900. The style of that music is characterized by:

1. A tonal center or tonic defined for an entire piece in terms of major or minor scales. Modulations to other keys serve to confirm tonal unity (called "monotonality" by Schoenberg).

2. Harmonic vocabulary of triads and seventh chords.

3. Chordal progressions defined by the bass line and harmonic function.

4. Voice leading (part writing) connecting chords smoothly while avoiding certain kinds of parallelism (no parallel octaves or perfect fifths).

5. Nonchord (nonharmonic) tones prepared and resolved with specified sanctioned formulas.

Although the influential theorist Heinrich Schenker took an all-or-nothing view of tonality, and viewed any music that did not meet all the conditions listed above as aberrant, many composers, not surprisingly, disagreed. Both Bartók and Stravinsky claimed that their music had a tonal center, though Schenker would have been hard-pressed to find much evidence of tonality in *Music for Strings, Percussion and Celesta*, or Stravinsky's Serenade for Piano, both works considered to be "in A" by their composers. Even twelve-tone works such as Schoenberg's Piano Concerto and Berg's Violin Concerto can sound tonal at times, and more so on repeated listening. Theorists sometimes use the terms "centric" or "polar" for such nontraditional but tonal-sounding harmonies, but perhaps we can better understand a wide range of harmonic idioms, diatonic and chromatic, sweet and harsh, functional and disjunct, as part of an evolving, expanding tonality. I'll reserve the term *atonality* for works—and there are plenty of fine ones—that don't use pitches at all or that aim to be "out," though, as "The Clothed Woman" demonstrates, even the "out" can sound tonal on repeated hearing.

We can test the proposition of expanded tonality on pieces by Debussy, Stravinsky, Schoenberg that seem to travel far from anything you learned in Harmony 101.

Let's start with "Et la lune descend sur le temple qui fut," from Debussy's second book of *Images,* composed in 1907. Its opening phrase breaks all the tonal commandments but one. In the first three bars we hear a melody of chords, but the chords are not triads built in thirds but three different trichords with either a perfect or diminished fifth between their outer notes and a major or minor second between their two top notes. We might hear the first chord (E–A–B, from bottom to top) as what jazz players call a "sus" chord, where the fourth takes the place of the usual third, and we might hear the last chord (F–A–B) as implying a dominant seventh, but they don't resolve in any way that would confirm these readings. There is also no bass line. The music appears nontonal in chord vocabulary, indication of harmonic function, and also voice leading, since the three voices most of the time move in forbidden parallel fifths. Despite the mysterious inconsistency of the chords, the melody is relatively simple. It outlines an octave from B to B using pitches from the e minor scale and even sounds a bit like "I Didn't Know What Time It Was" (Rodgers and Hart). If we listen to the harmonies from the top down rather than the usual way, upward from the bass, we can hear the lower voices as forming dissonances against the melody, which Debussy resolves in bar 5 by contracting the three voices to a unison B. As the piece unfolds, with nary a traditional chordal progression, it outlines a double tonality centered on E if we give the bass notes priority, and on B if we give greater weight to the melody in the upper voices.

The large structure becomes clear if we imagine that Debussy, anticipating audio editing, spliced together two pieces. Piece I, centered on the pitch B, is heard in bars 1–5, 12–19, 25–26, 41–42, 46–52, and 56–57. Piece II enters in bars 6–11 with parallel triads over a pedal harmony (E–B) in the bass, both textural effects absent from Piece I. These textures return in bars 20–24, 27–28, 39–40, 43–46, and 54–55. Unlike Piece I, which always affirms the pitch B, Piece II uses the device of the sequence, repetition at a changed pitch level, to create a sense of harmonic motion. We might say that Piece I functions as the tonic, Piece II as the dominant. At the close of the piece the bass line resolves Piece II on a low E, but the upper voice brings the piece to rest on three octaves of B, a resolution that the pianist can make clear by raising the pedal to release the E in the bass and then lowering it again to emphasize the

B, or *"faites vibrer,"* as Debussy suggests in the score. The word *atonal* seems out of place here, even though Debussy has upturned the usual way of hearing harmony and also redefined harmonic function as alternation rather than cause and effect.

For some listeners Debussy's groundbreaking piece may sound like orientalist mood music no matter how transgressive it might appear to the harmonic analyst, so let's look at a grittier piece, the "Pas d'action" from Stravinsky's 1947 ballet *Orpheus*. The score describes the action: "The Bacchantes attack Orpheus, seize him and tear him to pieces." Stravinsky, following his trademark practice, defined the movement with a single chord that sounds like it was discovered at the keyboard: G♯s in octaves in the bass, the pitches A and C, doubled in octaves, in the treble. Even though there are just three pitches the chord sounds harshly dissonant. By omitting the interval of the fifth, Stravinsky complicated interpretation of the chord. It could be heard either as implying an A♭ minor ninth, or as an inverted minor seventh chord, with the major seventh, G♯, in the bass. Either way, it has something of the blues about it. Like jazz pianists, and like Ravel, Stravinsky required that every harmony in this movement include the interval of the seventh, or its inversions, the second and ninth.

The initial and inscrutable *"objet sonore,"* however, becomes the harmonic building block for the piece. Theorists would define it as a pitch class set [0,1,4] that contains the intervals of minor second, minor third, and major third. In this movement its structure reappears transposed, inverted, and revoiced in well over 90 percent of the chords. Through repetition it becomes the harmonic norm, a substitute triad, and departures from its sound stand out clearly. The remaining harmonies are similarly derived mainly from two compressed variants of the "tonic' chord: [0,1,3], containing a minor second, a major second, and a major third; and [0,1,2], containing only minor and major seconds. In analysis I'll call the main chord X and these two others Y and Z, respectively.

Throughout the movement the notes in the bass sound like dissonances while the tonal center appears in the treble. I call this "clothes-line tonality"; we have already encountered it in "Et la lune descend," and it is a characteristic that links Stravinsky's music to Debussy's. Looking at the score of *Orpheus,* it is hard to explain this inverted center of gravity acoustically except by noting that the upper line moves in stepwise fashion while the bass always jumps. The melodic notes (beginning with a motive that sounds, appropriately, like another Rodgers and Hart tune, "This Can't Be Love") use the pitches of the a minor scale, while the bass line outlines triads of A♭ major and c minor. Stravinsky deployed this harmonic clash as part of a carefully designed plan of harmonic motion based on the polarity of A and E♭. In place of the extended ostinatos of his Russian works, Stravinsky composed this movement by alternating static harmonic plateaus with more unstable phrases of harmonic motion.

The movement closely resembles classical sonata form, albeit in a tightly coiled compression, and uses sonata-style strategies to achieve tonal contrast and tension. The poignant affect of the coda depends on our hearing its single harmony as a subdominant in relation to the tonic harmony (centered on A) announced at the beginning and affirmed climactically at the recapitulation. In its expressive use of harmonic relations the music could be by Beethoven, except for the fact that Stravinsky did not use any chords in the movement that Beethoven, or Brahms, or Schenker would have considered harmony. Monk, who wrote most of his tunes around the time that *Orpheus* appeared, would have felt right at home.

Let's venture still further out to the onset of Stravinsky's serial phase. The Bransle Double comes right in the middle of *Agon* and is the first movement based on a twelve-tone row. Previous movements used shorter rows, and in fact the Bransle Double combines two six-note rows that have already appeared:

Hexachord I: C D E♭ F E A

Hexachord II: G A♭ B♭ B D♭ G♭

As Peter van den Toorn points out, both of these hexachords contain recognizable chunks of the octatonic scale (alternating major and minor seconds), which underlies much of Stravinsky's music, especially of his Russian period.[7] But the Bransle Double doesn't sound Russian; it sounds like jazz. Hexachord I contains most of the notes you need for a blues in C. The first five pitches of Hexachord II make a nice jazz dominant with a flat fifth. This creates the possibility of a quasi-harmonic progression that Stravinsky gives us three chances to hear. The short movement consists of an eight-bar phrase (in $\frac{3}{2}$ time) written in two-part counterpoint, followed by its repetition with a third voice added in the bass. There follows a contrasting middle section, thirteen bars of $\frac{2}{2}$, then a repeat of the opening eight bars followed by a fourteen-bar coda in $\frac{2}{2}$. (If you do the math you'll see that each of the phrases contains about the same number of beats.) It is essentially an extended AABA pop tune form. This highly repetitive structure is not something you find in the music of the Viennese serialists, and neither is Stravinsky's manner of stuttering out the twelve-tone row, repeating two-note segments two or three times before moving on.

Around the time he wrote *Agon* Stravinsky stated that "the intervals of my series are attracted by tonality; I compose vertically and that is, in some sense at least, to compose tonally."[8] This music immediately sounds more tonal than most Schoenberg and Berg because Stravinsky used tonally affirming octave doubling of pitches, which the others usually avoided. If Stravinsky had followed serial rather than tonal logic in this Bransle he might have constructed his two-part counterpoint by superimposing the two hexachords to create a twelve-tone aggregate. He did combine a statement of I (in the violins) with II (in the brass), but the versions he used share three common pitches:

I: C–**D**–E♭–F–**E**–**A**

II: B♭–B–D♭–**D**–**E**–**A**

Stravinsky seems to have chosen his pitches not in order to get to twelve but to outline a tonal progression from C to G and back; he even used the inverted retrograde forms of both hexachords to crawl back to C at the cadence (where the trombone adds a Monkish minor second below the C in the violin.

In the short middle section Stravinsky did oppose two complementary hexachords:

D–E–F–G–F♯–B

A–B♭–C–D♭–E♭–A♭

He voiced them, however, to suggest two jazz chords: G7 (in the piano) and C7 (in the clarinets). Stravinsky himself pointed out the jazz character of this passage, a character perhaps most obvious in its rhythm and timbre, but underscored by its harmonies. He even ended the coda jazz style, with a G7 chord with two statements of Hexachord II in the bassoons:

A–B♭–C–D♭–E♭–A♭

D♭–E♭–E–F♯–G (C)

The second hexachord never sounds its final C, so we are left hanging both tonally and serially.

I am not trying to prove here that all music is in some sense tonal; music also needs a sense of risk and free fall; sometimes, as the old jingle goes, you feel like a nut. Or like Schoenberg. The piano piece Op. 23 no. 2 (written in 1920) is a two-part invention recast as a tantrum. Expressionist music employed two metaphors for portraying psychosis: the roller coaster for bipolar disorders and the assembly line for obsessive compulsion. On its surface Op. 23 no. 2 is a lurching roller coaster, a series of steep rises, gut-churning dips, and sudden swerves separated by deep breaths of anxiety. The meter and tempo constantly change; phrase lengths are unpredictable; nothing is repeated literally. Beneath the surface, though, it is a diabolical mechanism. Schoenberg plundered the first six bars to construct the music for the remaining sixteen. (The piece usually lasts around ninety seconds, though Glenn Gould stretched it almost to two minutes.) The rigor of the piece seems both obsessive and guilt-ridden. Everything comes back, but in unrecognizable forms, a perfect crime with a perfect cover-up.

The piece alternates two ideas so its formal plan could be likened to classical style alternating variations, although few listeners would detect the structure because the two themes are mainly defined by their pitch content but not their rhythms or textures. The only other hint that Schoenberg provides to make the contrast audible is in dynamic gesture; until the coda all the appearances of A are rising crescendos.

In a classical variation piece the harmonic progression would unify the structure. Op. 23 no. 2 has a lot of chords, but are they harmony? I've just backed into the central question about atonality, which, back in the day, also seemed like the central question about twentieth-century music. Theorists offer three different types of explanation for music like Op. 23 no. 2, which bears little recognizable relation to the harmonic practices and conditions of the tonal period. On one side Hindemith and Ulehla argued that any combination of tones produces a hierarchy; any music made from tones is tonal. Schoenberg actually made a similar point in 1923 in defending himself against the rival twelve-tone system of J. M. Hauer: "With tones, only what is tonal, in keeping with the nature of tones, can be produced; there must at least be that connection of tones based in the tonal, which has to exist between any two notes if they are to form a progression that is at all logical and comprehensible."[9] At the other side are the aesthetic arguments of Cage and Stockhausen. In their view the emancipation of the dissonance was just a first step toward a general emancipation of sounds; differences in harmony were mere statistics. And in the middle fall the Schoenbergian theorists, mainly American scholars influenced by the ideas of Milton Babbitt, George Perle, and Allen Forte. They see Schoenberg's harmonic development as evolutionary, but with a crucial turning point with the move, around 1921, from an idiom they term either "free atonal" or "contextual" to the twelve-tone method that Schoenberg developed in composing, simultaneously, the piano pieces Op. 23, the Serenade op. 24, and the piano suite Op. 25. The earliest twelve-tone piece, or at least the one with the lowest opus number, is the Waltz, op. 23, no. 5.

In much of his writings Schoenberg used the reasonable, omniscient voice of the teacher, claiming that the goal of his music was not revolution but comprehensibility: "I have not discontinued composing in the same style and in the same way as at the very beginning. The difference is only that I do it better now than before; it is more concentrated, more mature."[10] But he would also break into a religious and even mystical kind of discourse to defend his music in terms of divine inspiration. He alternatively portrayed himself as the successor to Bach, Mozart, Beethoven, Wagner, and Brahms, and, as in his 1911 essay on Liszt, compared himself to "Plato, Christ, Kant, Swedenborg, Schopenhauer and Balzac."[11] The twelve-tone method was not a logical path but a divine intervention: "The Supreme Commander had ordered me on a harder road."[12]

In practice Schoenberg's deep-seated dualism (style and idea, Moses and Aaron) rests on an unsteady foundation of jostling ideas. From the classical repertory Schoenberg derived an idea of organicism, in which all details of a piece are connected. "When one cuts into any part of the human body," he wrote with Kafkaesque imagery, "the same thing always comes out—blood."[13] From romantic music he derived an idea of unmediated, inspired writing, particularly in relation to a text. He claimed that he composed songs "inspired by the first word of the text . . . straight through to the end without troubling myself in the slightest about the continuation of poetic events, without even grasping them in the ecstasy of composing." Even though he had formulated the identity of compositional logic and spontaneous inspiration in 1912 at the moment of his decisive involvement with Kandinsky, he restated the argument in more concrete terms for a radio broadcast in 1932.[14] Schoenberg here explained his Four Orchestral Songs, op. 22 in terms of "the unconscious sway of musical logic." The first song, "Seraphita," begins with a long melody for the clarinets. Schoenberg shows first how it opens (like the bridge of "Prelude to a Kiss") with a series of minor seconds. This series ends, though, with a minor third. The combination of a rising minor third and a descending minor second produces what Schoenberg calls a "gestalt," but that shape immediately mutates to a rising minor third and a *rising* minor second, outlining a previously unstated interval, the major third. Pretty soon similarly inspired tropisms turn minor seconds into major sevenths, combine minor thirds into the tritone, and somehow generate "variations" that include the interval of the perfect fifth, which was not present in immediate succession in the initial phrase. Schoenberg here includes within the techniques of variation not only repetition and transposition and recombination of intervals but also their enlargement, so that a minor third can swell to become a major third. Inspiration knows no limits.

This radio lecture nicely illustrates the technique that Schoenberg termed "developing variation." When he cited this technique in the music of Brahms, it referred to the use of thematic elaboration rather than repetition. At the beginning of the Fourth Symphony Brahms followed his initial statement of the theme not with the usual repetition or counterstatement, but with a variation that introduced a new contrapuntal element to the phrase. Similar kinds of elaboration appear in Mahler's later symphonies. Both Brahms and Mahler, however, worked within the classical notion of a variation, which is also the basis of jazz improvisation—the rearticulation of a harmonic structure through melodic ornamentation. In his description of melodic development in Op. 22 no. 1, however, Schoenberg makes no mention of harmony, even though the melody is accompanied by chords of three to six pitches. In a music appreciation–style radio talk, such oversimplification may just be the nature of the beast, but Schoenberg certainly gave the impression that the rapid free-associational expansion of the melodic line was not constrained or contained by any notion of harmony.

This brings us to a third foundational idea, the emancipation of the dissonance, for which Schoenberg had to claim divine origins. Here too, though, Schoenberg offered a logical explanation. He described the history of music as a gradual expansion of the field of permitted harmonies, from perfect intervals, to triads, to seventh chords. Harmonies that once seemed dissonant, Schoenberg argued, later became consonances. Since dissonances created musical tension and heightened emotional expression, composers had to find new dissonances as the old ones lost their potency. Post-Wagnerian composers, like Wolf, Strauss, and Schoenberg, often created chords provocatively out of dissonances, in appoggiatura chords. In his early songs *Erwartung,* op. 2 no. 1, Schoenberg constantly restates such a brazen nonharmonic harmony in a five-pitch chord that looks like it is constructed in fourths rather than thirds (from the bottom up: E♭–A–D–G♭–C♭. Heard on its own, this combination of pitches would seem tonally illegible, but Schoenberg preceded it and followed it with an E♭ triad. The four upper pitches in his strange chord are neighbor tones to the notes of that triad. Heard as accented but passing dissonances they are both logical and pretty. And if they are so pretty, why call them dissonances? The richly expressive songs in Schoenberg's Opp. 2, 3, and 6 show a wide variety of techniques for avoiding, but ultimately confirming, the tonal structure. Schoenberg thought that he had attained a mature synthesis of advanced harmonic and melodic thinking in his *Kammersinfonie*, op. 9, written in 1906, which conspicuously absorbed whole-tone and quartal harmonies associated with his French rivals, into the synthesis of Brahmsian and Wagnerian ideas he had already achieved in his First String Quartet. The comforting idea that he had finally arrived at a personal style, however, "was as lovely as a dream as it was a disappointing illusion."[15] The next step, the result of an "unconscious process," was to abolish the distinction between dissonances and consonances; from now on all harmonies were to be created equal. Even before Schoenberg portrayed his role as musical emancipator in the operatic figure of Moses, the phrase "emancipation of the dissonance" carried a lot of baggage from the book of Exodus, and in particular the lesson that emancipation itself would be just the beginning of a long and difficult journey, a painful cultural revolution. As in Orwell's parable, after emancipation some intervals would have to be more equal than others. Schoenberg and his students increasingly emphasized the previously dissonant intervals of the second, fourth, seventh, and tritone while repressing the older consonances like the octave, fifth, and major triad as emblems of the previous enslavement.

Schoenberg's new harmony would grow out of this unpromising mix of academicism, genius worship, and utopianism, but perhaps the confluence of these ideas only looks strange if you expect the results to sound like normal music. To my ears the Waltz that ends Op. 23 and announces the twelve-tone method sounds all too normal, neither expressive nor ironic nor even, as it unfolds, particularly interesting, let alone divinely inspired. It seems more perishable than Irving Berlin's contemporary *valse triste* "What'll I Do?" Op. 23 no. 2, on the other hand, shows what Schoenberg could do when the lightning really struck. The system is not necessarily at fault here. Like other superfluent composers (Strauss, Hindemith, Shostakovich), Schoenberg couldn't always distinguish works that were merely competent from those that hit the bull's-eye.

Op. 23 no. 2 seems compelling even though it wavers between strict serial development and freer developing variation. Even its rigorous restatements of pitch material vary so much in rhythm that the connections are not obvious—nor should they be. Schoenberg's other biblical hero was Jacob; in the years leading up to the invention of the twelve-tone method he struggled with and failed to complete a vast cantata called *Jacob's Ladder*. Op. 23 no. 2 sounds like a man wrestling with an angel. Its harmonies are at once visionary and tactile; even the clustering of adjacent melody notes into chords calls attention to the physicality of fingers, muscles, and arm weight, and the gradually slowing coda is a picture of bodily exhaustion. In ending with a bare but reconfigured restatement of the opening motive it still clings to a hope of transcendence, the promise that this seedling might again spring to life.

Schoenberg believed that the twelve-tone method would sustain larger forms without compromising the emancipation of the dissonance. Other composers of the interwar period, however, felt that the new harmonic possibilities created by emancipation could also retain some aspects of older tonal thinking. Bartók and Berg worked out complex syntheses of tonal and atonal idioms. Although much has been written about both composers, their achievements have become enshrouded by arcane systematic elements either of their own devising or imagined by their proponents. Even today many of the riches of their harmonies remain untapped.

Let's look at a movement by Bartók that has achieved masterpiece status and yet remains resistant to harmonic analysis: the third movement, Lento, of his Quartet no. 2, composed in 1917, just a few years before Schoenberg's Op. 23 no. 2, and similarly impacted by the Great War. The movement might be described as a modified sonata form:

1. Opening to rehearsal no. 2: Theme I

2. Rehearsal no. 2 to no. 4: Theme II (sounds, vaguely, like a variation of Theme I)

3. Rehearsal no. 4 to three bars after no. 6: Theme III

4. Fourth bar of rehearsal no. 6 to six bars before no. 7: Development

5. Five bars before rehearsal no. 7 to six bars after no. 8: Episode

6. Seven bars after rehearsal no. 8 to end: compressed recapitulation of Themes I, III, and II.

The problem with this generic description, however, is that, in addition to its odd proportions, all three themes are in the same tonality of A.

I hear the movement in different terms, as a tone parallel to a funeral:

1. Gathering of mourners (the theme in violin I three bars after rehearsal no. 1 represents the deceased)

2. Dirge

3. Hymn

4. Cortege

5. Interment

6. Departure and dispersal of mourners with a climactic recall of the Hymn.

In his book on Bartók's chamber music János Kárpáti identifies the melody of the dirge as a "Transdanubian lament melody" from the collection made by Bartók and Kodály.[16] Bartók's great dirges form a Mahleresque subgenre that is as characteristic of his personality as his better-known night musics. (Perhaps Bartók was as scarred by the loss of his father, when he was just seven, as Mahler was by the premature deaths of many of his siblings.) We might term these despairing pieces the shadows of those ecstatic nocturnes. His early symphony *Kossuth* contained his first funeral march, but a more original style of elegy appeared in his piano music of 1907–10, Bagatelles no. 6 and 13 from his op. 6, the two Elegies, the last of the Seven Sketches, and the Four Dirges. All of these increasingly desolate pieces prepare for two greater examples written during the war, the last movements of the Suite for Piano and the Quartet no. 2, and these in turn prepare for the great elegiac movements of his later years, in the Divertimento, Quartet no. 6, and Concerto for Orchestra. Also part of the subgenre is the seventh Improvisation on Hungarian folk songs, written in 1920, which Bartók dedicated to the memory of Debussy.

To understand the harmonic idiom of the string quartet movement we first need to note the distinctive stylistic features of Bartók's dirge genre. Their source in folk music is clear both in the volume of transcribed laments and, more accessibly, in the second series of *For Children,* based on Slovak folk songs, which ends with the Mourning Song and Funeral Song. In these two dirges Bartók combined a plaintive melody with a simple dronelike accompaniment. This texture, which resembles the relation of bluesman and guitar, appears in most of the composed dirges as well and is clearly elaborated in the *Four Dirges,* op. 9a. All four pieces contrast a folk melody with an accompaniment that is less a harmony than an Other; the two elements seem to go their own way, so that, for instance, at the end of the last Dirge the melody cadences on the pitches C♯ and A♯ while the accompaniment ends on a G major triad. In all these pieces the accompanying harmonies serve to set off and amplify the expressive intensity of the melody rather than assimilating it to tonal progressions. To a large extent, therefore, melody and harmony use different pitches. Reversing usual tonal practice, shared notes, or melodic notes that complete a triad with the accompaniment, often resolve to nonharmonic tones, an effect first heard at the end of Bagatelle op. 6 no. 6.

In the Lento of String Quartet no. 2 Bartók presents the opposition of melody and drone clearly at the very opening by separating the two violins musically from the viola and cello. This opposition reappears in what I term the Dirge section, and in the Cortege, and at the very end. According to Kárpáti, Bartók composed his thematic ideas first and then added the connecting sections. The two main themes, which I call the Dirge and Hymn, contrast sharply in texture; the first is the folk-like contrast of melody and drone, the second a chorale. The Interment episode has its own uniquely woven texture, a two-part counterpoint in which the first violin plays one line in octaves while the second violin and cello play the other, a unique occurrence. Bartók linked these carefully differentiated textures with mediating transitional passages that also have the most directional sense of harmony, and, not incidentally, the most traditional voice leading.

Like Schoenberg's Op. 23 no. 2, the Lento of Bartók's Quartet no. 2 breaks with nearly all the conditions of earlier tonality. Not a single major or minor triad appears. The most coherent and affirmative-sounding harmonies, heard in the Hymn, are built out of fourths rather than thirds. Also like the Schoenberg, but more consistently, Bartók pursued "developing variation." Ideas do not repeat but evolve or mutate. We hear this at the very opening, where the violins state an idea four times: a held note and a descending interval that gradually expands, in each statement, from a minor third to a perfect fifth.

In keeping with this movement's theme of loss, its musical ideas rarely sustain their initial form. Even the relatively affirmative-sounding rising

fourth that begins the new section at rehearsal number 4 shrinks to a
major third when it begins to be developed after rehearsal number 6.
The wraithlike, insubstantial quality of the themes becomes even more
apparent when we begin to notice how they are related to motives from
the previous two movements. The main motive of the first movement,
E–A–D–C♯, returns in shriveled form three bars after rehearsal number
1 in the first violin, G♯–C♯–F–E, and in a distended variant in the cello
four bars before rehearsal number 2, C♯–F–B–A. The melody played by
the first violin at rehearsal number 2 is a beheaded version of the opening theme of the first movement, but it also recalls the ironic, acerbic
melodic idea from the trio of the central Scherzo, drained, however, of
its sassiness. The episode at the center of the movement sounds like an
even more distant allusion, to the opening of the lachrymose fifth act
of Debussy's *Pelléas et Mélisande*.[17] Piling despair on despair Bartók
quoted a motive, note for note, E–F–A♭–F, which itself is a shrunken,
death-ridden version of the leitmotif associated with Mélisande in the
opera: E–F♯–A–F♯.

Harmonically the movement similarly presents a ghost tonality of
A, a tonal center more clearly, if not traditionally, affirmed in the first
movement with a memorable cantabile theme. In creating a ghostly,
"deceased" tonality Bartók reinvented the traditional distinction between minor and major modes and between harmonic stasis and motion. The Dirge and Hymn represent grief and hope with two different
kinds of static harmony, the drone on the pitches A and C, implying the
minor mode, and chords constructed in fourths, which sound here like
a parallel major mode. This opposition appears in stark contrast in the
climax, seven bars after rehearsal number 9, where a five-note chord in
fourths (E–A–D–G–C), all on the white keys, alternates with intensify-
ing fourth chords, climaxing in a six-note tower of fourths (A♯–D♯–G♯–
C♯–F♯–B). The harmonies convey some sense of progression and also
present a clear range, from the relatively consonant to the dissonant.

Somehow Bartók also preserved the distinction between chord tones
and nonchord (or nonharmonic) tones, distinctions lost in Schoenberg's
music, even while he avoided familiar chordal types. In the dirge-style
passages melody and drone use different pitches; we might say that
Bartók constructed his dirge melodies entirely from nonharmonic tones,
but since the melodies came first it would be more accurate to say that
he constructed the drone so that it would form dissonant intervals with
the melodies, a process cognate with Charles Mingus's harmonization
of the blues in "Goodbye Pork Pie Hat."

Bartók, by most accounts, was as humble as Schoenberg was megalomaniacal (one graphologist interpreted Schoenberg's handwriting as the work of someone who thought he was the emperor of China).[18] In many ways they pursued similarly grandiose ambitions of musical renewal. Bartók's quest, which the Second Quartet reflects in midcourse, was perhaps more visionary even than Schoenberg's. Bartók reanimated musical diversity in an idiom that allowed different styles (and even different species) to interact rather than flattening them into an all-encompassing unity. Small wonder, then, that when opportunity knocked he was ready to compose his *Contrasts* for Benny Goodman.

PART TWO

Entr'acte: "Sepia Panorama"

I am just getting a chance to work out some of my own ideas
of Negro music. I stick to that. We as a race have a good deal
to pay our way with in a white world. The tragedy is that so
few records have been kept of the Negro music of the past. Is
has to be pieced together so slowly. But it pleases me to have
a chance to work at it.

—Duke Ellington

Timbre, rhythm, melody, and harmony are means to an end. Composers, like poets, novelists and filmmakers, have a story to tell, though most
prefer just to say it with music. Duke Ellington, however, spelled out
the terms of his expressive project throughout his career and summed
it up with the title of his radio theme "Sepia Panorama." As early as
1930 he announced his intention to compose a suite that would be "an
authentic record of my race *written by a member of it.*"[1] Mark Tucker
traced the source of this project back to the historical pageants of Ellington's childhood in Washington, D.C. In 1911 the Howard Theater put
on a production called "The Evolution of the Negro in Picture, Song,
and Story," divided in four parts: Overture, Night of Slavery—Sorrow
Songs, Dawn of Freedom, and Day of Opportunity.[2] The format looks
forward to *Black, Brown and Beige,* but in works like the *Perfume Suite*
and *Night Creature* Ellington took his music far beyond the model of
a civics lesson. Keeping his eyes on the prize, Ellington never allowed
his works to become generically didactic; although he often appeared
at left-leaning events, he marched to his own political beat and told his
story in his own way and on his own far-reaching terms. With more than
a little help from the members of his orchestra, he contained multitudes.

His music evoked a panorama of people, places, and moods, and, while focusing on African American experiences, it also addressed a broad American and international audience.

Ellington's phrase *written by a member of it* indicates the urgency of his project. Whether for base or noble reasons, in minstrel shows or *Uncle Tom's Cabin,* the history and experience of African Americans had been scripted by whites. In the 1920s Broadway was ablaze with secondhand accounts of black experience by Eugene O'Neill *(The Emperor Jones)* and DuBose and Dorothy Heyward, whose *Porgy* was destined, just a few years after Ellington's statement, to become the most enduring and problematic picture of African American life in the musical theater.

The institutions and habits of American racism thwarted the musical careers of Ellington's African American predecessors, especially Will Marion Cook and James P. Johnson. The stereotypes of the minstrel show still poisoned entertainment; puritanism, high-minded sacralization, and, most of all, segregation contaminated education. For Ellington to realize his ambitions he would have to redefine pleasure and uplift and everything in between.

Scholars and critics have found it easier to cite Ellington's many statements about his project than to describe how it actually took shape in music that defies the norms of jazz and classical idioms. At times Ellington himself muddied the waters; some works, like the opera *Boola,* which promised to fulfill his most ambitious goals, never appeared. Others, most notably *Black, Brown and Beige,* had a confusingly protean performance history, never settling down to one finished form.[3] Ellington's nonstop gig-filled schedule made his determination to take on large historical and cultural issues all the more heroic, if not quixotic; usually he found time to compose only after a show, between 3 A.M. and 7 A.M.[4] Even when writing the extended pieces that were meant to bear the burden of his expressive goals he composed on the fly, phoning in music for musical theater and movie projects from the road and leaving elements large and small to his musical alter ego Billy Strayhorn and Tom Whaley, the band's copyist.[5] While Leonard Bernstein could take a yearlong sabbatical from his reign at the New York Philharmonic to compose the eighteen-minute *Chichester Psalms,* Ellington spent little time away from the band. He never applied for a Guggenheim Fellowship and never received any awards equivalent to a "genius" grant.

Finding his extended compositions either pretentious or slapdash, critics like John Hammond and James Lincoln Collier cited Ellington's apparently casual attitude toward thematically important works like *Jump for Joy* or the *Deep South Suite* as a symptom of artistic failings, particularly in regard to large forms. Ellington's odd behavior (relative to some Platonic notion of how composers are supposed to behave) can serve as proof, however, of an integrity that was principled and tenacious. Ellington never composed "crossover" music. In pursuing his artistic project he sidestepped the available European genres of high seriousness: symphony, opera, oratorio. When a work like *Harlem* or *Night Creature* would involve an orchestra, he farmed out the orchestration (usually to the Juilliard-trained Luther Henderson) and made sure that the music that mattered was assigned to his own musicians.[6] Though it still maddens some critics, he never played the role of the isolated genius. For Ellington composition was collaborative and open-ended; his reluctance to terminate things (compositions or marriages), often described as a superstition, can also be taken as an aesthetic stance. Refusing to merge the idiom of jazz with the forms and ensembles of European concert music, he set himself on a different course from Gershwin or Copland or William Grant Still. From "Reminiscing in Tempo" onward his extended forms, both secular and sacred, were sui generis. Perhaps ironically, Ellington's quirkiness made him a kind of modernist; like Schoenberg, Stravinsky, and Bartók, he believed that form was inextricable from content. European forms, however, were simply irrelevant, even inimical, to the experiences he strove to represent musically. The scope of ideas, images, and emotions of his music was panoramic, from political protest ("Jump for Joy") to religious faith ("Heaven"), from the African past ("Ko-Ko") to the American present ("The Air-Conditioned Jungle"), from Rio to Tokyo. We'll consider his project, and its relation to other twentieth-century music, under three rubrics: love, history, and God.

CHAPTER 5

"Warm Valley": Love

While driving along the south shore of the Columbia
River east of Portland, Oregon, we had a good view of the
mountains on the north shore. They had the most voluptuous
contours, and to me they looked like a lot of women reclining
up there. "Warm Valley" came directly from that experience.

—Duke Ellington

INTRO: LOOKING FOR LOVE IN ALL THE WRONG PLACES

Though Ellington garnered prestige through concert performances,
most of his gigs were at dance halls and nightclubs, where his music
propelled couples, rocking in rhythm or gliding cheek to cheek, around
the floor. Music can move us both physically and emotionally; this
double power links it to love in multiple and mysterious ways. Musicians are sometimes asked to play *"con amore,"* but what does that
mean? One answer, by way of example, would be "Warm Valley," a
slow instrumental ballad that Johnny Hodges intoned *"con amore"* to
the delight of thousands of slow-dancing couples. Despite Ellington's
charmingly risqué account of its inspiration, "Warm Valley" is not obviously descriptive of either geography or anatomy; instead of observing love from the outside, it turns listeners into lovers. Long before
Nietzsche termed this phenomenon "Dionysian," musicians recognized
the erotic power of their art in the genres of the serenade and nocturne.
Much of Ellington's oeuvre (like Mozart's or Chopin's) is music of the
night, enveloping the listener in the sensuality of sound. When Johnny
Hodges keened a melody with vibrato and rubato, hesitations, swells,
and slides, his tone was like an intimate touch.

Modernist classical music, by contrast, often served up sex on the rocks. When Tom Rakewell, the young protagonist of *The Rake's Progress*, heads down the road to perdition by losing his virginity at Mother Goose's brothel, librettists Auden and Kallman and composer Stravinsky give the scene all the erotic charge of a trip to the dentist; even the pretty chorus "Lanter-loo" sounds like Muzak piped in to anesthetize a painful but necessary procedure. Rakewell seems more turned on by the prospect of getting rich than getting laid. The libretto dwells more on his utopian delusions than on the kind of dalliances we might expect of a rake. If he ever has sex with his bearded wife, Baba the Turk, whom he marries in an existentialist *acte gratuit,* we never hear about it. Oddly enough in the century of Freud and Kinsey, a lot of twentieth-century music seems similarly antierotic; apparently *Tristan und Isolde* and *La Bohème* were hard acts to follow. As early as 1907, in his comic opera *L'Heure espagnole,* Ravel portrayed sex as just a normal part of a Spanish lunch hour, no agony, no ecstasy. It still looks like fun, though, which is more than can be said for the depictions of deranged romance in *Pelléas, Salome, Lulu, Mahagonny,* or *Lady Macbeth of the Mtsensk District.* Or, for that matter, *Madama Butterfly* and *Turandot.*

In their treatment of eros, popular and classical music in the twentieth century sent conflicting messages. While popular songs celebrated falling in love and dancing in the dark, modern operas charted the course of love as a sequence of pathologies from infatuation to suicide, death in childbirth, or insanity. Forged in the cauldron of fin de siècle Decadence, Salome, Mélisande, and Lulu were daughters of the Yellow 1890s. Pierrot and Petrouchka were its sons. Modernist operas and ballets figured sexuality through the thematics of decadence: hysteria, femmes fatales, castration anxiety, the battle of the sexes. Modern popular song, by contrast, took shape in jazz age America, which was also the era of Prohibition. Songs mirrored the national duplicity. They pictured sex in contrasting sweet and lowdown images of boy-meets-girl puppy love and torch song degradation. The binarisms of American popular song up to 1960 resemble the map of a typical racially zoned American city:

Sweet	Hot
Puppy love	Sex
Middle class	Lower class
White	Black
Legit	Illicit

Public	Private
Times Square	Harlem
Above the waist	Below the waist

These contrasts mirrored larger anxieties about the erosion of Victorian values and white political dominance. Sexual liberation ("Let's do it!") implied political liberation. Fear of either form of liberation could spawn anxious fantasies of inverted power, black over white. Americans, and Europeans as well, conflated jazz and sex, and imagined jazz as a black Dionysus, like the title character of *Jonny Spielt Auf,* or Crown and Sportin' Life in *Porgy and Bess.* No wonder that Ellington, even in the racist décor of the Cotton Club, tried to detach his own music from the rubric of jazz and strove to construct a counternarrative free of Euro-American racial and sexual fixations. Those fixations, however, shaped musical modernism both high and low.

In the USA love was not racially blind. Black artists who gained a presence in the national media, such as Ellington, Louis Armstrong, Paul Robeson, Ethel Waters, Eddie "Rochester" Anderson, Lena Horne, and Nat King Cole, faced particular racist restrictions, most obviously in the movies, where they were never allowed to appear in romantic situations. For all her glamour, Lena Horne was rarely granted an on-screen lover; in the one exception, *Stormy Weather,* Bill "Bojangles" Robinson looks old enough to be her father. Broadway, Hollywood, and the radio perpetuated the stereotypes of the mammy, the lazy serving man, and the "high yellow" prostitute. Black actors had to choose to accept work in shows like *Green Pastures* or *Cabin in the Sky* or *St. Louis Woman* that softened the stereotypes slightly, or turn down roles and end their film careers. After a decade of being forced to walk through movie sets like an isolated visiting royal, Horne called it quits and developed her artistry in the freer setting of cabaret, or listening to recordings with her best friend, Billy Strayhorn.

"LOVE YOU MADLY": THE DUKE'S MUSICAL LADIES

I want to tell you what I think the sex act is. I think it is like a lovely piece of music, conceived quietly in the background of mutual affection and understanding, made possible by instincts which lean toward each other as naturally as the sunflower slowly turning its lovely face to the sun. I think it is an aria of the sex symphony, an aria which begins beautifully certain in its rightness, moves with that certainty to a distinct tempo of feeling, sings itself happily, steadily,

working, working, to a screaming, bursting climax of indescribable
beauty and rapture then throbs, spent and grateful in a rededication
for the next movement of its perfection.
—Duke Ellington

In order to demolish the toxic stereotypes of African American sexuality, Ellington created new images of black lovers. Ellington's erotic
oeuvre appears in two genres: romantic ballads and evocatively titled
portraits. "Black Beauty," one of his first portraits, was both a great
tune and a strong, if implicit, political statement. Ellington later called
it a "Portrait of Florence Mills" to honor the internationally famous
black singer and actress who died suddenly in 1927. The actress most
associated with the song, however, was Fredi Washington, who played
the female lead in *Black and Tan,* the only film where Ellington himself
played a dramatic role, albeit of himself.[1] The two-reel short, directed
by Dudley Murphy for RKO in 1929, employed a startling range of
period styles, including urban realism, art deco nightclub scenes, and
a deeply shadowed expressionist funeral. Breaking with stereotypes,
Washington and Ellington, and Arthur Whetsol as well, appear young,
good-looking, talented, and utterly normal, perfect emblems of the
Harlem Renaissance's New Negro.[2] Together they conspire to promote
Ellington's hot-off-the-piano masterpiece "Black and Tan Fantasy." In
a Harlem cabaret that appears both chic and sleazy, the character Fredi,
named after Washington but modeled on Mills, dances to Ellington's
music despite a heart condition. She falls fatally ill in the middle of her
routine. When the white manager demands that the show go on and
sends out a group of light-skinned Cotton Club beauties to continue
her dance, Ellington orders the band to stop and rushes to her bedside.
On her deathbed she asks to hear one last performance of "Black and
Tan Fantasy."

For all its obvious contrivances the short film was nevertheless a culturally revolutionary depiction of Ellington as a black creative genius.
Likewise, the film and the song "Black Beauty" presented "Fredi" as a
glamorous, intelligent, strong-willed, and dignified black woman, the
first in a long line of sophisticated ladies (and satin dolls).

Ellington's first extended portrait of a lady was "Reminiscing in
Tempo," an elegy for his mother, Daisy Kennedy Ellington (known to
the family as "Aunt Daisy"), who died in May 1935; Ellington wrote
that "no one else but my sister Ruth had a mother as great and as
beautiful as mine."[3] This work, twelve minutes of music spread over
four record sides, elicited some of the harshest criticisms Ellington ever

received. John Hammond called it "formless and shallow,"[4] and the English critic Spike Hughes termed it "a rambling monstrosity that is dull as it is pretentious and meaningless.[5] These objections may have stemmed from cultural discomfort about both form and content. While "Reminiscing" sounded nothing like classical music, it contained no hot solos, indeed little improvisation of any kind. Its style seemed far removed from Ellington's more familiar "jungle music" or the blues, or even from the spiritual, a genre Ellington had recently invoked for the "Hymn of Sorrow," a dirge accompanying a baby's funeral in *Symphony in Black,* a short sequel to *Black and Tan.* By contrast, the singular musical idiom of "Reminiscing in Tempo" served notice that Ellington's mother was no mammy and no floozy, neither Aunt Jemima nor Bess; she was simply "the most beautiful mother in the world."[6]

"Reminiscing" has baffled even sympathetic critics like A. J. Bishop and Gunther Schuller, who had the disadvantage of working from a single recording, without access to any written material. John Howland's recent analysis, making use of Ellington's sketches and parts in the Ellington Archive, outlines the work in two unequal parts, sides one through three of the original 78 rpm recording and side four. Howland concludes that side four, which sounds complete in itself, was composed first and served as "a template that was deconstructed to build Parts I–III."[7] He also locates the work's style provocatively within the framework of Paul Whiteman's genre of symphonic jazz. The music, however, lacks the modernistic markers characteristic of the symphonic jazz style and is devoid of the gushy buildups and climaxes typical of the crossover works of Gershwin and Grofé. If we need some classical parallel for its style we might say that "Reminiscing" feels more like Mahler in his ruminating Adagietto mode than Whiteman. It's non-mawkish Mahler, if such a thing is imaginable; a Mahlerish fox-trot. Ellington himself pointed out the ruminative character of the piece: "I wrote 'Reminiscing in Tempo' that year [of his mother's death]. It was one of my first ambitious things. It was written in a soliloquizing mood. My mother's death was the greatest shock. I didn't do anything but brood. The music is representative of that. It begins with pleasant thoughts. Then something awful gets you down. Then you snap out of it and it ends affirmatively."[8]

Perhaps like Ellington's own emotional recovery, the music sounds less straightforward than the simple sequence he described. We can understand "Reminiscing" better if we note how drastically Ellington restricted himself here, and then ask why he chose these particular constraints. The first three parts avoid the forms found in Ellington's earlier music such as blues or the AABA form, and they present no stylistic contact with the spiritual, or even with prayer, although later in life Ellington described his mother's broad-minded piety: "She was mainly interested in knowing and understanding about God, and she painted the most wonderful word pictures of God. Every Sunday she took me to at least two churches, usually to the Nineteenth Street Baptist, the church of her family, and to John Wesley A.M.E. Zion, my father's family church. It was never made clear to me that they were of different denominations, and to her, I'm sure, it did not matter. They both preached God, Jesus Christ, and that was the most important thing."[9] The blues would have been inappropriate for a woman of Daisy Ellington's religious devotion and middle-class background; her father had been a captain in the District of Columbia police. The absence of music suggesting a spiritual or hymn indicates that "Reminiscing in Tempo" was intended less as a eulogy for the dead than as a celebration of a life along lines that Ellington made explicit many years later in *My People*:

> The men before them worked hard and sang loud
> About the beautiful women in this family of mine.[10]

Excluding the forms of blues or hymn, the remaining option would have been the popular song. Here, too, Ellington's refusal was based on his mother's upright character. While Daisy Kennedy Ellington might have been termed a "Black Beauty" or a "Sophisticated Lady," her son chose not to portray her within the idioms used for Cotton Club dancers. He would not eulogize his mother within the thirty-two-bar framework of a commercial tune.

Soon after the recording appeared, however, the English critic Leonard Hibbs astutely pointed out that side four approximated the AABABA form of an expanded popular song and sounded complete in itself. Hibbs came up with an imaginative program for the earlier parts of the piece. According to him, they represented Ellington's compositional process, his search for a tune that was "just out of reach": "He can't nail it down. It's there but it won't take shape."[11] Hibbs's account is a sympathetic way of hearing the piece, but it fails to describe the thematic material accurately, although in passing it makes the lovely suggestion that the music has something to do with "proper clothing."[12]

Ellington began the portrait of his mother and her proper clothes with three ideas presented contrapuntally: a four-note "dirge" motive moving in parallel fifths in the bass; a two-note motto, a rising minor third repeated gently on the trumpet (which names the subject of the music either as Daisy or mother or mama); and a figure in lightly swung eighth notes on the piano (which could represent her proper clothes adorned with the strands of pearls that set off her face in the *Music Is My Mistress* photograph).

Critics undervalued "Reminiscing" by following only the main tune, an eight-bar idea that occurs fifteen times in the piece, without noticing the subtle variations Ellington rings on it, and its evolving relation to contrasting material. In between the rondo-like returns of the main tune Ellington inserted three different kinds of phrases, one that sounds like a B or bridge and usually comes between statements of the main theme, another that is a closing phrase built on a transformation of the four-note dirge theme, and, most intensely, a phrase in which the two-note Daisy theme is heard as a sequence of rising half steps in rhythmic augmentation, four times as slow as the original statement. This third idea, heard only twice, stands out from the rest of the work as a powerfully rendered acknowledgment of grief, but the essence of the music, its portrait of a great lady, appears in the varied, reorchestrated restatements of the eight-bar idea, which allow each member of the band to pay Ellington's mother a personal tribute. The eighth-note "strands of pearls" motive embellishes these melodic restatements either as a counterpoint or response, enriching the melody both horizontally and vertically. The pearls in the photograph and in the music proclaim Daisy's regal bearing, as would befit the mother of a duke.

Ellington's complicated marital and extramarital history suggests that no woman ever really replaced Daisy in his affections, but his devotion to her memory did not inhibit his musical portrayals of erotic themes. His next two extended works with romantic subjects, "The Blue Belles of Harlem" and the *Perfume Suite,* involved significant collaboration with Billy Strayhorn. The *Perfume Suite* premiered at the Carnegie Hall concert on December 19, 1944. Ellington signaled the collaborative effort obliquely with what may have sounded like a papal locution: "In the Perfume Suite our aim was not so much to try to interpret the mood . . . implied by the label on the commercial projects, but more so to try to capture the character usually taken on by a woman who wears different brands of perfume—or rather different blends of perfume. . . . We divided them into four categories: Love, Violence, Naiveté and Sophistication."[13] The first movement, first titled "Sonata" and later "Balcony Serenade," was in fact Strayhorn's reworking of material he had written for other purposes; the second, a vocal number

called "Strange Feeling," was also mainly by Strayhorn, though Ellington scored the instrumental chorus. Ellington composed the third
movement, "Dancers in Love," and performed it as a piano solo (with
bass). The final movement, "Coloratura," showcased the upper register
screech trumpet of Cat Anderson, who had just joined the band. It is
an Ellington work completed by Strayhorn in the handoff method the
two composers had established in "Jack the Bear." As Walter van de
Leur notes, the *Perfume Suite* became the model for later extended,
multimovement pieces "consisting of a mix of (retitled) old and new
compositions by Ellington and Strayhorn, unified by a programmatic
title and explanatory remarks."

The *Perfume Suite* overturned racial and sexual stereotypes through
unexpected and disturbing juxtapositions of mood. "Balcony Serenade"
sounds like a continuation of Strayhorn's "Sugar Hill Penthouse" from
Beige; its lush reed choir voicing is as Glenn Miller–ish as its title. Strayhorn's music won the praise of Miller's arrangers Bill Finnegan and
Billy May, as well as Ralph Burns, composer of "Early Autumn," a
Woody Herman hit—all masters of slow, cheek-to-cheek compositions.
Just when the mainly white Carnegie audience may have been lulled
into comfort, however, Al Hibbler appeared to sing "Strange Feeling"
in an impassioned, almost operatic baritone perfectly suited to the
song's scary intensity:

> This strange feeling is seeping through my blood.
> This strange feeling is sleeping cuddled up
> Somewhere inside me . . .

The instrumental chorus, scored by Ellington, combined jungle, modernistic, and psycho styles. It's almost an American *Wozzeck;* the closest
parallel is "Lonely Room," the creepy, revelatory (and usually omitted)
monologue by the pathological Jud Fry in *Oklahoma!*

The third movement, "Dancers in Love," subtitled "Stomp for Be-
ginners," sustains the *Wozzeck* mania with a twelve-tone melody but
is otherwise a delicious tribute to James P. Johnson. The music returns
to normalcy but moves north of Central Park. Again, the easygoing
nature of this movement is a setup for even greater eccentricity. "Coloratura" sounds like an operatic cadenza transcribed for trumpet, an
idea made famous by Roy Eldridge in his recording of "Rockin' Chair."
Here, though, the cadenza neither precedes nor follows a melody; it's
a pure diva moment. Anderson's trumpet sounds like an upward extension of Hibbler's voice, transforming Hibbler's masculine baritone

into an image of feminine star power. However it was written, the *Perfume Suite* turned black into white and male into female, and, in under twelve minutes, it presented the full spectrum of love, from tenderness to obsession.

SUCH SWEET THUNDER: OTHELLO REDUX

Theseus: We will, fair Queen, up to the mountain's top
And mark the musical confusion
Of hounds and echo in conjunction.
Hippolyta: I was with Hercules and Cadmus once
When in a wood of Crete they bay'd the bear
With hounds of Sparta. Never did I hear
Such gallant chiding; for besides the groves,
The skies, the fountains, every region near
Seem'd all one mutual cry. I never heard
So musical a discord, such sweet thunder.
—*A Midsummer Night's Dream,* Act IV, Scene I

Throughout his career Ellington challenged the dehumanizing stereotypes of black male sexuality by living up to the nickname he had earned when he was fourteen, when his friend Edgar McEntree dubbed him "Duke." "I think he felt that in order for me to be eligible for his constant companionship I should have a title," Ellington recalled modestly in *Music Is My Mistress.*[14] It's hard to find a photograph where he appears less than regal; even in a portrait from 1906 he looks like the heir apparent. In live performance he was better dressed and better spoken and infinitely cooler than anyone else in the room—even, to judge by the photos, the British royal family. Paul Whiteman looked more like the bridegroom on a wedding cake than the King of Jazz, and Benny Goodman, King of Swing, cut a less regal figure than a haberdasher. Ellington seemed to the manor born. In later years, when his face took on its aristocratic world-weary mask, people attending an Ellington performance felt privileged to be granted an audience by visiting royalty. Of course it was an act, but no more so than the similarly grand personae created by Leopold Stokowski or Leonard Bernstein. We're talking, after all, about show business.

Two of Ellington's tone parallels celebrate fellow black entertainers Bert Williams and Bill "Bojangles" Robinson, who had also cast off the demeaning trappings of minstrelsy. A third, "Menelik, The Lion of Judah," paid tribute (perhaps ironically) to Haile Selassie, emperor of Ethiopia and an African opponent of European aggression.[15] Ellington's ultimate tone parable of the vulnerable romance of black star and white audience—and, by extension, of Africa and America—demanded an even more extended framework and also a more global stage—the Shakespearean stage of the Globe itself.

Such Sweet Thunder, a suite in twelve movements composed by Ellington and Strayhorn for the Shakespearean Festival in Stratford, Ontario, premiered at a Music for Moderns concert titled "Twelve-tone to Ellingtonia," at New York's Town Hall on April 28, 1957, a day before Ellington's fifty-eighth birthday. (At Town Hall Ellington humorously called the final piece "Cop Out" because it was a placeholder for the yet-to-be-written finale; "Cop Out" was a minor blues that the band had recorded a month earlier and also a Gonsalves vehicle.) The band played the suite again at Stratford on September 5, 1957, with "Circle of Fourths" as a conclusion, as it is on the recording.[16] Later Music for Moderns concerts that season paired the Modern Jazz Quartet with Virgil Thomson, Mahalia Jackson with Martial Singher, and Chico Hamilton with Carlos Surinach. At Town Hall Kurt Weill's early, astringent Violin Concerto op. 12, played by Anahid Ajemian and members of the New York Philharmonic under Dmitri Mitropoulos, served as curtain raiser. Weill's music was having a posthumous boom thanks to the revival of *The Threepenny Opera,* but his concerto gave only a foretaste of the jazz-influenced Weill; Ross Parmenter, the *New York Times* critic, found the new Ellington/Strayhorn work far more persuasive and "thoroughly winning."

Ellington was on a roll. The premiere came less than a year after the band's triumphant "rebirth" at the Newport Jazz Festival on July 8, 1956. Ellington soon appeared on the cover of *Time* (August 19, 1956) and won a new contract with Columbia Records. On March 15, 1957, he appeared, with his sister Ruth and son Mercer, on Edward R. Morrow's *Person to Person.* His musical-theater fantasy of jazz history, *A Drum Is a Woman,* aired during the United States Steel Hour on CBS a week after the *Such Sweet Thunder* premiere; Ellington, who was fond of anagrams and verbal inversions, personified jazz as Madame Zajj. Six weeks later the band recorded *The Duke Ellington Songbook* with Ella Fitzgerald; Ellington's popular tunes, just a small part of his oeuvre, now took their rightful place along with the songs of Gershwin, Kern, Porter, Berlin, Arlen, and Rodgers in Ella's canon-defining albums on Verve records. Still later that summer the band would play the Ravinia Festival in Chicago, the summer home of the Chicago Symphony, then in its Fritz Reiner heyday. Surrounded by honors from the white cultural world, Ellington had good reason to liken himself to the original black superstar: Othello.

Although the phrase "I never heard so musical a discord, such sweet thunder" came from *A Midsummer Night's Dream,* Ellington described the title movement of the suite as "the sweet and singing, very convincing story Othello told Desdemona. It must have been the most because when her father complained and tried to have the marriage annulled, the Duke of Venice said that if Othello had said this to his daughter, she would have gone for it too."[17] Many of the instrumental parts, however, bear the title "Cleo." Somewhere along the line the music had changed genders while retaining an African setting and protagonist. The plots of both *Othello* and *Antony and Cleopatra* involved a high-stakes romance between European and African lovers. In *Music Is My Mistress,* Ellington wrote that "When Nobody Was Looking" from the *Deep South Suite* of 1946 "illustrated the theory that, when nobody was looking, many people of different extractions are able to get along together." He described the movement as a parable about a puppy and a flower following their "natural tendencies." A decade later Ellington, shielded by the Bard, presented a bolder representation of interracial sex, which was still illegal in many American states both North and South. (The Supreme Court would not declare antimiscegenation laws unconstitutional until 1967; sixteen states still had such laws at the time.)

Such Sweet Thunder revived the political themes Ellington had pursued in *Jump for Joy, Black, Brown and Beige, New World A-Comin', Deep South Suite, Liberian Suite, and Harlem.* The time gap between *Harlem* and *Such Sweet Thunder,* however, reflects a double crisis of the postwar years: the implosion of the market for big band music and the anticommunist crusades of the House Un-American Activities Committee and Senator McCarthy. In the November 5, 1952, issue of *Down-Beat* Leonard Feather claimed that the only functioning bands left were Ellington's, Woody Herman's, Count Basie's, and Stan Kenton's. The economics and demographics of music were changing, though critics were at a loss to explain how or why. The narrowed field of competition meant that the Ellington band was kept busy, though many of its gigs took place in provincial movie theaters and dance halls. Even in concert halls, however, some critics detected a precipitous decline and fall in musical relevance. After the Ellington band played the Civic Auditorium in Portland, Oregon, in March 1952, a review in *Down-Beat* by Ted Hallock dismissed Ellington impertinently as a "gross old man," speculated that Ellington was not the composer he claimed to be, and concluded that "if Ellington is Shakespeare, then I am beginning to wonder if there isn't a Roger Bacon somewhere in the woodpile."[18] Apparently even the leading jazz publication of the time had no problem insinuating the "N" word into its columns—but Hallock may unwittingly have planted the seed of *Such Sweet Thunder*. Although the magazine's readers, including Charles Mingus, protested Hallock's review, Ellington's humiliating decline seemed to continue. In the summer of 1955 the Ellington Orchestra was featured along with dancing waters, ice snow, water snow, and fireworks at the "Aquashow" at Flushing Meadow Park, and for most of the months surrounding that gig the calendar was empty. The most popular recording of the summer was "Rock Around the Clock" with Bill Haley and the Comets. On "race" labels the biggest hits were Fats Domino's "Ain't That a Shame" and Little Richard's "Tutti Frutti." Big band music seemed dead.

Ellington suffered political misfortunes as well. In the early 1950s he was caught up in two public political disputes that showed how times were changing. Throughout the 1940s Ellington had aligned himself with the leftist Popular Front, and the 1943 Carnegie Hall concert had been a benefit for Russian War Relief. After the war ended, however, any pro-Russian sympathies became suspect. When the *Daily Worker* claimed that Ellington had signed the Soviet-sponsored Stockholm Peace Petition, he wrote a statement for *The New Leader,* an anticommunist social democratic weekly, under the title "No Red Songs for Me," published September 30, 1950. In it, Ellington stated, "The only communism I know of is that of Jesus Christ."

Ellington's guarded political stance placed him out of sync with the emerging civil rights movement. In the fall of 1951 Ellington's band toured as part of The Big Show of '51, which also featured Sarah Vaughan and Nat King Cole. The NAACP picketed their appearances at segregated theaters in Richmond, Virginia, and in Atlanta. The black press seized on several statements attributed to Ellington that seemed to oppose the protest: blacks were "not ready" for integration; protest "is for the Negro at the bottom. It isn't doing the Negro who's got something any good."[19] However Ellington's words may have been misconstrued, it would take him a few years to mend fences with the movement. In the early 1960s he was honored by the Urban League, the NAACP, and the Congress of Racial Equality.

Well before these honors, though, Ellington was able to rekindle the politically ambitious side of his music because of a fundamental change in the way jazz was marketed. In the 1950s jazz was no longer the popular music of white or black audiences it had been in the swing era. Rock and roll and rhythm and blues took its place, particularly with younger listeners. The jazz scene now migrated to college campuses and destination festivals like those at Newport, Rhode Island, and Monterey, California. The new venues combined classy locales with high art ambitions; George Wein, one of the founders of the Newport Festival, predicted that it would be to jazz what Salzburg is to Mozart and Bayreuth is to Wagner.[20] In a sense the festival settings, captured in the aptly arty documentary film *Jazz on a Summer's Day,* replaced racial segregation with economic segregation, but they also offered jazz a safe haven well suited to the sophisticated music of the Ellington Orchestra and the refashioned Basie band of "April in Paris" and "Shiny Stockings." Both bands had moved far from their swing-era styles. While critics bewailed Ellington's decline and noted the departure of such signature players as Cootie Williams and Sonny Greer, Ellington modernized his sound with the significant arrivals of Paul Gonsalves, Clark Terry, Louie Bellson, and Sam Woodyard. Johnny Hodges also returned to the band in 1956 after a five-year hiatus, and at the beginning of that year Ellington lured Billy Strayhorn back to the fold after a brief parting of the ways. Strayhorn told a friend, "I talked to Edward. He would like me to be more *engaged* again. He asked *me* what sort of project I would like."[21]

The updated Ellington sound arrived, like a comet, in the unlikely guise of a nineteen-year-old composition, "Diminuendo in Blue and Crescendo in Blue," first recorded in 1937. The two sections were originally connected by an Ellington piano solo, but as early as 1951 Paul Gonsalves took over the moment with what became known as the "wailing interval." The live recording from the Newport festival remains one of the most soul-stirring moments in jazz history. John Fass Morton astutely notes that the performance broke down the stylistic barrier between jazz and rhythm and blues: Gonsalves played a honking R&B sax.[22] The performance made a subtler point as well: it demonstrated that Ellington's music transcended the pigeonhole periodization of so-called jazz history. "Diminuendo and Crescendo" was not a relic of the swing era; it was the most contemporary-sounding piece of the festival.

The explosive appearance of the new Ellington at Newport on July 7, 1956, came to be associated with a photograph that appeared on the live recording. George Avakian described the historical moment in Paul Gonsalves's twenty-seven-chorus solo in "Diminuendo and Crescendo in Blue": "At about his seventh chorus, the tension, which had been building both onstage and in the audience since Duke kicked off the piece, suddenly broke. A platinum-blond girl in a black dress began dancing in one of the boxes (the last place you'd expect that at Newport!) and a moment later somebody else started in another part of the audience. Large sections of the crowd had already been on their feet; now their cheering was doubled and redoubled as the interreacting stimulus of a rocking performance and crowd response heightened the excitement."[23] The blond in question was, as John Fass Morton discovered, Elaine Anderson, whose life as a dancer, starlet, and jazz enthusiast had prepared her for her iconic close-up. Symbolically, though, we might name her Desdemona.

The 1950s also witnessed a boom in Shakespeare festivals. The Stratford (Ontario) Shakespeare Festival, directed by Tyrone Guthrie, began in 1953. Joseph Papp founded the New York Shakespeare Festival in 1954, and the American Shakespeare Festival opened in Stratford, Connecticut, in 1955. In the United States the Bard served as an antidote to anticommunist cultural pressures. Joseph Papp, once a Communist Party member, first hatched the idea of presenting Shakespeare without an admission charge in 1953; his plans evolved into Shakespeare in the Park while he was tailed by the FBI and ordered to testify before HUAC. When Papp was subpoenaed by the HUAC in 1958 he was asked whether he injected Communist philosophy into his Shakespeare productions. Papp responded, "Sir, the plays we do are Shakespeare's plays. Shakespeare said: 'To thine own self be true,' and various other lines from Shakespeare can hardly be said to be 'subversive' or of 'influencing minds.' I cannot control the writings of Shakespeare. He wrote five hundred years ago. I am in no position in any plays where I work to influence what the final product will be, except artistically and except in terms of my job as a producer."[24]

By linking Shakespeare's uncontroversial standing and his own prerogatives as an artist Papp demonstrated the way Shakespeare could serve as a shield for political protest in the 1950s, whether at Shakespeare in the Park, or in *Such Sweet Thunder* or *West Side Story*. Without changing a word of the text Papp gave Shakespeare's plays a ripped-from-the-headlines buzz a decade before Jan Kott's book *Shakespeare Our Contemporary* appeared. He sought "blood-and guts actors" and ethnically diverse casts.[25] His American actors spoke in their own voices rather than affecting British speech and worked in the visceral "Method" style familiar from the film performances of Marlon Brando

and James Dean. Among them were Roscoe Lee Browne, Colleen Dew-
hurst, James Earl Jones, and George C. Scott. They made Shakespeare
sound as relevant to the 1950s as Clifford Odets had been to the '30s.

The time seemed ripe for celebrating the connection between jazz
and the Bard. On his Omnibus show "The World of Jazz," which aired
on October 16, 1955, Leonard Bernstein (who shared Papp's left-wing
background) demonstrated that the blues was a poetic form by singing
a blues to lines from *Macbeth*:

> I will not be afraid of death and bane
> Till Birnam forest come to Dunsinane.

Less than a fortnight after its Newport "rebirth" the Ellington Orchestra played two concerts for the Shakespearean Festival in Stratford,
Ontario, along with Dave Brubeck, the Modern Jazz Quartet, and the
Art Tatum Trio. According to David Hajdu's detailed account the festival had hoped for a major new work from Ellington, but not surprisingly he arrived with the same program he had played at Newport. After
the Stratford performances two members of the festival staff, Louis
Applebaum and Barbara Reed, asked Ellington to compose something
unusual and Shakespearean for Stratford. Ellington proposed the suite
form, and, according to Hajdu, "Strayhorn took it on excitedly, glow-
ing to his friends about having an Ellington Orchestra project geared especially to him." Strayhorn's knowledge of the Bard had already earned
him the nickname "Shakespeare."[26]

Both Ellington and Strayhorn brushed up their Shakespeare (as Cole
Porter had recently advised in *Kiss Me, Kate*), but their calendar was
full of other projects, particularly *A Drum Is a Woman*, a fanciful jazz
history conceived for television. Two of Strayhorn's movements, "The
Star-Crossed Lovers" and "Half the Fun," were retitled versions of
preexisting songs ("Pretty Girl" and "Lately"). Ellington's "Circle of
Fourths" had already been recorded (on January 29, 1957) without
any Shakespearean connection. Ellington composed "Sonnet to Hank
Cinq" between sets at Birdland, where the band played from April 18 to
May 1. The band recorded the new suite for Columbia in three sessions
before the Town Hall premiere on Sunday, April 28:

April 15: "Sonnet for Caesar," "Sonnet in Search of a Moor,"
"Madness in Great Ones," "Sonnet for Sister Kate"

April 24: "Up and Down, Up and Down," "Such Sweet Thunder,"
"Lady Mac"

May 3: "The Star-Crossed Lovers," "Madness in Great Ones," "Sonnet to Hank Cinq," "The Telecasters," "Circle of Fourths," "Half the Fun"

According to the producer, Irving Townsend, many of the movements were recorded under temporary titles ("Cleo," "Ham," "Puck"); Townsend claimed that he had found the title "Such Sweet Thunder" in *Bartlett's Quotations*.[27] Although the original recording credited the music to Ellington and Strayhorn, it did not make the authorship of individual movements clear. According to Walter van de Leur, only the title track was cowritten, and even that one only slightly; he attributes three bars (73–75) to Strayhorn. "Up and Down, Up and Down" was entirely Strayhorn's work, as were "The Star-Crossed Lovers" and "Half the Fun." Van de Leur credits Ellington with the remaining eight movements, but material in the Ellington Archive indicates that Clark Terry's extended solo in "Lady Mac" may also have been written by Strayhorn. Ellington and Strayhorn did not hear the entire suite in order until the Town Hall performance.

Here are the movements with the Shakespearean parallels as given on the original liner notes:

1. "Such Sweet Thunder" (*Othello*, though the words come from *A Midsummer Night's Dream*)
2. "Sonnet for Caesar" (*Julius Caesar*)
3. "Sonnet to Hank Cinq" (*Henry V*)
4. "Lady Mac" (*Macbeth*)
5. "Sonnet in Search of a Moor" (*Othello* again, but note the pun in the title)
6. "The Telecasters" (the Witches from *Macbeth* meet Iago from *Othello*)
7. "Up and Down, Up and Down (I Will Lead Them Up and Down)," originally titled "Puck" (*A Midsummer Night's Dream*)
8. "Sonnet for Sister Kate" (*The Taming of the Shrew*)
9. "The Star-Crossed Lovers" (*Romeo and Juliet*)
10. "Madness in Great Ones" (*Hamlet*; written comments in some of the parts imply that the band assumed that the piece was also a portrait of trumpeter Cat Anderson)
11. "Half the Fun" (*Antony and Cleopatra*)

12. "Circle of Fourths" (the four Shakespearean genres: tragedy, comedy, history, and sonnet)

However rushed its composition may have been, *Such Sweet Thunder* emerged as a richly varied yet coherent statement, at once a concept album and a showcase for the band.[28] The suite astutely balanced genres and grooves. There are two contrasting solos for Hodges, three swinging numbers, a rockabilly waltz, three avant-garde compositions, and four sonnets, poems without words that follow the meter and structure of the Shakespearean sonnet: fourteen lines of ten syllables. (Critics have speculated without agreement about what particular sonnets Ellington might have had in mind.) The self-imposed rigor of these musical sonnets suggests an analogy to the strict formal constraints of the blues. The suite also gave virtually every member of the band a star turn. The soloists, by track, were

1. Ray Nance, trumpet; John Sanders, trombone;

2. Jimmy Hamilton, clarinet (in some of the parts this movement is titled "Hamson," meaning "Hamilton sonnet");

3. Britt Woodman, trombone;

4. Russell Procope, alto sax; Clark Terry, flügelhorn;

5. Jimmy Woode, bass;

6. Harry Carney, baritone sax;

7. A concerto grosso : Jimmy Hamilton, clarinet; Ray Nance, violin; Russell Procope, alto sax; Paul Gonsalves, tenor sax; Johnny Hodges, alto sax; John Sanders, trombone; and, explicitly as Puck, Clark Terry;

8. Quentin Jackson, trombone (he is often referred to in the score and parts by his nickname, "Butter");

9. Johnny Hodges, alto sax (Hodges's parts are often labeled "Rab," short for his nickname, "Rabbit");

10. Cat Anderson, trumpet;

11. Johnny Hodges, alto sax;

12. Paul Gonsalves, tenor sax.

Ellington's approach to Shakespeare was radically revisionist. Irving Townsend wrote that Ellington's summaries of the plays and characters were unlike any he had heard before.[29] The misreadings were deliberate;

just as Papp was doing at Shakespeare in the Park, Ellington and Strayhorn presented a contemporary Shakespeare with no Elizabethan trappings. They made their stance clear in the very first bar when the trombones announce Othello's presence with a habanera-rock groove much closer to Fats Domino than John Dowland. Except for "The Star-Crossed Lovers," a typical Hodges ballad, and "Circle of Fourths," a romp based on the harmonic changes of "How High the Moon," the movements were innovative even in relation to the Ellington and Strayhorn oeuvres. Strayhorn's "Up and Down, Up and Down" and Ellington's "Madness in Great Ones" pushed jazz far beyond its usual forms and harmonies, right to the brink of free jazz.

The music of the suite and Ellington's sparse comments about it nevertheless implied a bold political statement, a demonstration, by way of the Bard, of black power, a phrase first used in 1954 as the title of Richard Wright's nonfiction book about the emergence of Africa from colonialism. By composing a Shakespearean work for a Canadian festival Ellington was placing questions of black identity outside American history and geography, taking his case to the court of world opinion. The suite equated the idiom of jazz with the language of Shakespeare through the syllable-to-syllable equivalence of the four sonnets, and through an overarching theme of music as seductive communication in the stories Othello tells Desdemona or the trumpeted version of Puck's "Lord, what fools these mortals be." (Through some glitch, Clark Terry's statement does not appear on the remastered release of the recording.) The suite also declared its equal standing with the Shakespearean canon by favoring composition over improvisation. Like a Shakespeare play, or like a symphony, *Such Sweet Thunder* is a text to be performed *come scritto*. Ellington made the comparison explicit in his program note for the Stratford premiere: "Anyone who listens to a beautifully performed symphony for the first time gains something from it. The next time he hears it, he gains more; when he hears the symphony for the hundredth time, he is benefited to the hundredth power. So it is with Shakespeare. The spectator can't get it all the first time; repeated viewings multiply the satisfaction. There is a perfect parallel with jazz, where repeated listening makes for enjoyment."[30]

Once they had leveled the playing field with the Bard (and Beethoven), Ellington and Strayhorn foregrounded black sexuality in the characters of Othello and Cleopatra, but also in Lady Macbeth, Henry V (alias Hank Cinq), "Sister" Kate, Puck, and Hamlet, all of whom speak in the language of the blues. The title track and "Half the Fun" portray cross-race relationships, but not as a pas de deux. The music speaks to the white Other, not for it. The two Othello movements address Desdemona but do not represent her except as the implied listener; the title "Half the Fun" and Strayhorn's exotically static music indicate that the movement portrays Cleopatra but not Antony. The two movements share a habanera rhythm, which, thanks to *Carmen,* serves as a musical metaphor for difference and sexuality, but Ellington and Strayhorn have reversed the usual hierarchy of difference, reversing roles, with two African characters telling their stories to silent, passive European partners. Black speaking to white, Africa speaking to Europe, jazz speaking to Shakespeare, the music presents half of the story—the half we haven't heard before.

All but three of the movements are monologues, soliloquies. "The Star-Crossed Lovers," of course, gives us a dialogue, though with casting that reminds us that Shakespeare's company, like the Ellington band, was all-male; in the liner notes Ellington says that Hodges's alto sax is Juliet and Gonsalves's tenor is Romeo (though I don't hear this in the music). "Up and Down, Up and Down" superimposes Puck's monologue on a babbling counterpoint of romantic confusion. The third exception to the rule, "The Telecasters," may be an in-joke. Ellington said that the movement combined characters from two plays, the witches from *Macbeth* and Iago, portrayed by a trombone trio and Harry Carney, respectively. The witches, however, sound more like passing car horns, and Iago's tune is surprisingly lacking in any hint of malevolence, though his phrases are separated by suggestive silences. In addition to anchoring the band's sound with his baritone sax, Carney served as Ellington's driver; the rest of the band took the bus. I hear the movement as a double portrait of Ellington (Othello) and Carney (Iago) in transit between gigs, Carney at the wheel, Ellington in the passenger seat, composing in silence.[31]

Such Sweet Thunder demands close scrutiny. Let's examine it movement by movement.

"Such Sweet Thunder"

A blues in a Phrygian-tinted G, the title track wavers between minor and major. There are six choruses with a four-bar shout chorus (by Strayhorn) inserted between choruses three and four:

Chorus 1: The bass instruments lay down an altered habanera rhythm spiked by backbeats on the drums and R&B-style triplets on the piano. In the even-numbered bars the long-short rhythm of the habanera reverses to short-long, prolonging the already provocative A♭s.

Chorus 2: The three muted trumpets superimpose a wa-wa-ed, chromatic chord-melody on a restatement of Chorus 1.

Chorus 3: Saxes enter in a riff chorus in dissonant five-note harmonies over a walking bass.

Chorus 4: A call-and-response alternation of saxes and improvised trumpet solo by Nance. In the last two bars the trombones reprise the opening habanera figure.

Shout insert: Four bars tutti, *fortissimo*. (This may have been intended by Strayhorn as a conclusion, then inserted as a climactic interlude instead.)

Chorus 5: A composed legato trombone solo played against a swung version of the habanera rhythm in the saxes, all *pianissimo*. The last two bars quietly reprise the habanera idea, harmonized and played by the reeds.

Chorus 6: Repeat of Chorus 2, plus a fatal low F on the piano.

Othello is a play about race ("an old black ram is tupping your white ewe") and about being and seeming. Othello seals his doom early by believing in the self-evident facts of his existence: "My parts, my title and my perfect soul, / Shall manifest me rightly." Iago acts out the opposite principle: "I am not what I am." Othello's tragic pride stems from a failure to understand that his noble character is as much a product of eloquence as is Iago's malignant fabrications; Othello's military and amatory success depends on the power of his discourse. When he says "Rude am I in my speech," he is deploying a classical tool of rhetoric, *humilitas*. Unlike Oedipus, Othello also falls because of racism. To the Venetians he is a hero one moment and a "black ram" the next. As a minority of one, he is particularly vulnerable to Iago, his white "manager"; they interlock in a fatal codependence:

Iago: I humbly do beseech you of your pardon,
For too much loving you.

Othello: I am bound to thee forever.

Ellington's career depended on his own silken eloquence and on services rendered by a number of rough Iagos, but "Such Sweet Thunder" tells a different tale, a swerve signaled, as Brent Hayes Edwards points out, by the title, which links the music "with an entirely different moment from a different play."[32] Tragedy only enters with the last note, a concise fate-motive. The music inverts the play's poisonous hatred and instead limns Othello's "constant, noble, loving nature," which inspires Desdemona's fierce love ("That I did love the Moor, to live with him,/My downright violence, and score of fortunes,/May trumpet to the world") and Iago's equally fierce strangelove.

Shakespeare portrayed Othello in five acts; Ellington needed just six twelve-bar blues choruses. Each chorus gives us a significant part of the picture. Chorus one figures Othello's proud stride exotic background. Previsioning Isaac Hayes's funk groove for "Shaft," Othello's rhythmic theme adds a kick of swagger to the usual habanera rhythm, but its connotations, like those of the other "topics" that Ellington employs, should not be reduced to a caption. Besides refashioning Othello in the image of Joe Louis or Sugar Ray Robinson, the rhythm reminds us of the meter of Shakespearean verse, thereby equating the temporal structures of the two art forms. Chorus two, with its echoes of jungle music, reveals the African inflections of Othello's voice with alternating G major and g minor chords. The chorus sounds the trumpets that Desdemona, defying difference, will echo in her proclamation of love. The sudden change of gait (from gutbucket habanera to walking bass) and timbre (from brass to reeds) in chorus three moves us from the public theater of the Venetian council chamber (act 1, scene 3) toward the private bedchamber (act 5, scene 2), a scenic jump cut that compresses the story almost as compactly as the three words "such sweet thunder." The music now reveals the man behind the public mask. Much as Ellington was "Duke" to the public, "Edward" to friends and family, Othello's thunderous and sweet aspects may be the two sides of celebrity, or they may also refer to W. E. B. DuBois's famous definition of African American double consciousness, or "twoness—an American, a Negro; two souls, two thoughts, two unreconciled strivings." Othello's strivings, though interrupted by the inserted shout phrase, do not sound disjunct. Ellington may be questioning DuBois's formulation, or affirming it by portraying an integral non–American African.

The central choruses present two aspects of Othello's private side, divided by a brief flare-up. Perhaps Ray Nance's seductive talking blues solo in chorus four is the Ellington/Othello known to a few intimates, while the almost whispered trombone solo of chorus five is the man known only to himself. Chorus six places the hero back on stage: The Moor of Venice, the Duke of Ellington.

"Sonnet for Caesar"

The first of the four sonnets is also the furthest from usual notions of jazz; its groove suggests a military dirge, a suggestion evocatively filled out by Sam Woodyard's percussion. Sketches indicate that Ellington first composed a tentative melody that established the rules for translating the sonnet form into music; each melodic phrase of two bars contains ten notes, the equivalent of the syllables in a line of iambic pentameter. The structure also mirrors the sonnet form:

> Introduction: Four bars of piano, four bars of trombone chorale with drums.

> Octave (two quatrains): Two statements of an eight-bar harmonic structure (articulated by chords in the trombones). The tonality hovers somewhere between D♭ Lydian and B♭ Dorian over a drone on B♭ and F throughout. The clarinet melody is different in each quatrain, but the saxophones punctuate the ending of each line with a three-note "comma."

> Sextet (one quatrain and one couplet): In the first eight bars the texture thins to two lines (clarinet and sax), with sparse entries of the bass offering only a hint of harmonic framework. The trombones return for the couplet, suggesting at first a harmony of e♭ minor. The second line of the couplet does not "rhyme" with the first but offers a surprising, discomforting contrast. The first couplet phrase is the melodic peak and harmonically the most conventionally structured progression of the work, but the second phrase clouds the certainty of the first with melodic chromaticism. The final cadence on a D♭ chord in second inversion leaves us hanging.

Who is Caesar? He certainly would not be mistaken here for Othello. Ellington assigned the melody to his most classical-sounding player; Hamilton bends pitches to a blues inflection only once in the movement. The saxophones and trombones similarly play it straight. Commentators have guessed that Ellington was alluding either to the warning about the Ides of March or Mark Antony's oration, but the movement is neither ominous nor rabble-rousing. The music speaks to Caesar in a stately, proper language, only slightly tinged by the vernacular. Perhaps it is addressed to a president rather than an emperor. Townsend described the piece as "imperial," a term also suited to much of the architecture of Washington, D.C. As of April 1957 President Dwight Eisenhower's support for civil rights was lukewarm and ambiguous, but the Republican Party was still the party of Lincoln. In his 1957 State of the Union address Eisenhower urged passage of a bill that would create a civil rights commission and strengthen the enforcement of voting rights. Eisenhower, however, was powerless to overcome the opposition of Southern Democrats in Congress. A much watered-down bill passed only on September 9, 1957, a week after Governor Faubus ordered the National Guard to block the integration of Central High School in Little Rock, Arkansas. In this context we might hear the calm, serious demeanor of "Sonnet for Caesar" as a legal brief addressed to the highest authority in the land, with no certain outcome.

"Sonnet to Hank Cinq"

Heard after "Sonnet for Caesar" this movement sounds like its negative image, an impetuous sonnet in black. The clarinet filigree of the introduction unleashes Jimmy Hamilton's wild and crazy side. The structure balances sonnet form against blues (in A♭):

Intro

Quatrain: Trombonist Britt Woodman plays four blustering ten-note phrases. The rhythm mimics the short-long alternations of iambic meter as a cross-rhythm to the walking pulse in the bass. The four lines correspond to the first two lines of a blues stanza. The expected third blues line, completing the thought, goes unspoken over a two-bar turnaround in double time.

Quatrain: Two lines for the solo trombone (eleven and ten notes, respectively) over the double-time groove, repeated by the section.

Quatrain: Repeat of the first quatrain in the original tempo.

Couplet: An out-of-time cadenza for Woodman, in two ten-note phrases, followed by a two-note "fatal" cadence.

Perhaps this sonnet is meant to show Caesar how a real leader would act, or to portray a less polite strategy for protest. Ellington wrote that "the changes in tempo have to do with the changes of pace and the map as a result of wars." The two tempos conflate the two Hanks, the riotous Prince Hal and the slightly more measured Henry V. As he did in "Such Sweet Thunder," Ellington upends Shakespeare's dramatic oppositions. Henry, Hal, and Hank are one and the same.

"Lady Mac"

Structure: A (twenty bars), A′, A″, X (eight bars), B (sixteen bars) A‴, B′, X, A‴′.

Listeners who might not have noticed Ellington's subversions get a wake-up call with this spiky gospel-inflected waltz in F, a weird sister to Kay Ballard's 1955 hit "Rock and Roll Waltz" and Brubeck's "It's a Raggy Waltz" of 1961. Ellington coyly explained the raucous mood by explaining that though Lady Macbeth "was a lady of noble birth, we suspect there was a little ragtime in her soul." The portrait is more complicated than it appears to be at first. The first phrase (A), played by piano and repeated by saxes, is twenty bars long, stretched by a menacing descent in the bass line under a two-beat cross-rhythm in the melody. When the brass enter for a third statement of the phrase the violence escalates and is then developed in a new eight-bar riff theme (X). Russell Procope defuses the tension in a sweet-toned sixteen-bar solo that acts formally like a bridge (B). Clark Terry seems to take up where Procope leaves off, but his solo covers both the twenty-bar phrase structure of A and sixteen bars of B and takes the music into a post-bop sound world far from its raggy roots. X returns followed by the most clangorous statement of A—and another fate motive.

Ellington's refashioning of Shakespeare's prime villainess as a spunky sister takes black power over a sexual divide. Without pushing things too far, I might suggest that the sequence from Procope's sax to Terry's flügelhorn recalls Lady Macbeth's moment of gender-bending:

> Come, you spirits
> That tend on mortal thoughts, unsex me here,
> And fill me from the crown to the toe top-full
> Of direst cruelty! make thick my blood;
> Stop up the access and passage to remorse,
> That no compunctious visitings of nature
> Shake my fell purpose, nor keep peace between
> The effect and it! Come to my woman's breasts,
> And take my milk for gall, you murdering ministers,
> Wherever in your sightless substances
> You wait on nature's mischief!

If we recall this reference "Lady Mac" further intensifies the political stance of the two previous sonnets.

"Sonnet in Search of a Moor"

Ellington pointed out the pun in the title (a Moor = *amour*). The sonnet returns to the g minor tonality of "Such Sweet Thunder" but strips it of its modal exoticism. Ellington sets the mood with a tinkling piano solo. The sonnet proper is a plucked bass solo (Jimmy Woode) accompanied by three clarinets (Hamilton, Procope, Carney). It follows the same rules as the previous sonnets but feels more like a lightly swung pop tune:

> Octet: Eight ten-note lines
>
> Quatrain: Four ten-note lines, beginning like a restatement of the octet
>
> Couplet: A ten-note line followed by a nine-note line; the piano adds the missing note

The music shows Ellington or Othello relaxing at home and far less complicated or exotic or scary or Other than you might have expected.

"The Telecasters"

Ellington said that this movement brought together the three witches from Macbeth with Iago, but see above (p. 175) for my quite different reading. The mood and texture relate closely to the previous movement; again a low melody instrument plays against a trio (trombones here). The form also resembles a pop tune: Intro, A (eight bars), A, A (tutti), B (twelve bars), A, outro.

"Up and Down, Up and Down (I Will Lead Them Up and Down)"

> Puck: Up and down, up and down
> I will lead them up and down.
> I am fear'd in field and town.
> Goblin, lead them up and down.
> (*A Midsummer Night's Dream,* Act III, Scene II)

This movement was Strayhorn's one new contribution to the suite. It is probably the most complicated piece he ever wrote,[33] and it may also be the greatest musical response to *A Midsummer Night's Dream* since Mendelssohn. In the play Puck, attempting to do the bidding of his master, Oberon, creates two mismatched couples, Helena and Lysander and Titania and Bottom (the weaver given the head of an ass by Puck's spell), and disrupts a third, Hermia and Demetrius, then undoes the damage by leading them all "up and down." Instead of telling the story, Strayhorn's music, like Mendelssohn's, captures the mood of giddy moonlit confusion. Strayhorn divided the band into "characters" portrayed by groups of instruments. There are three instrumental couples: Jimmy Hamilton on clarinet and Ray Nance on violin; Russell Procope on alto and Paul Gonsalves on tenor; and Johnny Hodges on alto and John Sanders on valve trombone. There are also a reed trio (clarinet, alto, tenor) and a mostly brass quintet (two trumpets, two trombones, baritone sax—perhaps representing the mechanicals). The bass and drums keep things moving throughout; the pianist just listens. The only character we can recognize consistently is Puck, impersonated by Clark Terry, who increasingly takes charge of the action as the piece unfolds and concludes the music by "speaking" the line "Lord, what fools these mortals be." Throughout the piece Puck's style is freer and bluesier than the other characters.

Because of its contrapuntal design "Up and Down" feels more like a baroque concerto grosso than a typical jazz chart. Contrapuntal sections alternate a ritornello in the form of an eight-bar straight-ahead jazz tune in F. The layout is as follows:

Bars 1–8: Main subject first played by clarinet, alto, and tenor, then by clarinet and violin in thirds over tonic (C) pedal in bass.

Bars 9–10 (letter A in score): Interjection by "rude" mechanicals (playing sophisticated harmony).

Bars 11–13: Double canon on main subject over dominant pedal in bass: clarinet and violin lead, alto and tenor follow down an octave one bar later; alto and trombone enter a bar later playing the inversion.

Bars 14–15: Second brass interjection.

Bars 16–24: Contrapuntal development of three couples over ostinato riffs in brass and bass; harmony wavers between A♭ and G dominant thirteenths. Each couple now plays inverted (mirror) imitations rather than parallel thirds. At bar 24 the three couples play the "rude" figure, perhaps indicating even greater confusion.

Bars 25–29 (letter B in score): Double contrary motion between couples.

Bars 30–33: Puck leaps in, brings the couples together, and clarifies the harmony (C7).

Bars 34–41 (letter C in score): Eight-bar call-and-response tune in F played twice (abab). In the first four bars the trumpet follows, and in the last four it takes the lead. This is the first time in the piece where the bass articulates a clear chord progression.

Bars 42–53 (letter D in score): Call-and-response dialogue between each couple and ad lib trumpet, over C pedal in bass, two bars for each call-and-response.

Bars 54–61 (letter E in score): Contrapuntal *imbroglio* over a dominant pedal (G7) ostinato by the mechanicals. The sax and trombone couple, trombone now muted, play a new chromatic choralelike figure (Oberon?).

Bars 62–65: Puck and mechanicals recall the tune.

Bars 66–75 (letter F in score): Call-and-response between Puck and couples who now appear to imitate his calls.

Bars 76–81: Second *imbroglio* over ii–V alternation in bass. Clarinet and alto bring back mirror figure from bar 17; alto and mute trombone play the menacing "Oberon" theme; clarinet and violin play the squeaky riff from bar 7; Puck tries to reassert leadership with a rising diminished seventh arpeggio.

Bars 82–93 (letter G in score): Return of F major tune beginning with its second four-bar phrase then restating the original eight-bar form (bab) with Puck leading (reverse of first time).

Bars 94–101 (letter H in score): Recap of bars 1–8 (minus tenor sax in first four bars).

Bars 102–3: Final cadence, like a compressed version of the "rude figure." Above the sustained F major 7 (or C major over F major) the trumpet "plays the quotation."

The outline shows, I hope, how carefully Strayhorn shaped the music as a concerto for Puck, and why it looms much larger than its actual temporal dimension of just over three minutes. Strayhorn may well have thought of the piece as a self-portrait, with Ellington off in the background as Oberon. We can read the implications in several different ways. Strayhorn played a Puck-like role in relation to Ellington's music, which he was often handed in a state of disorder and asked to complete (as he did here with "Such Sweet Thunder"). As David Hajdu writes, Strayhorn's gift for order complemented Ellington's personality: "Ellington resisted completion. . . . 'As long as something is unfinished,' Ellington said, 'there's always that little feeling of insecurity, and a feeling of insecurity is absolutely necessary unless you're so rich it doesn't matter.' With Strayhorn on hand, Ellington could keep that insecurity and gain the security of knowing that something he dropped could now not only be finished but possibly improved."[34]

The confused couples and the band of mechanicals may both portray the band itself; some of its members barely spoke to each other for years, and many lived rough lives that comported oddly with their musical sophistication. Admired by all, Strayhorn may have served as a peacemaker, while Ellington preferred just to look the other way. Because Strayhorn often did not tour with the band but remained in New York he was in some way a breed apart, above the fray and the frayed nerves of constant touring. Strayhorn was also a breed apart sexually, as the band knew and accepted, and Ellington supported unconditionally. As George Greenlee, Strayhorn's close friend, told David Hajdu, "Duke didn't question his manliness." Puck's quotation can be heard as a gay comment on the follies of the straight world, a reversal of hierarchies that perfectly matches the overturning of values already seen in "Such Sweet Thunder" and "Lady Mac."

"Sonnet for Sister Kate"

Quentin "Butter" Jackson "speaks" the final sonnet on his muted trombone accompanied by a sax trio and rolled cymbals. The title conflates Shakespeare's shrewish Katherine with the shimmying Sister Kate of A.J. Piron's song, which Ellington had echoed in "East St. Louis Toodle-Oo." If Lady Macbeth had some ragtime in her, Kate speaks with a deep knowledge of the blues. Whatever words we may imagine for this sonnet, they are probably not those of Katherine's apology, which Cole Porter had set to music in *Kiss Me, Kate:*

> I am ashamed the women are so simple
> To offer war where they should kneel for peace,
> Or seek to rule, supremacy, and sway
> When they are bound to serve, love and obey.

Ellington's sketch explicitly divides the piece into fourteen lines:

Introduction: Two bare phrases, hazily recalling the opening of "Such Sweet Thunder" on the piano, each with ten notes.

Octave: Eight ten- or eleven-note phrases over a choralelike harmonization wavering between C major and a minor in the saxes. The end of the octave is indicated by a repeated melodic couplet.

Quatrain: Four phrases in d minor.

Couplet: The highest note and the sassiest sound. Cadence (with four saxes) on an added sixth chord combining C major and a minor.

Outro: Piano.

The music sounds neither shrewish nor apologetic but more like an elegy for Joe Nanton, who made the "talking trombone" a signature sound for the band, and in particular the voice of its African heritage. In the eleventh phrase Jackson plays a figure with an echo of "Swing Low, Sweet Chariot" that Nanton played, in the same key, in *Black, Brown and Beige*.[35]

"The Star-Crossed Lovers"

According to David Hajdu, Ellington suggested that Strayhorn base his Romeo and Juliet number on his song "Pretty Girl," which Johnny Hodges had recorded a year earlier. Strayhorn was less than amused when he found himself sharing credit with Ellington in the published sheet music,[36] though on the recording Ellington framed Strayhorn's song with two passionate cadenzas. The song is an AABA' in D♭; on the recording it is played twice, with Gonsalves playing the melody on AA and Hodges returning for the rest. A brief chromatic interlude links the two iterations; the second statement is completely rescored with a prominent role for Carney in the bridge. The sensitively plush scoring throughout shows how Strayhorn served as a model for Gil Evans. The piece also exemplifies Strayhorn's harmonic and melodic finesse. It begins on a IV major 7 chord rather than the tonic, saving a more traditional harmonization for the last phrase. The harmony toys throughout with G♮, the raised fourth degree. Strayhorn also creates his personal version of the blue note by raising a pitch rather than lowering it; the melody moves to A♮ and D♮ as if it were tightening up the pitches of the D♭ scale to a greater intensity. Hodges explores every corner of the tune's writhing dissonances.

"Madness in Great Ones"

In a blindfold test you might guess that this was a Thelonious Monk tune arranged by Dizzy Gillespie (or perhaps Bob Graettinger). It portrays Hamlet as the father of the jazz avant-garde, and perhaps was written to remind the jazz world that Ellington was still the king of the cats. The piece sounds so unhinged that it is surprising to see how precisely Ellington sketched it. Contrasted with "Up and Down" it illustrates Ellington's collagelike approach to composition as opposed to Strayhorn's finely woven method. "Madness" seems to follow no logic but its own north by northwest lunacy. Ellington's sketch shows a sequence of carefully composed phrases that seem to get shuffled and reshuffled, with letter names and arrows added later on to indicate the final order of events. As in "Up and Down" a single conventional jazz phrase, played twice, serves to rein in the chaos, though here the chaos, Cat Anderson's manic raving, wins out.

"Half the Fun"

Although it is the penultimate movement of the suite, "Half the Fun" forms a bookend with "Such Sweet Thunder," a portrait of Cleopatra (minus Antony) as counterpart to Othello. The double relation is shown by rhythmic similarity, a habanera slowed down to the tempo of a beguine, and harmonic polarity, an exoticized D♭ to balance the opening movement's modal G.

Like "Star-Crossed Lovers," "Half the Fun" sprang from an older Strayhorn number, "Lately," and somehow gained a collaborative credit.[37] "Half the Fun" is the third avant-garde piece of the set; it predicts modal jazz in general and *The Far East Suite* in particular. There are no chord changes. The outer sections rest on a constant ostinato in D♭ (with a flatted sixth: D♭, A, A♭, G♭); the middle section just moves the ostinato up a fourth to G♭. The harmony, texture, and mood recall Debussy's Iberian pieces, especially "La Puerta del Vino" from the second book of preludes. In the central section we hear another side of Johnny Hodges, not far from free jazz; and in the transition back to the main section Strayhorn presents a chain of dissonant six-note chords heard beneath an inverted D♭ pedal. The star of the movement, though, is Sam Woodyard, who covers the canvas in evocations of ancient evenings.

"Circle of Fourths"

Ellington reached into his own book for this boppish romp, which was said to honor the four Shakespearean genres: tragedy, history, comedy, and sonnets. After "Half the Fun" it pulls us smartly out of the East and out of the Bard and back to Manhattan, back to business. It is the only movement of the suite that sounds like a head chart; it feels like a company bow. Ellington launches the piece with a four-bar, eleven-note motto and then it takes off. The piece, a showcase for Paul Gonsalves, has two structural components. The first is a twenty-four-bar harmonic progression around the circle of fourths, similar to the changes of "How High the Moon," by Morgan Lewis. The progression is: C–F7–B♭7–E♭7–A♭7–D♭7–B7–E9–A7–D7–d7–G7. The second element is an eight-bar blues-tinged call-and-response idea built on the opening motto.

In retrospect this section on *Such Sweet Thunder* might have appeared in a chapter on politics rather than one on love, but in African American music, as in African American literature, the two subjects are inseparable. In the writings of Richard Wright, Ralph Ellison, Malcolm X, James Baldwin, and Alice Walker the freedom to love demands a reclamation of manhood and womanhood. In *Such Sweet Thunder* Ellington and Strayhorn replaced the degraded images of Porgy and Bess with regal portraits of Othello and Cleopatra. In these figures sexuality is both public and private, both powerful and tender.

SECRET LOVE: THE LISTENER AS VOYEUR

Music is miraculous in that one can say everything in such a way that
those in the know can understand it all, and yet one's own secrets,
those which one will not even admit to oneself, remain undivulged.
—Arnold Schoenberg

In 1977 composer and theorist George Perle rocked the staid world of musicology with a document that was one part Rosetta stone, one part *National Enquirer.* He had tracked down a copy of the score of Alban Berg's *Lyric Suite* annotated in the composer's hand. The published score already contained some tantalizing clues, including musical quotations from the *Lyric Symphony* of Alexander von Zemlinsky (to whom the work was dedicated) and the famous opening of Wagner's *Tristan und Isolde,* as well numerical oddities; both the metronome markings and the number of bars in each movement were derived from the numbers twenty-three and ten. The long-hidden annotations explained the meanings of pitches, themes, and even bar numbers and revealed that the final movement was based on a poem by Baudelaire, "De profundis clamavi"—not vaguely, but word for word, syllable for syllable, implying the need for an additional performer, a singer, following the precedent of Schoenberg's Quartet no. 2. The most important pitches of the work, H (B in German) F, A, and B (B♭ in German) were a cryptogram for Hanna Fuchs and Alban Berg. Berg likewise associated the numbers ten and twenty-three with these two masked characters. Perle found the score in the possession of Dorothea Robettin, daughter of Herbert and Hanna Fuchs-Robettin, a wealthy and cultured couple with whom Berg stayed in May 1925 when his *Three Fragments from Wozzeck* was first performed in Prague, conducted by Alexander Zemlinsky. Berg returned chez Fuchs in November 1925 en route to the Berlin premiere of *Wozzeck,* by which time he felt the need to respond to his wife's anxieties about his relations with Frau Fuchs, a.k.a. Mopinka: "(. . . may I die of distemper if I ever sin against faithfulness!). Faithfulness towards you, and also towards myself, Music, Schoenberg (and *he* makes this really hard for one) even towards Trahütten."[38]

Despite Berg's reassurances, rumors of the affair circulated in Vienna, even though the annotated score remained hidden; shortly after Berg's death in 1935, his student T. W. Adorno advised his widow "not to worry about the affair with Hanna since Berg 'didn't write the *Lyric Suite* because he fell in love with Hanna Fuchs but fell in love with Hanna Fuchs in order to write the *Lyric Suite.*'"[39] Adorno was recycling an old argument about the relation of Wagner's affair with Mathilde Wesendonck to the composition of *Tristan und Isolde,* but he may have been right.[40]

I was present when Perle revealed his discovery at a musicological meeting in New York. He looked like the cat that had swallowed the cream and the room crackled with the sense of a historic moment. A few days later the final movement was performed for the first time with voice, and many listeners felt they were finally hearing the work as Berg intended. Today I'm not so sure. Perle had decoded the piece by assuming the truth-value of Berg's annotations, but a man who could lie to his wife with the ease demonstrated in Berg's letter might just as easily deceive his mistress, or posterity. Taken on its own, the annotated score might have been just an over-the-top thank-you note to a gracious hostess with whom Berg had shared perhaps no more than some kind of moment. (Or perhaps Berg, an overnight celebrity, attracted cultured groupies all over Europe.) Berg scholars, moreover, had resented Helene Berg's protective guardianship over her husband's papers and her longstanding refusal to allow for the completion of his opera *Lulu*. Perle's paper explained Frau Berg's diffidence all too conveniently; his mean-spirited portrait of Frau Berg in the third part of the *Lyric Suite* article verges on libel.

As for the composer's intentions, Perle gave the impression that the annotated copy represented the real piece ("My own belief is that the composer would not have been opposed to a vocal performance of the finale"), even though Berg never showed it to anyone except Hanna Fuchs-Robettin. Had he really wanted it performed at some future time, when it would not embarrass either Mrs. Berg or Mrs. Fuchs, he could have sent a copy to his good friend Alma Schindler Mahler Gropius Werfel, who was married to Hanna's brother and certainly would have understood any romantic situation that might have existed. On the fine recording of the vocal version of the finale by Dawn Upshaw and the Kronos Quartet, the reconstructed voice line often sounds awkward in its tessitura and in its relation to the accompaniment. Most tellingly, the text ("Not even brook and tree, nor field nor flock") and vocal line written above the score's quotation of the opening of Tristan do not clarify or even exploit the allusion but just cover it over. The annotated score may be less an urtext than a billet-doux.

Perle's revelation of the secret program marked a turning point in the hermeneutics of twentieth-century music from modernist formalism to postmodernist semiotics. Perhaps as an unforeseen consequence Perle revived long-repressed habits of programmatic reading, which modernists had consigned to the middlebrow milieu of musical appreciation. Post Perle, critics and scholars have routinely described the *Lyric Suite* as a cinema verité depiction of the affair between AB and HF, and soon enough scholars found other secret programs in Berg's music, without benefit of the composer's own notes.[41] Programmatic speculation became an even bigger business just a few years later with the publication of *Testimony*, said to be the work of Dmitri Shostakovich, which similarly claimed a decisive role for secret programs in an important and apparently misunderstood oeuvre. Arid formalism had turned into vulgar literalism overnight.

As an alternative to reductive styles of interpretation, and in pursuit of a Sontagian "erotics of listening" I propose that we read the *Lyric*

Suite in relation to a work rarely mentioned in the same breath, or even the same paragraph, "Jeux de vagues," the second movement of Debussy's *La Mer*. Like the *Lyric Suite, La Mer* coincided with tumultuous romantic events. During the three years of its composition, 1903–5, Debussy left his first wife, Rosalie ("Lilly") Texier, whom he had married just four years earlier, and began a relationship with Emma Moyse Bardac. Debussy's biographer, Marcel Dietschy, interpreting the music in Perle's manner, though without the smoking gun, presents *La Mer* as both a premonition and product of the dissolution of one marriage and the creation of another. As Debussy began work on the piece in the summer of 1903, Dietschy writes, "He had no idea that exactly twelve months later the turning-point would be reached. A ground swell would wash away all the past. He was preparing himself for it involuntarily; he hoped for it without knowing it."[42]

Dietschy's *Portrait of Claude Debussy* (originally titled *La Passion de Claude Debussy*, but retitled and toned down in translation) exemplifies *cherchez la femme* musical criticism, perhaps well suited to a composer noted for his wandering eye, but, like Perle's account of the Berg-Fuchs affair, reductive and naïve in its readings. Its account of *La Mer*, though, suggests some intriguing parallels with Berg's *Lyric Suite*. Let me present them schematically:

Composer	Debussy (1862–1916)	Berg (1885–1935)
Work	*La Mer*	*Lyric Suite*
Age at completion	43	41
Opera premiere	*Pelléas*, 1902	*Wozzeck*, 1925
Musical father	Wagner	Schoenberg
Counterinfluences	Mussorgsky, Satie	Mahler, Debussy
Marriage	Rosalie Texier (1899)	Helene Nahowski (1911)
Affair	Emma Bardac (1904)	Hanna Werfel Fuchs-Robettin (1925)
Other women	Marie-Blanche Vasnier	Marie Scheuchl
	Gabrielle Dupont	Alma Mahler Gropius Werfel
	Mary Garden (?)	Several others (see Simms)

| *Pelléas* | Opera | Analysis of Schoenberg's tone poem, 2nd movement, *Kammerkonzert* |

La Mer and the Lyric Suite, both associated with multidimensional life crises, blurred genre distinctions. Debussy called his work "symphonic sketches" rather than a symphony, just as Berg would reject the title of string quartet for its symphonic, developmental implications. Their extrasymphonic titles comport with the extramarital events that surrounded them. The course of these events was similar despite the fact that Debussy traded one wife for another, ruptured his important circle of friends, and transformed his lifestyle from bohemian disorder to anxiously high bourgeois comfort, while Berg apparently never contemplated divorce and was better at keeping up appearances. At age forty, the two composers passed from relative obscurity to worldwide fame with the premieres of their operas. Soon after these successes they both became involved with wealthy and cultured married women— "trophies," we might say today—more suited to their new eminence. Similar patterns can be found in the marital history of Stravinsky and Schoenberg, and, possibly, your accountant. In addition to their physical and personal charms, both Emma Bardac and Hanna Fuchs-Robettin were far more knowledgeable about music than the women they replaced (or, in Hanna's case, supplemented); the very fact that Berg prepared an annotated score for Mrs. Fuchs attests to her musical literacy. (The large literature on the Berg-Fuchs affair is stunningly uninformative about Hanna; mainly we learn that she was ten years younger than Berg and a "flirt.") Both composers celebrated their new alliances, or their newfound celebrity, with works that combined monumental and provisional aspects in novel musical structures.

These are the intriguing factual parallels, but rather than reducing La Mer and the Lyric Suite to reportage, I suggest that we read them as complex symbolic statements about the interplay of the sensual and semiotic both in love and in music. Both works subvert older forms of erotic representation in music. As post-Wagnerian composers, Debussy and Berg knew that their musical depictions of love would have to coalesce in a climactic mimicry of orgasm, following the overwhelming model of the second and third acts of *Tristan*. Climactic moments, or *"Höhepunkte"* as Berg sometimes labeled them in his scores, were both mimetic and formal, imitating the curve of sexual activity and shaping the curve of musical form; the high point marked the sexual union of composer and listener. After *Tristan* the representation of sexual climax became a musical game in which composers could juggle evocative devices to take the music to the brink of good taste—or over it. Standing at the brink myself, I suggest that in pursuit of their formal and expressive secrets we hunt for the Big O in each work.

At its premiere *La Mer* baffled most critics, who judged it either as a defective symphony or an inaccurate weather report; I suspect it was also badly played. Debussy, who, unlike Berg, never discussed the technical or thematic aspects of his own music, gave the three movements the evocative titles "From Dawn to Midday at Sea," "Play of the Waves," and "Dialogue of the Wind and the Sea." Let's dub them more symbolically "Birth and Growth," "Love," and "Death and Rebirth." We can hear *La Mer,* the only work in which Debussy engaged such fundamental existential issues on a symphonic scale, as Debussy's riposte to Strauss's *Also sprach Zarathustra* and as a Bergsonian interpretation of Nietzsche, in which change and transformation replace the illusions of certainty. Just as the sea, for Verlaine, was more beautiful than cathedrals, the inner self, for Bergson, was "a continuous flux, a succession of states, each of which announces that which follows and contains that which precedes it."[43] Bergson's philosophy and Debussy's life experience demanded a formal approach different than the cathedral-like certainties of the symphony. "Jeux de vagues," the centerpiece of *La Mer,* restates Bergsonian metaphysics in erotic terms.

For much of its duration "Jeux de vagues" defies formal analysis; it is even hard to tell where it starts, since the opening phrase seems to continue the harmony ($D\flat = C\sharp$) of the previous movement, and the breathless flute filigree of the opening phrase never returns. Flux itself seems more thematic than any of the musical themes. The tempo changes constantly and the meter, although written mainly in $\frac{3}{4}$, implies $\frac{3}{4}, \frac{3}{8}, \frac{6}{16}$, and $\frac{2}{4}$ simultaneously in many places. Although the movement takes the place of a symphonic scherzo, it does not exhibit the expected tripartite ABA scherzo form. It falls instead into a multisectional form shaped by two orgasmic climaxes on a $B\flat$ dominant ninth chord:

1. Introduction (mm. 1–8)

2. Exposition (mm. 9–88)

3. Compressed restatement (mm. 89–114)

4. Restatement interrupted and then building to first climax (mm. 115–59)

5. Quasi-recapitulation leading to second climax (mm. 160–215)
6. Coda (mm. 216–58)

This scheme is unusual in several ways. The exposition presents a succession of six different thematic ideas without repetition or much sense of tonal direction. Although two shortened restatements seem to give more shape to the music, the irruption of a new theme in the trumpet at measure 124, almost exactly halfway through the piece, alters the mood radically. Introducing a new idea midway through a movement violates classical notions of form, but here it recalls Wagnerian precedents, like the appearance of the sword motive (also in the trumpet) at the end of *Das Rheingold*. There is a Debussyan precedent as well. At measure 131 Debussy follows the trumpet motive, call it X, with a chromatic trilled idea in the clarinet, call it Y. The source for both new motives is the erotically charged action in *Pelléas* act 3, scene 1, where Mélisande leans out a window and lets Pelléas lose himself in her hair. The Y motive bubbles up when she sings "Je suis affreuse ainsi" as she unpins her hair, and it returns as Pelléas asks to kiss her hand. The first part of the X motive appears a moment later when their hands meet. The recollection of these moments in "Jeux de vagues" transforms its free-floating eroticism, splitting it into male and female components *(X and Y)* whose counterpoint sets off a sensual tsunami.

After this first climax the quasi recapitulation begins. Instead of repeating the loose thematic succession of the exposition, however, the music becomes a spiraling waltz, urged on by restatements of the trumpet theme. It achieves its second climax at measure 212 with a superimposition of X and Y. I leave an anatomical assessment of these musical climaxes to the reader, but at least one of them represents a sexual climax. Just as the succession of events in the first half of the movement only hinted at the ecstatic buildup to come, the coda, evoking at once detumescence and afterglow, suddenly takes the music to a new sphere of harmony, melody, and timbre, with the music finally resolving to a Lydian-tinged E major.

The climactic moment in "Jeux de vagues" feels simultaneously like a moment of sensual bliss and as a fleeting revelation—but of what? Here love, or at least sex, is no redemptive *Liebestod*, but, in the words of Cole Porter, just one of those things.

Debussy exhibited an aversion bordering on phobia about discussing his musical technique; Berg's obsession with form, by contrast, resembles the compulsive behavior of one of his operatic characters. His

Byzantine, overdetermined formal schemes pushed the music over the edge of rationality, and nowhere more clearly than in the *Lyric Suite*. The six-movement structure of the quartet is unusual for Berg in its avoidance of odd-number symmetry. In many of Berg's compositions a dramatic central moment serves as a defining point. In the *Lyric Suite*, as in the later Violin Concerto, however, the central event is a silent pause between movements, a sounding silence during which the action of the music up to that point takes a fatal turn.

The erotic action of the *Lyric Suite* appears in its third and fourth movements, marked "Allegro misterioso" (with an episode marked "Trio estatico") and "Adagio appassionato," respectively. The introduction to the score points out the "developmental character" of the Adagio, and most scholars hear it as a development of the Trio estatico since it quotes most of its material. Schoenberg, as Berg noted in his analysis of his teacher's *Kammersinfonie*, had similarly placed the development section after an intervening scherzo. The *Lyric Suite* may be less the "latent opera" that Adorno took it to be (all of Berg's instrumental works have that character) than a fragmented one-movement symphony portraying an off-kilter wild ride from musical certainty to the abyss.

The published score of the *Lyric Suite* exposed, however obliquely, the double nature of its vertiginous downward journey. The movement titles and the overt citations of Alexander von Zemlinsky's *Lyric Symphony* and Wagner's *Tristan und Isolde* pointed to an erotic subtext. The Zemlinsky quote would not be obscure to anyone who has heard his *Lyric Symphony;* sung to the words "Du bist mein Eigen" (You are my only one), it's the most memorable theme. Zemlinsky's seven-movement song-symphony, based on poems by Tagore, traced a love affair from tentative beginnings to explosive passion to dissolution. Berg borrowed its trajectory as well as its love theme.

The alternating presence and absence of the twelve-tone method, also duly noted in the introduction, suggested a musical conflict alongside the erotic one. Only two of the six movements (the first and last) employ the method throughout. The movements and sections with the strongest romantic character (Andante amoroso, Trio estatico, Adagio appassionato, and Presto delirando) were composed "freely." The serial sections of the piece, by contrast, progress from jovial to desolate, becoming ever more menacing as the piece goes on. Berg clearly differentiated the expressive character of free and serial passages throughout the work. As the music unfolds the serial method becomes associated with mechanical, relentless, antihuman sounds. The free/serial conflict meshes with the erotic drama. The alternation of serial and free sections also corresponds to masculine and feminine stereotypes. Through its apparent inconsistency of technique the work pursues a complex dialectic about gender and music, mastery and submission, freedom and order.

Methodologically Berg, who had published an analysis of Schoenberg's tone poem *Pelleas und Melisande* and had quoted its Melisande theme in his own Kammerkonzert, played the treacherous role of Pelleas to his teacher's Golaud. Berg proudly informed Schoenberg of his initial use of serialism in the *Lyric Suite* in his letter of July 13, 1926, but he may have poisoned the pill by pointing out that the series he employed was an all-interval set discovered by his student Fritz Heinrich Klein.

Most of the serial devices derived from Klein occur in the first movement of the suite; its jovial character can be heard as a friendly parody of Schoenberg's newly achieved twelve-tone normality. In its ordered form Klein's series (F–E–C–A–G–D–A♭–D♭ E♭–G♭–B♭–B♮) contained all eleven intervals; both Klein and Berg mistakenly thought it was unique in this aspect. Berg, however, also pointed out its nonordered properties. The pitches of each of its hexachords could be presented as a cycle of fourths (E–A–D–G–C–F/E♭–A♭–D♭–G♭–B) or as a diatonic hexachord (C–D–E–F–G–A/G♭–A♭–B♭–B–D♭–E♭). In unordered form the second hexachord just transposed the first up an augmented fourth; this meant (as AB did not point out to AS) that rows beginning on the pitches B and F were equivalent. These hexachords could mimic the scales of C and G♭ and also produce triadic harmonies like the G♭ major and minor triads heard in bars 5 and 6. The series, properly manipulated, could produce the sounds of tonality, polytonality, or atonality; given the liberties that Berg took—reorderings, selective verticalizations, superimpositions to create triads—virtually any row might produce these effects. No wonder Berg felt jovial.

To mark the lucidity of the work's harmonic technique Berg wrote the movement in the so-called sonatina form, an exposition and recapitulation without the mature gravitas of a development section. Actually, though, the movement is anything but simple. The exposition contains four thematic groups. The recapitulation feels like an inverted, transposed restatement, mirroring the structure of the row, though it is actually a developed variation, different in every detail. According to Willi Reich, Berg exhorted his students to "develop, do not write sequences, and intensify,"[44] just as he had learned from his teacher. Fluently serial and emotionally well adjusted, the movement presents Alban Berg as a very good boy indeed.

If the first movement depicts a happy composer and his new toy, the second, as the annotated score revealed, portrays a happy *Hausfrau mit Kinder*. Stein says the movement is in rondo form, but it sounds like a Mahler scherzo (ABA'CA") with contrasting trios in a variety of dance rhythms, including minuet, furiant, and waltz. (Berg admired Mahler's Sixth Symphony, whose rhythmic complexities supposedly represented his own two children at play.) Reich claims that the movement is based on an altered row (A–G–E♭–A–B♭–F–C–E–F♯–B–C♯–D) in which the pitches A and C have exchanged places. This mutation deprives the row of all its Kleinian properties, making it more like a Schoenberg series. Had Reich written out the row a step higher, another reason for the exchange of pitches would have become obvious; the first four notes would then be B♭–A–F–B, or, in German, B–A–F–H. It is difficult, however, to find much trace of the row in the movement, which more conspicuously uses whole-tone and half-diminished harmonies familiar from Berg's Seven Early Songs, op. 1 Sonata and op. 2 Songs. Perhaps the row is only present as an irritant, because the movement becomes increasingly agitated as it progresses. The final appearance of the main section of the piece twice becomes wildly animated, as if a childish game had gotten out of hand and Mama had to intervene—a forecast of a greater loss of control just around the corner.

We have almost reached the sexy bits, but first let's note how Berg's story differs from "Jeux de vagues." Debussy began with undifferentiated eros, slowly moving toward a sense of form. Berg began with difference, with the opposition of male and female, serial and free, in a presexual state of children's games, a gemütlich middle-class Eden before the fall. Gender differentiation appears in the "immature" forms of sonatina and rondo and in a contrast of highly rational and apparently improvised idioms. It also appears in the most clearly articulated cyclical theme of the quartet, scalar patterns harmonized as three- or four-note chords. We hear their ascending, masculine form at the two structural cadences of the first movement, and the descending, feminine form at the cadences of the three A sections of the second movement.

The onset of the third movement changes everything. Perle reported that the annotated score was prefaced by the date "20.5.25," five days after Berg's arrival chez Fuchs and a day after he had written his wife that he hoped she was on her way to join him in Prague (perhaps hoping to confirm she was not). The music is almost inaudible, barely musical; bowed on the bridge, the instruments produce more scratchy noise than pitch. If we could hear the pitches we might notice that their sequence was strictly serial, but the music sounds like the diary of a plague of flies, or a muted hubbub of whispers. (Berg's annotation is *"wie geflüstert"*)[45] that might fill a Viennese café during one of Berg's favorite activities, *Jause,* afternoon gossip. And what is all the buzzing about? The cello makes the subject (or at least the pitches) clear in bar 6 by plucking the strings rather than scratching them; it plays three different orderings of the pitches (in German) B–A–F–H. Rumors seem to be flying ahead of actual (or imagined) events.

The buzzing texture Berg created out of the various series harkens back to Schoenberg's expressionist period, in particular to the thirteenth movement, "Enhauptung" (Decapitation), from *Pierrot Lunaire,* especially bars 10–16.[46] Berg, whose literary sophistication surpassed even his teacher's, would have appreciated the subtext of castration anxiety in Schoenberg's lurid vignette.

Berg excelled in expanding lightning-flash moments of Schoenberg's music into sustained structures. Here he inflated Schoenberg's seven-bar phrase into a sixty-nine-bar paragraph followed by its forty-six-bar retrograde, played *pianissimo* throughout. To make the retrograde audible he structured the initial section as a succession of contrasting textures and timbres: *murmurando* imitation played on the bridge, pizzicato statements of rows hocketing (alternating) between instruments, *tremolando* homorhythm, double canon in augmentation using harmonics in rhythms based on seven beats, repeated notes played by striking the string with the wooden side of the bow *(col legno),* and an imitative stretto mixing notes bowed and struck *col legno,* with a final codetta based on the ascending chromatic scale from F to B. The memorable timbre of each of these phrases keeps them recognizable even when played backward.

Out of this superorganized nonmusic the Trio estatico erupts, *"plötzlich ausbrechend,"* in two loud gasps, as if music itself, like a nearly drowned swimmer, was struggling for breath. In bars 76 and 77 Berg reprised and conjoined the gendered rising and falling scale patterns as an arch, but he also reshaped the scales according to the "master array" of intervals, Berg's contribution to atonal theory. The brief section unfolds in waves, a veritable *jeu de vagues,* plummeting and rising again. Although there are plenty of A–B–H–F sightings, the peaks, notably the motive in the violins at 86, do not state that tetrad either horizontally or vertically but instead state a new idea, a falling major third followed by a rising major third one half step lower. Berg will bring this new motive (which is imitated upside down by the viola and cello) back at the climax of the fourth movement, but here it appears as an epitome of the warm third-based harmonies that suffuse the entire trio and keep it on the verge of tonality. Had Berg presented the motive with the pitches A–F–E–G♯ we might recognize it as the first four notes of *Tristan,* an association strengthened by the four-note chromatic countermelody, which, when inverted, as it is by the cello, announces the "Yearning" theme. (Berg presents both ideas at their correct pitches in the final movement, *zu spät.*) Before desire or tonality have much of a chance to expose themselves the buzzing music returns, almost as if a broadcast of *Tristan* suddenly emerged from and disappeared back into a sea of static; Berg often remarked on the quality of radio transmission in his letters. Aberrant electronics drown out human voices.

The Trio estatico figures love as the dissolution of self, both anagrammatically and texturally. The Adagio appassionato, which Berg annotated as "the next day," presents itself as both a symphonic development and a love scene, but what do these genres have in common? In the classical sonata form the development prolongs the structure by postponing recapitulation; a love scene, like that of act 2 in *Tristan* (which Berg would parody in *Lulu*), attempts to prolong the moment of bliss and postpone the inevitable, which, in Wagner, entails both sexual climax and death. In romantic musical aesthetics the development section was also synonymous with freedom. A subtle example of developmental freedom is the new motive that appears in the viola on the upbeat to bar eight. This figure expands the two-note oscillation that opens the movement in ever-widening intervals: D–C♯–E♭–C–E♭–B–F, from a half step to a diminished fifth. We might say that Berg has turned his "worm" motive into an aroused "screw" motive, which, aptly enough, he will bring back (in bar 51) to generate the final climax at bar 57, a coincidence of mathematics, implicitly lewd sexual imagery, and dramatic overkill that suggests that Berg and perhaps Mrs. Fuchs shared an objective sense of humor about their affair. At the climactic moment, heralded by *tremolandos* on A–B–H–F in the violins, Berg transformed the "screw" motive into a rhythmic idea, with a rhythmic series of thrusts that diminish in number (4, 3, 2, 1) as they increase (by a Fibonacci series) in density (two notes, three, five, eight). A second rhythmic series follows with a six-note spasm on A–B–H–F, receding to five notes and then to four. In different performances this passage sounds either like a nearly simultaneous double orgasm or like a death rattle. The coda that follows, the most tender moment of the entire score, muted throughout, sounds like a ghostly aubade from beyond the grave.

I leave to the reader the pleasures of reading the remaining two movements; in short, it's downhill, romantically but not musically, all the way. I hope that I have already demonstrated how the *Lyric Suite,* like *La Mer,* is no sordid snapshot but a richly textured contemplation of matters of life and death or, perhaps, even civilization and its discontents, to borrow the title from Berg's Viennese neighbor. I also leave to the reader to pursue an aspect of erotic representation not present in this chapter. All of the composers discussed here—Ellington, Strayhorn, Debussy, and Berg—were men. The forms and materials they created to represent erotic experience, complex and varied as they are, nevertheless represent a partial view, as does my analysis as well. The idea that meaning resides in form may be a male prejudice. What would be its female counterpart?

CHAPTER 6

Black, Brown and Beige: History

The historical sense involves a perception, not only of the
pastness of the past, but of its presence.

—T. S. Eliot, "Tradition and the Individual Talent"

"Ladies and gentlemen," he cried. "At the request of Mr.
Gatsby we are going to play for you Mr. Vladimir Tostoff's
latest work, which attracted so much attention at Carnegie
Hall last May. If you read the papers, you know there was
a big sensation." He smiled with jovial condescension, and
added: "Some sensations!" Whereupon everybody laughed.
    "The piece is known," he concluded lustily, "as Vladimir
Tostoff's *Jazz History of the World.*"

—F. Scott Fitzgerald, *The Great Gatsby*

History is only his story. You haven't heard my story yet.

—Sun Ra

INTRO: CONTROVERSIAL SUITES

Almost as soon as they had thrown off the shackles of convention to
represent the "century of aeroplanes" modernist composers retreated
back to the past, or back to the future; neoclassicism and futurism were
two sides of the same coin that showed a different side up every decade. After the First World War many composers, acting either as high-
minded custodians of tradition or "bad boy" musical grave robbers,
practiced neoclassicism, buttressing their musical innovations with audible reminders of Bach or Haydn or Beethoven. The post–World War

II avant-garde rereversed the flow of history forward with a renovated vanguardism, back-to-Busoni, or what I term "neomodernism." Both of these strategies betray a certain anxiety about the present, often viewed as the worst of all possible worlds filled with the worst of all possible music. This catastrophic view shaped T. W. Adorno's essay "Perennial Fashion—Jazz."[1] More a projection of cultural paranoia than music criticism, it painted jazz as the negation of history. As his title indicated, Adorno placed jazz in a logically contradictory historical state: "For almost fifty years the productions of jazz have remained as ephemeral as seasonal styles." In other words, jazz was transitory and, even worse, permanent. Adorno's rant, which does not cite a single piece of music, shed little light on jazz but evinced a deep-seated frustration from within modernist music at its own failure to connect with the everyday present, a sphere in which European concert music sat commandingly throughout the nineteenth century.

Jazz, virtually on arrival, became synonymous with the present moment. European music of the 1920s, *Gebrauchsmusik* or *Zeitoper* or *Les Six*-ism, summoned up the sound of "today" with the saccharine buzz of an alto saxophone or, as in Erik Satie's *Parade,* a half-remembered Irving Berlin tune while alienating these allusions with modernist dissonances. Figuring a return to the everyday by putting "jazz" in quotations, these modernist styles distanced themselves from it. Works like Milhaud's *La création du monde* or Hindemith's Suite 1922 treated the new vernacular as an amusing foreign language. More radically the Brecht/Weill *Mahagonny* presented jazz as the musical jargon of hell.

Euro-jazz, at least in its most overt forms, was short-lived. By the late 1920s modernists replaced pop references with conspicuous displays of historical authority. Modern music, as Hindemith said, was no longer a laughing matter. Bach, famous for being unappreciated during his own time, now served as an emblem of belated historical justice. Composers spelled out the letters of his name by their pitch equivalents like a seal of approval (or a cry for help). BACH appeared to guarantee the value of Schoenberg's Variations for Orchestra, or Stravinsky's Symphony of Psalms, or Webern's String Quartet. By implication, these claims of impeccable lineage and high seriousness consigned popular music to a state of ahistorical moon/June/spoon mindlessness. While Adorno cleverly placed all popular music on a metaphorical runway of fashion (as if its appeal were limited to the chic rich), the concert world's prejudice against jazz often bared its racism more brazenly. In 1943 Winthrop Sargent, later the music critic for *The New Yorker,* wrote that "jazz is graphic and colorful, but, in poetic resources, it is about as rich as pidgin English."[2]

Giving the lie to Adorno's charge of "eternal faddishness," jazz had demonstrated a consciousness of its past as early as James P. Johnson's "Carolina Shout" and Joe Oliver's "Dippermouth Blues." Barely a quarter century after the first jazz recordings appeared, historically minded critics were debating its "evolution and essence" (to borrow André Hodeir's title) and evaluating new styles like swing and bop either as betrayals of the past or authentic heirs of tradition.[3] Even as the jazz imitations of the early 1920s lost their glow, the impact of jazz on concert music as varied as Antheil's *Jazz Symphony,* Schoenberg's *Moses und Aron* (where the orgy around the golden calf sounds like a nightmarish parody of a Weimar cabaret), and Hindemith's Symphonic Metamorphoses showed that, far from being ahistorical, the jazz idiom had become a necessary part of historical representation in music. The question that remained on the horizon was whether historical representation in music still required a classical component. In January 1943 Ellington's *Black, Brown and Beige* answered that question from the stage of the concert world's ground zero, Carnegie Hall.

The role of history in twentieth-century music is a large subject with its own complex history—which I leave to the historians. In this chapter, I focus on two nearly contemporary instances of historical narrative in American music: *Black, Brown and Beige,* from 1943, and *Appalachian Spring,* from 1944. Both of these momentous works appeared during an ongoing conflict that raised questions about the meaning of the past and prospects for the future. In wartime, at the cusp of neoclassicism and vanguardism, history itself was up for grabs. Not surprisingly, both works faltered in their original forms as they tried to imagine a resolution. Both were revised after the war ended, downsized to suites, one in a way that critics took as an admission of failure, the other in a way that refashioned music and history in the image of victory.

BLACK, BROWN AND BEIGE: GETTING TO CARNEGIE HALL

D. W. Griffith's *Birth of a Nation,* the most popular and influential film of the silent era, premiered early in 1915 and received a private screening at the White House for the president, his cabinet, and their wives. The film, based to some extent on the historical writings of President Wilson, celebrated the growth of the Ku Klux Klan. Historian Thomas Cripps describes three of its scenes as follows:

1. A scene set in the South Carolina legislature in the early 1870s (introduced with an intertitle that suggests that what is to follow is drawn from "historic incidents"), which depicts newly elected black legislators lolling in their chairs, their feet bare, eating chicken and drinking whiskey, leering at white women in the visitors' gallery.

2. A scene in which one of the film's white southern heroes witnesses a group of white children donning white bed sheets, inadvertently scaring several black children playing nearby, which provides him with "The Inspiration" for the Klan's infamous outfits.

3. A scene of Klansmen, dressed in white sheets and astride horses, dumping the body of the character Gus, an African American whom they had killed for causing Flora, the little sister of the story's southern white protagonists, to hurl herself off a cliff.

After viewing the film a white man in Lafayette, Indiana, shot a teen-age African American boy to death. Houston audiences, according to historian David Levering Lewis, "shrieked 'lynch him!' during a scene in which a white actor in blackface pursued Lillian Gish."[4] President Wilson reportedly told Griffith that the film was "like writing history with lightning. And my only regret is that it all is so terribly true."[5] The wild success of the film confirmed a version of American history already accepted by nearly the entire spectrum of white Americans, from Ivy League history professors to Southern lynch mobs. Anticipating the strategies of fascism, the film packaged racism with populism and paranoia, calling "for an alliance of the common folk from the formerly warring sections to overthrow a tyranny based on Northern commercial corruption allied with African Americans."[6] The film made visible the ideological subtext of the Democratic Party's "Southern Strategy," an alliance of Northern blue collar workers, Southern small farmers, and property owners to which Wilson gave the name "New Freedom" and which the Republican party, no longer the party of Lincoln, would appropriate later in the century. Wilson's strategy fortified the reversal of the Union victory in the Civil War that began with the end of Reconstruction. White Americans imposed second-class citizenship on blacks throughout the country, justifying the denial of rights and the constant threat of violence with the scarifying accounts of Reconstruction that Griffith dramatized using the most advanced artistic technology of the time. Although he claimed to be surprised and even offended by accusations of racism, Griffith was so animated by fear of miscegenation that he forbade "any 'black blood' among the players who might have to touch white actresses. Those actors were always whites in blackface."[7]

Whatever else it may have done, *Birth of a Nation* demonstrated as never before the incendiary persuasive power of the film medium. As soon as it came out the NAACP, then led by W. E. B. DuBois, attempted to counter its impact. After the failure of campaigns to cut racist scenes or ban the film altogether, plans were made for a rebuttal film, to be called *Birth of Race,* that would be based on Booker T. Washington's autobiography, *Up from Slavery.* Respected and well connected, Washington died before the film could be completed and adequately financed; as Nelson George writes, "The film slipped into the hands of con men, swindlers and incompetents."[8] Its opening was a fiasco. The racist historical narrative of *Birth of a Nation* would remain unchallenged in the popular media until the appearance of the television series *Roots* in 1979.

Ellington was sixteen when *Birth of a Nation* appeared, and the humiliating failure to oppose its version of history may well have motivated his lifelong project of composing a history of African Americans. As Mark Tucker showed, the historical pageants that had already appeared during his school days in Washington, D.C. provided templates for Ellington's historical compositions. In 1911 the Howard Theater presented a musical production called *The Evolution of the Negro in Picture, Song and Story* in four sections: Overture, Night of Slavery—Sorrow Songs, Dawn of Freedom, and Day of Opportunity. Even more elaborate was *The Star of Ethiopia,* produced by DuBois in 1913 and brought to D.C. in October 1915. It covered "ten thousand years of the history of the Negro race" in five scenes—"Gift of Iron," "Dream of Egypt," "Glory of Ethiopia," "Valley of Humiliation," and "Vision Everlasting"—in a multimedia spectacle with music, lights, and dancing.[9]

These pageants gave Ellington a model for narrating black history, but their theatrical forms left open the question of whether the story could also be told through instrumental music without words, actors, dancers, and spectacle. Ellington later explored a variety of media, composing music for film, ballet, political revue, musical comedy, and television, and he often spoke of writing an operatic presentation of African American history titled *Boola.* In 1958 *A Drum Is a Woman,* a history of jazz told through a fantastic mixture of allegory, music, and dance, appeared on television; in 1963 the historical pageant *My People,* a theatrical blend of religious service and history lesson that anticipated Leonard Bernstein's *Mass,* was performed twice a day over a three-week period as part of a Century of Negro Progress exhibition. While Ellington pursued these mixed-media forms he also narrated black history in instrumental compositions. Between 1943 and 1950 he presented what might be termed chapters of an historical epic: *Black Brown and Beige, New World A-Comin', Deep South Suite, Liberian Suite,* and *Harlem.* All these works provoked intense critical controversy that continues today. Most critics, however, measured them in terms of their genre (sizing them up either as jazz or symphonic compositions) rather than their content, or they claimed that their form and content were fatally mismatched.

In composing these concert works Ellington took his music into two different contested areas. *Black, Brown and Beige* and *Harlem* (a.k.a. *A Tone Parallel to Harlem* and *Harlem Suite*) appeared as program music, or tone parallels, as Ellington called them. By the 1940s the concert world had come to think of program music as a dated genre that had peaked in the tone poems of Richard Strauss. Most modernist composers rejected the idea of musical storytelling in favor of more abstract designs; the tone poem devolved into such midcult works as Gershwin's *An American in Paris* or Grofé's *Grand Canyon Suite.* Many of the narrative techniques of program music also became clichés of movie music and cartoon music. Educated listeners unthinkingly branded most program music as kitsch and assumed that its composers were either naïve, provincial, or, in the case of Hollywood composers, willfully exploitative. Predictably, critics accused Ellington's tone parallels of technical ineptitude and narrative pretentiousness, and these charges have clouded the music for years. James Lincoln Collier's biography of the composer, written in 1987, summarily dismissed all of Ellington's extended works.

Ellington risked even greater acrimony in giving musical shape to the African American experience. The black community had long debated the lessons to be drawn from its history. At the turn of the century Booker T. Washington and W. E. B. DuBois laid down contrasting goals of self-sufficiency and equality, economic power and civil rights. Their positions evolved as the center of African American life moved from the rural south to northern cities. Older black leaders such as DuBois and Alain Locke encouraged African American artists to seek a new maturity of expression by pursuing European high art standards of "discipline, restraint, austerity and resolution."[10] They were suspicious of jazz and the blues. Younger artists like Langston Hughes and Zora Neale Hurston, however, embraced the new music and all it represented. Hughes wrote, "We younger Negro artists who create now intend to express our dark-skinned selves without fear or shame."[11] After the flourishing of the Harlem Renaissance and its vision of the "New Negro" in the 1920s, the Depression devastated black communities everywhere. Many black intellectuals and artists, like Paul Robeson, Richard Wright, and Langston Hughes, joined the Communist Party and at times viewed the Soviet Union as a better friend than the United States. Relations with the party, though, were complex. As Martin Duberman wrote, the party's "aggressively secular scorn for Christian institutions and values, so central to the culture of Afro-Americans, seriously constricted its appeal to the black masses." As part of its Popular Front stance in the late 1930s, however, the party "threw itself into pronounced support for black arts, helping to sponsor a variety of efforts to encourage black theater, history and music."[12]

Once the United States entered the war racial tensions escalated. A segregated army, perpetuating American racism, drafted young black men to fight Nazi racism. While white workers found employment in the burgeoning defense industry, blacks were barred from these jobs; as white America suddenly prospered, the Depression only deepened in Harlem. The *Amsterdam Star-News* described an "upsurge of rebellion, bordering on open hostility" within its community.[13] Meanwhile, the Communist Party (which had already lost much credibility due to the Hitler-Stalin pact) made Russian relief a greater priority than improving conditions for African Americans. Even as black political leaders pressed the administration to increase opportunities for black workers, Harlem erupted in riots. How would *Black, Brown and Beige* mirror this complex and fast-changing political climate?

BLACK, BROWN AND BEIGE: WHAT ARE WE FIGHTING FOR?

Black, Brown and Beige premiered on January 23, 1943, at a benefit concert for Russian War Relief, and thus appeared at the crossroads of two different and competing causes. The audience may have expected to hear something suitably patriotic. Owing to the propaganda power of radio broadcasts, music played an unprecedented wartime role, whether in the classical form of Shostakovich's Symphony no. 7 ("Leningrad"), which had been smuggled out of the besieged Soviet Union, or in the popular music of the Andrews Sisters and Glenn Miller. Even before the war, didactic anti-Nazi works like Kurt Weill's *Eternal Road*

and *Ballad for Americans* by Earl Robinson and John La Touche established a genre of inspirational populist music that would continue with
Copland's *Lincoln Portrait*, Blitzstein's *Symphony: The Airborne*, and
Schoenberg's *Survivor from Warsaw*. Although Ellington had been con-
templating *Black, Brown and Beige* since the early 1930s, it premiered
in the context of these wartime works at a time when, as Ellington said
to the audience, the Black, Brown, and Beige would once again fight for
the Red, White, and Blue. Given the nature of the occasion he could not
say explicitly that he hoped they would be rewarded for their services
better than they had been in previous wars, but the message was encoded, perhaps too deeply, in the music.

A sold-out, celebrity-packed house cheered the Ellington band's first
Carnegie Hall concert, and it received wide attention in the press. Eleanor Roosevelt was in attendance, and Frank Sinatra greeted Ellington
backstage during a break from his own show at the Paramount. (Ellington wrote Sinatra's name, address, and phone number at the top
of his first sketch for *Black*. He had begun composing the new work
a month earlier in Hartford, Connecticut, where the band shared the
bill with the emerging blue-eyed singer.) Ellington's manager, William
Morris, who was also active in the Russian relief movement, had declared January 17–23 National Ellington Week, and midway through
the sold-out concert Ellington received a plaque signed by such lumi-
naries of American music as Louis Armstrong, Benny Goodman, Cab
Calloway, Earl Hines, Count Basie, Lena Horne and Paul Whiteman,
Leopold Stokowski, Walter Damrosch, Marian Anderson, Paul Robeson, Roy Harris, Aaron Copland, Kurt Weill, Jerome Kern, and Chico
Marx.

The concert reinstated Ellington's place of honor in the jazz world
after two years of disruption. Jimmy Blanton's early death in July 1942
and the departures of Cootie Williams, Ivie Anderson, and Barney Bigard threatened to terminate the achievement of the "Blanton/Webster"
band of 1940 and 1941. Battles between ASCAP, the musicians' union,
and the broadcast and recording industries interrupted the development
of repertory and records. Responding to obstacles creatively, Ellington
had relocated to Hollywood in January 1941. In addition to the usual
schedule of ballroom performances the band made five short films and
performed in the musical review *Jump for Joy*, which ran from July
10 to September 27, 1941. As Michael Denning points out, the show
mixed the revue format of Ellington's Cotton Club shows with the edgy
political commentary of *Pins and Needles*, the union-sponsored topical

musical that opened in New York in 1937 with its theme "Sing Me a Song with Social Significance."

By 1941, however, the war had already altered the tone and terms of political protest. Anticipating that the war effort against Nazi racism might finally bring an end to racial discrimination in America, *Jump for Joy* celebrated (with Paul Webster's lyrics) the imminent death of Uncle Tom, blackface, and the other stereotypes that still reigned in the American theater:

> Fare thee well, land of cotton,
> Cotton lisle
> is out of style,
> Honey chile,
> Jump for joy.

Jump for Joy took shape just as A. Philip Randolph was planning a march on Washington to protest employment discrimination in the defense industries. Ellington showed his support of the cause on Lincoln's birthday in 1941 in the radio address "We, Too, Sing America," its title echoing Langston Hughes's poem. Ellington declared, "The Negro is the creative voice of America. . . . We fought America's wars, provided her labor, gave her music, kept alive her flickering conscience, prodded her on toward the yet unachieved goal, democracy."[14] During the run of the show Ellington also supported such leftist groups as the Veterans of the Lincoln Brigade, the Hollywood Democratic Committee, and the Independent Citizen's Committee of the Arts, Sciences and Professions, and along with Herb Jeffries and Ivie Anderson he performed excerpts from the show on NBC's *Salute to Labor*.

Even though a few of its songs ("I Got It Bad," "Chocolate Shake," "Rocks in My Bed") became popular, *Jump for Joy* never made it to Broadway; after Pearl Harbor its irreverent tone may have seemed out of line. Protest now had to take a backseat to patriotism. Ellington spent most of 1942 on the road, returning to Hollywood in the fall for two full-length films, *Cabin in the Sky* and *Reveille with Beverly*, and also making recordings for the Armed Forces Radio Service. The January 1943 Carnegie Hall benefit concert was simultaneously a triumphant return to New York and a high point in Ellington's political visibility. The stakes were high.

The live recording demonstrates that the Ellington Orchestra was more than up to the occasion; the critical sniping that ensued may simply illustrate the danger of giving an audience too much of a good thing, though it also exposed the usual cultural prejudices. In the *Herald Tribune,* Paul Bowles, while noting the vociferous approval of the audience, warned that "the whole attempt to fuse jazz as a form with art music should be discouraged. . . . One might say they operate on different wave lengths; it is impossible to tune them in simultaneously."[15] Heard today the concert sounds like a peak moment in the history of American music, a nonstop display of virtuosity and creativity (with new works by Ellington, Strayhorn, Mercer Ellington, Juan Tizol, and Mary Lou Williams) compared to which Paul Whiteman's far more celebrated Experiment in Modern Music of 1924 was, with the exception of one piece, *Rhapsody in Blue,* an overhyped dud. The program opened with "The Star-Spangled Banner" (begun solemnly, but gradually speeding up and ending with a brazen added six chord, which Stravinsky may have imitated at the conclusion of his 1945 Symphony in Three Movements), followed by Ellington's own anthem, "Black and Tan Fantasy," in its epically slo-mo rearrangement of 1938. Although it featured such chestnuts as "Black Beauty," "Rockin' in Rhythm," and "Mood Indigo," most of the other pieces on the program were of recent vintage.

Avoiding the expected, Ellington's program broke with the quasi-historical scenarios of earlier crossover concerts. Paul Whiteman's Experiment in Modern Music, for instance, had laid out a didactic evolution from the "primitive" jazz of "Livery Stable Blues" to Gershwin's sleek symphonic jazz. Two concerts at Carnegie Hall in the late 1930s, produced by John Hammond, figured jazz history as a move from spirituals to swing.[16] By contrast, Ellington's program looked like a sprawling patchwork quilt of familiar and novel jazz numbers wrapped around a monumental and original trilogy that defied the very category of jazz. Placed at the center of the concert, before the intermission, *Black, Brown and Beige* lasted some forty-eight minutes; the three-part suite was Ellington's long-promised panorama, or "tone parallel," of African American history.

In its length (four times that of "Reminiscing in Tempo") and the burden of its content, *Black, Brown and Beige* was unprecedented in jazz composition. Comparable African American works like William Grant Still's Symphony no. 1 or James. P. Johnson's *Harlem Symphony,* both composed for symphony orchestra, mixed jazz elements with symphonic gestures within familiar formal outlines. Ellington, though, scored *Black, Brown and Beige* for his own jazz orchestra, did not call it a symphony, and did not follow any of the formal structures found in European concert music. To help his audience Ellington briefly introduced each of the three movements (with an uncharacteristic nervousness); program notes by Irving Kolodin and well-placed preview articles in *DownBeat* and the *New York Times Magazine* further spelled out Ellington's intentions.[17] *Black* portrayed the distant past in three sections: "Work Song," "Come Sunday," and "Light." *Brown* described events from the Revolutionary War to the Spanish American War in three sections: "West Indian Dance," "Emancipation Celebration," and "The Blues," the only music with a singer and lyrics. Neither Ellington nor Kolodin attempted to outline the sections of *Beige,* but the notes said that it covered the period from the First World War to the present, contrasting the misconceived exotic Harlem of the 1920s with the community's actual educational, economic, and spiritual aspirations.

The program notes shared content with a long poetic script that Ellington wrote out by hand and carefully revised but never published (though parts of it appear in *Music Is My Mistress*); the original is preserved in the Ellington Archive.[18] The copies of the poem in the Ellington Archive are undated. It is likely but not completely evident that the poem preceded the music; Ellington could have used it as a blueprint for composing the suite, but he also may have written it afterward in the hopes of clarifying the political content of the music, which went virtually unnoticed in the concert's reviews. In 1956 Ellington said that he was working on a new version of *Black, Brown and Beige* with a narration based on "a thing I wrote a long time ago";[19] a few years later the revised version had evolved into the musical show *My People,* which included important sections of *Black, Brown and Beige.*

The poem (as Mark Tucker pointed out in 1993, after it surfaced in the Ellington Archive) clearly links *Black, Brown and Beige* and Ellington's long-promised opera. To chronicle the African American experience, Ellington had imagined a transhistorical black everyman named Boola. His story, told in three parts titled "Black," "Brown," and "Beige," is also the story of his people. This narrative device is similar to the role of the "American" that Robeson sang in *Ballad for Americans* (Ellington would collaborate with John La Touche in the 1946 show *Beggar's Holiday*), or the narrator/participant in Schoenberg's *Survivor,* but it might also be compared to HCE, the polymorphous progenitor of *Finnegans Wake.* Ellington's poem weaves together Boola's personal story, including his marriage to Voola, with scenes and figures from black history: the "seeds of the first civilization" in Egypt, the African discoveries of "agriculture, law, literature, music, natural sciences, medicine," and "basketry, pottery, cutlery, sculpture": "Whence came the art of Greece? . . . out of black Africa." Some lines in "Black":

> Look, now, is this not the same golden sun
> Which fired your brain along the calm Euphrates?
> And smiled upon your seeking, searching sorties
> As you followed the course of the Ganges?

echo Langston Hughes's poem "The Negro Speaks of Rivers":

> I bathed in the Euphrates when dawns were young.
> I built my hut near the Congo and it lulled me to sleep.

Hughes's poem had appeared in *The Crisis* in 1921, and in the 1930s Hughes and Ellington had discussed a collaboration that would have featured Paul Robeson as a "wandering Negro minstrel."[20] Hughes also contributed lyrics to *Jump for Joy.* (The poet also introduced Ellington to the young Ralph Ellison.)

The "Black" section of Ellington's poem traces Boola's story from African childhood to the horrors of the Middle Passage and the slave market and then charts his discovery of the Christian religion and, with it, the light emanating from the Bible, his recognition "as early as 1652" of the call for freedom:

> Boola's spirit rising from the dusty fields.
> Heroes . . . strong and firm . . . rising from the fray.
> Chains breaking . . . Hopes rising . . . Boola fighting
> For or with anybody . . . for FREEDOM!

In the section titled "Brown" Ellington turns the focus from Boola to specific figures in African American history: Crispus Attucks, Barzillai Lew, the Fontages Legion of Free Haitians, Frederick Douglass, Harriet Tubman, the black soldiers who fought on San Juan Hill. Moving suddenly inward from this historical panorama, the section concludes with the words Ellington set in "The Blues." In the final part of the poem, "Beige," Boola disappears altogether and the poetic style changes. Its first section echoes Vachel Lindsay's "Congo," the clichéd jungle world of "Hot Harlem," but then the poem shifts to the uplifting idiom of James Weldon Johnson, cursing the false view of Harlem with the stern tones of a biblical prophet:

> Who draped those basement dens
> With silk, but knaves and robbers
> And their ilk?

Who came to prostitute your art
And gave you pennies
For your part . . .
And ill-repute?
Who took your hunger
And your pain
Outraged your honor
For their gain?

Ellington's script often reads more like a radio narrative than polished poetry, but its counterpoint of subjective states and historical facts recalls other American literature of the time, the cinematic effects of Hart Crane and John Dos Passos, the blues poems of Langston Hughes, and the folk sermons of James Weldon Johnson. The opening of "The Blues":

The Blues . . .
The Blues ain't
The Blues ain't nothin'
The Blues ain't nothin' but a cold grey day . . .

even recalls T. S. Eliot's "Ash Wednesday":

Because I do not hope to turn again
Because I do not hope
Because I do not hope to turn . . .

But perhaps Langston Hughes, with whom Ellington had planned to collaborate in the 1930s, had set down the clearest challenge to write *Black, Brown and Beige* in his poem "Note on Commercial Theatre," published in *The Crisis* in 1940. White culture, both high and low, Hughes decried, had stolen the blues and rearranged it according to its own purposes, "mixed 'em up with symphonies . . . so they don't sound like me." Hughes predicted, though, that someone would reclaim the blues "and write about me—black and beautiful—and sing about me."

Boola, the "me" of Ellington's poem, stood for the entirety of black experience. It is hard to imagine how he could have appeared in a conventional opera. In his "tone parallel" Ellington would deploy a counterpoint of soloists and instrumental choirs to weave together the poem's strands of history lesson and personal story. *Black, Brown and Beige,* as we will see, can be heard as a new kind of opera, an opera conceived mainly for instrumental voices.

While Ellington's poetic scenario retold African American history, it also contained ideologically sensitive elements that may have clashed with the varying political agendas of a Popular Front audience like the one assembled at Carnegie Hall. After spelling out the horrors of en-slavement, Ellington emphasized the nobility of work:

> Boola put down his heavy load and gazed about.
> He's been looking at this tree-swept land
> Reclaimed by steady swinging of his ringing axe
> And was proud of what he saw there. Honest toil
> Was not without reward. Had not this toil
> Restored the steely muscles rippling
> 'Neath the black satin smoothness of his skin.

The poem stressed the African American role in building America—clearing its forests—but also portrayed slaves as a revolutionary prole-tariat whose work songs would be "used as a weapon . . . / To slash the ties of bondage!" Those lines might have pleased the Communists in the audience, but with "Come Sunday" Ellington celebrated the redeeming role of Christianity. From the Bible, Boola learns:

> Something to live for.
> Something to work for.
> Something to hope for.
> Something to sing about.
> Something to SHOUT about.

That something, the "kindly light" of Scripture, is the message of freedom. Yet even though he affirmed Christian values, Ellington's faith was nonsectarian. In his eulogy for Billy Strayhorn Ellington would ex-pound his creed in terms of freedom: "freedom from hate, uncondi-tionally; freedom from self-pity (even throughout all the pain and bad news); freedom from fear of possibly doing something that might help another more than it might help himself; and freedom from the kind of pride that could make a man feel he was better than his brother or neighbor."[21] For Ellington the central message of Christianity was jus-tice for all in this world rather than salvation in a world to come.

Despite its generally hostile critical reception, the lack of a well-engineered recording of the original score, and the even more glaring lack of a critical edition of the music, there is a large literature on *Black, Brown and Beige*.[22] These writings pursue three topics: critical evalu-ation, musical structure, and, to a lesser extent, ideological content. Putting aside evaluation for the moment, I would suggest that the form is only understandable in terms of the content; the genre of "tone par-allel" was not a marketing device but a considered strategy for giving

African American experience musical form. The content of the music, however, is not necessarily the same as the content of the poem; the two artifacts are complements, not duplicates. Large sections of the poem, particularly the celebration of black heroes in "Brown," never found their way into the music, but the quirkiness of the poem often points to unnoticed expressive and ideological twists in the music. Instead of using the poem as a simple pony for the music, I want to look at the way the music itself writes history. This exploration will combine musical analysis and interpretive reading.

Before proceeding, though, let's stop and ask how *any* music writes history. Coupling music and history may first bring to mind works like the "1812 Overture" that use sound effects and musical quotations to set the scene and identify the opposing sides. These devices are powerful: just a few notes of *La Marseillaise* tell us who is fighting. There are a couple of moments in *Black, Brown and Beige* that employ historically resonant "source" sounds in a similar way. The chimes Sonny Greer played at the beginning of "Come Sunday" immediately moved the musical action from the cotton fields to a church.

But music can also represent history, the past as interpreted by the present, without specific allusions, and it can shape history in its own way; indeed, sometimes it writes history so transparently that we barely notice. As an example as far from the "1812 Overture" as possible, consider Irving Berlin's 1914 song "Play a Simple Melody." Actually it is two songs that can be sung separately or together, a trick Berlin repeated later in his career with "You're Just in Love." The two songs of "Play a Simple Melody" figure the past and present in their music and words:

Singer 1:

Won't you play some simple melody?
Like my mother sang to me . . .

Singer 2:

Musical demons
set my honey a-screaming.
Won't you play me some rag?

The words and music for the first singer evoke the Victorian parlor; the second singer, moving twice as quickly, summons up ragtime syncopations and contemporary urban slang. Berlin's song indulges in nostalgia, then sabotages it, then weds it to its opposite contrapuntally.

The song shows us how the past and present are different—one smooth, the other choppy—but also how they denote interwoven, interdependent feelings of rootedness and spontaneity. In its own miniature way the song forecasts the complex historical metaphors of neoclassicism, especially in the way it uses jazz as an image of the present.

Writing history, music can also link the past to the future, and with a good dose of irony, as in the Beatles' "When I'm Sixty-Four."

> When I get older
> Losing my hair
> Many years from now . . .

Connecting 1927 to 1967 to 2007, the song evoked the style of the English music hall to represent the music of forty years in the future, when the surviving Fab Four, shorn of their defining mops, would attain geezer status and turn into their fathers. It deftly illustrated the weight of the past and anxieties about the future with music that spoke powerfully of the present.

Through a similar manipulation of styles Ellington would contrast the past and future more elaborately (and critically) in his *Controversial Suite* (1951). Signifying on the dispute that raged, at least in the pages of *DownBeat*, between preservationists (or "moldy figs") and progressives, Ellington called the two movements of the *Controversial Suite* "Before My Time" and "Later." They are usually heard simply as parodies of the popular Dixieland-revival style of Bob Crosby and the equally popular jazz modernism of Stan Kenton; *Controversial* appeared after Bob Graettinger's "Thermopylae" (but before his masterpiece "City of Glass"). In sending up these self-styled preservationists and sci-fi prophets, Ellington staked out the middle ground, the present, and yet the suite also demonstrated, with a gentle humor, how Ellington's music had been there and done that; his music already contained past, present, and future. Graettinger's brash dissonances owed a lot to "Diminuendo in Blue," but Ellington had also anticipated the Dixieland revival in "Clarinet Lament," a New Orleans–flavored concerto for Barney Bigard built on the changes of "Basin Street Blues." Ellington's satire may have been aimed less at other musicians than at critics who claimed to discern the hidden shape of jazz history.

These examples illustrate some of the devices music uses to represent history: allusion, quotation, evocation, parody, prophecy, juxtaposition, superimposition, sequence. These devices enable music to write history not just by illustration and allusion but by formal process as well. They give music the ability to articulate, criticize, or subvert the historical ideas and myths that shape its cultural milieu. They all play a role in *Black, Brown and Beige.*

BLACK, BROWN AND BEIGE: A READING

Let's begin by mapping out the large design. Ellington outlined the work in groups of three: there are three movements, and the first two of these are clearly divided into three parts each.[23] *Beige* also has a tripartite structure, but, as we will see, Ellington may have considered its 1943 form provisional; he never revived its original structure. All of these trinities relate to the implicit ambiguity of the title: Do the three shades represent a sequence of events or simultaneous states? Does the music tell a tale of assimilation, a progression from black to beige, or does it portray a synchronous spectrum? Or both? The title might simply be a description of the range of flesh tones in the Ellington Orchestra, or it might stand for the entire nonwhite population of the planet. To articulate the complex relations implied by his title, Ellington employed the resources of his orchestra and its distinctive timbral syntax. The Ellington Orchestra appeared as three choirs: reeds, trumpets and trombones with the rhythm section (drums, guitar, bass) serving as foundation, and the piano as a kind of presiding consciousness. The band also serves as the source of solo voices to create a dialogue between individuals and groups. Many parts of *Black, Brown and Beige* spotlighted his famous soloists as he had already done in his various "concertos." Ellington carefully deployed the particular expressive styles of Harry Carney, Joe Nanton, Ray Nance, Rex Stewart, Johnny Hodges, Ben Webster, and Betty Roché, who had recently replaced Ivie Anderson. By juxtaposing solo playing and instrumental choirs Ellington gave *Black, Brown and Beige* the dramatic shape of an opera. The soloists portray the main characters, but, as in folk opera, the ensemble, the people, have the final say because they are the real subject. *Black, Brown and Beige* thereby fulfilled the purposes of Ellington's projected opera "Boola" and became his answer to *Porgy and Bess* as well as to *The Birth of a Nation.*

Black: *"Work Song"*

Summing up his larger project in a musical motto, Ellington began *Black* with a clarion drums and winds theme that we might call "Fanfare for the Common Black Man," a companion to (and perhaps a sly commentary on) Copland's contemporary fanfare. Ellington, however, had already composed similar motives to animate "Creole Rhapsody" and *Symphony in Black*. (Indeed, he used the opening phrase of *Symphony in Black* to launch the opening medley of the Carnegie concert.) While it functions mainly as a refrain, the *Black* motto was also built for variant usage. It counterpoints two separable ideas, the pounding "boom boom boom boom" of the drums and the nobly insistent summons to attention in the winds. In the course of "Work Song" and "Light" the motto appears as an eight-bar phrase over a choralelike harmonization in the trombones, and in melodic fragments as short as five notes that still retain its defining character. A three-note rhythmic encapsulation of the motto—quarter, quarter, half—links many of the movement's melodic ideas. Its two quarter note upbeats establish a recurrent rhythmic motive (not unlike the three upbeat eighth notes of Beethoven's Fifth) that gives *Black* a distinctive stride even in the face of many changes in tempo. The subtext of this rhythm becomes clearer when the trombones present it as a new theme that seems to set the words "Jump for Joy." *Black* doesn't need a singer to sing.

Because Ellington did not recycle the fanfare theme in *Brown* and *Beige* its very absence in those movements poses a question: if it is missing, what has taken its place? Progress seems inseparable from loss. The tripartite structures of *Black* and *Brown* figure this conundrum in contrasting historical patterns. *Black* is structured in clear Hegelian terms: thesis ("Work Song"), antithesis ("Come Sunday"), and synthesis ("Light"). With "West Indian Dance" and "Emancipation Celebration," *Brown* at first seems even more concretely historical and clearly chronological in structure, but with the concluding section, "The Blues," it counteracts its own sense of progression with a palindromic structure that defies history. Heard in sequence *Black* and *Brown* thus appear as a large thesis and antithesis of spiritual and blues, setting up a possible synthesis in *Beige*. Ellington reinforced these patterns through a contrast of high and low instruments and gender. Black builds its dialectic on a timbral contrast of Joe Nanton's growling "jungle-style" trombone, the leading role in "Work Song," and Johnny Hodges's sophisticated or "dicty" alto sax solo (or aria) in "Come Sunday." This contrast intensifies with the entry of a woman's voice in "The Blues," which genders *Brown* as a female counterpart to *Black*. (On the 1965 recording, though, "The Blues" was sung by a man, and "Come Sunday" was played down an octave by Harry Carney.)

Given its historical subject, *Black, Brown and Beige* required an idiom that differed from ordinary jazz because jazz itself was part of the history it was writing. Earlier analyses have used terms from European music like "thematic development" and "recapitulation" as if they carried no cultural baggage, but the only overt contact the music makes with Europe is a passing two-degrees-of-separation allusion in "Come Sunday" to "Swing Low, Sweet Chariot," which Dvořák had appropriated in his "New World" Symphony and which Ellington neatly takes back long before the quotation by reabsorbing it into a whole family of related motives that fill the collagelike structure of "Work Song."

To differentiate the music of the distant past from contemporary jazz, "Work Song" avoids the usual phrase structures of jazz, the thirty-two-bar AABA structure of the pop tune, or the twelve-bar structure of the blues. Ellington also withheld his trademark chromaticism, which would have carried an anachronistically modernistic flavor. *Black* figures the pre-European past through diatonic melodies (with the exception of a single blues-scale motive) and static harmonies, rarely straying from E♭ major for the first two thirds of the movement. Apart from the fanfare theme, the other melodic material seems to come and go almost haphazardly, but at the climactic moment of the movement, Joe Nanton's solo in C major against the "grunts" of the orchestra (a moment that Ellington brought to the audience's attention in his introductory remarks), the music suddenly attains a sense of unity.

The first four notes of Nanton's tune, C–E–G–A, reveal the genetic connection between the other melodic ideas. I'll label the main motives of "Work Song" as:

1. Fanfare
2. Riding on a Blue Note
3. Blues Riff
4. Jump for Joy
5. Sax Section Work Song
6. Epiphany Motive
7. Ain't That Good News

The melodic "gene" appears in all of these motives except for the Fanfare. If we invert the melodic figure C–E–G–A we get E–C–A–G, a melodic motive (reminiscent of "Swing Low") that appears throughout (transposed, in E♭, to the pitches G–E♭–C–B♭) and which Ellington had previously used at the very opening of "Riding on a Blue Note." Once we hear the relation of these two figures, its connection to the "Work Song" melody played by the saxes becomes clear, and with a little more attention we can also hear the motive embedded and embellished in the nine-note blueslike riff that also floats up periodically in the movement. The four-note "germ" also functions as a harmony; in the Sax Section Work Song every chord in the five-part voicing states the pitches G– E♭–C–B♭.

Retrospective revelation, giving sense to musical events after they have happened, is a subtle effect of musical storytelling that is very difficult to pull off. There are precedents in such classical works as the first movement of the "Eroica" Symphony, Chopin's *Ballades,* Sibelius's Fifth Symphony, and also Sousa's "Stars and Stripes Forever." In a different way, though, this effect also appears in great jazz solos, beginning as early as Joe Oliver's solo in "Dipper Mouth Blues." Ellington's narrative strategy in *Black* resembles both of these precedents. As with Sibelius's "Swan Theme," Nanton's melody (and the harmonic move from E♭ to C that it announces) is not a logical development but a lightning bolt that suddenly clarifies the musical meaning. Ellington set the epiphanic moment up through a succession of solos that articulate the large formal divisions of the movement, and which tell its story in terms of the idiosyncratic blues timbres and inflections of his players. The music clearly contrasts the personal styles of these solos with the more communal ensemble passages for sax, trumpet, and trombone choirs. Once we hear the importance of the solo voices, the many short phrases of the movement coalesce into a simpler large-scale design.[24] Using the bar numbers from Maurice Peress's version of the score, I would divide the movement as follows:

Part 1: mm. 1–62 (binary, divided at m. 27, with a coda at m. 57)

Part 2: mm. 63–114 (Harry Carney baritone sax solo)

Transition: mm. 115–26 (Harold Baker trumpet solo)

Part 3: 127–79 (Joe Nanton solo beginning at m. 139)

Climax and coda: 180–210 (Nanton solo in C major, followed by brass section amplification in D♭ major and reaffirmation, at m. 204, through counterpoint of Nanton and fanfare motive in saxes)

Transition to "Come Sunday": 211–16

Further simplifying this plan, we might think of the movement as an extended aria (from the opera "Boola"), almost like a Verdian cabaletta, with an introduction, a first solo section, a recitative-like transition, a second solo section, and a triumphant conclusion. We can hear the single solo voice of this aria articulated by three instrumentalists: Carney, Baker, and Nanton. If we lean on the poem they may be said to represent three phases of Boola's consciousness: his recollections of the black past, his union with Voola, and his realization that the work song could be "used as a weapon . . . /To slash the ties of bondage!" And if we hear the music in these terms we may hear the introductory section as a picture of the communal African past that is severed traumatically with the whiplash dissonances at bar 57, perhaps the remnant, reduced to a single image of pain, of sections Ellington had intended to write to describe the slave ship and slave market.

Black: *"Come Sunday"*

Just as the audience was getting a grip on "Work Song" it segued into "Come Sunday." In his introductory remarks Ellington briefly referred to the section as a spiritual that was closely related to the work song; he must have known that further words were not necessary because he had two winning cards up his sleeve, a great tune and Johnny Hodges, whose solo voice had not yet been heard. The structure of "Come Sunday" mirrors that of "Work Song" in two respects: it places its defining theme last, and it unfolds with three solo instrumental voices, Juan Tizol's valve trombone, Ray Nance's violin, and finally Hodges's alto sax. The melodic presentation reverses the usual jazz or symphonic practice of exposition followed by development. Here, instead, the theme is heard first in fragmented form and then finds its true shape.

Ellington chose to write his own spiritual rather than quote from a well-known and revered repertory of "sorrow songs." Surprisingly, he created a hybrid of spiritual and pop tune, following the AABA form of Tin Pan Alley, which is not characteristic of the spiritual literature. With a deceptively plain-style diatonic melodic line over rich harmonies, the tune has resonances of both "Sometimes I Feel Like a Motherless Child" and "Summertime." (To hear the first, sing the words "motherless child" and then "Sunday O Come" or "Please look down and" to Ellington's melody. To hear the second, play the progression F9–E♭9.) Its AABA design, moreover, suggests an ironic parallel to "Old Man River," which Ellington had already mocked with his "Old Man Blues," part of which will appear at the end of "Light."

Writing "Come Sunday" in a hybrid style, Ellington lifted its spirituality out of the chronological frame; he would bring the theme back at the end of *Beige* as an emblem of Harlem's living piety, not as a vestige of the past. Before its full statement, though, he used instrumental colors to convey the story line of the poem, where Boola sits outside the master's church:

> The music was soothing and sweet . . .
> Even from the outside looking in.
> He longed to enter and be a part
> Of this silv'ry tongued
> Ding! Dong! Ding! Dong!

At the opening of the original "Come Sunday" Ellington superimposed the chimes (a timbral metamorphosis of the opening drumbeats) over an organlike chorale played by the brass, and echoed by the saxes, that hints at the melody to come. The melody next appears solemnly intoned on the valve trombone, the "whitest" instrument in Ellington's orchestra; a brief interjection by the alto sax (Otto Hardwick) may represent Boola's commentary on its alien sound. After the trombone solo concludes with a bit of "Swing Low, Sweet Chariot," the sax section seems to recall some of its "Work Song" music. The harsh labors of the workweek return, but time has a new organization, measured from Sunday to Sunday. In the next section Ray Nance plays an expressive obbligato over the trombone tune. The counterpoint may represent the group of slaves worshipping outside the church and their dawning recognition of the liberating content of Scripture, its call for justice:

> "A false balance is abomination to the Lord;
> But a just weight is his delight . . ."
> "When pride cometh, then cometh shame,
> But with the lowly is wisdom."
> "The integrity of the upright shall guide them:
> But the perverseness of transgressors
> Shall destroy them."

The distant promise of liberation, though, appears only in a short passage of "train effect" music at the close of the violin solo; in spirituals the train signified the network of escape known as the Underground Railroad. And then Hodges steps out and finally plays the entire melody to the bare accompaniment of guitar and bass. The poem presents this climactic performance, the keystone of the trilogy's arch, as both a religious and musical calling:

> God was good, but in his infinite wisdom
> Would allow one blessing at a time. . . .

He touched Boola's heart
And gave those golden sounds a lilt . . .
A depth . . . that no one else could duplicate.
He nudged the whites
And said to them: "LISTEN!"

The programmatic storytelling that sets up Hodges's solo allows the tune to expand its expressive domain to include the secular and the sacred. It is at once a ballad, a prayer, and a protest.

Black: *"Light"*

In the last parts of the poetic script for "Black" Ellington pursued the idea that the development of black music paralleled the evolving consciousness of the cause of freedom. Boola discovers that his songs placated his master but also could manipulate him:

It is not true . . . that all his songs
Were songs of sorrow. Tantalizingly
His humor slyly touched upon
His master's gullibility.
"Yassa, boss!" Simple, wasn't it?

This story, though, is not immediately apparent in the music of "Light" that brings *Black* to a close, yet more than the previous sections, "Light" shapes a musical narrative through the devices of thematic recall, embellishment, and superimposition and constantly weaves together melodic ideas from the previous two sections. It achieves this new synthesis by building on a platform of repeated phrase structures; in other words, it fuses work song and spiritual through the medium of jazz.[25] Finally endowing the music with both the physiognomy and drive of his three-minute compositions, Ellington was also cryptically rewriting jazz history, backdating its origins by a century.

Expanding on the thematic superimpositions Ellington deployed in "Harlem Air Shaft," "Light" is a virtuosic display of contrapuntal *ars combinatoria*. A detailed outline is needed to map out the polyphony:

Introduction (mm. 1–16): Beginning with a solo trumpet cadenza by Rex Stewart, which serves as a transition from "Come Sunday," this section restates the Riding on a Blue Note and Blues Riff ideas from "Work Song" and ends with an allusion to the bridge of "Come Sunday."

First chorus (mm. 17–56): A forty-bar AABBA in B♭ that begins with the shout chorus from Riding on a Blue Note. In the first A the trumpet superimposes the Fanfare motive from "Work Song." In the second A it superimposes the sax section Work Song theme. In the first B a reprise of the trombone section's Jump for Joy theme takes the place of the piano solo bridge heard in Riding on a Blue Note. The second B combines a shout in the trumpets, riffs based on the bridge of "Come Sunday" in the saxes, and statements of the Fanfare motive and the Blues Riff motive in the trombones. The final A is a harmonized unison shout chorus for all three choirs. On the last bar the bass enters with the Riding on a Blue Note motive.

Second chorus (mm. 57–77): Bass solo, ABA, but with a harmonic twist. The bass continues its solo with four bars by quoting four bars from Nanton's solo in "Work Song" that recall the spiritual "Good News"; the next four bars uses the Blues Riff motive to modulate to A♭. The equivalent of a bridge consists of a four-bar variant of the Blues Riff in A♭ followed by a restatement of the Sax Section Work Song in C major, the key of Nanton's "Work Song" Epiphany. A shortened, four-bar A returns the music to B♭ by way of the Blues Riff.

Mm. 77–119: This section contains a thirteen-bar phrase that sounds like a condensed AA, followed by a four-bar reinterpretation of the Fanfare motive by the trumpet section in counterpoint to an augmentation of "Swing Low" in the saxes. The AA begins by superimposing the Good News motive in the saxes on Riding on a Blue Note in the trombones. In the first B phrase the sax section recalls the bridge of "Come Sunday." The second bridge phrase brings in the solo trombone (Lawrence Brown) against a new sax riff. In the extended ten-bar A that follows, Brown recalls the melody of "Come Sunday" against "Riding on a Blue Note" in the saxes.

Transition (mm. 120–25): The music suddenly broadens.

First coda (mm. 126–165): A series of climactic superimpositions of the motives of "Work Song" and "Come Sunday" beginning in B♭ then modulating to C with a faux final cadence in the saxes.

Second coda (mm. 166 to end): Suddenly the music starts up again at a faster tempo and in A♭, with a three-way superimposition: the Riding on a Blue Note motive in the saxes, Nanton's Epiphany in the trumpets, and the Fanfare in the trombones.

Much of this section is driven by repeated trumpet notes, alternatingly muted and open, that recall a figure from "Old Man Blues."[26] Just as that earlier piece inverted "Old Man River" into a celebratory shout, this second coda blows the blues away and serves as an apt summary of the path *Black* has traveled (in around twenty minutes) from enslavement to enlightenment.

"Light" celebrates freedom and jazz at the same time. In backdating jazz, Ellington also backdates freedom; the understanding of liberation precedes emancipation. Freedom, the music says, was not something bestowed on blacks by whites. It is the rightful claim of all humanity as proven by Scripture:

> The master carried his fear with him . . .
> Clutched to his bosom, into the haven of love.
> Boola sang his way into the gallery of the church,
> He could sing . . . yes . . .
> But he couldn't sit with the worshippers
> Of the Christ who said: "Peace on earth
> To men of good will." Boola sat upstairs,
> In the "Crow's Nest" they called it.
> Did they not realize he was above them . . .
> Closer to that Heaven they were shouting about?

The idea that freedom is a counterpoint of faith and justice may sound awkward in words, but it translates powerfully into a musical texture. Ellington's polyphony sounds improvised but had to be calculated in advance; it's not an effect a composer can leave to chance. At the same time, though, the constant interplay of allusions recalls the techniques of scat singing.

Brown: *"West Indian Dance," "Emancipation Celebration," "The Blues"*

If we briefly allow ourselves to think of *Black, Brown and Beige* as a kind of symphony, *Brown* combines scherzo and slow movement;[27] like Mahler's Second and Third, it has two scherzos, "West Indian Dance" and "Emancipation Celebration." Heard in operatic terms, it feels like two ballets followed by a substantial aria, a fine second act. Unlike the complexly interwoven parts of *Black*, *Brown* presents itself as three freestanding vignettes, with no thematic exchange between sections. We therefore need to interpret them in terms of contrast rather than continuity, and the contrasts are provocative. Generically Caribbean rather than specifically Haitian, "West Indian Dance," originally prefaced by a brief snatch of Revolutionary War fife and drum sounds and post-faced with fragments of "Old Folks at Home" and "Yankee Doodle," expands the African American story beyond the United States, placing it within the larger story of the African diaspora. Coming before the "Emancipation Celebration," it makes the jubilant mood of "Emancipation" feel provincial, of one place and one time. Ellington told the audience that the "Emancipation Celebration" illustrated "two sides of a story," the hopes of the younger generation and the exhaustion of "a small group of old people who had earned the right to sit down and rest on somebody's property and of course their song was a very plaintive but tragic one." The music, however, hardly sounds tragic and is only vaguely plaintive; it feels like a catchy swing number. Listening to the live recording, I sense that the warm applause that followed this section may have expressed a sense of relief that Ellington was finally playing the kind of music the audience had come to hear; Ellington's little parable about young and old may really have been a well-masked critique of a public who just wanted to hear the same old songs. Or it could allude to the contrasting political ideas of DuBois and Washington.

"The Blues" contrasts sharply in mood and style with "Emancipation Celebration," a contrast complicated by the fact that, as the words tell us, much of "The Blues" "ain't the blues." The chronological sequence of "Emancipation" and "The Blues" is historically accurate, at least in terms of current research, yet it is emotionally perplexing: if people were free, why were they feeling so sad? Again Ellington's words, seemingly at odds with the music, contained a veiled message. He announced that the "third part of Brown, which we call 'Mauve,' is 'The Blues,' after the many love triangles that developed in the life of the great Negro heroes of the Spanish-American War." Nothing in the music recalls the battle of San Juan Hill, but the idea that the blues was created by returning heroes rather than marginalized rural folk musicians was a cunning bit of anti-Hammond historical revisionism. (John Hammond predictably bemoaned that Ellington "saw fit to tamper with the blues.")[28] In these terse comments Ellington reminded his wartime audience of the failure of America to recognize and honor black participation in all of its past wars, and he was also giving notice that no one would define the blues for him. If anyone in the audience expected a country blues à la Lead Belly or a "territory" blues in the style of Jimmy Rushing they were in for a rude surprise; the opening of "Mauve" sounds more like Berg than Basie.

In *Stomping the Blues* Albert Murray distinguishes between "the blues as such, the feeling inside your head that tries to make you wish that you were dead or had never been born," and the "blues as music," which "by its very nature and function is nothing if not a form of diversion. With all its preoccupation with the most disturbing aspects of life, it is something contrived specifically to be performed as entertainment." Ellington announced the ineffable mystery of his subject with a series of cautionary negations:

> The Blues . . .
> The Blues ain't
> Then Blues ain't nothing . . .
> Ain't nothin' like nothin' I know.

"Know" even sounds like "no." The blues is not knowable, but it can be negated, through the blues. Or not.

Ellington brandished his contrarian intentions with the very opening of "The Blues," a modernistic brass fanfare followed by a counterintuitive blues motive, not the expected "blue" minor third but an ambiguous descending major third, heard first in whole-tone harmonies, which the singer, Betty Roché, revealed as a diminished fourth, E♭ to B♮ resolving to C—a potently dissonant melodic interval but not at all bluesy. The first two stanzas are sung virtually without a sense of beat, like a recitative. There is no suggestion of a blues scale until a G♭ appears in the sixteenth bar. Just at the point when listeners may have decided that this blues "ain't the blues," Ben Webster leapt in (with the rhythm section) as if to prove otherwise. He played a seventeen-bar solo, lifted from "Jump for Joy," with a blues inflection, but the harmonic structure drifts impressionistically between the keys of c minor and D♭ rather than following the usual blues pattern. Once again, the blues ain't. The blues "as music" (and in D♭) only arrives at bar 52, as a call-and-response between pitch-bending trombones and growling trumpets (a passage Ellington soon expanded into a stand-alone piece, "Carnegie Blues"). Just as the music established its groove and seemed to prepare the singer to tell us how her baby left her, Webster intervened again with a short cadenza. Roché then reentered, but with an eight-bar phrase that led back, in retrograde, to the opening negations:

> The Blues ain't nothin'
> The Blues ain't
> The Blues.

The overall form resembles a Bartókian arch, symmetrical but fore-shortened:

Recitative (two stanzas, each moving from c minor to f minor)
Webster solo
Carnegie blues
Webster solo
Recitative (moving from D♭ to c minor)

("Emancipation Celebration," perhaps less casual than it first appears, has a similar structure.)

In *Stomping the Blues* Murray places the "blues as music" in a double relationship, one historical, the other spiritual. On one side the blues is a response to suffering inflicted by history, but blues also repre-sents one side of a dualism that Murray frames in terms of the Saturday Night Function and the Sunday Morning Service. These two opposites are so mutually dependent that the boundaries can get blurred and con-tested. Murray, for instance, praises James Brown for performing "as if he were a spellbinding Evangelical preacher" but criticizes the way Ray Charles "bootlegged" sacred music into profane: "the assumption seems to be that sacrilege can be nullified by sentimentality."[29] By composing "The Blues" as a monumental concert aria, Ellington counterposed it to "Come Sunday" and again raised the question of whether this opposi-tion signified progression or codependence. Ellington understood the complex cultural tensions presented by the opposition of spiritual and blues. When he recorded *Black, Brown and Beige* with Mahalia Jack-son in 1958, he omitted "The Blues" along with all the music for *Beige,* which he replaced with a new setting of Psalm 23.

Beige

Ever since the premiere of *Black, Brown and Beige, Beige* has been the most problematic part of the triptych. While Ellington continued to program parts of *Black* and *Brown* for the rest of his career, *Beige* mainly lived on as a movement titled "Sugar Hill Penthouse." In the 1965 studio recording Ellington revived the opening sections of *Beige,* but he never performed or recorded its dramatic ending. Walter van de Leur has conjectured that Ellington simply ran out of time and brought Strayhorn in to help complete the movement; otherwise the music of

Black, Brown and Beige is all by Ellington. Strayhorn composed a long cadenza for Ben Webster, accompanied by a series of chords based on earlier parts of the suite, and interpolated his own older composition, "Symphonette-Rhythmique, which now became "Sugar Hill Penthouse." When Ellington later performed and recorded a piece by that name, however, it was sometimes Strayhorn's composition and at other times was just its last section, which uses the same melody that Ellington used for a waltz in the earlier part of *Beige.* It is not clear if this phrase, with its distinctive scoring for clarinets and saxes that reminded many critics of Glenn Miller, was collaborative; the Ellington archive contains a sketch for this passage in Ellington's hand.

As presented in January 1943, however, *Beige* was a sizable movement in many contrasting sections:

1. Modernistic, dissonant, fast introduction
2. Ragtime-style piano solo that Ellington later called "Bitch's Ball"
3. Waltz
4. Interjection of a trumpet solo
5. Waltz continued
6. Saxophone cadenza
7. Short piano solo, leading to . . .
8. "Symphonette," a.k.a. "Sugar Hill Penthouse," ending with reed chorus
9. Coda: Fanfares, reprise of "Come Sunday," portentous piano solo, *Meistersinger*-style thematic summation, like an anthem; up-tempo codetta

Ellington never stated his self-critical thoughts about *Beige;* its performance history, however, suggests that he was happier with Strayhorn's contributions than his own. "Sugar Hill Penthouse" soon entered the band's repertory. The poem reveals that Ellington had set himself a difficult task, contrasting the fake view of Harlem with the real one. The opening sections of *Beige* show that, as we might expect, Ellington had no problem evoking the 1920s fantasy Harlem of "Mongrel Manhattan." He had been there, and his music, particularly in its jungle substyle, had defined the era. If we compare the music of *Black, Brown and Beige* with that of *Symphony in Black,* however, we can see how far Ellington had evolved in musical technique and in historical awareness. The score for the short film, a mix of new music and old, illustrated scenes from black life that were clichés of 1920s theater and nightclubs—a little bit of *Show Boat,* a little Cotton Club, a little *Green Pastures.* The stylized visual language of much of the movie treated black bodies as aesthetic objects, African sculptures, with one-dimensional emotions: sorrow, jealousy, revelry. The "Laborers" section just revived the imagery of "Old Man River." The song of sorrow featured a preacher with arms stretched upward like De Lawd in *Green Pastures.* The central "Jealousy" section, known for its performance by Billie Holiday, linked the blues in a stereotyped way to a fallen woman, an association Ellington excoriated in *Porgy and Bess.*

Much of the music in *Beige* departed from the two contrasting voices—one satiric, one prophetic—found in the poem, suggesting that Ellington was pursuing a different musical program. In his memoirs Mercer Ellington suggested an angle in the music not present in the poem: "It also embodied a criticism of his own race and its caste system."[30] Roi Ottley spelled out that system in a chapter titled "The Café-au-Lait Society" in *New World a-Comin',* which also appeared in 1943: "Social distinctions developed among Negroes as early as slavery. At first, house servants drew the line against field-hands; later the mark of distinction was the amount of aristocratic 'white' blood one possessed, and finally the length of time one was freed."[31] In Harlem the light-skinned elite lived in the elegant apartment buildings on Sugar Hill, "the most modern and beautiful residential area for Negroes in Black America."[32] Ottley, though, further distinguished between the older Negro elite, professionals who moved in their own segregated world, and the "café society" of Harlem's artists and intellectuals who might be heard discussing "the relative merits of Count Basie and Benny Goodman, or the possible musical importance of Duke Ellington's 'Concerto for Cootie.'"[33]

We may hear Ellington's tone parallels for both of these "beige" elites in the two extended lyrical sections of *Beige,* the waltz and "Sugar Hill Penthouse." These sections may also represent two different generations. Though Ellington's parents were middle class, they emulated the tastes and decorum of the black aristocracy. They lived in Northwest Washington, whose residents, according to Rex Stewart, "were the lighter complexioned people with the better-type jobs, such as schoolteachers, postmen, clerks or in government service."[34] We can hear the waltz as an affectionate portrait of his parents, both his father, who "raised his family as though he were a millionaire" and was, Ellington recalled, " a great dancer (ballroom that is), a connoisseur of vintages, and unsurpassed at creating an aura of conviviality,"[35] and his mother, whom he thought of as "the most beautiful mother in the world."[36] Ellington viewed their social aspirations in a kindly manner; after all, they were the source of his own nobility. The waltz, an extended lyrical "concerto" for trumpeter Harold Baker, gradually loses its inhibitions and reveals a "ragtime" subtext that Ellington deployed more overtly later in the waltz depicting Lady Macbeth. His parents also must have had a less inhibited, down-home side.

If his parents aspired to the life of the African American elite, Billy Strayhorn, who was around the same age as Ellington's son, Mercer, represented the other facet of the upper crust, its café society. Unlike Daisy Ellington, Billy Strayhorn was by no means beige in complexion, nor was he conventional in his lifestyle. A free spirit, not deterred by his short stature, dark skin, or homosexuality, he was as at home in Paris or Hollywood as he was in Harlem. His music demonstrated an equal disregard for convention; his "Dirge," which was performed at Carnegie Hall after the intermission, barely seemed like jazz at all. Barry Ulanov wrote that it "stumped the audience and sounded more like Milhaud and the latter-day Stravinsky than Ellington," but the "Stomp" that followed, more familiar as "Johnny Come Lately," was as swinging a number as could be imagined. Strayhorn could be seen as an embodiment of the freedom that Boola had first perceived as a possibility hundreds of years before. What better way to illustrate that freedom than through Strayhorn's own music? Ellington may have incorporated "Symphonette" into *Beige* not as an act of last-minute bricolage but as a deliberate tribute. Strayhorn, after all, would also contribute significantly to the *Perfume Suite* and the *Deep South Suite* without the impetus of a looming deadline.

Emblems of a past and future unfettered by prejudice, Ellington's parents and Billy Strayhorn represented aspects of the unseen Harlem that Ellington hoped would dislodge the old stereotypes. But in giving so much of *Beige* over to these intimate portraits, Ellington had strayed far from the much more public and political agenda he outlined in the poem, and when the more rhetorical closing section of *Beige* finally arrived, it sounded tacked on. Rather than rewrite the movement, however, Ellington soon composed two works that stayed focused on its political goals and also worked out some unresolved musical problems. We can hear Ellington's critique of *Beige* in two of its sequels, *New World A-Comin'* and *Harlem*.

When the Ellington Orchestra returned to Carnegie Hall in December 1943 it did not reprise any of *Black, Brown and Beige* but instead presented the premiere of *New World A-Comin'*, which Graham Lock aptly terms its "conceptual successor, the evocation of the visionary future." The new work, a compact piano concerto in one movement, took its title from Roi Ottley's book about Harlem, which had appeared in August 1943 and would win the Peabody Award for literature. Born in Harlem, Ottley had a successful career as an athlete and journalist, eventually becoming a regular columnist for the *Chicago Tribune*. His charmingly knowledgeable book was a far more sophisticated work of literature than Ellington's poem and a more nuanced history; it might be considered an uptown equivalent of Frederick Lewis Allen's *Only Yesterday,* a masterfully written account of New York in the roaring 1920s. Where Allen, writing in 1931, described a recent past that suddenly seemed remote, Ottley's book looked toward a future: "The Negro may not be able to predict the future, but he knows what he wants—liberty and peace, and an enriched life, free of want, oppression, violence and proscription."[37]

Ottley's words were not hollow rhetoric. His book contained a specific agenda, the "Eight Point Program" that black leaders had presented to the President demanding the end to all laws that distinguished citizens on the basis of color, the guarantee of civil liberties, abolition of the poll tax, an end to lynching, and "representation for Negroes on all missions, political and technical, which will be sent to the peace conference." Ottley also documented how Nazi and Japanese agents were already exploiting widespread if not majority disaffection with the war in the black community. The war would only be won, Ottley argued, as a shared fight for American freedom: "This war, undeniably, belongs to the Negro as well as to the white man. To this extent, it may be called a 'People's War'—for in spite of selfish interests a new world is a-coming with the sweep and fury of the Resurrection.[38]

Though it used Ottley's title, Ellington's composition surprisingly leapfrogged across the burning rhetoric of the present to the imagined future. Ellington was once again demonstrating musically the ideological point he had made in "Light," that freedom had to be imagined in order to be realized. In sharp contrast to the militant fanfare of *Black,* the opening theme seems to sing Ottley's title with a comforting, almost nostalgic warmth. It represented, as Ellington said, a vision of the "beautiful things to come that have already been enjoyed." Instead of mounting a fight for equality Ellington composed music for a time when that fight would be only a memory.

New World A-Comin' also fulfilled the transmuted operatic ambitions of *Black, Brown and Beige.* The one instrumental voice that had not come to the fore in *Black* and *Brown* was Ellington's own. He had reserved this personal statement for *Beige,* but it appeared half-formed in the piano solo, which Ellington later identified as "Bitch's Ball," a piece he had written in 1914, and in the Gershwinesque cadenza that serves as a transition to the final section of the movement. Ellington would include piano solos similar to "Bitch's Ball" in the *Perfume Suite* ("Dancers in Love") and the *Deep South Suite* ("There Was Nobody Looking"); in *Beige,* however, it seems all too short and unrelated to the extended waltz that follows. The modernistic cadenzas in *Beige* sound like vestiges of an anxious rivalry with Gershwin that went back at least as far as "Creole Rhapsody." If the piano were to assume a leading role in *Beige* it would unavoidably risk a comparison with *Rhapsody in Blue.* In *Beige,* though, that starring role emerged only tentatively; in *New World A-Comin'* it appears in terms that are so thoroughly Ellingtonian that further comparison to Gershwin is irrelevant. The piece is a free-flowing dialogue between a piano and orchestra equally steeped in the Ellington style; the orchestra does not oppose the soloist but amplifies its ideas.

Although it was composed in 1950 (aboard the *Île de France* on the way back from a European tour), *Harlem* (commissioned by the NBC Symphony and premiered at the Metropolitan Opera House) captured the mood and scope of Ottley's book even more powerfully than *New World* and can be heard as the ultimate realization of *Beige.* Ottley, whose parents emigrated to Harlem from Grenada, emphasized the diverse communities of Harlem in his provocatively titled chapter "How Colored Is Harlem?" In *Beige,* Ellington had shaped African American history so that it all seemed to lead to magenta-hazed Sugar Hill and its privileged inhabitants. That may have been *his* story, but it was only part of a far broader picture.

Harlem, we might say, turns time into space; it is geography rather than history, traversing neighborhoods populated by black, brown, and beige rather than moving from past to future. And yet, more successfully than any of Ellington's extended works, it tells a musical story, a transformation and reevaluation of the poetic "Beige." The poem set out to contrast false and true views of Harlem. The music offers a different and inclusive vision, more parallel with Ottley's description:

Harlem! The word itself signifies a vast, crowded area teeming with black men. Its population is pushing hard toward a million, and is crammed into two square miles. Some are foreign born and come from diverse racial, religious and national origins. Though their skins may be black, brown, yellow or white they are all seeking a way out of the impasses of Negro life. To this end, the Negro community is a big forum of soapbox oratory. Day-to-day living seems to be an endless vigil of picket lines, strikes, boycotts, mammoth mass meetings, as well as a series of colorful parades, jazzy picnics, and easy stomping at the Savoy Ballroom. But comes Sunday, everybody praises God—faithfully, noisily.[39]

For his tone parallel, Ellington created an unusual form: two sets of free variations, back to back. The first half of the piece develops a melody that begins with a musical intonation of the word "Harlem." The variations present the melody in constant flux, with a new groove in every phrase, alluding to a variety of jazz and Latin rhythms; the music seems to get ever faster and louder, and then it suddenly breaks off with a slow, plaintive clarinet solo that initiates the second wave of variations. The new theme has something of the quality of New Orleans funeral music and a certain suggestion of the morning after; it picks up countermelodies slowly, wistfully, gradually regaining its strength. By 1950 the fake Harlem was a vague memory; whites from downtown no longer arrived in ermines and pearls. Instead of counterposing fake and real, Ellington portrayed a daily cycle of the secular and sacred, nighttime and daytime, two faces of the same community, both essential to its identity. *Harlem* solved the problems in *Beige* by reimagining its dualisms as complements, thereby redeeming the historical past of both Harlem and Ellington from the scars of otherness.

SQUARE DANCE: THE TWO SIDES OF
APPALACHIAN SPRING

One minute and thirty-six seconds into the ballet *Appalachian Spring* a single gesture foretells the action to come. Or does it? Watching the video we see a story about gender, about men and women, their connections and their differences. It is also a story about spaces, interiors and exteriors, delicately but rigidly mapped out by Isamu Noguchi's spare set. Almost as soon as the music starts a man enters, clad in the black garb and wide-brimmed hat of a nineteenth-century American preacher. He walks calmly, steadily. Behind him a woman enters, moving with a similarly stately gait. They both walk past the outlines of a house. He strides toward the front of the stage, steps up on a circular platform, like a tree stump, and stands erect, looking confidently outward. This is his land. She walks to the side of the stage and sits facing away from the audience, as if opposite a spinning wheel. This is her domain. Throughout the ballet her billowing skirt and circling motion will give her the quality of an earth mother (the "prevailing spirit" as May O'Donnell described her),[40] even though her actual relation to the other characters is not clear. A second man now enters, dressed with rural formality in a vest and tie but no jacket. As he walks past the house he touches its wall, stroking it gently. This is his house. He strides toward the preacher then takes up a position on the fence, looking outward. A second woman enters. In her dress and movements she seems younger than the first woman. She enters the house, looks across at the younger man, and suddenly recoils, taking a step backward before walking forward to embrace him. This is her fate. The recoil is seismic; it is the one moment of uncertainty in the unfolding action. What does she fear?

I questioned whether this moment actually occurred because it is in no way present in the music. Copland's famously atmospheric opening betrays not a quarter note of anxiety. It employs only the notes of the A major scale in a steady pulse of half and quarter notes without syncopation, and with a veiled timbre that Copland refers to in the score as a "white tone." Listeners to the music would never suspect that the Bride (as the second woman is designated) had wavered in her simple devotion to the Husbandman (as Graham termed the second man). Nor would they imagine that the danced action for which Copland created his music describes what Lynn Garafola has termed a "netherworld of evil."[41]

The dance historian Marta Robertson has pointed out the conceptual issues raised by *Appalachian Spring.* Is it a work of dance theater or a musical composition? The title applies to a large family of works: the ballet "conceived and choreographed by Martha Graham" (as it says in the video), with music by Aaron Copland and set by Isamu Noguchi; the original Copland score, subtitled "Ballet for Martha," for thirteen instruments (a number dictated by the small size of the auditorium at the Library of Congress, where the premiere of the ballet took place in October 1944); and the various instrumental works that Copland drew from that score: a suite for the original instrumentation, a suite for full orchestra, and *Variations on a Shaker Theme* for orchestra or band.[42] Copland completed the suite for orchestra in May 1945, right after the ballet score received the Pulitzer Prize for music on V-E Day. Arthur

Rodzinski conducted the premiere with the New York Philharmonic in October 1945; the suite was soon played by major orchestras around the country and around the world. Within a few years Copland's final variation on the Shaker tune "Simple Gifts" would attain the status of an unofficial national anthem.

As Robertson points out, the music world assumed that Copland's score "had transcended its choreographic origins."[43] As the music entered the orchestral repertory, Graham's choreography, like Nijinsky's for *Le sacre du printemps,* appeared as just part of the birthing process of a musical masterpiece, even though, like *Le sacre,* the original *Appalachian Spring* was the product of collaboration, created as a work of musical theater. When Graham produced a video of the ballet in 1958, fearlessly dancing the role of the Bride at the age of sixty-four, the opening credits gave her own creative role precedence over Copland's. She was attempting to reclaim her own work, whose dark vision had been buried under the runaway success of Copland's score.

Because *Appalachian Spring* evolved during the war years it offers an instructive counterpoint to *Black, Brown and Beige* in its representation of American history and ideology, and in its critical reception. In many ways Martha Graham's career paralleled Ellington's, and the similarities may shed light on the way critics framed their achievements. Like Ellington, Graham developed a body of work for her own company and had little interest in having it performed by others. Like Ellington she built her works out of the specific qualities of the members of her company, including herself. Like Ellington she evolved her own idiom that broke with European tradition. (Copland called the work "Ballet for Martha," but technically speaking it was not a ballet but a work of modern dance using a movement vocabulary distinct from classic balletic practice.) Finally, like Ellington she devoted herself to representing the experience of a part of human society that had not been able to tell its own story; in her case this meant telling the story of women from Medea and Clytemnestra to the present. Critics attacked her dances with the same barbs aimed at Ellington's longer works; they were termed pretentious, overloaded with message, too idiosyncratic to last. Even today the fate of Graham's oeuvre, like Ellington's, remains uncertain. How should they be preserved? How can they be reinterpreted? These questions never arise in relation to Copland's music.

If music can write history it can also erase it. In its development and subsequent history, *Appalachian Spring* gradually covered over all of its discordant elements in favor of a picture of American innocence

with which it quickly became synonymous. The process of erasure pre-
dates even the earliest discussion of a commission in 1942. *Appalachian Spring* was Copland's third ballet with a Western theme, after
Billy the Kid (1938) and *Rodeo* (1942). Prior to these scores Copland
was not a "Western" composer but a quintessential New Yorker whose
music emulated the syncopations and sonorities of jazz, at first overtly,
as in his *Music for the Theatre* (1925) and Piano Concerto (1926),
and later more abstractly, as in the Piano Variations (1931) and Short
Symphony (1934). *Music for the Theater* evoked the sleazy mood of
a Bowery burlesque show; *Statements* (1934) quoted "The Sidewalks
of New York." In his three Western ballets, however, the jazz element
disappeared, replaced by cowboy melodies and the Scots-Irish lilt of the
square dance.

Copland's westward turn can be explained in several ways; Copland
himself liked to point out that although his father was born in Russia,
on his mother's side he was related to one of the founders of Neiman
Marcus, the famed Dallas department store. Virgil Thomson, on the
other hand, accused Copland of stealing the idea from Thomson's score
for the film *The Plow That Broke the Plain,* which made use of cowboy
songs, including "I Ride an Old Paint," which Copland used in *Billy the
Kid* and *Rodeo.* That film, though, illustrates a more general trend in
historical representation. It told the story of how the American plains
were turned into a dust belt due to the market demands of the First
World War and the economic speculation that fueled the boom of the
1920s. The film portrayed the excesses of the '20s with fleeting shots
of black jazz musicians crosscut with ticker-tape machines spinning out
of control. Pictorially and musically, it seemed to blame the dustbowl
equally on capitalism and blacks. Jazz, the musical idiom of the 1920s,
was now counterposed against the sufferings of "real" Dust Belt Americans, Western and white.

In the 1930s the defining status of frontier America appeared in the
murals of Thomas Hart Benton, cowboy movies, the songs of Woody
Guthrie, and the music of Roy Harris, who was born in a log cabin in
the Indian Territory that would become Oklahoma. All of these works
redefined American national identity away from the conflict of North
and South and toward the opening of the West and the experience of
the frontier. In doing so, moreover, they erased African Americans and
their music from American history. Although there were, in fact, many
African Americans in the American West, they would not appear in a
cowboy movie until *Blazing Saddles,* Mel Brooks's Western parody,

which featured a black sheriff and a cameo by the Count Basie Orchestra playing "April in Paris."

With *Billy the Kid* Copland did not just jump on board the Wild West bandwagon; he hijacked it.[44] Despite its Western theme *Billy the Kid* was the brainchild of a wealthy Bostonian impresario, Lincoln Kirstein. Its composer was Brooklyn-born, and its choreographer, Eugene Loring, hailed from Wisconsin; Billy the Kid himself was born as Henry McCarty in an Irish slum in New York City. According to Lynn Garafola, Kirstein was attracted to the subject out of a left-leaning politics he shared with Copland. Billy "belonged to a new breed of American working class heroes popularized in proletariat dramas like *Stevedore.*"[45] Kirstein provided Copland with a book of cowboy tunes, but Loring created the scenario, and, infusing the ballet with ideas from modern dance, he created a movement vocabulary for the work that was "weighted rather than light, angular as opposed to rounded and full of percussive punch."[46]

Two themes emerged strongly from the ballet: the inexorable movement of Americans westward, presented as a "horizontal trek across the stage" (inspired by an earlier work by Martha Graham, *American Document*) set to Copland's weighty saraband rhythm, and Billy's isolation and tentative existence, spelled out in brief scenes that are "terse, rapid and cinematic." While the opening "prairie music" echoed Roy Harris in its open texture and primitive-sounding parallel fifths, much of Billy's music is modernistic and nervous; the famous gunfight scene could take place as easily in a Brooklyn alley as at the O.K. Corral. The new immediacy of expression in these passages owes as much to the film music of Prokofiev as to Copland's westernizing contemporaries.

If Kirstein's choice of American subjects for his Ballet Caravan reflected the Popular Front slogan, "Communism is twentieth-century Americanism," Copland's score, insinuating the composer's own New York sensibility into a frontier setting, demonstrated that musical modernism could be as American as a Conestoga wagon. Not everyone was convinced, though. In his influential survey *Our American Composers,* written in 1941, John Tasker Howard wrote that Copland's music "brings us the sophistication of the cosmopolitan cities on the seaboard."[47] Copland, though, might have considered that a compliment. His second Western ballet, *Rodeo,* choreographed by Agnes de Mille, once more portrayed a misfit, this time a cowgirl rather than a cowboy.

At the time of its premiere in 1942 with the Ballet Russe de Monte Carlo, *Rodeo* appeared as a crowd-pleasing comedy, "The Taming of the Shrew—cowboy style," as de Mille described it, with a common-sensical plot premise: "the problem that has confronted all American women . . . how to get a suitable man."[48] Copland's music, too, sounded more folkloristic than in *Billy the Kid.* As Howard Pollack notes, the folk songs that Copland borrowed from various anthologies "appear in their entirety and in relatively traditional settings."[49] The suite from the ballet, and especially its "Hoe-Down," finally earned Copland popular success beyond the confines of new music. The score remains a staple of both symphony and pops concerts, and the ballet, alone of the trilogy, continues to be danced in its original form.

Seen today, however, its action, if not its music, reveals a psycho-logical complexity that no longer seems like a joke. It is a story about gender roles that can be read several ways. The Cowgirl (danced by de Mille herself) is a jeans-clad tomboy who finally puts on a dress to land a husband. Before the change in outfit, though, she shows that she can keep up with any of the guys by outdancing them all, yet she finally conforms. Garafola writes that "to the extent that it was about the curbing of female independence," the ballet "anticipated the postwar ideology that sent Rosie the Riveter back home."[50] Comic though it may seem, *Rodeo* represented wartime anxieties about the redistribu-tion of power on a home front devoid of "suitable" men. De Mille would develop this theme further in the Dream Ballet of *Oklahoma!* Rodgers and Hammerstein asked her to choreograph their new musical after seeing *Rodeo;* the Dream Ballet at the end of act 1 was her con-ception. It portrays Laurey's despair at having to choose between two defective men, the violently sexual Jud and the sweetly asexual Curly. Laurey can be considered a link between the Cowgirl in *Rodeo* and the Bride in *Appalachian Spring.* But what is a cowgirl, or a tomboy? Is she a lesbian who finally yields to the pressures of society? Or does "she" represent a closeted gay man who, donning that dress, finds a way to come out? Or a woman more in touch with her masculine side than men can tolerate? The ballet endures today because it accommo-dates all these possibilities, and with a smile on its face. At the same time, though, the Cowgirl, Laurey, Rosie the Riveter, and the Bride in Copland's next ballet were, without knowing it, women poised on the uncharted frontier of feminism.

Rodeo must have seemed like a diversion from the war; *Appala-chian Spring* was intended from the start as a commentary on it.[51] In-deed, Copland's third Western ballet was at the outset not Western at all. Graham's first scenario, "Daughter of Colchis," was set in New

England in the time of Hawthorne; Graham, who called the second script (after Copland rejected the first) "House of Victory," placed the action slightly westward, in Pennsylvania, and moved the timeframe up to the Civil War. The characters included the "Citizen," whom Graham associated with the abolitionist John Brown, and a fugitive slave; in a revision Graham added an Indian girl inspired by Hart Crane's vision of Pocahontas. These early dramatic ideas would shape the later music: the New England setting suggested a musical and scenic relation to the Shakers, a sect not found in Pennsylvania, and the distant sound of war would appear in the suggestion of a fanfare in the opening clarinet solo. While Graham would end up with a more abstract, almost mythic, treatment of the story, her drafts included specific period episodes such as a retelling of *Uncle Tom's Cabin* (an idea picked up by Jerome Robbins for *The King and I*), a charade of John Brown's attack on Harpers Ferry, and a scene that would suggest a Negro church.[52]

Copland began composing even as Graham sent him these evolving concepts. After she received his final score, however, Graham altered the scenario significantly, as Copland would discover to his surprise a few days before the premiere; Graham also gave the work its title, based on a line from Hart Crane. Graham, after all, had commissioned the music (though the money came from Elizabeth Sprague Coolidge).

Copland, who, like Ellington, knew the value of a smiling public face, said that the fact that Graham had used "music composed for one kind of action to accompany something else, doesn't bother me a bit," but, as Howard Pollack notes, his letters to Carlos Chavez were less sanguine and cautioned that Graham was "becoming more and more psychoanalytic in her motifs."[53] Copland had expressed no unhappiness with the Freudian aspects of the two previous ballets.

In its final form *Appalachian Spring* had just eight characters, with no Fugitive or Indian woman:

The Revivalist (danced by Merce Cunningham)

The Pioneer Woman (May O'Donnell)

The Husbandman (Erick Hawkins)

The Bride (Graham)

The Revivalist's Followers: Nina Fonaroff, Marjorie Mazia, Yuriko [Kikuchi], and Pearl Lang

(The fact that Copland's score managed to upstage three of the giants of American dance testifies to its power and cogency.) The two minority figures were absorbed into white characters; the Pioneer Woman took on some of the traits of the Indian girl, and the Revivalist channeled some of the rage of the Fugitive. The action was similarly streamlined to a presentation of the characters, a wedding followed by a "charivari" or shivaree accompanied by variations on "Simple Gifts," and a fiery sermon by the Revivalist ("Fear in the Night") followed by "Day of Wrath" and "Moment of Crisis," with the action and music returning to its calm pastoral tone in a concluding "Lord's Day." Graham turned three large sections of the score into solos for the Bride, her own role. These solos foregrounded the Bride, transforming the external story into what Howard Pollack has termed a "psychological monodrama," a continuation, so to speak, of the Dream Ballet in *Oklahoma!* In the section of the score marked "Wedding Day II," the Bride makes an insistent gesture that seems to ask "What about me?" Although she does not dance with the Husbandman here, she seems to cradle their child near the end of the solo, but she hands off the baby to the Pioneer Woman. In addition to dropping the specific Civil War references, Graham also made the narrative less explicit. It is hard to say when the wedding ceremony takes place or when the child is born. At the temporal and spatial center of the ballet the two male principals shake hands and the two women principals embrace, as if in accord, but the terms of their social compact are not clear, especially since the Pioneer Woman makes little contact with the other characters and the Bride acknowledges the Revivalist only once.

The music for the Fear, Wrath, and Crisis sections is unfamiliar because Copland omitted them from the orchestral suite. The action in these sections, however, is crucial to the story. The Revivalist, previously appearing as an almost comic figure despite a suspect relationship to his four female followers, who flutter around him like a flock of small birds, suddenly becomes terrifyingly stern. Graham told Merce Cunningham, "I don't know if you are a preacher, a farmer, or the devil."[54] His sermon demands that the Husbandman leave for war, which he does after first consulting the Pioneer Woman rather than the Bride. In my reading of the ballet he does not return alive but only as a ghostly memory. In the climactic reprise of "Simple Gifts" the Bride and Husbandman do not dance together. He seems at once present and absent. At the end, as Howard Pollack writes, "The Husbandman—or rather his spirit—stands behind the Bride, as she stretches her arm out toward the horizon, a remarkable gesture conjoining private and public destinies."[55]

If Graham's choreography told a story of a woman's love, fear of abandonment, and inner strength, what story was Copland telling in the music, much of it written for different characters than those of the final version? Pearl Lang, one of the original Followers, described the score as "joyous," "without a tragic moment in it—there is only the hint of one."[56] May O'Donnell recalled that the music had a "gentleness and sweetness" untypical of Graham's other dances.[57] Copland's score was heard, quite aptly, as a utopian vision, well suited to the original name for the setting, Eden Valley. The music subliminally places the action in an idyllic fantasy world just after the opening when the violins echo Stephen Foster's "Beautiful Dreamer." Whatever tensions might have appeared onstage, the music (or at least the parts of the score the people remembered) pictured a community where man was one with nature, woman was one with man, labor meshed with faith, the past gave strength to the future. A cynic might say that Copland's utopia crossed a Shaker village with a Labor Zionist kibbutz.

To represent Eden as simultaneously a legacy of the past and a hope for the future, Copland reinvented neoclassicism by way of traditional American fiddle music. This folk style preserved the straightforward harmonic logic and clear-cut phrase structure of the classical period. The music evokes American spaces through its own spaciousness of phrasing. Dissonances are rare, and Copland restricted his habitual irregular rhythmic groupings to two and three eighth notes, a device he derived from jazz, to a few moments of intensification; unusually for Copland, a lot of the music unfolds without metrical changes. No matter what convoluted situations Graham offered him, Copland seemed to perceive that his goal was to give his audience the quality that Stendhal had defined as the essence of art: the promise of happiness. It is quite likely that Copland understood that this luminous approach would serve well as a foil to Graham's darker expressionism.

Like *Black, Brown and Beige,* the ballet *Appalachian Spring* questioned the war effort under a camouflage of patriotism. While Ellington reminded his audience of the black heroes of America's earlier wars and implicitly called for a new social order, Graham portrayed the impulse to war itself in terms of demonic male fanaticism. By loosening the historical representation of the original scenario, she heightened its contemporary relevance at a time when many American women did not know if they would ever see their husbands again. In its reception and revisions, *Black, Brown and Beige* itself became a battlefield between Ellington and his mainly white critics. In its development and dual history as ballet and concert work, *Appalachian Spring* remained a contested zone in a gendered battle. In the contrasting entrances of the principals Graham not only set up the drama to come but also characterized her working relationship with Copland.

The most potent and disputed feature of the score was its treatment of "Simple Gifts." Despite the stamp of authenticity that it lends to the action, the Shaker hymn was wildly inappropriate, as Copland enjoyed pointing out: since the Shakers were celibate, a Shaker wedding was a contradiction in terms.[58] As Pollack notes, Copland may have viewed the Shakers sympathetically as protocommunists; Graham, by contrast, saw them as a typical American religious cult whose fanaticism sprang from "hidden desires." Copland made this dark side audible in the later sections of the ballet, whose style recalls the brittle tensions of the gunfight in *Billy the Kid,* but hardly any of this mood emerged in the suite, which omitted around three hundred measures from the original score.

In the ballet the four variations on "Simple Gifts" function much like the parts of a traditional pas de deux:

Theme: The Bride

Variation I: The Husbandman

Variation II: The Bride

Variation III: The Husbandman

Variation IV: Bride and Husbandman

The Husbandman's movements become increasingly outgoing and athletic in his variations. At the end of Variation IV the Bride and Husbandman enter the house, and she sits in the chair where the Pioneer Woman had sat at the opening. In the coda to the variations, however, the action shifts to the Revivalist and his flock. Suddenly the Revivalist begins to spin like a tornado, his arm jabbing out from time to time like an accusatory bolt of lightning. With the blessing of the Pioneering Woman, but without bidding his Bride farewell, the Husbandman steps across the fence that has so far bounded the action. The Revivalist and his followers pray for him and return to their regular business. Suddenly the Husbandman reappears, but no one seems to see him; perhaps he is only the image of the Bride's concern. She launches into a distraught solo in which she seems to tell her child about his or her father and recall their wedding dances. When the fifth, climactic variation of "Simple Gifts" sounds everyone dances joyously, except the Bride, who sits on the side, alone. For most of the quiet, prayerlike music that follows, she dances alone while the others are still. As the opening music returns the Husbandman joins her as the other characters depart; it is not clear whether they will face the future together, as many early accounts of the ballet assumed, or if she is alone with her memories.

However we interpret the action, the choreography for the final variation comes as a theatrical shock, and, if we only know the suite, a musical one as well. By placing the Bride off to the side, Graham stressed her alienation just as the music resonated with communal accord and marital affirmation. Indeed, watching the ballet I find myself continuously taken aback by moments of tension and pathos that I had not perceived in the music, a testimony, it might be said, to the artistry of both of its creators; there was no need for Copland to "mickey-mouse" the action. And yet, as Marta Robertson warns, the fact that music and dance seem to tell such different stories might also be termed an artistic failure on the part of the composer. The concert suite, Copland's pentimento, achieved its momentous success, we might speculate, precisely because it replaced Graham's story with a plotline more familiar in the concert hall. By lopping off the episodes of Fear, Wrath, and Crisis Copland allowed the fifth variation to appear as the defining and logical completion of the series, a triumphant resolution. Instead of appearing as a midballet divertissement, the sequence of theme and variations was now the goal of the entire composition, on the model of Beethoven's Ninth, whose theme Copland must have realized has a clear kinship with "Simple Gifts." The timing was perfect. With the war over, America (or at least its noninvisible population) was ready to sing its own "Ode to Joy." Years later Copland made no bones about his good fortune in mirroring the national mood: "I must admit I'm influenced by public opinion!"[59]

"Simple Gifts" was an odd anthem for a newly emerged nuclear superpower. Copland had no interest in actual Shaker doctrine; he had voided the song of its content just as he and Graham had bleached the discordant racial elements out of their vision of the American past. At war's end none of the demands that black leaders had made for fair employment and civil rights had been implemented; indeed, the reforms would not come about for another twenty years. Due to a large extent to the continuing power of Southern Democrats in Congress, the American Armed Forces remained segregated until the Korean War. A new world of equality was once again a "dream deferred." Late in the twentieth century conductors began to preface performances of Beethoven's Ninth with Schoenberg's *Survivor from Warsaw,* a chronologically inverted attempt to assert the Ninth's continuing relevance. Perhaps conductors might someday consider a similar pairing of Copland's *Appalachian Spring* with the Ellington/Strayhorn *Deep South Suite,* which premiered at Carnegie Hall in January 1946. Its first two movements, Ellington's satiric "Magnolias Dripping with Molasses" (titled "Psuedo" *[sic]* in the parts) and Strayhorn's grimly dissonant "Hear Say," contrast illusion and reality in a way that parallels the interplay of Copland's bright music and Graham's dark drama. And its final movement, "Happy-Go-Lucky Local," presents a vision of hope just as powerful as Copland's but far more reflective of the conditions over which hope would have to triumph.

OUTRO: THE ELLINGTON ARCHIVE

The study of history combines evidence and interpretation. Today much of the written evidence about Ellington's music is housed at the Smithsonian Museum of American History on the National Mall in Washington, D.C. The Archive Center is located on the first floor of the museum, just across the hall from a much-visited re-creation of Julia Child's television kitchen. For most of Ellington's compositions the Ellington Collection contains the composer's sketches, full scores, and original sets of the parts used by players. The Ellington Collection is just one of many in the care of the devoted and helpful staff of the Archive Center, though most of the other collections contain what is called "material history." While I was looking at the original instrumental parts for Ellington's scores, a researcher across the table might be examining maps of the national power grid, or nineteenth-century cookbooks, or early twentieth-century advertisements. It seems fitting and proper that Ellington's legacy resides in the city of his birth, surrounded by such seemingly modest yet essential Americana.

The papers of American composers can be found in the Library of Congress, in the New York Public Library, or at the Paul Sacher Stiftung in Basel, Switzerland—all places where I have worked and been spoiled rotten by superb librarians and their support staff. The Ellington Collection, though, has a particular importance, which I would like to discuss briefly in terms of the future rather than the past. Unlike the music of Copland or Carter, very little of Ellington's music was published. Many of the arrangements that are commercially available today were created without the benefit of the written materials now in the archive but were instead transcribed, painstakingly to be sure, from the recordings, especially in the pioneering efforts of David Berger. These arrangements, though, were educated guesses. Unfortunately, the lack of published scores fueled rumors that Ellington lacked the techniques of a trained composer, a slander developed at great length in James Lincoln Collier's mean-spirited biography. The Ellington Collection disproves this libel with mountains of manuscript in Ellington's distinctive hand (easy, most of the time, to distinguish from the writing of Strayhorn and Ellington's copyist, Tom Whaley). More than documenting Ellington's compositional process, the materials are essential for understanding the artistry of jazz orchestra composition as well as the working methods of its creators and performers.

To view this collection is an awesome privilege. While a researcher on, say, Mahler would use archives of sketches as a supplement to the published scores, the Ellington collection is currently the only place where you can see the music on the page as the members of his orchestra saw it, and in the precise form that Ellington composed it. Every day I spent there presented more revelations than I could assimilate. I remember in particular a day when I asked for the boxes containing the *New Orleans Suite,* one of Ellington's last works. Written in 1970, the suite once again figured the past with musical portraits of Sidney Bechet, Louis Armstrong, Wellman Braud, and Mahalia Jackson—the New Orleans roots of his New York music. My favorite movement, and the one that has become a jazz standard, is "The Second Line," which commemorates a New Orleans social institution that endures even today.

The *New Orleans Suite* seems like the fitting completion of Ellington's historical project, which took a different turn after *Harlem,* a turn from political history to musical history signaled by the radically whimsical historical deconstruction of *A Drum Is a Woman.* Beginning in the late 1950s Ellington pursued a number of projects that would redefine his place in jazz history. Now that he no longer had to prove the distinctiveness of his own approach it was time to reaffirm the values it shared even with artists whom jazz critics had positioned as Ellington's adversaries. The first steps in this new direction were the collaborations with Count Basie, Louis Armstrong, Ella Fitzgerald, Coleman Hawkins, and John Coltrane. Hawkins's performance of "Mood Indigo" and Coltrane's version of "In a Sentimental Mood" demonstrated how these works resonated with a far larger repertory than even that of the Ellington Orchestra; both soloists imbued Ellington's music with their own very recognizable styles, and each song took on a new life. We can detect a similar refashioning of jazz history in the two albums that recalled the music of the big band era and, in a very different way, in the suites based on Tchaikovsky's *Nutcracker* and Grieg's *Peer Gynt*. In both instances Ellington was reopening a dialogue that defied the boundaries of jazz history. Even more ambitious were such encounters with world music as the *Far East Suite* and the *Latin American Suite*, which took jazz beyond America's geographical and cultural borders. Far from novelty exercises in exoticism, these works demonstrated in musical terms the ties in African American history to the Ganges, the Euphrates, and the Caribbean that Ellington had celebrated in the script for *Black, Brown and Beige*. Having pushed the boundaries of jazz outward in so many directions, Ellington now returned, in 1970, to honor its birthplace, New Orleans.

In researching the *New Orleans Suite* I carefully worked my way, one folder at a time, through the materials, many of them the originals professionally copied in India ink. Each part was identified by the name of the player, not the instrument, and many of them included the players' own comments and doodles. When I opened folder 5 of box 242, though, I came upon the holy grail, Ellington's sketches for "The Second Line," written, as was his habit, very distinctly in pencil with full indications of all the harmonic voicings. Often these pencil sketches show signs that they were written on the road; they may appear on the back of another piece of music and are often full of arrows that reorder the phrases between different pages. With familiarity, though, it becomes clear that Ellington and Strayhorn both worked in a systematic way that allowed Tom Whaley to extract parts from a score set out on four or five staves. The sketches look casual, but in fact they are complete (with the provision that neither Ellington nor Strayhorn wrote out a drum part and rarely indicated much about the piano part, which, of course, they would be playing). In the middle of sketches for different phrases I found Ellington's first entry for the great tune that serves as its refrain, a defiant melody that seems to capture the essential spirit of jazz. My hands began to tremble. I felt like I was witnessing the moment when the notes first hit the page. For a second Edward Kennedy "Duke" Ellington seemed to be looking over my shoulder, pointing to his sassy tune with pride.

The weight of that encounter suggested to me that the Ellington Archive may be only in its formative, provisional state. The entire collection, so much of which is in pencil, needs to be put in digital form, safe from the wear and tear it now receives on a daily basis, and at the same time made more accessible. (As an example, today you can access most of the Copland holdings in the Library of Congress through the Internet.) Critical and performing editions need to be carefully prepared from the materials, an effort that would at least equal those that have gone into the great scholarly monuments of European music. Since the Smithsonian already has a branch institution in New York City (the Cooper-Hewitt National Design Museum), I can imagine a time when the collection might be housed in its own building, an Ellington Institute, located, with all due respect for his birthplace, on the heights of Sugar Hill. Ellington may have been born in D.C., but his music is inseparable from Harlem.

CHAPTER 7

"Heaven": God

We commit fewer musical sins in church.

—Igor Stravinsky

It has been said once that a man, who could not play the
organ or any of the other instruments of the symphony,
accompanied his worship by juggling. He was not the world's
best juggler but it was the one thing he did best. And so it
was accepted by God.

—Duke Ellington

INTRO: AIN'T BUT THE ONE

When I first envisioned closing this book with a chapter on religious
music (a.k.a. the "God chapter"), I thought that I would examine Ellington's three Concerts of Sacred Music, which premiered in 1965,
1968, and 1973, in the context of other spiritual works of the time.
There's no shortage of impressive sacred music from that era: John Coltrane's *A Love Supreme*, Mary Lou Williams's *Mass for Peace*, Messiaen's *Et Exspecto Resurrectionem Mortuorum*, Britten's *War Requiem*,
Stravinsky's *Requiem Canticles*, and Leonard Bernstein's *Mass* are
just the beginning of a long list. Many of these works—intense, dis-
quieting, pious, questioning, epic, modest, ritualistic, theatrical—reflect
the transformations of religious thought and practice brought about
by Vatican II, the civil rights movement, and the Vietnam War. These
transformative historical events, however, would have overshadowed
the attention I wanted to draw to the special character of Ellington's
sacred concerts. They are far less appreciated, even in the jazz world,

than many of the musical works listed above. Most classical listeners, I have found, don't even know they exist—and don't know what they are missing. Fulfilling many of Ellington's lifelong expressive projects, the three Concerts of Sacred Music exemplify an Ellingtonian "late style" that brought his music to its rightful home, the church.

As Janna Tull Steed has written, the three Concerts of Sacred Music are best characterized as a continuously evolving work in progress.[1] Only the Second Sacred Concert shares no significant material with other works. Ellington did not treat any of the concerts as a finished composition; the many performances that the band gave of them varied enormously in content and the order of numbers.[2] I would suggest, though, that all the concerts were emanations, extensions, and developments of *Black, Brown and Beige* and that there were really five sacred concerts.

By my count the first Concert of Sacred Music was not a concert proper but a recording. In 1958 Ellington released an album titled *Black, Brown and Beige* that differed substantially from the original suite. Ellington omitted all of *Brown*, replaced *Beige* with a setting of the 23rd Psalm, and added a vocal version of "Come Sunday," which was heard for the first time with lyrics. The ostensible reason for these changes was the presence of the great gospel singer Mahalia Jackson. For Jackson, as for many others in the black community, gospel and blues were inimical, and Ellington showed his respect for that view here. In doing so, though, he reshaped the earlier musical representation of African American history away from the complex interplay of work song, spiritual, blues, and jazz found in the original suite and toward a picture of ascending faith. The music and its story now found their goal in the church, not in a Sugar Hill penthouse.

Ellington never hid his religious feelings. He wore a gold cross around his neck at all times, he traveled with a well-thumbed Bible (his "little brown book," to quote the Strayhorn song), and he carefully annotated copies of *Forward Day by Day,* a spiritual guide published by the Episcopal church.[3] Yet Ellington's turn to the realm of gospel music in the late 1950s also reflected contemporary developments in black music and politics. Moving beyond church gospel music began to reinvigorate the wider cultural climate. In 1957 and 1958 Mahalia Jackson appeared at the Newport Jazz Festival. That same year Art Blakey's recording of Bobby Timmons's tune "Moanin'" became an anthem for a jazz style that earned the awkward name "funky hard bop regression" from its emphasis on both blues and gospel. The sound of gospel music was soon popularized in Charles Mingus's "Saturday Night Prayer Meeting" and Horace Silver's "Sister Sadie." Critics pegged hard bop as a black reaction to the cool West Coast jazz of Jimmy Giuffre and Chet Baker, but, more than another perennial attempt to take jazz back from popular white imitators, hard bop mirrored a profound change within black culture that allowed artists to travel across the previously impermeable barrier between sacred and profane styles. Gospel singing, as performed by the Clara Ward Singers or James Cleveland, had become increasingly blues inflected; Sam Cooke and Ray Charles took the gospel style over into the realm of popular music. In 1961 Ellington's friend Langston Hughes brought gospel music successfully to Broadway with the show *Black Nativity*. With the formation of Dr. Martin Luther King's Southern Christian Leadership Conference in 1957, religious leaders had become the spearhead for the movement; musical developments quickly followed the new political alignment. In the civil rights struggle spirituals were reborn as freedom songs. At the March on Washington on August 28, 1963, the day Dr. King delivered his "I have a dream" speech, Mahalia Jackson sang, "I've been 'buked and I've been scorned." Five years earlier, though, when she recorded "Come Sunday" with its new lyrics, politics were already interlaced with theology:

> Lord, dear Lord above,
> God Almighty, God of Love,
> Please look down and see my people through.

Ellington's next protosacred concert, in 1963, was *My People*, not a concert but a musical theater "spectacular" that was performed twice a day at the Century of Negro Progress Exposition in Chicago from August 16 to September 2, 1963, at the five-thousand-seat Arie Crown Theater. The exhibition celebrated the centennial of the Emancipation Proclamation and was also exactly contemporary with the March on Washington, which demanded that the promise of emancipation finally be implemented. *My People*, which Ellington dedicated to Dr. King, remade *Black, Brown and Beige* as multimedia music theater; in addition to composing the music, Ellington directed, arranged the choreography, and even helped paint the set.[4] *My People* could be termed Ellington's *Gesamtkunstwerk*.

Although Ellington downplayed the political aspect of the show, saying that the message was insinuated "here and there,"[5] it amplified the political themes from the earlier versions of *Black, Brown and Beige*, most importantly the interdependence of faith and freedom.[6] The show opened as if in church with three new gospel-style numbers, "Ain't But the One," "Will You Be There?" and "99%," sung by the Irving Bunton Singers and Jimmy McPhail. The Christian message of these songs might have seemed surprising in the context of a nonreligious exhibition, and even more surprising at an event associated with a jazz musician, not a gospel musician or a religious leader. These songs, however, would have appeared narrowly doctrinaire only to listeners unfamiliar with the coded language of the spirituals, which gave salvation a double meaning, celestial and terrestrial. The oneness of God testified to the oneness of mankind; the question "Will You Be There?" demanded a full commitment ("99% won't do") to political struggle as well as to the demands of Scripture. The gospel tunes set down a political agenda in a language its audience would have understood.[7] Following these numbers Ellington reprised the vocal version of "Come Sunday" (now performed by McPhail) but then transformed it into a new up-tempo number, "David Danced," for the choir and the tap dancing of Bunny Briggs. Here the walls separating church and theater came tumbling down. The music hinted at the familiar spiritual melody about Joshua that would appear later in the show to honor Dr. King, explicitly: "King Fit the Battle of Alabam.'"

With the song "My Mother, My Father" (a.k.a. "Heritage"), Ellington took another unexpected turn, charming the audience with a pop-style autobiographical ballad/hymn that might have seemed self-indulgent without its clear political dimension:

> My mother—the greatest—and the prettiest.
> My father—just handsome—but the wittiest.

Ellington later told an interviewer that this was "everybody's song";[8] it celebrated love and origins just before "black is beautiful" became a slogan. Ellington underscored the politics, or at least reinsinuated them, by following the song with "Montage," a retitled version of "Light," the original third section of *Black*. The new title drew attention to the cinematic scope of the music, its depiction of an entire people on the verge of freedom. At many performances Ellington literally climbed up on a soapbox as an orator to make that message explicit: "My people—singing—dancing—praying—thinking about freedom." Now, as he had done at Carnegie Hall, Ellington acclaimed the contribution African Americans had made as workers: "Cotton—sugar—indigo—iron—coal—peanuts—steel—the railroad—you name it. The foundation of the United States rests on the sweat of my people."

Ellington's oration then segued into a reprise of The Blues from *Black, Brown and Beige* sung by Joya Sherrill. Just as he had earlier opened up the content of *Black,* Ellington followed his artful meditation on the blues with four short blues vignettes ("Workin' Blues," "My Man Sends Me," "Jail Blues," and "Lovin' Lover") that were as down-home as "The Blues" was not. Never before had Ellington made such an incursion into the rival stylistic domain of Count Basie; once again Ellington was pushing his own stylistic spectrum ever wider to encompass experiences and forms of expression that rarely before had shared the same theatrical space. Finally the show turned from insinuation to explicit statement with a calypso-groove freedom song, "King Fit the Battle of Alabam,'" that harshly recalled the misdeeds of Eugene "Bull" Connor, the commissioner of safety of Birmingham, Alabama, who had turned police dogs and fire hoses on black citizens earlier that year: "Little babies fit the battle of police dogs—mongrel police . . . / And the dogs came growling—howling—growling." Ellington could have ended on this note, but he had one more stylistic twist to play, the category-defying "What Color Is Virtue?" which sounds like a perfect Broadway vehicle for Lena Horne. The two contrasting final numbers gave a new face, or perhaps two new faces, to the militant ending of the original *Black, Brown and Beige.* The dizzying stylistic range of *My People* challenges its audience to be as proudly and unconditionally inclusive as its composer.

My People was a version of the historical pageants of Ellington's childhood, updated musically and politically, but by its very nature—it was part of a temporary exposition—it was provisional. Too religious to run on Broadway, too full of the blues to be performed as a church service, its music imagined a hypothetical theatrical framework, at once sacred and profane, timely and eternal, that fused and transcended the usual ideas of entertainment, education, and worship. Only the largest sacred space, a cathedral, could possibly contain its vision, though perhaps it required the *idea* of a cathedral, the largest, most inclusive monument to God, more than the acoustic reality. As it happened, those spaces were also looking for new music to reinvigorate worship.[9] In 1962 the Reverend C. Julian Bartlett and the Reverend Jon S. Yaryan invited Ellington to compose music for the dedication of Grace Cathedral on San Francisco's Nob Hill, an invitation that led to the first Concert of Sacred Music on September 16, 1965. Eventually Ellington's Concerts of Sacred Music would rattle the gothic arches of

Grace Cathedral, the Cathedral of Saint John the Divine in New York, and Westminster Abbey in London with amplified voices, blaring brass, and ricocheting drum solos, filling the vast spaces like a dense, pungent musical incense. *Time* magazine wrote that the devilish acoustics turned the music into an "impenetrable mass." (On the other hand, Gary Giddins praised the music's "aural affinity for the cavernous architecture of great churches.")[10] The physics may have been problematic but the metaphysics rang out loud and clear.

The three Concerts of Sacred Music shared certain features that pushed them in the opposite direction of the contemporary jazz masses of Ellington's friend Mary Lou Williams.[11] Her religious music drew on traditional Catholic liturgy, though it also added contemporary commentary on their words. Even when the music rocks, Williams intended it for worship. The Ellington concerts, by contrast, were not masses, and, if we heed Ellington's exhortations, they also were not jazz; he asked that the four-letter "J" word not appear in any of the programs or publicity. They were concerts, not services; the only liturgical text Ellington set was the Lord's Prayer. Yet, as Janna Tull Steed notes, all three concerts were conceived for performance in sacred spaces that helped "define the meaning of these events and their impact on performers and audiences, too."[12]

The concerts would have been provocatively eclectic in their range of musical styles in any setting. The first concert featured two gospel singers, Esther Marrow (incorrectly listed as "Esther Merrill" in the program and much of the literature and later known as Queen Esther Marrow) and Jimmy McPhail, the jazz singer John Hendricks, and tap dancer Bunny Briggs.[13] The second featured the high soprano voice of the Swedish singer Alice Babs, a blues solo for Ellington's longtime trumpeter Cootie Williams, and a prominent role for an African American children's chorus (Les Jeunes Voix, directed by Roscoe Gill). As the criticism reveals, all three concerts contained something to please or ruffle the religious or nonreligious sensibilities of just about every listener. People who loved the intensity of "Come Sunday" were baffled by the Bacharach-like slickness of "Something about Believing" or the appropriately childlike Sunday school offerings of the children's choir. Even Gary Giddins, the first critic to sense the full scope of Ellington's achievement in these works, seemed to bridle at the "outright proselytizing" of the second concert, even though the texts were notably nonsectarian. All religious music is by its very nature preachy, but it is often easier for outsiders to encounter musical spirituality either without words or in a foreign language. Ellington, however, was not satisfied with making things easy.

To amplify Giddins's appreciation of the concerts and to answer his objection, let's look at each of the concerts to see what Ellington preached and how.[14]

FIRST CONCERT OF SACRED MUSIC:
IN THE BEGINNING GOD

Perhaps, like a medieval craftsman, intent on offering God only his best work, Ellington built the first sacred concert, entitled *A Concert of Sacred Music,* on well-tested material from *Black, Brown and Beige, New World A-Comin',* and *My People:* "Come Sunday" (in both instrumental and vocal versions), "Montage," "Will You Be There?" "99%," "Ain't But the One," "Heritage," "New World A-Comin'" (performed as an extended piano solo), and "David Danced." In the case of *New World,* Ellington conferred sacred status on the music retroactively. In the program he wrote that the work "is really the anticipation of a very distant future place on land, at sea, or in the sky where there will be no war, no greed, no nonbelievers, and no categorization . . . where love is unconditional and no pronoun is good enough for God."[15] The new material was a gospel song, "Tell Me It's the Truth" (sung by Esther Marrow), and an extended multisection concert piece titled "In the Beginning God" for jazz vocalist John Hendricks (of Lambert, Hendricks and Ross), the Ellington band, and the Herman McCoy Choir, and a gospel-style setting of the Lord's Prayer, again by Marrow. To classical listeners Ellington here appeared to take on a subject already given musical form by Haydn in *The Creation,* by Schoenberg in the *Genesis Prelude,* and, most recently, by Stravinsky in *The Flood* (1962)—but the music might be better heard as his retort to "It Ain't Necessarily So." It began with a six-note motive, the musical equivalent of the divine tetragrammaton in Hebrew; Ellington also placed this motive at the very opening of his memoir, *Music Is My Mistress.* The six notes stand for the six opening syllables of Genesis, "In the beginning God," but when the lyrics are sung they swerve away from the Bible:

> In the beginning God.
> No heaven,
> No earth,
> No nothin'.

As he had done in *Harlem,* Ellington used a recurring motive to announce and reiterate his theme, with or without actual words; it is even "spoken" by the drums.

Rather than being a depiction of chaos and creation akin to those offered by classical composers, "In the Beginning God" is an extended meditation on the first principles, God and the Bible, from which all else flows. The sections of the piece are as follows:

Piano introduction hinting at the six-note theme (e♭ minor).

Slow, out-of-time statement of theme on the baritone sax (Harry Carney), repeated and extended in tempo.

Clarinet solo (Jimmy Hamilton) ushered in by a harsh dissonance that, to my ears, evokes the words "the spirit of God moved upon the face of the waters." Clarinet continues the theme in a moderate tempo. Clarinet cadenza.

Singer intones the opening words (b♭ minor).

Hendricks sings the motto over a swung accompaniment then begins an Ellingtonian rap: "No mountains, no valleys/No main streets, no back alleys . . ."

Hendricks again intones the opening melody slowly, ending on a climactic high F.

Swung music returns with a solo for Paul Gonsalves over which the choir reels off the titles of the books of the Old Testament.

A fanfare followed by a trumpet solo (Cat Anderson) that gradually moves to the highest possible note (I think this solo announces the incarnation of Christ).

Piano interlude.

Over a soft drumroll and piano punctuations the choir declaims the titles of the books of the New Testament.

An extended drum solo (Louis Bellson) initiated by the six-note theme played on the cymbals.

Choral restatement of the opening motive. Final chord combines notes of the e♭ minor and D♭ major scales.

Although all this material was new, we can hear how it continues the practice of earlier Ellington, particularly in its deployment of motivic unity to knit together a wide variety of tempos and solo voices, including, most theatrically (especially given the cathedral acoustics), the voice of the drums and cymbals. As usual, Ellington knew how to make the most of each of his soloists. Carney's weighty tone established the work's foundation, Hamilton's ethereal, cool-sounding clarinet evoked a sense of intergalactic emptiness, and Anderson's screech trumpet literally scaled the heights. Ellington brought in Bellson especially for the occasion, knowing well his instinctive ability to stop the show. He told the drummer, "You are thunder and lightning," and that was all that needed to be said.[16] The knowing simplicity of late Ellington and Bellson's artistry turned one of the oldest clichés of jazz, the big, loud drum solo, into a cosmic event. Much of Bellson's solo feels more like an ecstatic aria than a percussive display. It sets the stage for further lyric utterances: two versions of "Come Sunday," first the 1958 vocal version, sung by Marrow, and then the original, played, as it was in 1943, by Johnny Hodges (the two separated by the new setting of the Lord's Prayer), and then Ellington's solo performance of *New World A-Comin'*, which has a meditative intensity in its execution reminiscent in feeling if not in style to the last part, "Psalm," of Coltrane's *A Love Supreme*. The only thing that could possibly top that solo would be the tap dancing of Bunny Briggs. As Gary Giddins wrote, Ellington had brought the Cotton Club into the cathedral, but it was a Cotton Club cleansed of its sins.

Two days after the premiere Ellington performed much of the music in the very different setting of the Monterey Jazz Festival. The entire concert (plus a new Christmas surprise performed by Lena Horne and Billy Strayhorn) came to New York's Fifth Avenue Presbyterian Church on December 26, 1965, and two months later it was heard in England at Coventry Cathedral, where Britten's *War Requiem* had premiered three years before. In *Music Is My Mistress* Ellington proudly pointed to the nearly fifty performances of *A Concert of Sacred Music* heard around the world.

SECOND SACRED CONCERT: FREEDOM

New York's Episcopal Cathedral of Saint John the Divine, the birthplace of the *Second Sacred Concert*, overlooks the southern part of Harlem from Morningside Heights; its site is a sacred counterpart to Sugar Hill two miles to the north. The cathedral has also remained unfinished by choice. Its leaders decided that healing their community was more important than completing the building, which, if it were ever finished, would be the largest Gothic cathedral in the world. Ellington may well have identified personally with the idea of the never-to-be-completed project, a symbol of human imperfection and constant striving. The cathedral would be the site of Ellington's funeral service on May 27, 1974.

In *Music Is My Mistress* Ellington wrote that the *Second Sacred Concert* was "the most important thing I have ever done," a claim not to be taken lightly. First performed on January 18, 1968, the work derived its special character from three seemingly unrelated elements. Like *My People,* much of it seems designed for the edification of children, and Ellington gave an important role to a children's chorus, in this case the choirs of St. Hilda's and St. Hugh's School, an Episcopal private school a few blocks from the cathedral. There were children's voices in the first concert, but here their voices imbued much of the music with a disarming (or disconcerting) innocence, most notably in the spoken episode where a young boy retold the story of the fall from the unusual point of view of the apple:

> I was swinging.
> Ripening in peace and quiet,
> And who do you think came crawling down that limb?
> That little old serpent.

Your first reaction may be that this is the kind of school performance you tolerate only if your own kid is onstage, if then; but, as we will see, the naïveté served a larger goal.

The second new element was Alice Babs, the Swedish soprano who first performed with Ellington in Stockholm in February 1963. Babs was the Ellington singer in excelsis; her voice combined the classical quality Ellington admired in Kay Davis with a range that matched the stratospherics of Cat Anderson's trumpet; she could also read Ellington's unpredictable melodies at sight. "Heaven," the most enduring tune from the *Second Sacred Concert,* and the wordless "T.G.T.T." (Too Good to Title) took full advantage of all of Babs's musical strengths.

The third shaping element of the *Second Sacred Concert* hovered over it in absentia. After a long illness Billy Strayhorn had died, on May 31, 1967. He was already ill when Ellington was writing the theme for the first concert, and Ellington had consulted with Strayhorn: "On the telephone I told him about the concert and that I wanted him to write something, 'Introduction, ending, quick transitions,' I said. 'The title is the first four words of the Bible—"In the Beginning God."' He had not heard my theme, but what he sent to California started on the same note as mine (F natural) and ended on the same note as mine (A♭ a tenth higher). Out of six notes representing the six syllables of the four words, only two notes were different."[17]

Ellington read a eulogy at Strayhorn's funeral, and for the *Second Sacred Concert* he would recite part of it to illustrate freedom, the overarching theme of the entire program, which somehow unified the contrasting elements of naïveté, transcendence, and commemoration. (Ellington printed the entire text in *Music Is My Mistress*, though not in the same order heard on the recording.) The seemingly impossible thematic triangulation produced a score even more varied in style than the first concert. As Harvey Cohen writes, "The Second Sacred Concert itself was a study in musical freedom, with wildly varying transitions within compositions and influences from jazz, gospel, the black spirituals, classical choral music, Latin music, show tunes and more."[18]

The repeated successful performances of the first concert must have emboldened Ellington both musically and spiritually in preparing the second. In the original program notes he described himself as "a messenger boy, one who tries to bring messages to people, not people who have never heard of God, but those who were more or less raised with the guidance of the Church." All the music on the recording of the *Second Sacred Concert* was newly composed, although the actual performance also included a reprise of "99%." Much of the music was also far more secular sounding than the first concert. "Almighty God" and "Don't Get Down on Your Knees to Pray until You Have Forgiven Everyone" were the only gospel-style numbers on the program. "The Shepherd (Who Watches over the Night Flock)," intended as a portrait of John Gensel of St. Peter's Lutheran Church, who was known as the "pastor of New York's jazz community," featured a growling blues performance by Cootie Williams. "Something about Believing" reminded Giddins and others of the hackwork of "Broadway tunesmiths,"[19] but its easygoing pop language masks a typically Ellingtonian harmonic complexity. Its simple melodic line, moreover, might be considered an identifying element of Ellington's Mozartian late style; similar tunes would proliferate in the *Third Sacred Concert*.

On first hearing the *Second Sacred Concert* can sound like a bewildering (but tuneful) miscellany; its unity and form only become clear with repeated listening. To better understand it we need to consider its overall plan rather than just ticking off its long list of styles. Ellington framed the concert with two statements of Psalm 150 (slightly amended). The first is instrumental, once again giving Harry Carney the job of establishing a musical foundation, while the second is sung by the entire company as a finale. We might say that the concert is a journey that gradually readies the audience for the words of praise implied by the opening music. Psalm 150, "Praise God with the sound of the trumpet,/Praise God with the psaltery and harp," has long been a favorite of composers; Stravinsky set it in the third movement of his *Symphony of Psalms*. Ellington, however, building on the idea of "David Danced," added movement to the instruments of praise: "Praise God and Dance, Dance, Dance, Dance, Dance, Dance."

Within this framework of praise the concert traces the gradual maturing of religious understanding from childlike wonder to the more adult values of compassion and forgiveness. This growth in spiritual and moral understanding subliminally parallels the unfolding history of the Bible. The second movement, "Supreme Being," retells the opening chapters of Genesis in a recitation by the children's chorus framed by passages of modernistic music for the band. The instrumental music seems to develop ideas from the opening of "In the Beginning God" but is much more sustained and dissonant. It sounds like a cross between "Later," from the *Controversial Suite* (though without any suggestion of parody), and Billy Strayhorn's "Dirge." The sophistication of the instrumental music makes for a sharp contrast with the wide-eyed recitation of the story of creation and the fall by the children. The second instrumental statement, however, metamorphoses from dissonance to the comforting sounds of a slow gospel chorale; the scoring gives the band the sound of an organ. This dramatic transformation suggests that the children's words have taught the band how to pray: "And a child shall lead them . . ."

As he had done in the first concert, Ellington confounded expectations with unexpected stylistic juxtapositions. With "Heaven," which follows right on the heels of "Supreme Being," the voice of Alice Babs changed the tone of the conversation, or launched a new one, for "Heaven" has its own dialectical structure. There are three choruses: in the first, an out-of-tempo recitative-like statement by Babs (and Ellington) pictures the sublime through an angular melody full of dissonant leaps; the second lays down a slow groove and softens the angles so that the melody becomes a quintessential Johnny Hodges ballad; and the third time around Babs returns as the groove becomes a celebratory bossa nova. In the cadenzalike outro Babs ascends to a heavenly high D. As in "Supreme Being" Ellington used stylistic contrast to create an upward spiraling spiritual conversation in which contrasting voices seem to inspire one another to higher awareness and higher joy. We expect to find this kind of religious drama in Bach's cantatas, but it takes a little careful listening, and a change in our habitual ways of listening to jazz, to see that Ellington's sacred music achieves a comparable goal of enlightenment and uplift in his own idiom.

The next three numbers, "Something about Believing," "Almighty God," and "The Shepherd," present different styles of prayer in contrasting voices: a pop tune for the chorus, a gospel-pulsed prayer for Alice Babs's coloratura soprano and Russell Procope's throaty New Orleans–style clarinet, and, for Cootie Williams, a bluesy instrumental "tone parallel" that sounds like a slowed-down, stretched-out version of "Moanin'" with a hint of "St. James Infirmary." "Something" begins with a jolt as Ellington enters on an electric keyboard instead of his customary acoustic grand piano; each of these numbers has a sound that defines its scene, from the "cool" world of "Something" to the smoky after-midnight world of Pastor Gensel's congregation of "night people." If these three prayers are responses to Genesis, they also pave the way to Exodus, the advent of freedom.

"It's Freedom" is the centerpiece of the *Second Sacred Concert*. Its first musical theme, Ellington wrote, "was suggested by an old lick of Willie 'The Lion' Smith, who helped us when we came to New York in 1923." "It's Freedom" is a concert-within-a-concert, a series of episodes that include Ellington's own sermon:

Two statements of an AABA tune in c minor: Freedom, Freedom, Freedom, Freedom

Slow chorale in E♭ major (ends on a half cadence)

Keyboard solo on original tune

Upbeat choral tune (Freedom, Freedom, Freedom's what you thought you heard) on harmonic structure of the chorale (E♭)

Instrumental version of previous chorus with Johnny Hodges solo

Repeat of chorale tune

New chorale

Sax solo leads to new jazz tune ("Freedom is sweet") in F

Recitation of the word *freedom* in twenty languages

Ellington sermon (spoken)

New chorale (in c minor) behind continuation of sermon, which speaks of Billy Strayhorn's understanding of freedom

Reprise of opening chorus

Like the biblical exodus, the attainment of freedom is both the end and the beginning of a story. Childhood has ended and messy maturity begins. After an intermission the music seemed to starts up anew with three wordless numbers, a solo piano meditation, a sizzling instrumental interlude, and "The Biggest and Busiest Intersection," which featured a drum solo to represent the "fire and brimstone" of a "sermonette" rather than the thunder and lightning of the first concert. Then came "T.G.T.T" an ethereal floating vocalise for Alice Babs with Ellington on electric keyboard. Taken together, the three movements could represent a growth in consciousness, an awareness of the dangers and pleasures of the flesh, and the responsibilities of the spirit. They might also mark the passage from the Old to the New Testament. The message becomes explicit in "Don't Get Down on Your Knees to Pray until You Have Forgiven Everyone," which was sung by Tony Watkins and reinforced in "Father Forgive," which brings home, once again, the inseparable interdependence of faith and social justice:

Father Forgive, Father Forgive
The hatred which divides nation from nation,
Race from race, class from class.
The covetous desires of men and nations
To possess that which is not their own.

These words, sung in January 1968, would resonate with events that would soon follow in the momentous and tragic year. (Oddly, both tracks were dropped from the CD reissue.) If Ellington had now become "strenuously verbal," as Gary Giddins wrote, the times demanded such a prophetic voice.[20]

After these stern calls for justice, the concluding "Praise God and Dance," launched with Alice Babs's repeated exhortations to praise God, combined the jubilation of the psalm with the prophetic vision of Isaiah in a blaze of C major affirmation comparable in spirit to the end of Mahler's "Resurrection" Symphony—imagine what Mahler would have done with Cat Anderson's high E. At the premiere, Stanley Dance reported in DownBeat, "two sets of dancers . . . surprised the audience by erupting down the center aisle. The first group, colorfully dressed and coached by Geoffrey Holder, moved with gestures symbolic of worship in the idiom of modern dance. The second, issuing from behind the band, was swinging all the way with steps and rhythms right out of the Savoy Ballroom." Since Ellington had choreographed My People, it is quite likely that he also conceived and directed this final coup de théâtre.

THIRD SACRED CONCERT: THE LORD'S PRAYER

But thou, when thou prayest, enter into thy closet, and when thou
hast shut thy door, pray to thy Father which is in secret; and thy
Father which seeth in secret shall reward thee openly.

—Matthew 6:6

The *Third Sacred Concert* premiered at Westminster Abbey on October
24, 1973, six months before Ellington's death and in the shadow of
death and illness. Johnny Hodges had died in 1970; Dr. Arthur Logan,
Ellington's personal physician and closest friend, would die (under
suspicious circumstances) a month after the premiere. Ellington was
already ill at the time of the premiere, although he did not allow his
condition to become known and he did not let it interfere with the
band's European tour (which included a performance of the *Third Sacred Concert* at the Basilica de Santa Maria del Mar in Barcelona) or his
composing, especially his work on the comic opera *Queenie Pie* and the
ballet *Three Black Kings*. Mercer Ellington described his father's condition as the premiere approached:

> It was then, for the first time, that I began to understand how gravely ill he
> was. He was terribly tired, and after a couple of hours of rehearsal he had to
> sit down or go back to the hotel. Flying the Atlantic at his age and going into
> rehearsal without much sleep required strength, but he knew that he always
> did his best work under pressure. He had a pace he was used to, a norm, that
> really set him working, and he gauged himself so that he would have that
> pace just prior to the performance, but I think for the first time in his life he
> knew he wasn't capable of it.[21]

The recording of the *Third Sacred Concert* shows signs of Ellington's
condition and of his band's weariness after flying in from Chicago two
nights before the premiere (although Ellington's piano playing seems
unimpaired). Like the first concert and unlike the second, the third reprised older compositions: "Tell Me It's the Truth," "Praise God and
Dance," and "In the Beginning God."[22] The concert was recorded live,
and Ellington was dissatisfied with much of it, so some sections were
never released commercially. Despite these conditions, many critics have
recognized the distinctive tone of the *Third Sacred Concert,* its move, as
Janna Tull Steed wrote, "from preachment and toward prayer."[23]

Although the *Third Sacred Concert* was titled "The Majesty of God"
on its recording, it might more accurately have been called "Medita-
tions and Variations on the Lord's Prayer." Ellington's opening piano
solo is a wordless version of that prayer, anticipating the variations

found in the extended movement "Every Man Prays in His Own Language." Two new songs for Alice Babs (Ellington's "personified muse," as Steed calls her) are more like mantras than conventional ballads or prayers. "My Love" and "Is God a Three-Letter Word for Love?" repeat the same phrases over and over, as if each repetition will yield a higher understanding. (The brief and very un-Handelian "Hallelujah," based on rhythm changes, pursues a similar spiritual strategy, with a little sly humor, considering the regal setting.) Both songs have an inner calm that transfigures their pop tune formats, though listening to Ellington's interludes I have the sense that he was proud to produce, so late in the day, two more songs destined to become standards.

"Every Man Prays in His Own Language" intones the Lord's Prayer seven ways:

1. Instrumental (Harold Ashby, tenor sax solo, fast tempo)

2. A cappella choir (slow, in chorale style)

3. Instrumental (reeds and cymbals, also in chorale style), with a choral "amen"

4. Alice Babs unaccompanied singing in Swedish to her own melody

5. Recorder solo played by trombonist Art Baron

6. Alice Babs and the John Alldis Choir, vocalise

7. Ellington's homily with choral background:

> In a raging storm
> When the captain gives the abandon ship alarm
> Are we sure that the ocean
> Has not taken a notion
> To demonstrate the Hundred-and-fiftieth Psalm?
> When a baby screams out after the doctor's first spank
> Are we certain that the baby is not trying to say "Thank
> God."

This easily could have been the last word, but Ellington needed to show Westminster Abbey his down-home gospel side with "Ain't Nobody Nowhere Nothin' Without God," a catalogue of negations in the service of affirmation sung by Tony Watkins. The final number, "The Majesty of God," feels like a threefold closing benediction (by Ellington, Carney, and Babs) framed by a modern-style processional, the kind of music you might hear as you walked out of a Broadway musical while the cast took curtain calls. This mellow, casual-sounding ending, so different from the time-stopping cadences of Stravinsky or from the ecstatic conclusions of the two earlier concerts, has its own theological significance, Ellington's equivalent to the exaltation of minutiae in Gerard Manley Hopkins's "Pied Beauty." Like the earlier modestly scaled Hallelujah, the ordinary-sounding tune challenges the listener to find the majesty of God in ordinary things. Ceasing rather than arriving, circular rather than linear, the *Third Sacred Concert* does not progress in spiritual understanding; it just basks in its glory.

OUTRO ULTIMO

I never had the privilege of hearing the Ellington Orchestra perform one of the Concerts of Sacred Music live, but I have attended performances by the Seattle Repertory Jazz Orchestra, which has been presenting the music annually since 1989. These concerts were exhilarating and rapturous, even for the unchurched. The Seattle version, available on CD, combines numbers from all three concerts, very much in the work-in-progress spirit in which the music was conceived. Their selection of tunes is a nonstop hit parade. The SRJO recording, along with that of the Big Band de Lausanne, answers resoundingly the question I often hear about Ellington's music from people in the classical world: how can we perform it? Concert musicians who have no trouble assembling the complex forces needed for a *War Requiem* or Bernstein's *Mass* get weak in the knees at the thought of playing Ellington's music. In some ways their trepidation is well-founded. Most classically trained players have no idea how to read an Ellington part; in the orchestrated versions of his music made during his lifetime the music too often sound like the generic offering of a symphonic pops concert and not at all Ellingtonian. Classical musicians who don't even know where to turn for advice on how to perform the music need to break out of their segregated sphere and begin a conversation with jazz musicians who possess the requisite skill and·spirit to bring the music to life. And they have to stop thinking of Ellington's music as a repertory they don't need to know. The Concerts of Sacred Music demand all the resources of a musical community, from a coloratura soprano to a tap dancer; preparing them for performance can create a new community out of previously non-communicating musical subcultures.

As with classical music, performance of Ellington's work raises all sorts of questions of textual authenticity, performance practice, and interpretation.[24] As the music continues to be played we will doubtless see a range of responses comparable to those we are used to in performances of, say, Beethoven, though I would prefer to see a much broader spectrum of possibilities. I can imagine bands dedicated to reproducing the music as it was first played, others modernizing the beat, and still others putting the Ellington oeuvre through an electronic remix. Ellington himself updated much of his music, even classics like "Black and Tan Fantasy." It would be academic in the worst sense of the word to treat the Ellington repertory only through the aesthetic of "early music" and perform the music by mimicking old recordings, though, to be academic in the best sense, every note of those recordings has something to teach the musicians of the future. Ellington's music, however, was written for and played by giants: Hodges, Nanton, Webster, Bigard, Babs, and others. It requires masterly musicians, just as Bach's music does. We expect such musicians to bring music to life on their own terms; otherwise there would be no point in hearing new performances. On the Lausanne recording, Jon Faddis, a latter-day giant, splendidly remakes the solos of both Cootie Williams and Cat Anderson in his own image. To paraphrase Stravinsky, love trumps respect.

The jazz orchestra itself may be an endangered species. Or not. There are astonishingly virtuosic ensembles today at Lincoln Center and at many of the universities and conservatories that teach jazz performance. These ensembles, rarely money making, may continue to thrive just because of the desire to preserve the rich musical legacies of Ellington, Basie, Henderson, Lunceford, Woody Herman, Stan Kenton, and Gil Evans, among many others, as living repertories, not just as recordings. But those legacies might also evolve within other musical contexts, some of which no doubt will leave the moldy figs of the future shaking their fists in fury. One fine example of creative Ellington performance can be heard on a recording of the *Far East Suite* made by the Asian American Orchestra, directed by Anthony Brown, in 1999. They add the colors of Persian and Chinese instruments to Ellington's timbral palette with imagination and conviction. And they swing. Perhaps a similar treatment awaits the *Latin American Suite.*

The biggest challenge of all, perhaps neither possible nor even desirable, may be the long-delayed acceptance of Ellington's music, not just its tunes, but its totality, by the concert world. Ellington's lone CD of his symphonic music includes a piece titled "Non-Violent Integration." That would be a good place to begin.

Notes

The following acronyms are used for the sources most frequently cited.

DER   Mark Tucker, ed., *The Duke Ellington Reader*

EJ   Gunther Schuller, *Early Jazz*

JCAC   Robert O'Meally, ed., *The Jazz Cadence of American Culture*

MBA   Eileen Southern, *The Music of Black Americans*

MIMM Duke Ellington, *Music Is My Mistress*

SE   Gunther Schuller, *The Swing Era*

UC   Robert O'Meally, Brent Hayes Edwards, and Farah Jasmine Griffin, eds., *Uptown Conversation*

VJ   Gary Giddins, *Visions of Jazz*

PART I

Epigraphs, p. 1: Mercer Ellington, quoted in Perlis and Van Cleve, *Composers' Voices from Ives to Ellington*, p. 371; Claude Debussy, quoted in *Debussy on Music*, p. 297.

    1. Denby, *Dancers, Buildings and People in the Streets*, p. 110.
    2. Tick, *Ruth Crawford Seeger*, p. 214.
    3. Ibid., p. 357.
    4. Thompson, *The Soundscape of Modernity*, pp. 237–38.

1. "BLUE LIGHT": COLOR

Epigraphs, pp. 11–12: Billy Strayhorn, *DownBeat*, November 5, 1952; Aaron Copland, *Copland on Music*, p. 31; André Previn, quoted in Giddins, *VJ*, p.

105; Cecil Taylor, in A.B. Spellman, *Black Music,* p. 74; Arnold Schoenberg, *Theory of Harmony,* p. 421; O'Meally, ed., *JCAC,* p. 178. Epigraphs, pp. 26–27: Rainer Maria Rilke, *Sonnets to Orpheus* XV; Mahler to Alma on Puccini's *Tosca,* quoted in de la Grange, *Gustav Mahler,* p. 601; Zola, *Au bonheurs des dames,* pp. 86–87.

1. Ellington, *MIMM,* p. 17.

2. De Long, *Pops,* pp. 80–81.

3. Tucker, *Early Years,* p. 250.

4. Hasse, *Ragtime,* p. 134.

5. Tucker, ed., *DER,* pp. 339–40.

6. A transcription appears in Porter, Ullman, and Hazell, *Jazz: From Its Origins to the Present,* p. 104.

7. Schuller, *SE,* p. 109.

8. The piano solo sheet music, published for copyright purposes, I assume, contains little of what is heard on the recording apart from the trombone melody of the third chorus. Curiously, it is in A♭, while the recorded performance is in G.

9. Tucker, ed., *DER,* p. 70.

10. Southern, *MBA,* p. 192.

11. Ibid., p. 334.

12. Ellington, *MIMM,* p. 47.

13. Ibid., p. 33.

14. Titon, *Early Downhome Blues,* p. 144.

15. Olly Wilson, "The Heterogeneous Sound Ideal in African-American Music," in Wright, ed., *New Perspectives on Music.*

16. Floyd, *Power of Black Music,* p. 80.

17. Brothers, *Louis Armstrong's New Orleans,* p. 43.

18. Ibid., p. 57.

19. Tucker, ed., *DER,* p. 172.

20. Ibid., p. 369.

21. Chilton, *Sidney Bechet,* p. 40.

22. Stewart, *Jazz Masters of the Thirties,* p. 98.

23. Timner, *Ellingtonia,* p. 39. See Schuller, *SE,* pp. 105–7, for a discussion of the differences between takes.

24. See the transcription in Schuller, *SE,* p. 107.

25. See the transcription in ibid., pp. 124–25.

26. Lawrence Gushee in Tucker, ed., *DER,* p. 430.

27. Ellington had employed vocalise earlier, in "Creole Love Call," recorded in 1927 with Adelaide Hall, and in "Rude Interlude" with Louis Bacon in 1933. Bacon scatted Armstrong-style.

28. See the liner notes by Andrew Homzy to *Black, Brown and Beige.*

29. Tucker, ed., *DER,* p. 249.

30. Ibid., p. 145.

31. Ulanov, *Duke Ellington,* p. 253.

32. Looser, faster performances can be heard on recordings from Fargo, North Dakota (November 7, 1940) and Carnegie Hall (January 23, 1943). A study score, transcribed from the first recording by David Berger and Alan

Campbell, is published by United Artists Music; a simplified piano version appears in Hasse, *Beyond Category*.

33. Rattenbury, *Duke Ellington, Jazz Composer*, p. 105.

34. See Bushell and Tucker, *Jazz from the Beginning*, p. 55.

35. Peinkofer and Tannigel, *Handbook of Percussion Instruments*, p. 43.

36. Fulcher, ed., *Debussy and His World*, p. 161.

37. See Katz, *Capturing Sound*, pp. 74–77.

38. See the accounts of Schoenberg's life in Hahl-Koch, *Arnold Schoenberg/Wassily Kandinsky*, and Meyer and Wasserman, eds., *Schoenberg, Kandinsky and the Blue Rider*.

39. Meyer and Wasserman, eds., *Schoenberg, Kandinsky and the Blue Rider*, p. 25.

40. Hahl-Koch, *Arnold Schoenberg/Wassily Kandinsky*, p. 21.

41. Ibid., p. 23.

42. Meyer and Wasserman, eds., *Schoenberg, Kandinsky and the Blue Rider*, p. 30.

43. Ibid., p. 50.

44. Schoenberg and Stein, *Style and Idea*, p. 145.

45. Kandinsky, *Concerning the Spiritual in Art*, p. 9.

46. Ibid., p. 13.

47. Hahl-Koch, *Arnold Schoenberg/Wassily Kandinsky*, p. 149.

48. Kandinsky, *Concerning the Spiritual in Art*, pp. 38–41.

49. See Covach, "Schoenberg and the Occult," pp. 103–18.

50. Hahl-Koch, *Arnold Schoenberg/Wassily Kandinsky*, p. 96. See Meyer and Wasserman, eds., *Schoenberg, Kandinsky and the Blue Rider*, p. 107, for Schoenberg's scale of colors.

51. Hahl-Koch, *Arnold Schoenberg/Wassily Kandinsky*, p. 111.

52. Theosophical music was brought to the United States in 1916 by a French composer, Dane Rudhyar, who became an important figure among the American "ultra-modernists" and whose ideas would influence Ruth Crawford, John Cage, Lou Harrison, and James Tenney (Oja, *Making Music Modern*, pp. 99–100).

53. Joseph, *Stravinsky and Balanchine*, p. 89.

54. Ibid., p. 144.

55. Ibid., p. 68.

56. Lederman, ed., *Stravinsky in the Theater*, p. 81.

57. Kirstein, *Thirty Years/The New York City Ballet*, p. 65.

58. Walsh, *Stravinsky: A Creative Spring*, p. 469.

59. Edmund Wilson's 1930 study *Axel's Castle* remains the best introduction to the Symbolist movement.

60. C..F. MacIntyre, trans., *French Symbolist Poetry*, p. 12.

61. See Rosemary Lloyd, "Debussy, Mallarmé, and 'Les Mardis,'" in Fulcher, ed., *Debussy and His World*, pp. 255–69.

62. Lockspeiser also compares this song to the ironic poetry of Debussy's friend Jules Laforgue, who mocked the enforced boredom of Parisian Sundays in his collection of poems entitled *Dimanche*. Lockspeiser, *Debussy*, vol. 1, p. 133.

63. Nichols, *Debussy Remembered*, p. 83.

64. Ibid., p. 84.

65. Lockspeiser, *Debussy*, vol. 2, pp. 45–46.

66. Roberts, *Images*, p. 143.

67. Paul Jacobs suggested that the first follows the model of Liszt's *Transcendental Etudes* (perhaps no. 2 in a minor) (liner notes to Nonesuch recording); Roger Nichols proposes a relationship to a Hans Christian Anderson story, "The Garden of Paradise," about the four winds, or to Shelley's "Ode to the West Wind," which Debussy knew in translation (liner notes to recording on DGG by Krystian Zimerman); and Paul Roberts hears a connection, which I don't, to "Orage" from Liszt's *Années de pèlerinage*. The clearest musical precedent, though, is the third movement, "Dialogue of the Wind and Sea," from Debussy's own *La Mer,* a tumultuous representation of death and rebirth; both pieces could refer to paintings by Turner.

68. Debussy composed several other snowscapes, two of which employ the rising four-note motive from *Tristan* to convey contrasting qualities of tristesse: *"Le Tombeau des naiads,"* from *Trois chansons de Bilitis,* and "Snow Is Dancing," from *Children's Corner.* In two works from his last years, the third movement of *En Blanc et Noir* and the "Etude in Chromatic Steps," the dance of snow seems to transcend human suffering and becomes a gently whirling interplay of the natural world and the human imagination, Wallace Stevens's "Snow Man" avant la lettre.

69. In her article "Tristan in the Making of Pelléas," Carolyn Abbate noted that Debussy often alludes to Wagner's opera through puns. The *"triste"* landscape evoked here in the opening performance instruction and repeated, with a different nuance, later (*"Comme un tender et triste regret"*) points to the desolate (but not wintry) stage décor that Wagner calls for in the third act of *Tristan:* "The whole scene gives the impression of being deserted, ill-tended, here and there in poor repair and overgrown." But behind that hidden allusion is another, a hothouse or *"Treibhaus"* as described in a poem by Mathilde Wesendonck, which Wagner set as a compositional study for the prelude to act 3. This hothouse is also surprisingly "triste":

> Weit in sehnendem Verlangen
> breitet ihr die Arme aus,
> und umschlinget wahnbefangen
> öder Leere nicht'gen Graus.

> Wide, in yearning desire
> you spread your arms,
> and in the bonds of delusion you embrace
> the futile horror of a desolate void.

(Wagner's song is in the same key as Debussy's prelude. Debussy had written the words and music for his own hothouse prose poem "De fleurs . . ." in his *Proses lyriques,* but it sounds more like *Parsifal* than *Tristan.* Symbolists preferred hothouse flowers to the lilies of the field.)

70. Lockspeiser, *Debussy*, vol. 2, p. 46.

71. Thompson, *The Soundscape of Modernity*, p. 118.

72. Ibid., p. 49.

73. Giddins, *VJ*, p. 348.

74. Zak, *The Poetics of Rock*, pp. 88, 87.

75. Ibid., p. 35.

76. Ibid., p. 88.

2. "COTTON TAIL": RHYTHM

Epigraphs, p. 50: Zora Neale Hurston, "Characteristics of Negro Expression," in O'Meally, ed., *JCAC*, p. 302; Murray, *Stomping the Blues*, p. 144; Irving Mills, lyrics to "Don't Mean a Thing (If It Ain't Got That Swing)," also attributed to Bubber Miley. Epigraph, p. 000: Louis Armstrong, quoted in Teachout, *Pops*, p. 280. Epigraphs, pp. 71–72: Igor Stravinsky, *Stravinsky in Conversation with Robert Craft*, pp. 128–30; Gene Krupa, in Gottlieb, ed., *Reading Jazz*, p. 774; Stravinsky, *Memories and Commentaries* (2002), p. 136; George Antheil, cited in Albright, *Modernism and Music*, p. 395; Mercer Ellington, quoted in Nicholson, *Reminiscing in Tempo*, p. 124.

1. Octave Mirabeau in 1908, quoted in Kern, *The Culture of Time and Space 1880–1918*, p. 113.

2. Walter Lippman in 1914, quoted in ibid., p. 124.

3. Porter, Ullman, and Hazell, *Jazz*, p. 464. For spurious definitions see Virgil Thomson's articles "Swing Music" and "Swing Again," which appeared in *Modern Music* in 1936 and 1938; Thomson trots out his much-used theories about "quantitative" rhythms.

4. Murray, *Stomping the Blues*, p. 138. See Michael Denning's discussion of the broader political resonances of swing in *The Cultural Front*, pp. 328–38.

5. Schuller, *SE*, p. 129.

6. As with many other works in the Ellington repertory, there is some debate about authorship, despite Ellington's unshared listing as composer on all published versions. Webster told Milt Hinton that he had composed the tune (Büchmann-Møller, *Someone to Watch over Me*, p. 69). Rex Stewart, in a lovingly limned portrait, wrote that Webster was its composer *and* arranger, and, somewhat contradicting that claim, "also wrote the now-famous saxophone section chorus" (Stewart, *Jazz Masters of the Thirties*, p. 129). Mercer Ellington, on the other hand, wrote that the chart sprang from a "device" of Webster's (Ellington and Dance, *Duke Ellington in Person*, p. 87).

7. Büchmann-Møller, *Someone to Watch over Me*, p. 61.

8. In later jazz the sectional sax solo has come to be called "supersax" after a Charlie Parker tribute band formed by Med Flory and Buddy Clark that debuted in 1972 featuring harmonized arrangements of Parker's solos.

9. A score of the full composition as transcribed from the recording by David Berger is published by Jazz at Lincoln Center. Webster's solo is transcribed (somewhat differently) by Gunther Schuller in *SE*, pp. 582–83. An incomplete set of parts and detailed sketches for the shout chorus are in the Ellington Archive at the Smithsonian, but there is no complete manuscript score and parts. A superb Ellingtonian performance of "Cotton Tail" as a "head" followed by improvised solos appears on *Duke Ellington's Jazz Violin Session*. Two other

recordings of the six-chorus composition with Webster were made in Fargo, North Dakota, in November and at Carnegie Hall in January 1943, the latter at a much faster clip than the studio recording. Not by Ellington but not to be missed: the vocalized version of the 1940 recording by Lambert, Hendricks, and Ross.

10. Oliver, *Blues Fell This Morning*, p. 66.

11. See Schuller, *SE*, p. 128.

12. Sublette, *Cuba and Its Music*, p. 80.

13. You can find extensive descriptions of African rhythms in Jones, *Studies in African Music*; Chernoff, *African Rhythm and African Sensibility*; Floyd, *Black Music in the Harlem Renaissance*; Arom; *African Polyphony and Polyrhythm*; and Floyd, *Composing the Music of Africa*, as well as clear accounts of the relation between African and Cuban rhythms in Fernandez, *From Afro-Cuban Rhythms to Latin Jazz*; and Sublette, *Cuba and Its Music*. See also Wilson, "The Significance of the Relationship between Afro-American and West African Music"; and Agawu, "The Invention of 'African Rhythm.'" Many listeners today will be familiar with the minimalist appropriation of West African rhythms found in such Steve Reich pieces as *Drumming* and *Music for Eighteen Musicians*. There are now many recordings of traditional Ewe music, but for a Caribbean perspective I recommend the CD released as *Our Man in Havana*, produced originally by Mongo Santamaría in the 1950s, which presents rural Cuban music very close to its African origins and also to modern Cuban popular music.

14. A classic statement of this misunderstanding appears in Richard Waterman's "'Hot' Rhythm in Negro Music."

15. I wonder if a similar experience of temporal terror underlies the phase-shift pieces of Steve Reich, such as *Clapping Music*, which start in phase, go out, and gradually come back, something that might happen in West African music if you got totally lost and tried, step by step, to find your way back.

16. Chernoff, *African Rhythm and African Sensibility*, p. 51.

17. Malcolm Floyd, *Composing the Music of Africa*, p. 58.

18. The sheet music is reprinted in Jasen, ed., *"For Me and My Gal" and Other Favorite Song Hits, 1915–1917*.

19. Schuller, *EJ*, 186.

20. The resilient "bones" of the four-phrase structure are still evident in the most famous "Tiger Rag" descendant, Jerry Herman's "Hello Dolly!"

21. Schuller, *EJ*, p. 111.

22. Tucker, ed., *DER*, p. 36.

23. Ellington's repeated use of "Tiger Rag" was noted in 1970 by Martin Williams in *The Jazz Tradition*.

24. Tucker, ed., *DER*, p. 111.

25. The solos are listed by Stanley Dance in the liner notes for *The Okeh Ellington*.

26. Schuller, for instance, termed it "ephemeral" (*SE*, p. 483).

27. Schuller, *EJ*, p. 346.

28. Hasse, *Beyond Category*, p. 55.

29. Quoted in notes by John Szwed to *Jelly Roll Morton: The Complete Library of Congress Recordings.*

30. Jones, "Blues People," p. 108.

31. Floyd, *The Power of Black Music*, p. 110.

32. See Magee, *The Uncrowned King of Swing.* p. 131.

33. Schuller, *EJ*, p. 268

34. Southern, *MBA*, p. 135.

35. Ibid., p. 99.

36. Ibid., p. 160

37. The caveats are raised by Wayne Shirley (in his 1978 introduction to the reissue of *Afro-American Spirituals, Work Songs, and Ballads*), so they are serious. Shirley pointed out Lomax's way of manufacturing an air of primitive authenticity in his field recordings and noted that the performance of "Run, Old Jeremiah" on *Afro-American Spirituals, Work Songs, and Ballads*, while a ring shout, the style with the clearest connections to African practice, traces no straight line from Africa to this 1934 recording: the Louisiana community heard here had only "recently reintroduced the ring-shout as a means of attracting" a younger, dance-oriented generation to the church.

38. See http://historymatters.gmu.edu/d/5759/.

39. For an extended theoretical discussion of shout, see Samuel A. Floyd Jr., "Ring Shout, Signifyin(g), and Jazz Analysis," in Walser, ed., *Keeping Time.*

40. Ibid., p. 21.

41. Blesh and Janis, *They All Played Ragtime*, p. 188.

42. Copland, *The New Music*, p. 66. See also my chapter, "Copland and the Jazz Boys," in Dickinson, ed., *Copland Connotations.*

43. See rehearsal number 86 in the coda of *Apollo*, rehearsal number 92 in the boogie-woogie Pas d'action of *Orpheus*, and bars 352–64 of *Agon.*

44. Laki, *Bartók and His World*, p. 52.

45. The idea that Bartók's music springs from binary oppositions was first proposed by Erno Lendvai. Although recent scholarship has questioned many of Lendvai's claims, particularly that Bartók employed Golden Section proportions systematically, they often reconfigure the dialectics outlined by Lendvai rather than rejecting them. Botstein's restatement is typical. See also Kárpáti, *Bartók's Chamber Music*, p. 213.

46. The ethnomusicologist Timothy Rice claims that 3 + 3 + 2 meter does not exist in Bulgarian music and that therefore two of the six studies from *Mikrokosmos* were really meant to "capture the syncopated rhythms of American popular music and jazz" (Antokoletz, Fischer, and Suchoff, eds., *Bartók Perspectives*, p. 198). In klezmer music, however, the pattern is common and is called either "Freylechs" or "Bulgar." Bartók, moreover, uses the 3 + 3 + 2 rhythm in a folklike style that does not sound like jazz or klezmer in *Music for Strings, Percussion and Celesta*. Bartók had used 3 + 3 + 2 patterns in pieces based on Romanian folk music as early as the popular *Romanian Dances* of 1915.

47. See Tirro, *Jazz: A History*, p. 336.

48. Ulanov, *Duke Ellington*, p. 231.

49. Taruskin, *Stravinsky and the Russian Traditions*, p. 1357.

50. See Van den Toorn, *The Music of Igor Stravinsky,* pp. 99–100.

51. Jones, *Studies in African Music,* vol. 2, p. 71.

52. Taruskin, *Stravinsky and the Russian Traditions,* 1306–7. Taruskin confuses matters, though, by anachronistically comparing Stravinsky's ragtimes with Joplin's. The dotted rhythms in the *Histoire* "Ragtime" and the 1918 *Ragtime for Eleven Instruments* show that Stravinsky was keeping up with more advanced evolutions of the form; both works are really fox-trots (a dance rage launched by Vernon and Irene Castle and their musical director James Reese Europe in 1914) rather than rags, though the confusion of nomenclature persisted for some time on both sides of the Atlantic. Stravinsky cubisticly rearranged the elements of the fox-trot just as he would with many other historical styles.

53. The pairing is analyzed in Crawford, *American Musical Landscape.*

54. Thomson and Kostelanetz, *A Virgil Thomson Reader,* p. 164.

55. Ibid.

56. See Oja, *Making Music Modern,* p. 143.

57. Tick, *Ruth Crawford Seeger,* pp. 217–21.

58. Nicholls, *American Experimental Music,* p. 55.

59. The complex relation of the Cage avant-garde to jazz is explored in detail in Lewis, *A Power Stronger Than Itself.*

60. Tirro, *Jazz: A History,* p. 377.

61. For Gunther Schuller's "out" genealogy, see "The Avant-Garde and Third Stream," in his *Musings,* pp. 121–33.

62. The movement is surveyed in the important studies Litweiler, *The Freedom Principle;* Jost, *Free Jazz;* Spellman, *Black Music;* and Lewis, *A Power Stronger Than Itself.*

63. Litweiler, *The Freedom Principle,* p. 75.

64. Tucker, ed., *DER,* p. 334.

3. "PRELUDE TO A KISS": MELODY

Epigraph, p. 89: T. W. Adorno, *Introduction to the Sociology of Music,* p. 25.

1. Stravinsky, *Poetics of Music.* p. 43.

2. "Heart and Brain in Music," in Schoenberg and Stein, *Style and Idea,* p. 69.

3. Hamm, *Yesterdays,* pp. 285–86. For accounts of the rise of Tin Pan Alley see Hamm, *Yesterdays,* and Goldberg, *Tin Pan Alley,* still informative and fun to read despite its age. See also Hamm's commentaries in the three-volume *Irving Berlin's Early Songs,* published by MUSA.

4. Hamm, *Yesterdays,* p. 290.

5. Ibid., p. 294.

6. In discussing Ellington's songs (and Strayhorn's), I will refer to the versions found in "The Great Music of Duke Ellington," first published by Belwin Mills in 1985.

7. Wilder and Maher, *American Popular Song,* p. 412.

8. Ellington was listed as composer of two musicals and one opera, the 1946 *Beggars' Holiday,* with lyrics by John Latouche, based, like *The Threepenny*

Opera, on *The Beggars' Opera.* According to Walter van de Leur, Billy Strayhorn did most of the composing, "occasionally conferring with Ellington over the telephone" (*Something to Live For,* p. 98). The musical *Pousse-café,* based on *The Blue Angel,* appeared briefly in 1966. *Queenie Pie,* an opera buffa, was produced only after Ellington's death. None of these shows had a successful run or produced enduring songs.

9. Tucker, *Ellington: The Early Years,* chapter 8.

10. Ibid., pp. 126–33.

11. Reprinted in Nicholson, *Reminiscing in Tempo,* pp. 152–59.

12. Giddins, *VJ,* p. 117.

13. When I wrote my book on *Rhapsody in Blue* I noted that "Black Beauty" begins with the same harmonies as the opening piano solo in the Gershwin; it's even in the same key. I hadn't noticed, though, that "Swampy River," which Ellington recorded at the same piano solo session as "Black Beauty," began with an even more explicit allusion to *Rhapsody in Blue.* I also hadn't noticed that Gershwin returned the compliment, because the bridge of "I Got Rhythm," written two years later, recalls the second strain of "Black Beauty." Tipping his hat to Gershwin, Ellington flaunted his compositional and pianistic chops. Both pieces are complex multistrain piano compositions in the manner of James P. Johnson. But the main melody in "Black Beauty" is neither Gershwinesque nor Johnsonesque, and it does not display the creamy chromaticism of many Ellington tunes.

14. Collier, *Duke Ellington,* p. 118.

15. Wilder and Maher, *American Popular Song,* p. 414.

16. For a more modern and much sexier vocal rendition, check out Sarah Vaughan's recording on the Smithsonian *Jazz Singers* collection. Johnny Hodges's exultant 1957 recording, with what sounds to me like a Strayhorn arrangement, appears on *Duke Ellington Indigos.*

17. Furia, *Ira Gershwin,* p. 72.

18. Pollack, *George Gershwin,* p. 456.

19. Furia, *Ira Gershwin,* p. 72.

20. Tucker, ed., *DER,* p. 341.

21. A great sampling of twentieth-century performance styles across a wide spectrum can be heard on *I Got Rhythm: The Music of George Gershwin,* a four-CD set from the Smithsonian Collection of Recordings.

22. See Pleasants, *The Great American Popular Singers;* and Friedwald, *Stardust Melodies.*

23. Taylor's 1929 performance leads off the album *The Jazz Singers,* edited by Robert G. O'Meally, who describes her as a "pre-jazz singer with a vaudeville twist."

24. Ken Romanowski, liner notes for *Mamie Smith: Complete Recorded Works in Chronological Order,* vol. 1, Document Records DOCD-5357.

25. Jasen and Jones, *Black Bottom Stomp,* p. 219.

26. Friedwald, *Stardust Melodies,* p. 32.

27. See van de Leur, *Something to Live For,* pp. 152–59, for an extensive discussion of Strayhorn's arrangement.

28. Giddins, *VJ,* p. 113.

29. Van de Leur, *Something to Live For*, p. 63.

30. Ibid., p. 27.

31. Ibid., p. 171.

32. Kahn, *Kind of Blue*, p. 71.

33. See Slonimsky, *Perfect Pitch*, pp. 173–80.

34. Berliner, *Thinking in Jazz*, p. 192.

35. For late Renaissance divisions, see William Byrd's "My Ladye Nevels Grownde"; for a twentieth-century version, see Prelude no. 21 from Shostakovich's Preludes and Fugues, op. 87. For a romantic and more dissonant expansion of Bach's *moto perpetuo* technique, see Chopin's Prelude in B♭ Minor, op. 28, no. 16.

36. Published by Hal Leonard in 2001.

37. O'Meally, ed., *JCAC*, p. 269.

38. According to Kahn, *Kind of Blue* (p. 110), he quotes a melodic line from Junior Parker's 1957 R&B tune "Next Time You See Me."

4. "SATIN DOLL": HARMONY

Epigraphs, p. 120: Duke Ellington, in Tucker, ed., *DER*, p. 42; Ferruccio Busoni, "Sketch of a New Esthetic of Music," in Debussy, Busoni, and Ives, *Three Classics in the Aesthetic of Music*, p. 93; Igor Stravinsky, *Poetics of Music*, p. 37.

1. Tucker, *The Early Years*, p. 243.

2. Transcribed by John Mehegan in *Tonal and Rhythmic Principles*.

3. In Mingus, *Charles Mingus: More Than a Fake Book*.

4. See Orenstein, *Ravel*, p. 209, and Orenstein, ed., *A Ravel Reader*, pp. 519–20.

5. Orenstein, ed., *A Ravel Reader*, pp. 519–20.

6. Baraka, *Blues People*, pp. 229–30.

7. Van den Toorn, *Music of Igor Stravinsky*, pp. 407–8.

8. Stravinsky and Craft, *Stravinsky in Conversation with Robert Craft*, p. 38.

9. Schoenberg and Stein, *Style and Idea*, p. 210.

10. Ibid., p. 30.

11. Ibid., p. 446.

12. Ibid., p. 109.

13. Ibid., p. 144.

14. Reprinted in liner notes for *The Music of Arnold Schoenberg, Vol. III*.

15. Schoenberg and Stein, *Style and Idea*, p. 49.

16. Kárpáti, *Bartók's Chamber Music*, pp. 96 and 286.

17. Ibid., p. 34.

18. Robert Craft, "The Emperor of China," *New York Review of Books*, November 5, 1987.

PART II

Epigraph, p. 153: Duke Ellington, in Tucker, ed., *DER*, p. 43.

1. Tucker, ed., *DER*, p. 50.

2. Ibid., p. 12.

3. For the history of many of these pieces, see Lock, *Blutopia;* Early, *Tuxedo Junction;* and Cohen, *Duke Ellington's America.*

4. Ellington's schedule is documented in Stratemann, *Duke Ellington,* and Vail, *Duke's Diary.*

5. See Alvin Ailey's account of *The River* in Perlis and Van Cleve, *Composers' Voices from Ives to Ellington,* pp. 400–404. Van de Leur, *Something to Live For,* and Hajdu, *Lush Life,* offer many detailed descriptions of the Ellington/Strayhorn collaboration.

6. For Ellington's frank assessment of his work with Henderson see Howland, *"Ellington Uptown,"* p. 165.

5. "WARM VALLEY": LOVE

Epigraph, p. 157: Duke Ellington, in Ellington, *MIMM,* p. 53. Epigraph, pp. 159–60: Duke Ellington, "Sex Is No Sin," *Ebony,* May 1954. Epigraph, p. 187: Arnold Schoenberg, quoted in Beaumont, *Zemlinsky,* p. 207.

1. See Stratemann, *Duke Ellington,* pp. 5–23.

2. See Metzer, *Quotation and Cultural Meaning in Twentieth-Century Music,* for a discussion of the film's cultural setting.

3. Ellington, *MIMM,* p. 6. Ellington's father died two years later; he suffered these two great losses just as the swing era was taking off.

4. Tucker, ed., *DER,* p. 120.

5. Lawrence, *Duke Ellington and His World,* p. 246.

6. Hasse, *Beyond Category,* p. 23.

7. Howland, *"Ellington Uptown,"* p. 176.

8. Tucker, ed., *DER,* p. 244.

9. Ellington, *MIMM,* pp. 12–15.

10. See Tucker, *Ellington: The Early Years,* p. 16.

11. Tucker, ed., *DER,* p. 124.

12. See also Gunther Schuller's thematic analysis in *SE.*

13. Van de Leur, *Something to Live For,* pp. 93–94.

14. Ellington, *MIMM,* p. 20.

15. See Appel, *Jazz Modernism,* pp. 225–27.

16. See Chambers, "Bardland," 43.

17. Liner notes for original album.

18. Vail, *Duke's Diary,* p. 35.

19. Quoted in Nicholson, *Reminiscing in Tempo,* p. 290.

20. See Gennari, in O'Meally, Edwards, and Griffin, eds., *UC,* p. 129.

21. Hajdu, *Lush Life,* p. 148.

22. Morton, *Backstory in Blue,* p. 147.

23. Tucker, ed., *DER,* p. 291.

24. Epstein, *Joe Papp,* p. 127.

25. Ibid., p. 167.

26. Hajdu, *Lush Life,* p. 155.

27. Tucker, ed., *DER,* p. 321.

28. Its precedent as an album-long composition was soon followed by the Miles Davis/Gil Evans *Miles Ahead* and Charles Mingus's *Black Saint and the*

Sinner Lady. Both albums acknowledged their debt to Ellington/Strayhorn. *Miles Ahead* included Evans's arrangement of Dave Brubeck's "The Duke"; on *Black Saint* Mingus asked saxophonist Charles Mariani to imitate Johnny Hodges.

29. Tucker, ed., *DER*, p. 321.

30. Ellington, *MIMM*, p. 192.

31. See Dyer, *But Beautiful*, pp. 3–4.

32. O'Meally, Edwards, and Griffin, eds., *UC*, p. 336.

33. See an analysis in van de Leur, *Something to Live For*, pp. 159–61.

34. Hajdu, *Lush Life*, p. 82.

35. See Tucker, ed., *DER*, p. 191.

36. Hajdu, *Lush Life*, p. 160.

37. You can find the music in Ellington, *The 100th Anniversary Collection*.

38. Berg and Berg, *Alban Berg: Letters to his Wife*, pp. 341–42.

39. See Jarman in Pople, ed., *The Cambridge Companion to Berg*, p. 177.

40. For an updated, clear-eyed assessment of both the affair and the music, see Simms, "Alban Berg and Hanna Fuchs."

41. See Douglas Jarman, "Secret Programmes," in Pople, ed., *The Cambridge Companion to Berg*, pp. 167–79.

42. Dietschy, Ashbrook, and Cobb, *A Portrait of Claude Debussy*, p. 127.

43. Quoted in Kern, *The Culture of Time and Space 1880–1918*, p. 25.

44. Reich, *Alban Berg*, p. 71.

45. Perle, *The Operas of Alban Berg*, p. 710.

46. In September 1925 Berg wrote Schoenberg, "Casting a glance at our new score [the Wind Quintet, op. 26] a while back was immeasurably exciting. How long will it be before I understand the music as thoroughly as I fancy, for example, that I understand *Pierrot?*"

6. *BLACK, BROWN AND BEIGE:* HISTORY

Epigraphs, p. 200: T. S. Eliot, "Tradition and the Individual Talent"; F. Scott Fitzgerald, *The Great Gatsby*; Sun Ra, quoted in Graham Lock, *Blutopia*, p. 140.

1. Adorno, *Prisms*, pp. 119–32.

2. Tucker, ed., *DER*, p. 207.

3. See Anderson, *Deep River*, pp. 221–25.

4. Lewis, *W. E. B. Dubois*, p. 507.

5. Cripps, *Slow Fade to Black*, p. 52.

6. May, *Screening out the Past*, pp. 81–82.

7. Ibid., 83.

8. George, *The Death of Rhythm and Blues*, p. 7.

9. Tucker, *Ellington: The Early Years*, p. 8.

10. Gennari, *Blowin' Hot and Cool*, p. 29.

11. Ibid., p. 30.

12. Duberman, *Paul Robeson*, p. 250.

13. Ottley, *"New World A-Coming,"* p. 289.

14. Tucker, ed., *DER*, p. 147.

15. Ibid., p. 166.

16. For a detailed account of these concerts and Hammond's role in shaping jazz history, see Anderson, *Deep River*, chapter 5.

17. Tucker, ed., *DER*, pp. 155–65.

18. See Tucker, "The Genesis of *Black, Brown and Beige*"; Cohen, *Duke Ellington's America*.

19. See Edwards in O'Meally, Edwards, and Griffin, eds., *UC*, p. 345.

20. Denning, *The Cultural Front*, p. 310.

21. Tucker, ed., *DER*, p. 504.

22. See Ulanov, *Duke Ellington*; Tucker, ed., *DER*; Giddins, "In Search of Black, Brown and Beige" in Tucker, ed., DER,; Tucker, "The Genesis of *Black, Brown and Beige*"; DeVeaux, "'Black, Brown and Beige' and the Critics"; Lock, *Blutopia*; Peress, *Dvořák to Duke Ellington*; Cohen, *Duke Ellington's America*; Knauer, "Simulated Improvisation"; Howland, *"Ellington Uptown."*

23. The critical literature covers the considerable and varied formal history of *Black, Brown and Beige*. Here I will consider the work as heard on the January 1943 recording with the help of Maurice Peress's version of the score, which, however, is not a critical edition. I discuss this version of the piece because of its historical importance, not because I think it represents an urtext or is definitive either in its composition or performance.

24. The short phrases are outlined by Howland, *"Ellington Uptown,"* p. 188.

25. Brian Priestley and Alan Cohen note how the work uses material from the 1938 version of "Riding on a Blue Note." Tucker, ed., *DER*, p. 193.

26. You can see this effect in the 1930 film *Check and Double Check*.

27. See Tucker, ed., *DER*, p. 197.

28. Ibid., p. 172.

29. Murray, *Stomping the Blues*, p. 36.

30. Ellington and Dance, *Duke Ellington in Person*, p. 94.

31. Ottley, *"New World A-Coming,"* p. 168.

32. Ibid., p. 180.

33. Ibid., p. 176.

34. Hasse, *Beyond Category*, p. 23.

35. Ellington, *MIMM*, p. 12.

36. Hasse, *Beyond Category*, p. 23.

37. Ottley, *"New World A-Coming,"* p. 343.

38. Ibid., p. 347.

39. Ibid., p. 2.

40. Copland and Perlis, *Copland*, p. 44.

41. Oja and Tick, eds., *Aaron Copland and His World*, p. 137.

42. See William Brooks, "Simple Gifts and Involuntary Accretions," in Dickinson, ed., *Copland Connotations*.

43. Robertson, "A Gift to Be Simple," p. 30.

44. See Levy, "From Orient to Occident," for a detailed account of Copland's westward turn and its erasure of black history in "Music for Radio."

See Lynn Garafola, "Making an American Dance," for detailed histories of the three ballets. Both chapters are in Oja and Tick, eds., *Aaron Copland and His World*.

45. Oja and Tick, eds., *Aaron Copland and His World*, p. 125.

46. Ibid., p. 128.

47. Cited in Levy, "From Orient to Occident," p. 337.

48. Cited in Garafola, "Making an American Dance," p. 132.

49. Pollack, *Aaron Copland*, p. 367.

50. Garafola, "Making an American Dance," p. 135.

51. See Robertson, "A Gift to Be Simple," chapter 3.

52. Pollack, *Aaron Copland*, pp. 394–97.

53. Ibid., p. 393.

54. Copland and Perlis, *Copland*, p. 41.

55. Pollack, *Aaron Copland*, p. 403. I should note that the normally astute Edwin Denby assumed that the Husbandman was alive at the end; but, then, Denby's review of the premiere made no mention of any of its "netherworld" elements, instead praising it as a realistic (!) portrayal of "our country ancestors and inherited mores" (Denby and MacKay, *Dance Writings*, p. 314). On second viewing Denby praised the way the work "persuades you of the value of domestic and neighborly ties" and described the Revivalist as a cross between Saint Francis and Thoreau (ibid., p. 318).

56. Copland and Perlis, *Copland*, p. 43.

57. Ibid., p. 45.

58. Pollack, *Aaron Copland*, pp. 400–401.

59. Copland and Perlis, *Copland*, p. 45.

7. "HEAVEN": GOD

Epigraphs, p. 248: Igor Stravinsky, in *Conversation Robert Craft*, p. 136; Duke Ellington, *MIMM*, p. 262.

1. Steed, *Duke Ellington*, p. 140.

2. See Lloyd, "The Revival of an Early 'Crossover' Masterwork."

3. See Edwards in O'Meally, Edwards, and Griffin, eds., *UC*, pp. 348–49.

4. Nicholson, *Reminiscing in Tempo*, p. 348; Ellington, *MIMM*, p. 198.

5. Dance, *The World of Duke Ellington*, p. 26.

6. The recording does not include all the music from the show; most notably it omits "Work Song" from *Black, Brown and Beige*, which was danced by the Alvin Ailey company (Cohen, *Duke Ellington's America*, p. 395).

7. Harvey Cohen demonstrates that there is little evidence to support the claim by Stuart Nicholson that the show was criticized for a lack of political commitment (ibid., pp. 396–97).

8. Ibid., p. 396.

9. See ibid., pp. 456–60.

10. Tucker, ed., *DER*, p. 377.

11. See Murchison, "Mary Lou Williams's Hymn *Black Christ of the Andes (St. Martin de Porres)*."

12. Steed, *Duke Ellington*, p. 135.

13. See the program in Stratemann, *Duke Ellington, Day by Day and Film by Film,* p. 516.

14. I'll use the three RCA recordings as the basis for my discussion, even though all are incomplete in some way; Ellington performed the concerts differently on many occasions. There are also two fine recordings that combine numbers from different concerts by the Seattle Repertory Jazz Orchestra and the Big Band de Lausanne.

15. Stratemann, *Duke Ellington, Day by Day and Film by Film,* p. 516.

16. Nicholson, *Reminiscing in Tempo,* p. 366.

17. Ellington, *MIMM.* p. 156.

18. Cohen, *Duke Ellington's America,* p. 484.

19. Tucker, ed., *DER,* p. 378—but perhaps the real resemblance was to "The Girl from Ipanema."

20. Ibid., p. 376.

21. Ellington and Dance, *Duke Ellington in Person,* pp. 192–93.

22. Vail, *Duke's Diary,* p. 441.

23. Steed, *Duke Ellington,* p. 147.

24. See Lloyd, "The Revival of an Early 'Crossover' Masterwork," for a thorough account of the problems involved.

Bibliography

Abbate, Carolyn. "'Tristan' In the Composition Of 'Pelléas.'" *19th-Century Music* 5, no. 2 (1981): 117–41.

Abrahams, Roger D. *Afro-American Folktales: Stories from Black Traditions in the New World*. New York: Pantheon Books, 1985.

———. *Deep Down in the Jungle . . . : Negro Narrative Folklore from the Streets of Philadelphia*. Chicago: Aldine, 1970.

Adorno, Theodor W. *Introduction to the Sociology of Music*. New York: Seabury Press, 1976.

———. *Prisms*. Translated by Samuel and Shierry Weber. Cambridge: MIT Press, 1982.

Adorno, Theodor W., Juliane Brand, and Christopher Hailey. *Alban Berg, Master of the Smallest Link*. Cambridge: Cambridge University Press, 1991.

Agawu, Kofi. "The Invention Of 'African Rhythm.'" *Journal of the American Musicological Society* 48, no. 3 (Autumn 1995): 380–95.

Ahr, J. "Ashley Kahn, Kind of Blue: The Making of the Miles Davis Masterpiece." *American Music* 22 (2004): 319–20.

Albright, Daniel. *Modernism and Music: An Anthology of Sources*. Chicago: University of Chicago Press, 2004.

Anderson, Paul Allen. *Deep River: Music and Memory in Harlem Renaissance Thought*. New Americanists. Durham, NC: Duke University Press, 2001.

Andriessen, Louis, and Elmer Schönberger. *The Apollonian Clockwork: On Stravinsky*. Oxford: Oxford University Press, 1989.

Antokoletz, Elliott. *The Music of Béla Bartók: A Study of Tonality and Progression in Twentieth-Century Music*. Berkeley: University of California Press, 1984.

Antokoletz, Elliott, Victoria Fischer, and Benjamin Suchoff, eds. *Bartók Perspectives: Man, Composer, and Ethnomusicologist*. Oxford: Oxford University Press, 2000.

Appel, Alfred. *Jazz Modernism: From Ellington and Armstrong to Matisse and Joyce.* New York: Alfred A. Knopf, 2002.

Arom, Simha. *African Polyphony and Polyrhythm: Musical Structure and Methodology.* Cambridge: Cambridge University Press; Paris: Editions de la Maison des sciences de l'homme, 1991.

Attali, Jacques. *Noise: The Political Economy of Music.* Theory and History of Literature, vol. 16. Minneapolis: University of Minnesota Press, 1985.

Badger, Reid. *A Life in Ragtime: A Biography of James Reese Europe.* New York: Oxford University Press, 1995.

Bailey, Kathryn. *The Life of Webern.* Musical Lives. Cambridge: Cambridge University Press, 1998.

Baker, Houston A. *Blues, Ideology, and Afro-American Literature: A Vernacular Theory.* Chicago: University of Chicago Press, 1984.

Baraka, Imamu Amiri. *Blues People: Negro Music in White America.* New York: W. Morrow, 1963.

Barraqué, Jean. *Debussy.* Solfèges 22. Paris: Editions du Seuil, 1962.

Beaumont, Antony. *Zemlinsky.* Ithaca, NY: Cornell University Press, 2000.

Berg, Alban, and Helene Berg. *Alban Berg: Letters to His Wife.* New York: St. Martin's Press, 1971.

Berg, Alban, Arnold Schoenberg, Juliane Brand, Christopher Hailey, and Donald Harris. *The Berg-Schoenberg Correspondence: Selected Letters.* New York: W. W. Norton, 1987.

Berlin, Irving. *Early Songs I.* Madison, WI: A-R Editions, 1994.

Berliner, Paul. *Thinking in Jazz: The Infinite Art of Improvisation.* Chicago Studies in Ethnomusicology. Chicago: University of Chicago Press, 1994.

Berry, Wallace. *Structural Functions in Music.* Englewood Cliffs, NJ: Prentice-Hall, 1976.

Blesh, Rudi, and Harriet Grossman Janis. *They All Played Ragtime.* New York: Oak Publications, 1971.

Boretz, Benjamin, and Edward T. Cone. *Perspectives on Schoenberg and Stravinsky.* New York: W. W. Norton, 1972.

Bronner, Stephen Eric, and Douglas Kellner. *Critical Theory and Society: A Reader.* New York: Routledge, 1989.

Brothers, Thomas David. *Louis Armstrong's New Orleans.* New York: W. W. Norton, 2006.

Brown, Julie. *Bartók and the Grotesque: Studies in Modernity, the Body, and Contradiction in Music.* Aldershot, England: Ashgate, 2007.

Büchmann-Møller, Frank. *Someone to Watch over Me: The Life and Music of Ben Webster.* Ann Arbor: University of Michigan Press, 2006.

Buckley, Gail Lumet. *The Hornes: An American Family.* New York: Knopf, 1986.

Burton, Humphrey. *Leonard Bernstein.* New York: Doubleday, 1994.

Bushell, Garvin, and Mark Tucker. *Jazz from the Beginning.* Michigan American Music Series. Ann Arbor: University of Michigan Press, 1988.

Chambers, Jack. "Bardland: Shakespeare in Ellington's World." In *The International DEMS Bulletin* 05/1 (April–July 2005). Available at the Duke Ellington Music Society website, www.depanorama.net/dems/051f.htm.

Chernoff, John Miller. *African Rhythm and African Sensibility: Aesthetics and Social Action in African Musical Idioms.* Chicago: University of Chicago Press, 1979.

Chilton, John. *Sidney Bechet: The Wizard of Jazz.* New York: Oxford University Press, 1987.

Cohen, Harvey G. *Duke Ellington's America.* Chicago: University of Chicago Press.

Collier, James Lincoln. *Duke Ellington.* New York: Oxford University Press, 1987.

Copland, Aaron. *Copland on Music.* Garden City, NY: Doubleday, 1960.

———. *The New Music: 1900–1960.* New York: W. W. Norton, 1969.

Copland, Aaron, and Vivian Perlis. *Copland. Since 1943.* New York: St. Martin's Press, 1989.

Covach, John. "Schoenberg and the Occult." *Theory and Practice* 17 (1992).

Cowell, Henry, and David Nicholls. *New Musical Resources.* Cambridge: Cambridge University Press, 1996.

Craft, Robert. *Stravinsky: Chronicle of a Friendship.* Nashville, TN: Vanderbilt University Press, 1994.

Crawford, Richard. *The American Musical Landscape.* Berkeley: University of California Press, 1993.

Cripps, Thomas. *Slow Fade to Black: The Negro in American Film, 1900–1942.* Oxford: Oxford University Press, 1993.

Crouch, Stanley. *Notes of a Hanging Judge: Essays and Reviews, 1979–1989.* New York: Oxford University Press, 1990.

Cunningham, Mark. *Good Vibrations: A History of Record Production.* London: Sanctuary, 1998.

Dahl, Linda. *Morning Glory: A Biography of Mary Lou Williams.* New York: Pantheon Books, 1999.

Dance, Stanley. *The World of Duke Ellington.* New York: Da Capo Press, 2000.

Davis, Francis. *The History of the Blues.* New York: Hyperion, 1995.

De Long, Thomas A. *Pops: Paul Whiteman, King of Jazz.* Piscataway, NJ: New Century, 1983.

Debussy, Claude. *Debussy on Music.* Collected and introduced by François Lesure, translated and edited by Richard Langham Smith. Ithaca, NY: Cornell University Press, 1977.

Debussy, Claude, Ferruccio Busoni, and Charles Ives. *Three Classics in the Aesthetic of Music: Monsieur Croche the Dilettante Hater.* New York: Dover Publications, 1962.

Denby, Edwin. *Dancers, Buildings and People in the Streets.* New York: Horizon Press, 1965.

Denby, Edwin, Robert Cornfield, and William MacKay. *Dance Writings.* New York: Knopf, 1986.

Denning, Michael. *The Cultural Front: The Laboring of American Culture in the Twentieth Century.* London: Verso, 1998.

DeVeaux, Scott. "'Black, Brown and Beige' and the Critics." *Black Music Research Journal* 13, no. 2 (1993): 125–46.

Dickinson, Peter, ed. *Copland Connotations: Studies and Interviews.* Woodbridge, Suffolk, England: Boydell Press, 2002.

Dietschy, Marcel, William Ashbrook, and Margaret G. Cobb. *A Portrait of Claude Debussy.* Oxford: Oxford University Press, 1990.

Douglas, Ann. *Terrible Honesty: Mongrel Manhattan in the 1920s.* New York: Farrar, Straus and Giroux, 1995.

Duberman, Martin B. *Paul Robeson.* New York: Knopf, 1988.

Dyer, Geoff. *But Beautiful: A Book about Jazz.* New York: North Point Press, 1996.

Early, Gerald Lyn. *Tuxedo Junction: Essays on American Culture.* New York: Ecco Press, 1989.

Ellington, Duke. *Music Is My Mistress.* New York: Da Capo Press, 1976.

———. *The 100th Anniversary Collection.* New York: Alfred Publishing, 1999.

Ellington, Mercer, and Stanley Dance. *Duke Ellington in Person: An Intimate Memoir.* New York: Da Capo Press, 1979.

Ellison, Ralph. *Shadow and Act.* New York: Random House, 1964.

Epstein, Helen. *Joe Papp: An American Life.* Boston: Little, Brown, 1994.

Fernandez, Raul A. *From Afro-Cuban Rhythms to Latin Jazz.* Music of the African Diaspora 10. Berkeley: University of California Press; Chicago: Center for Black Music Research, Columbia College, 2006.

Finkelstein, Sidney Walter. *Jazz, a People's Music.* New York: International Publishers, 1988.

Floyd, Malcolm. *Composing the Music of Africa: Composition, Interpretation, and Realisation.* Ashgate Studies in Ethnomusicology. Aldershot, England: Ashgate, 1999.

Floyd, Samuel A. *Black Music in the Harlem Renaissance: A Collection of Essays.* New York: Greenwood Press, 1990.

———. *The Power of Black Music: Interpreting Its History from Africa to the United States.* Oxford: Oxford University Press, 1995.

Forte, Allen, Richard Lalli, and Gary Chapman. *Listening to Classic American Popular Songs.* New Haven, CT: Yale University Press, 2001.

Friedwald, Will. *Stardust Melodies: The Biography of Twelve of America's Most Popular Songs.* New York: Pantheon Books, 2002.

Frisch, Walter. *The Early Works of Arnold Schoenberg, 1893–1908.* Berkeley: University of California Press, 1993.

Fulcher, Jane F., ed. *Debussy and His World.* The Bard Music Festival Series. Princeton, NJ: Princeton University Press, 2001.

Furia, Philip. *Ira Gershwin: The Art of the Lyricist.* Oxford: Oxford University Press, 1996.

———. *The Poets of Tin Pan Alley: A History of America's Great Lyricists.* New York: Oxford University Press, 1990.

Gammond, Peter. *Duke Ellington: His Life and Music.* The Roots of Jazz. New York: Da Capo Press, 1977.

Garafola, Lynn. "Making an American Dance." In Carol J. Oja and Judith Tick, eds., *Aaron Copland and His World.* Princeton, NJ: Princeton University Press, 2005.

Gates, Henry Louis. *The Signifying Monkey: A Theory of Afro-American Literary Criticism*. New York: Oxford University Press, 1988.

Gennari, John. *Blowin' Hot and Cool: Jazz and Its Critics*. Chicago: University of Chicago Press, 2006.

George, Nelson. *The Death of Rhythm and Blues*. New York: Penguin, 2004.

Giddins, Gary. *Celebrating Bird: The Triumph of Charlie Parker*. New York: Beech Tree Books, 1987.

———. *Rhythm-a-Ning: Jazz Tradition and Innovation in the '80s*. New York: Oxford University Press, 1985.

———. *Riding on a Blue Note: Jazz and American Pop*. New York: Oxford University Press, 1981.

———. *Satchmo*. New York: Anchor Books, 1992.

———. *Visions of Jazz: The First Century*. New York: Oxford University Press, 1998.

Gilbert, Steven E. *The Music of Gershwin*. Composers of the Twentieth Century. New Haven, CT: Yale University Press, 1995.

Gillies, Malcolm. *The Bartók Companion*. Portland, OR: Amadeus Press, 1994.

Goldberg, Isaac. *Tin Pan Alley: A Chronicle of the American Popular Music Racket*. New York: John Day, 1930.

Gorrell, Lorraine. *Discordant Melody: Alexander Zemlinsky, His Songs, and the Second Viennese School*. Contributions to the Study of Music and Dance, no. 64. Westport, CT: Greenwood Press, 2002.

Gottlieb, Robert, ed. *Reading Jazz: A Gathering of Autobiography, Reportage, and Criticism from 1919 to Now*. New York: Pantheon Books, 1996.

Gushee, Lawrence. *Pioneers of Jazz: The Story of the Creole Band*. Oxford: Oxford University Press, 2005.

Hahl-Koch, Jelena, ed. *Arnold Schoenberg/Wassily Kandinsky: Letters, Pictures and Documents*. Translated by John C. Crawford. London: Faber and Faber, 1984.

Haimo, Ethan. *Schoenberg's Serial Odyssey: The Evolution of His Twelve-Tone Method, 1914–1928*. Oxford: Oxford University Press; New York: Clarendon Press, 1990.

———. *Schoenberg's Transformation of Musical Language*. Cambridge: Cambridge University Press, 2006.

Hajdu, David. *Lush Life: A Biography of Billy Strayhorn*. New York: Farrar, Straus and Giroux, 1996.

Hamm, Charles. *Yesterdays: Popular Song in America*. New York: Norton, 1979.

Hasse, John Edward. *Beyond Category: The Life and Genius of Duke Ellington*. New York: Simon & Schuster, 1993.

———. *Ragtime: Its History, Composers, and Music*. New York: Schirmer Books, 1985.

Headlam, David John. *The Music of Alban Berg*. Composers of the Twentieth Century. New Haven, CT: Yale University Press, 1996.

Hersch, Charles. *Subversive Sounds: Race and the Birth of Jazz in New Orleans*. Chicago: University of Chicago Press, 2007.

Hodeir, André, and David Noakes. *Jazz, Its Evolution and Essence*. New York: Grove Press, 1956.

Holloway, Robin. *Debussy and Wagner*. Eulenburg Books. London: E. Eulenburg, 1979.

Howland, John Louis. *"Ellington Uptown": Duke Ellington, James P. Johnson, & the Birth of Concert Jazz*. Ann Arbor: University of Michigan Press, 2009.

Hughes, Langston, Arnold Rampersad, and David E. Roessel. *The Collected Poems of Langston Hughes*. New York: Knopf, 1994.

Hyde, Martha M. *Schoenberg's Twelve-Tone Harmony: The Suite Op. 29 and the Compositional Sketches*. Studies in Musicology, no. 49. Ann Arbor, MI: UMI Research Press, 1982.

Jarman, Douglas. *The Berg Companion*. Boston: Northeastern University Press, 1990.

————. *The Music of Alban Berg*. Berkeley: University of California Press, 1979.

Jarocinski, Stefan. *Debussy: Impressionism and Symbolism*. London: Eulenberg Books, 1976.

Jasen, David A., ed. *"For Me and My Gal" and Other Favorite Song Hits, 1915–1917*. New York: Dover, 1994.

Jasen, David A., and Gene Jones. *Black Bottom Stomp: Eight Masters of Ragtime and Early Jazz*. New York: Routledge, 2002.

Jewell, Derek. *Duke: A Portrait of Duke Ellington*. New York: Norton, 1977.

Jones, A. M. *Studies in African Music*. London: Oxford University Press, 1959.

Jones, LeRoi. "Blues People." *Times Literary Supplement* No. 4834 (1995): 32.

Joseph, Charles M. *Stravinsky and Balanchine: A Journey of Invention*. New Haven, CT: Yale University Press, 2002.

Jost, Ekkehard. *Free Jazz*. The Roots of Jazz. New York: Da Capo Press, 1981.

Kahn, Ashley. *Kind of Blue*. New York, NY: Da Capo Press, 2000.

Kallir, Jane. *Arnold Schoenberg's Vienna*. New York: Galerie St. Etienne/Rizzoli, 1984.

Kandinsky, Wassily. *Concerning the Spiritual in Art*. New York: Dover Publications, 1977.

Kárpáti, János. *Bartók's Chamber Music*. Stuyvesant, NY: Pendragon Press, 1994.

Katz, Mark. *Capturing Sound: How Technology Has Changed Music*. A Roth Family Foundation Book on Music in America. Berkeley: University of California Press, 2004.

Keil, Charles. *Urban Blues*. Chicago: University of Chicago Press, 1966.

Kerman, Joseph. *Music at the Turn of Century: A 19th-Century Music Reader*. California Studies in 19th-Century Music 7. Berkeley: University of California Press, 1990.

Kern, Stephen. *The Culture of Time and Space 1880–1918*. Cambridge, MA: Harvard University Press, 1983.

Kirstein, Lincoln. *Thirty Years/The New York City Ballet*. New York: Knopf, 1978.

Knauer, Wolfram. "'Simulated Improvisation' in Duke Ellington's 'Black, Brown and Beige.'" *The Black Perspective in Music* 18, no. 2 (1990): 20–38.

La Grange, Henry-Louis de. *Gustav Mahler, Volume 2: Vienna: The Years of Challenge (1897–1904)*. Oxford: Oxford University Press, 1995.

Laki, Peter. *Bartók and His World*. Bard Music Festival Series. Princeton, NJ: Princeton University Press, 1995.

Lang, Paul Henry, ed. *Stravinsky: A New Appraisal of His Work with a Complete List of Works*. New York: W. W. Norton, 1963.

Lawrence, A. H. *Duke Ellington and His World: A Biography*. New York: Routledge, 2001.

Lederman, Minna, ed. *Strawinsky in the Theater; a Symposium*. Dance Index, vol. 6, nos. 10–12. New York: Dance Index–Ballet Caravan, 1948.

Lesure, François, and Roger Nichols, eds. *Debussy Letters*. Cambridge, MA: Harvard University Press, 1987.

Levine, Lawrence W. *Black Culture and Black Consciousness: Afro-American Folk Thought from Slavery to Freedom*. New York: Oxford University Press, 1977.

———. *Highbrow/Lowbrow: The Emergence of Cultural Hierarchy in America*. The William E. Massey, Sr., Lectures in the History of American Civilization. Cambridge, MA: Harvard University Press, 1988.

Levine, Mark. *The Jazz Piano Book*. Petaluma, CA: Sher Music Co., 1989.

Levy, Beth E. "From Orient to Occident." In Carol J. Oja and Judith Tick, eds., *Aaron Copland and His World*. Princeton, NJ: Princeton University Press, 2005.

Lewis, David L. *The Portable Harlem Renaissance Reader*. Viking Portable Library. New York: Penguin Books, 1995.

———. *W. E. B. Dubois—Biography of a Race, 1868–1919*. New York: H. Holt, 1994.

———. *When Harlem Was in Vogue*. New York: Knopf, 1981.

Lewis, George. *A Power Stronger Than Itself: The AACM and American Experimental Music*. Chicago: University of Chicago Press, 2008.

Litweiler, John. *The Freedom Principle: Jazz after 1958*. New York: W. Morrow, 1984.

Lloyd, Thomas. "The Revival of an Early 'Crossover' Masterwork: Duke Ellington's Sacred Concerts." *Choral Journal* 49, no. 11 (2009): 8–26.

Lock, Graham. *Blutopia: Visions of the Future and Revisions of the Past in the Work of Sun Ra, Duke Ellington, and Anthony Braxton*. Durham, NC: Duke University Press, 1999.

Locke, Alain LeRoy. *The New Negro*. New York: Simon & Schuster, 1997.

Lockspeiser, Edward. *Debussy: His Life and Mind*. New York: Macmillan, 1962.

MacIntyre, C. F. *French Symbolist Poetry*. Berkeley: University of California Press, 1964.

Magee, Jeffrey. *The Uncrowned King of Swing: Fletcher Henderson and Big Band Jazz*. Oxford: Oxford University Press, 2005.

May, Lary. *Screening out the Past: The Birth of Mass Culture and the Motion Picture Industry*. New York: Oxford University Press, 1980.

Mehegan, John. *Tonal and Rhythmic Principles.* New York: Watson-Guptill Publications and Amsco Publications, 1984.

Mellers, Wilfrid. *Music in a New Found Land: Themes and Developments in the History of American Music.* New York: Alfred A. Knopf, 1965.

Metzer, David Joel. *Quotation and Cultural Meaning in Twentieth-Century Music.* New Perspectives in Music History and Criticism. Cambridge: Cambridge University Press, 2003.

Meyer, Esther da Costa, and Fred Wasserman, eds. *Schoenberg, Kandinsky and the Blue Rider.* London: Scala, 2003.

Mingus, Charles. *Beneath the Underdog; His World as Composed by Mingus.* New York: Knopf, 1971.

———. *More Than a Fake Book.* New York: Jazz Workshop, 1991.

Moldenhauer, Hans, and Rosaleen Moldenhauer. *Anton von Webern: A Chronicle of His Life and Work.* New York: Knopf, 1979.

Moorefield, Virgil. *The Producer as Composer: Shaping the Sounds of Popular Music.* Cambridge, MA: MIT Press, 2005.

Morton, John Fass. *Backstory in Blue: Ellington at Newport '56.* New Brunswick, NJ: Rutgers University Press, 2008.

Murchison, Gayle. "Mary Lou Williams's Hymn *Black Christ of the Andes (St. Martin de Porres):* Vatican II, Civil Rights, and Jazz as Sacred Music." *Musical Quarterly* 86, no. 4 (Winter 2002): 591–629.

Murray, Albert. *Stomping the Blues.* New York: Da Capo Press, 1989.

Nicholls, David. *American Experimental Music.* Cambridge: Cambridge University Press, 1990.

Nichols, Roger. *Debussy Remembered.* Portland, OR: Amadeus Press, 1992.

———. *The Life of Debussy.* Musical Lives. Cambridge: Cambridge University Press, 1998.

Nichols, Roger, and Richard Langham Smith. *Claude Debussy: Pelléas et Mélisande.* Cambridge Opera Handbooks. Cambridge: Cambridge University Press, 1989.

Nicholson, Stuart. *Reminiscing in Tempo: A Portrait of Duke Ellington.* Boston: Northeastern University Press, 1999.

O'Meally, Robert G. *The Jazz Cadence of American Culture.* New York: Columbia University Press, 1998.

———. *Lady Day: The Many Faces of Billie Holiday.* New York: Da Capo Press, 1991.

O'Meally, Robert G., Brent Hayes Edwards, and Farah Jasmine Griffin, eds. *Uptown Conversation: The New Jazz Studies.* New York: Columbia University Press, 2004.

Oja, Carol J. *Making Music Modern: New York in the 1920s.* New York: Oxford University Press, 2000.

Oja, Carol J., and Judith Tick, eds. *Aaron Copland and His World.* Princeton, NJ: Princeton University Press, 2005.

Oliver, Paul. *Blues Fell This Morning: Meaning in the Blues.* Cambridge: Cambridge University Press, 1990.

Orenstein, Arbie. *Ravel: Man and Musician.* New York: Columbia University Press, 1975.

————, ed. *A Ravel Reader: Correspondence, Articles, Interviews*. New York: Columbia University Press, 1990.

Ottley, Roi. *"New World A-Coming": Inside Black America*. Boston: Houghton Mifflin, 1943.

Pasler, Jann. *Confronting Stravinsky: Man, Musician, and Modernist*. Berkeley: University of California Press, 1986.

Peinkofer, Karl, and Fritz Tannigel. *Handbook of Percussion Instruments: Their Characteristics and Playing Techniques, with Illustrations and Musical Examples from the Literature*. London: Schott, 1976.

Peress, Maurice. *Dvořák to Duke Ellington: A Conductor Explores America's Music and Its African American Roots*. Oxford: Oxford University Press, 2004.

Perle, George. *The Operas of Alban Berg*. Berkeley: University of California Press, 1980.

————. *Serial Composition and Atonality; An Introduction to the Music of Schoenberg, Berg, and Webern*. Berkeley: University of California Press, 1968.

Perlis, Vivian, and Libby Van Cleve. *Composers' Voices from Ives to Ellington: An Oral History of American Music*. New Haven, CT: Yale University Press, 2005.

Pleasants, Henry. *The Agony of Modern Music*. New York: Simon and Schuster, 1955.

————. *The Great American Popular Singers*. New York: Simon and Schuster, 1974.

Pollack, Howard. *Aaron Copland: The Life and Work of an Uncommon Man*. New York: Henry Holt, 1999.

————. *George Gershwin: His Life and Work*. Berkeley: University of California Press, 2006.

Pople, Anthony. *Berg, Violin Concerto*. Cambridge Music Handbooks. Cambridge: Cambridge University Press, 1991.

————, ed. *The Cambridge Companion to Berg*. Cambridge Companions to Music. Cambridge: Cambridge University Press, 1997.

Porter, Lewis. *John Coltrane: His Life and Music*. The Michigan American Music Series. Ann Arbor: University of Michigan Press, 1997.

Porter, Lewis, Michael Ullman, and Ed Hazell. *Jazz: From Its Origins to the Present*. Englewood Cliffs, NJ: Prentice Hall, 1993.

Priestley, Brian. *Mingus: A Critical Biography*. New York: Da Capo Press, 1984.

Ramsey, Guthrie P. *Race Music: Black Cultures from Bebop to Hip-Hop*. Music of the African Diaspora 7. Berkeley: University of California Press, 2003.

Rattenbury, Ken. *Duke Ellington, Jazz Composer*. London: Yale University Press, 1990.

Reich, Willi. *Alban Berg*. New York: Harcourt, Brace & World, 1965.

Rilke, Rainer Maria, and Stephen Mitchell. *The Sonnets to Orpheus*. New York: Simon and Schuster, 1985.

Roberts, Paul. *Images: The Piano Music of Claude Debussy*. Portland, OR: Amadeus Press, 1996.

Robertson, Marta Elaine. "'A Gift to Be Simple': The Collaboration of Aaron Copland and Martha Graham in the Genesis of Appalachian Spring." Ph. D. diss., University of Michigan, 1992.

Rosen, Charles. *Arnold Schoenberg*. New York: Viking Press, 1975.

Ross, Alex. *The Rest Is Noise: Listening to the Twentieth Century*. New York: Farrar, Straus and Giroux, 2007.

Saunders, Frances Stonor. *The Cultural Cold War: The CIA and the World of Arts and Letters*. New York: New Press, 2000.

Schmitz, E. Robert. *The Piano Works of Claude Debussy*. New York: Dover Publications, 1966.

Schneider, David E. *Bartók, Hungary, and the Renewal of Tradition: Case Studies in the Intersection of Modernity and Nationality*. California Studies in 20th-Century Music 5. Berkeley: University of California Press, 2006.

Schoenberg, Arnold. *Structural Functions of Harmony*. New York: Norton, 1954.

———. *Theory of Harmony*. Berkeley: University of California Press, 1978.

Schoenberg, Arnold, Wassily Kandinsky, and Jelena Hahl-Fontaine. *Arnold Schoenberg, Wassily Kandinsky: Letters, Pictures, and Documents*. London: Faber & Faber, 1984.

Schoenberg, Arnold, and Erwin Stein. *Letters*. London: Faber and Faber, 1964.

Schoenberg, Arnold, and Leonard Stein. *Style and Idea: Selected Writings of Arnold Schoenberg*. New York: St. Martin's Press, 1975.

Schoenberg, Arnold, and Gerald Strang. *Fundamentals of Musical Composition*. New York: St. Martin's Press, 1967.

Schorske, Carl E. *Fin-de-Siècle Vienna: Politics and Culture*. New York: Vintage Books, 1981.

Schrecker, Ellen. *Many Are the Crimes: McCarthyism in America*. Boston: Little, Brown, 1998.

Schuller, Gunther. *Early Jazz: Its Roots and Musical Development*. New York: Oxford University Press, 1968.

———. *Musings: The Musical Worlds of Gunther Schuller*. New York: Oxford University Press, 1986.

———. *The Swing Era: The Development of Jazz, 1930–1945*. New York: Oxford University Press, 1989.

Seldes, Gilbert. *The Seven Lively Arts*. New York: Harper & Bros., 1924.

Shawn, Allen. *Arnold Schoenberg's Journey*. New York: Farrar, Straus and Giroux, 2002.

Showalter, Elaine. *Sexual Anarchy: Gender and Culture at the Fin de Siècle*. New York: Viking, 1990.

Simms, Bryan R. "Alban Berg and Hanna Fuchs: The Story of a Love in Letters (Review)." *Notes* 65, no. 3 (2009): 507–10.

———. *The Atonal Music of Arnold Schoenberg, 1908–1923*. New York: Oxford University Press, 2000.

Slonimsky, Nicolas. *Perfect Pitch: A Life Story*. Oxford: Oxford University Press, 1988.

Somfai, Laszlo. *Béla Bartók: Composition, Concepts, and Autograph Sources.* Berkeley: University of California Press, 1996.

Southern, Eileen. *The Music of Black Americans: A History.* New York: W. W. Norton, 1971.

———. *Readings in Black American Music.* New York: W. W. Norton, 1983.

Southern, Eileen, Josephine Wright, and Samuel A. Floyd. *New Perspectives on Music: Essays in Honor of Eileen Southern.* Detroit Monographs in Musicology/Studies in Music, no. 11. Warren, MI: Harmonie Park Press, 1992.

Spellman, A. B. *Black Music: Four Lives.* New York: Schocken, 1973.

Stearns, Marshall Winslow, and Jean Stearns. *Jazz Dance: The Story of American Vernacular Dance.* New York: Macmillan, 1968.

Steed, Janna Tull. *Duke Ellington: A Spiritual Biography.* New York: Crossroad, 1999.

Stevens, Halsey. *The Life and Music of Béla Bartók.* New York: Oxford University Press, 1953.

Stewart, Rex William. *Jazz Masters of the Thirties.* New York: Macmillan, 1972.

Stratemann, Klaus. *Duke Ellington, Day by Day and Film by Film.* Copenhagen: JazzMedia, 1992.

Straus, Joseph Nathan. *Stravinsky's Late Music.* Cambridge Studies in Music Theory and Analysis 16. New York: Cambridge University Press, 2001.

Stravinsky, Igor. *Igor Stravinsky: An Autobiography.* New York: Norton, 1962.

———. *Poetics of Music in the Form of Six Lessons.* New York: Vintage Books, 1956.

Stravinsky, Igor, and Robert Craft. *Dialogues and a Diary.* Garden City, NY: Doubleday, 1963.

———. *Memories and Commentaries.* Garden City, NY: Doubleday, 1960.

———. *Memories and Commentaries.* London: Faber and Faber, 2002.

———. *Stravinsky in Conversation with Robert Craft.* Harmondsworth: Penguin Books, 1962.

Stuckenschmidt, Hans Heinz. *Schoenberg: His Life, World, and Work.* New York: Schirmer Books, 1978.

Sublette, Ned. *Cuba and Its Music: From the First Drums to the Mambo.* Chicago: Chicago Press Review, 2004.

Szwed, John F. *Space Is the Place: The Lives and Times of Sun Ra.* New York: Pantheon Books, 1997.

Taruskin, Richard. *Stravinsky and the Russian Traditions: A Biography of the Works through "Mavra."* Berkeley: University of California Press, 1996.

Teachout, Terry. *Pops: A Life of Louis Armstrong.* Boston: Houghton Mifflin Harcourt, 2009.

Thompson, Emily Ann. *The Soundscape of Modernity: Architectural Acoustics and the Culture of Listening in America, 1900–1933.* Cambridge, MA: MIT Press, 2002.

Thomson, Virgil, and Kostelanetz, Richard. *A Virgil Thomson Reader.* New York: Routledge, 2002.

Tick, Judith. *Ruth Crawford Seeger: A Composer's Search for American Music.* New York: Oxford University Press, 1997.

Timner, W. E. *Ellingtonia: The Recorded Music of Duke Ellington and His Sidemen.* Metuchen, NJ: Institute of Jazz Studies and Scarecrow Press, 1988.

Tirro, Frank. *Jazz: A History.* New York: Norton, 1993.

Titon, Jeff Todd. *Early Downhome Blues: A Musical and Cultural Analysis.* Urbana: University of Illinois Press, 1977.

Trezise, Simon. *Debussy: La Mer.* Cambridge Music Handbooks. Cambridge: Cambridge University Press, 1994.

Tucker, Mark. *Ellington: The Early Years.* Music in American Life. Urbana: University of Illinois Press, 1991.

———. "The Genesis of *Black, Brown and Beige.*" *Black Music Research Journal* 13 (Fall 1993): 67–86.

Tucker, Mark, ed. *The Duke Ellington Reader.* New York: Oxford University Press, 1993.

Ulanov, Barry. *Duke Ellington.* New York: Creative Age Press, 1946.

Vail, Ken. *Duke's Diary. Part Two: The Life of Duke Ellington, 1951–1974.* Lanham, MD: Scarecrow; Oxford: Oxford Publicity Partnership, 2002.

Van de Leur, Walter. *Something to Live For: The Music of Billy Strayhorn.* New York: Oxford University Press, 2002.

Van den Toorn, Pieter C. *The Music of Igor Stravinsky.* Composers of the Twentieth Century. New Haven, CT: Yale University Press, 1983.

———. *Stravinsky and* The Rite of Spring: *The Beginnings of a Musical Language.* Berkeley: University of California Press, 1987.

Walser, Robert, ed. *Keeping Time: Readings in Jazz History.* New York: Oxford University Press, 1999.

Walsh, Stephen. *The Music of Stravinsky.* Companions to the Great Composers. Oxford: Clarendon Press, 1993.

———. *Stravinsky: A Creative Spring: Russia and France, 1882–1934.* New York: Alfred A. Knopf, 1999.

———. *Stravinsky: The Second Exile: France and America, 1934–1971.* New York: Alfred A. Knopf, 2006.

Waterman, Richard A. "'Hot' Rhythm in Negro Music." *Journal of the American Musicological Society* 1, no. 1 (1948): 24–37.

Wilder, Alec, and James T. Maher. *American Popular Song: The Great Innovators, 1900–1950.* New York: Oxford University Press, 1990.

Williams, Martin T. *The Jazz Tradition.* Oxford: Oxford University Press, 1983.

Wilson, Edmund. *Axel's Castle: A Study in the Imaginative Literature of 1870–1930.* New York: C. Scribner's Sons, 1931.

Wilson, Olly. "The Significance of the Relationship between Afro-American and West African Music." *The Black Perspective in Music* 2, no. 1 (Spring 1974): 3–22.

Wilson, Sondra K., and the National Association for the Advancement of Colored People. *The Crisis Reader: Stories, Poetry, and Essays from the N.A.A.C.P.'S "Crisis" Magazine.* Modern Library Harlem Renaissance. New York: Modern Library, 1999.

Woideck, Carl. *Charlie Parker: His Music and Life,* Michigan American Music Series. Ann Arbor: University of Michigan Press, 1996.

Wright, Josephine, ed. *New Perspectives on Music: Essays in Honor of Eileen Southern.* Warren, MI: Harmonie Park Press, 1992.

Zak, Albin. *The Poetics of Rock: Cutting Tracks, Making Records.* Berkeley: University of California Press, 2001.

Zola, Emile. *Au bonheur des dames (The Ladies' Delight),* translated by Robin Buss. London: Penguin, 2001.

Index

Accademia Nazionale di Santa Cecilia (Rome), 121–22
Adams, Diana, 3
Adderley, Cannonball, 114, 116–17
Adorno, T. W., 90–91, 103, 137, 188, 194, 201–2
African American culture/music, 153–54; "black is beautiful," 251; and Christianity, 206, 211, 213–14, 221, 249–51; and civil rights movement, 137, 168, 179, 248, 250; and Great Migration, 24, 126; and harmony, 126, 137–38; and history, 202–6, 209–14, 219–22, 225, 228–33, 236–37, 239, 243, 246, 249–51; and melody, 91–94; and Middle Passage, 24, 211; and religious music, 249–51, 253; and rhythm, 51, 62–63, 69–71, 73–74, 83, 86; and social distinctions, 229–30; and tone colors, 12, 17–18, 24, 26; and Underground Railroad, 221. *See also* race relations; *names of individual African Americans*
African/West African music: African diaspora, 225; and clave, 58, 60–62, 66, 68–70, 73, 77–78, 272nn13,15; Ewe music, 60–62, 272nn13,15; and handbell, 58, 60–62, 83, 272nn13,15; Husago dance, 81; and melody, 109; and rhythm, 8, 56–62, 66, 68–69, 81, 86, 272nn13,15; in *Such Sweet Thunder,* 185; and tone colors, 18, 24, 28; and xylophone, 28

Afro-Cuban music, 58, 60, 73, 78, 272n13
airplanes, 8–9, 51, 200
Ajemian, Anahid, 5, 166
"Alexander's Ragtime Band," 92
Allen, Frederick Lewis, 231
"All Things Considered" (NPR program), 111
American Popular Song (Wilder), 92–94, 97
American Shakespeare Festival (Stratford, Conn.), 170
Amsterdam Star-News, 206
Andersen, Hans Christian, 270n67
Anderson, Cat, 58, 164, 173, 186, 255–57, 261, 265
Anderson, Eddie "Rochester," 159
Anderson, Elaine, 170
Anderson, Ivie, 107–8, 207–8, 216
Anderson, Marian, 207
Andrews Sisters, 206
Ansermet, Ernest, 20
Antheil, George, 8, 202; *Ballet mécanique,* 8; *Jazz Symphony,* 202
anticommunism, 167–68, 170
Antony and Cleopatra (Shakespeare), 167, 172, 174–75, 178–79, 186–87
Appel, Alfred Jr., 2
Applebaum, Louis, 171
"Aquashow" (Flushing Meadow Park), 168
Aragon, Louis, 118

TEXT:
10/13 Sabon

DISPLAY:
Sabon (Open Type)

COMPOSITOR:
BookComp, Inc.

INDEXER:
Sharon Sweeney

PRINTER AND BINDER:
Maple-Vail Book Manufacturing Group